To Vela,
my friend and connoisseur
Pierre.

Contemporary Macroeconomic Modelling

Contemporary Macroeconomic Modelling

Edited by

Pierre Malgrange *and* Pierre-Alain Muet

Basil Blackwell

First published 1984
Basil Blackwell Publisher Limited
108 Cowley Road, Oxford OX4 1JF, England

British Library Cataloguing in Publication Data

Contemporary macroeconomic modelling.
1. Macroeconomics—Mathematical models—Congresses
I. Malgrange, Pierre II. Muet, Pierre-Alain
339'.0724 HB135

ISBN 0-631-13471-9

Typeset by Santype International, Salisbury, Wilts.
Printed in Great Britain by T. J. Press Ltd, Padstow

Contents

Introduction

PIERRE MALGRANGE AND
PIERRE-ALAIN MUET

In the 1960s, macroeconomic modelling developed in the wake of macroeconomic theory and in relative harmony with it. The basic structure of macroeconomic models—a dynamic version of the IS-LM model with the evolution of prices and wages depending on goods and labour market disequilibria—seemed to be a relatively faithful reflection of the theory commonly held and taught, which was Keynesian in the short term and neo-classical in the long term.

In the decade of the 1970s, macroeconomic theory developed primarily in two directions:

(a) one was the neo-Keynesian fixed-price model, and
(b) the other was the full-equilibrium rational expectation model.

The academic nature of the development of macroeconomic theory has given exaggerated emphasis to the criticism of the earlier theory and at times has obscured the considerable progress that has been made in the quantitative knowledge of certain phenomena, such as, for example, the study of the constraints of an open economy. This criticism has, however, emphasized certain weak points of traditional macroeconomic modelling, namely:

(a) the specification of expectations, and
(b) the insufficient recognition of constraints other than demand in determining production and employment.

Has the quantitative knowledge of these phenomena made sufficient progress for it to be taken into consideration in macroeconomic modelling? This is one of the main themes to be explored in these papers. In all, there are ten main chapters, which have been grouped into three parts, an introductory chapter on macroeconomic modelling by Edmond Malinvaud and a conclusion by Edwin Kuh.

These contributions, and the comments accompanying them, were presented at the International Seminar on Recent Developments in Macroeconomic Modelling organized jointly by the Commissariat du Plan Français and the CEPREMAP from 13 to 15 September 1982, in Paris.

Edmond Malinvaud's preliminary chapter draws attention to a certain number of aspects of macroeconomic modelling which, in his view, have been somewhat neglected: the study of aggregation, the taking into account of non-conventional macroeconomic variables, and the need for more systematic testing.

Part one, devoted to the problem of specifying expectations, consists of three chapters. Robert Shiller, in 'Expectations and the prices of long-term assets', provides a historical analysis of the rates of a certain number of financial assets over a very long period. This leads him to question the validity of the different current theories that attempt to explain the great variability of these rates by means of rational expectations hypothesis. This paper is discussed by Alain Monfort.

The availability of data from qualitative surveys on the expectations of agents makes it possible, through a comparison with realizations, to construct direct tests of their rationality. This presupposes, however, a conversion from the qualitative to the quantitative. In this context, Hashem Pesaran presents, in 'Expectations formations and macroeconometric modelling', a new method of conversion which he uses to test whether inflation expectations in Great Britain are rationally formed. The paper is discussed by Christian Gourieroux and Jean Tirole.

Chapter 4, 'The aggregate labour market in the United Kingdom: some experiments with rational expectations models', by Samuel G. B. Henry and S. Wren-Lewis, consists of the explicit derivation of alternative models of labour demand, based on intertemporal optimizing behaviour with rational expectations. These models are then estimated, and their forecasting performance is compared. This paper is discussed by Jean Waelbroeck.

Part two of the work also contains three chapters, which are devoted to exchange rate models. Thus, Michel Aglietta and Gilles Oudiz, in 'Real exchange rates and structural transformations', have doubts about the long-term validity of the theory of purchasing power parity and, by using the Ricardian theory of international trade, they provide an econometric analysis of the medium-term deformations of real exchange rates, which they explain by structural differences among economies. This paper is discussed by Vivien Levy-Garboua and Uwe Westphal.

William H. Branson, in 'A model of exchange rate determination with policy reaction: evidence from monthly data', analyses the nature of exchange rate policies. The study of the correlations of the residuals of an autoregressive model for different countries allows him to show the contrast between the USA, where the exchange rate is determined by domestic monetary policies, and the UK and West Germany, where monetary policy reacts to exchange rate movements. This paper is discussed by Raymond Courbis and Paul de Grauwe.

Stephen J. Turnovsky, in 'Exchange market intervention in a small open economy: an expository model', shows that even within an extremely simple theoretical framework, the optimal stabilization policy of exchange rates can be, depending on the source of the uncertainty, either 'leaning with the wind' or 'leaning against the wind'. The paper is discussed by Jean-Pierre Laffargue and Jacques Melitz.

In part three, four chapters presenting new approaches to macroeconomic modelling or the analysis of models have been grouped together. The first three of these deal with small-scale models. The study provided by Albert R. Bergstrom in 'Monetary, fiscal and exchange rate policy in a continuous-time econometric model of the United Kingdom', consists of adjoining to his famous continuous-time model certain rules of political economy à la Phillips and of evaluating analytically the stabilizing properties through a calculation of the eigenvalues in the neighbourhood of a stationary path. This paper is discussed by Jean-Michel Charpin and Giancarlo Gandolfo.

Michel Deleau, Pierre Malgrange and Pierre-Alain Muet, in 'A study of short-run and long-run properties of macroeconometric dynamic models by means of an aggregative core model', present a theoretical model with numerical coefficients whose structure is of the IS-LM dynamic type. Its behaviour, supported by simulation runs shows it to be representative, both qualitatively and quantitatively, of a broad category of neo-Keynesian inspired econometric models. This paper is discussed by Gonzague d'Alcantara and Pierre-Yves Hénin.

The subject of the contribution of Richard Portes, Richard Quandt, David Winter and Stephen Yeo, 'Planning the consumption goods market: preliminary disequilibrium estimates for Poland, 1955–80', is the specification of a disequilibrium model, estimated for the Polish economy in which the usual condition of dynamic price adjustment has been replaced by a supply behaviour which is dependent upon previous realizations. This paper is discussed by Jean-Pascal Bénassy and Jacques Mairesse.

Ronald P. Smith's contribution, 'The evaluation and comparison of large macroeconomic models', proposes a systematic framework for the evaluation and comparison of the performance of models based on decision theory by taking into account the cost for the decision-maker of a forecast error. This paper is discussed by Pascal Mazodier and Clifford Wymer.

The work closes with a conclusion by Edwin Kuh which draws up a synthesis of the different papers by showing the contribution made by recent developments in macroeconomic modelling to the understanding of contemporary macroeconomic controversies.

The authors of the contributions to this volume were given an opportunity to revise their papers in the light of the comments made at the conference by the formal discussants, and in turn the discussants have based their written comments published here on the final revised versions of the papers.

The conference was financed by the Commissariat du Plan and held at CESTA, Ministère de l'Industrie et de la Recherche.

We would like to thank Michel Rocard, Minister of Planning, for opening the conference, Professor Claude Fourgeaud, Director of CEPREMAP and Chairman of the Programme Committee, and the other members of that Committee, who were responsible for arranging the conference. Our thanks also go to Paule Lasserre, Agnès Picard and Christiane Pillard for their secretarial work, and to Christine Laffargue and Patricia Hunter for translation during the conference.

1

Reflections on Macroeconomic Modelling

EDMOND MALINVAUD

Macroeconomics is in a state of crisis. Not only do our fellow countrymen feel that macroeconomic policies have failed, but strong schools of opinion among economists fundamentally disagree with orientations that have prevailed up till now for macroeconomic modelling and the estimation of macroeconomic models.

A brief look at the contents of this volume shows that we are going to pay little heed to these external disturbances. This book has a certain serenity, in that the various studies do not question previous achievements but aim rather to consolidate or enrich them. This is a good thing. Questioning is, of course, useful, but there is too much of it in econometrics at present. To restore a just equilibrium, it is by no means to be deplored that we should here devote little time to questioning.

Accepting the constructive mood of the book, I shall examine three directions in which I feel that macroeconomic modelling is failing to move fast enough. I do not claim to be original in what I have to say, but I think it is not said or considered often enough.

MORE WORK SHOULD BE DEVOTED TO AGGREGATION

For macroeconomic modelling the logical method consists of two phases: the representation of a certain microeconomic reality and the transposition of this representation into a model treating macroeconomic data. In practice, whereas the first phase is carried out attentively, the second is treated very lightly. Sometimes the microeconomic representation is merely transposed directly without consideration of the required conditions for this transposition or of an eventual change of significance that this would bring about for certain parameters. Sometimes, even, a model that did not claim to be anything other that a prototype for microeconomic reflection is treated as directly valid for econometric studies.

This state of affairs can no doubt be explained by the fact that aggregation theory has proved disappointing for those who have worked on it. A pragmatic reflex was to neglect it totally so as not to have to cope with it. This reflex is, of course, to be rebuked.

To summarize what is actually a complex picture, we can say that aggregation theory has established that only unrealistic conditions would justify the direct transposition of microeconomic representations to identical macroeconomic representations. Thus the conclusion should be that the nature of the aggregation to be carried out in each case must be studied for this particular case, as there exists no simple rule that can be systematically applied.

I obviously cannot claim to be the only person to bridge this gap, which I notice and deplore in our common efforts of macroeconomic modelling. But the time I have spent studying aggregation prompts me to believe that it has not been in vain. I will give two examples.

On the macroeconomic level and in work dealing with the middle or long term, a link has often to be recognized between the volume of capital stock and labour productivity: this is the link we refer to when speaking of an overall production function. We know that this function translates not only microeconomic substitutabilities but also the functioning of resource allocation. The result is that the overall production function changes when the allocation process is changed, while elementary substitutabilities are not affected. Examining closely the aggregation of production functions, as I did in writing my book, *Macroeconomic Theory*, suggests how the change is likely to take place, at least in some cases.

In the same way, if there is disequilibrium in the actual functioning of markets, perception of the global effects of this is complex, as every real situation is a combination of various disequilibria on the microeconomic level. A good macroeconomic model must not, therefore, merely identify a small number of regimes between which the observed situation would alternate; rather it should take into account a steady range of regimes, which naturally implies non-linear modelling with no discontinuity. I proposed this type of modelling; the method I used for it can be improved upon in several ways.

The sole aim of these two examples is to put across to you my conviction that now is the moment to be more explicit in our treatment of aggregation.

WE SHOULD RECOGNIZE THE IMPORTANCE OF NON-CONVENTIONAL MACROECONOMIC VARIABLES

Macroeconomic modelling had developed by focusing on all principal data computed by national accounts, and on the main indices calculated by traditional economic statistics. The equation systems of our present models rarely use anything but these data and these indices.

Two recent trains of thought in economic theory tend towards the introduction of new variables. On the one hand, the role of expectations and the complex interdependencies which relate the formation of expectations to actual economic evolution are stressed. On the other hand, there is a new emphasis on the importance of existing tensions and disequilibria on the various markets, on the degree of pressure or sluggishness of various demands, and on the perception that agents have of their situation.

The conclusion is inevitable: macromodels must use variables representing expectations, attitudes, disequilibria and tensions, and for all these variables data are increasingly available. In fact, a good many macromodels already contain this type of variable, although in an unambitious way.

Research into macroeconomic modelling should devote part of its work programme to the study of the introduction on these new variables.

I envisage two parts to this study. One is a fairly direct result of the recent orientation of theoretical reflection. This entails defining when and how expectations and tensions affect behaviour and adjustment processes. It also entails seeking the ways in which expectations and tensions are themselves determined. It is then necessary to improve behaviour and adjustment representation by the explicit introduction of factors which have often been ignored until now, and also to create new blocks which will explain the newly introduced variables.

But there is also another part to this study, of which I do not yet have a clear-cut idea. It is also essential to understand how actual data relate to the fundamental concepts that the theory has elaborated. At first sight, one might be tempted to proceed to the identification of such and such an indicator, from replies to a survey, for example, with such and such a related theoretical concept. The little time I have devoted to the question leads me to say that this identification is not as easy as might be thought.

This comes about, first, from the fact that the actual data refer to less rigidly defined notions than is usual in conventional statistics. The subjectivity of people interviewed can have an effect which can vary according to circumstances. Even an apparently objective notion, such as the degree of capacity utilization, leaves room for a fine appreciation of what is meant by capacity at any given time; this does not seem a purely physical notion and must be interpreted with reference to what the head of a firm considers to be normal operating conditions.

If the identification of concepts is difficult, this also comes from the fact that conceptual analysis retains categories which may not coincide with those of everyday experience. For example, if the head of a firm replies that he cannot produce more for lack of labour, this does not necessarily mean that he could not have a larger workforce if he wanted to, and therefore that the labour market is a supplier's market for the qualifications that he is interested in.

I have the feeling that macroeconomists are still not up to dealing adequately with these non-conventional variables which should be included more often in their models; more research work should be devoted to this.

WE SHOULD TEST MORE SYSTEMATICALLY

This third precept is no longer original. However, I think it is worth mentioning because, although the precept is now generally accepted, it is relatively seldom applied.

Most macromodels currently in use have fairly elaborate specifications, the validity of which depends on previous theoretical analyses rather than on hard facts. These analyses often concentrate on particular aspects of phenomena, so that we often have the feeling that these specifications may be somewhat arbitrary.

We must tackle this problem. Obviously we must not over-estimate its importance and follow in the footsteps of those who take this as an excuse for rejecting the use of econometric models or for claiming that their methodology should be entirely revised. We know very well that there are strong points in favour of these models; we have also had the opportunity of seeing that these models, developed during the period of rapid growth, have served well since the 1974 crisis and have on the whole been fairly reliable.

But we must admit that the validity of certain variantial effects is often dubious, albeit because of differences between results deduced from distinct models, all of which are considered to be admissible. The weak spots in the models—those most prone to specification whims and most sensitive for the direction of certain variantial effects—mainly concern investment, the explicative factors of its variations, as well as its effect on productivity and competitivity. This should not surprise us, as this has always been the most complex aspect to analyse in any effort to understand economic development.

Whatever the case may be, we must resort to facts to test our behaviour or adjustment equations, and especially to discriminate between alternative specifications which seem *a priori* admissible. Although the relevance of these tests is not questioned, I feel that in practice they do not have the place they deserve.

If I have properly understood the reason for this state of affairs, it stems from the small discriminatory power of the statistical tests that are proposed in the methodological literature. The sample of macroeconomic time series which is used for the estimation of our models is usually too small to lead to clear results on points that do in fact cause problems. Knowing that this is the case, econometricians are at a loss and cannot see how they can carry through the precept I am considering, even though they fully accept its value.

If my diagnosis is correct, the conclusion must be that tests should eventually be carried out on different data, which would be relevant to the problem in hand. We must set ourselves the aim of carrying out specific research programmes by isolating certain aspects of phenomena, investment, for example, and studying them by using less aggregated data; for instance, researchers might consider time series concerning various sectors experiencing different economic conditions; they might also deal with samples of individual data, or series concerning foreign countries.

Carrying out econometric research work of this kind successfully would not, of course, be new; but it must be done with the aim of using it to test, as directly as possible, the equations contained in macroeconomic models. At the very least, we must spare no effort to refine our judgement gradually as to the choice of better specifications; we cannot be satisfied with the present state of uncertainty concerning some of the laws embodied in our present models.

Devoting more attention to aggregation, making the most of unconventional data, and doing more systematic testing: these are the three general precepts that I have discussed, without in any way intending to undermine the importance of the many other points that will be considered in the remainder of this volume.

PART ONE

Expectations Specification

2

Expectations and the Prices of Long-Term Assets

ROBERT J. SHILLER

INTRODUCTION

I wish to give a broad overview here of some exploratory work that my colleague, Sanford Grossman, and I have been doing on the determinants of the variability of long-term asset prices (Shiller, 1979, 1981a, b; Grossman and Shiller, 1981, 1982). The discussion will serve as a broad introduction to our work and related work in the emerging 'intertemporal substitution' school of thought, and will attempt to offer some perspective on the literature.

Having been suitably impressed with the recent work in macroeconometric modelling, I feel a little out of place here presenting exploratory data analysis that is in many respects very simple in its techniques. With some of the work I plan to discuss, I feel a bit like an advocate of wood-burning stoves speaking at a seminar of heating engineers. At least, this wood stove has a rather different design. Simple methods have their place too.

The empirical work presented here might yet be of methodological interest, however. Advocates of serious exploratory data analysis (for example Tukey, 1977) would say that it is worthy of extensive discussion, and should not be regarded as something one does only in the privacy of one's office. While models are discussed here, no model is so carefully defined as to yield a likelihood function which might be the basis for formal statistical testing. Exploratory data analysis is intended as an early stage of model building when we are not ready to specify a model completely. At this stage, it may not be helpful to define a model in an arbitrarily narrow way just to allow formal statistical analysis to proceed. Instead, exploratory data analysis seeks to inform the reader of useful basic facts. As such it is more an art than a science. As an art it may be more instructive to practice it together than to discuss how to do it.

BASIC NOTIONS

Prices of long-term assets, i.e. assets which yield services over decades, are very variable. Figure 2.1 shows real price data for the USA on four major assets: corporate stocks, housing, land and long-term bonds (see the appendix for source of data). The standard deviation of the five-year real percentage price change for corporate stocks is enormous: 45 per cent. The standard deviation of five-year percentage price change for the other assets is smaller but still large: for the housing series 15 per cent, for the land series 18 per cent, for the long-term bond series 21 per cent. At the risk of comparing apples with oranges, note that the standard deviation of the

FIGURE 2.1 Basic US data series in real terms. All series are divided by a price index: the consumption deflator for non-durables and services. See appendix for sources of data

five-year percentage change in real per capita consumption on non-durables and services from 1894 to 1981 was only 8 per cent (and for 1955 to 1981 was only 3 per cent).

There is no received doctrine as to what accounts for these price movements. The absence of a generally accepted theory poses real problems for macroeconometric model builders. The problems are often dealt with only by ignoring these prices altogether.

Many people in the profession feel, however, that while we may not be able to predict these prices, we have a basic theory which describes qualitatively why they change and conveniently offers an excuse why we may be unable to forecast them. The theory I refer to attributes movements in real prices primarily to new information about future real dividends paid on the respective assets. For corporate bonds (for which the dividends are called coupons and repayment of principal) and stocks the dividends are observed. For land and housing we do not have good data on the dividends paid. In principle, their dividends could be measured by observing the amounts earned by these assets in rental markets.

In its extreme form, the theory attributes price movements *entirely* to information about future dividends, and asserts that the real price of the *i*th asset is the present value with constant discount rate r_i of expected future real dividends:

$$P_{it} = \sum_{k=0}^{\infty} \left(\frac{1}{1 + r_i}\right)^{k+1} E_t D_{it+k} \tag{1}$$

where P_{it} is the real price of a unit of the *i*th asset at time t, D_{it} is the real dividend paid on the *i*th asset at (let us say the end of) time period t and r_i is the real discount rate applicable to the *i*th asset. The symbol E_t refers to mathematical expectation conditional on all publicly available information at time t.

The assumption of a constant real discount rate r_i for each asset is extreme, of course, and the assumption is not always made. Some such assumption about discount rates is necessary, however, if the theory is to have content. Those who casually interpret price movement only in terms of new information about future dividends are probably implicitly relying on this theory.

Why is the theory in (1) popular? Some sorts of casual and inconclusive evidence for aspects of the theory might be offered which could be inferred from figure 2.1 alone. Note that the prices of the different assets shown in figure 2.1 do not seem to show much comovement. We tend to think of movements in the discount rate as economy-wide phenomena which should affect all assets together. Note also that the volatile prices of these assets could be explained as primarily due to discount rate movements only if discount rate movements are themselves quite variable, a possibility that many have felt implausible. Another fact, immediately apparent from figure 2.1, seems important: real stock price series roughly resemble real dividend series. This is what the model (1) would predict if dividends were generally expected to continue at their present level.

The most important evidence for (1) that has been offered, however, comes from evidence from numerous tests in the literature of 'efficient markets'. The outcome of these tests is described as finding that real returns on long-term assets whose dividends are readily measured, i.e. on stocks and long-term bonds, are unforecastable, i.e. that

$$E_t(R_{it}) = E_t\left(\frac{P_{it+1} - P_{it} + D_{it}}{P_{it}}\right) = r_i \tag{2}$$

where r_i does not depend on time t. Here $(P_{it+1} - P_{it})/P_{it}$ is the capital gain, and D_{it}/P_{it} the dividend yield. The sum of the two is the return R_{it}. Thus, (2) embodies the assumption that there is no 'good time' or 'bad time', in terms of expected returns, to buy any of the assets. Sometimes the efficient markets result is casually described as asserting that price changes $(P_{it+1} - P_{it})/P_{it}$ are unforecastable. That description is inaccurate. Prices of stocks predictably fall when the stock goes ex-dividend. The efficient markets theory asserts that returns, not price changes, are unforecastable.

It is accepted, incidentally, that r_i should differ from one asset to another because of risk. The mean-variance capital asset pricing model, for example, would attribute differences in r_i to different covariances with the 'market portfolio', or 'beta'. Empirical work with the capital asset pricing model usually assumes that (2) holds, with r_i constant at least over substantial time intervals.

The point is that (2) is a rational expectations model which, if solved, subject to a condition that prices do not explode in the face of stable dividends, yields (1). If we can regard the literature on efficient markets as having demonstrated that (2) is exactly true, then we can regard (1) as having been established.

There is a widespread feeling in the profession that efficient markets has been vindicated in the literature and by implication that (1) has been established. The successes of the notion of 'efficient markets' in finance have been so admired as to give rise to a dominant paradigm in empirical econometrics in the last two decades. One might speculate that the growth of the 'rational expectations' literature in macroeconometrics is an outgrowth of experience with tests of efficiency in financial markets. Anyone who has tried the standard methodology for testing for random-walk behaviour of prices of long-term financial assets has probably had a similar experience. If one regresses with the usual sample size stock market returns on various information variables one generally finds, on first pass, some information variables statistically significant. If one examines these significant variables carefully for timing, however, one generally finds that they were actually not completely known before the return was observed. If the timing is corrected (by lagging the information variable in the regression) the variable generally drops from significance. It has become almost a sport predicting when working papers claiming to forecast returns will reappear in revision with opposite conclusions! Such experiences with tests for efficient markets can be contrasted informally with experiences with tests of other theories in economics. One has the casual impression that dropping or adding a variable from a regression or changing a sample period slightly often radically alters the significance of crucial coefficients. It is not surprising, then, that those involved in applied econometrics are attracted to efficient markets models.

Unfortunately, it is not widely appreciated that the alternative hypotheses against which simple tests of efficient markets have power may not be very interesting. Moreover, the results of efficient markets testing are often described as discriminating between hypotheses for which the tests actually had little power to discriminate.

What is discovered most often in simple regression tests of efficient markets is that it is not possible to forecast well short-run returns on volatile financial assets. It is not surprising that one cannot forecast such returns well. If one could, one could make a lot of money fast. It is not surprising that those who do 'event studies' which test for the correlation with the outcome of an important event of the return on a stock over a very short interval of time (say an hour's time) over which the event occurred find a significant correlation, but find no correlations with the outcome of the event of subsequent returns. In the former instance, by choosing a very short time interval over which nothing much else happened but the event in question and during which the event was much discussed by market participants, it is not surprising that a significant correlation with returns is found. It is also not surprising that one cannot make a lot of money with little risk in subsequent days by using information about the event. The power of a test for an effect of the event on the price change over the next year is bound to be low since the variance of the one-year price change is vastly higher than the variance of the one-hour price change.

The interesting hypothesis that seems to be suggested by (1) and not by (2) is that price changes represent *information* about future dividends. Tests of the model by regressing returns on information variables may have little power to discriminate whether price movements represent such information. If price changes are very large and unpredictable, so as to swamp out changes in dividends as a component of returns, then returns might be hard to forecast even if price changes did not have anything to do with future dividends. Expression (2) itself does not say price changes have anything to do with information about future dividends. If (2) held exactly and if price changes did not represent such information, then prices would tend to drift away from dividends, i.e. prices would tend to explode even in the face of stable dividends. Since the dividend price ratio has shown no important drift over the past century, we can conclude that prices *have not* exploded away from dividends. Can we then conclude that (1) must be true? The conclusion is valid only if efficient markets tests have shown that (1) holds *exactly*.

To see that regression tests may not give much evidence that price changes represent information about subsequent dividends, consider the following scenario which I will call a 'fads' scenario. Suppose, to take an extreme case, the dividend D_{it} is constant through time: $D_{it} = \bar{D}_i$. Suppose the price of a share follows a stationary first-order autoregressive process:

$$(P_{it+1} - \bar{P}) = \lambda(P_{it} - \bar{P}) + \varepsilon_{t+1}$$

where $\bar{P}$ is the mean of P_{it}, $\lambda(0 < \lambda < 1)$ is the autoregressive parameter, and ε_t is the innovation in price uncorrelated with information. Prices move, let us say, because of fads among investors who spontaneously change their minds about the value of the stock. Since in this scenario dividends never change, price changes certainly do not represent information about dividends! Prices are also mean reverting so that there is no tendency for the price to explode. Yet simple regressions of returns on information will have little power to reject hypothesis (2) if λ is close to one. The theoretical R^2 in a regression of $P_{it+1} - P_{it} + D_{it}$ on P_{it} and a constant is $(1 - \lambda)/2$. If λ is, say, 0.9 for annual data, then this theoretical R^2 is 0.05. We know that power to reject is very small with such low R^2 unless we have many years data! Switching from annual to monthly, weekly or even daily observations will greatly increase the number of observations but will not substantially raise the power of the test, since as the time interval of observations shrinks the relevant value of λ approaches one.

VARIANCES BOUNDS FOR DIVIDENDS

The above example suggests that something is wrong with simple regression tests as tests of the model (1). In a case in which dividends are never observed to move, we ought to know with certainty that the model (1) is wrong! In fact, dividends do move but the present value of dividends, being a long moving average, behaves much like a simple trend.

One has the impression from the statistical literature, however, that regression tests have many desirable properties. Why do they seem to be failing us here? I discussed this point in the context of the likelihood principle in another paper (Shiller, 1981b). I pointed out there that the assumptions of the conventional regression model do not capture all we know about the model (1). They miss the fact that price changes must be justified in terms of subsequent dividends. Regression tests may then have little power and may fail to reject whether or not prices in fact explode in the sample.

Thus, we see that dividends must show some variability if the variability of prices is to be justified. I have in several papers (Shiller, 1979, 1981a, b) (as also LeRoy and Porter, 1981) devised simple tests of the model (1) based on this simple notion.

The easiest way to understand the basic notion behind such tests is to consider the model (1) in innovation form. Let $\delta_t \equiv E_t - E_{t-1}$ denote the innovation operator, so that for any variable x_t, $\delta_t x_t$ is the change in the conditional expectation of x_t between $t - 1$ and t. Applying this operator to both sides of (1) then gives us

$$\delta_t P_{it} = \sum \left(\frac{1}{1 + r_i}\right)^{k+1} \delta_t D_{it+k}. \tag{3}$$

Thus, the innovation in price at time t is the present value of the time t innovations in future dividends. We shall suppose that $\delta_t P_t$ and $\delta_t D_{t+k}$ are stationary stochastic processes in time t. Our model implies that we observe innovations in price:

$$\delta_t P_{it} = \Delta P_{it} + d_{it-1} - r_i P_{it-1}.$$

The innovation in price might be regarded as the change in price corrected for 'ex-dividend' effects or other effects of the current dividend. Unfortunately, the model does not tell us that we can observe the innovation in dividends. The difficulty in testing all implications of the model is that, conditional on the validity of (3), we do not know in which future time periods the dividend innovations implicit in the price innovations occur.

We do know that the variance of dividends which *is* observed (supposing dividends are a stationary stochastic process which has a variance) is the sum of the variance of its innovations:

$$\mathrm{Var}(D_{it}) = \sum_{k=0}^{\infty} \mathrm{Var}(\delta_{t-k} D_{it}). \tag{4}$$

In practice, since dividends apparently have a trend, the expression should refer to the variance of detrended dividends, but we disregard that complication here, for expositional purposes.

We may then ask the question for a given observed variance of the innovation in price $\delta_t P_{it}$: What is the minimum admissible variance of D_{it} that is consistent with the model (1)? It is easy to see from (3) that given any sequence $\mathrm{Var}(\delta_t D_{it})$, $\mathrm{Var}(\delta_t D_{it+1})$, $\mathrm{Var}(\delta_t D_{it+2})$, ... then the largest possible $\mathrm{Var}(\delta_t P_{it})$ consistent with this sequence occurs when $\delta_t D_{it}$ is perfectly correlated with $\delta_t D_{it+k}$ for all $k > 0$. This means that dividends are forecasted as simple moving average processes, i.e. forecasts are linear in lagged dividends only. In this circumstance

$$\mathrm{Var}(\delta_t P_{it}) = \left[\sum \left(\frac{1}{1+r_i}\right)^{k+1} \sqrt{\mathrm{Var}(\delta_t D_{it+k})}\right]^2$$

and the minimum value for $\mathrm{Var}(D_{it})$, for given value of $\mathrm{Var}(\delta_t P_{it})$, occurs when $\mathrm{Var}(\delta_t D_{it+k})$ is proportional to $(1 + r_i)^{-2k}$. This then gives us the inequality

$$\mathrm{Var}(D_{it}) \geq [(1 + r_i)^2 - 1]\mathrm{Var}(\delta_t P_{it}). \tag{5}$$

This inequality was the basis for testing the model in Shiller (1981a). Of course, to apply the inequality r_i had to be estimated and the variable D_{it} had to be detrended, a point we shall return to. Based on point estimates of trends and variances using essentially the stock price data of figure 2.1, the standard deviation of actual dividends around their trend was found to be less than one-fifth of the minimum possible standard deviation according to the inequality. Thus, dividends have not been nearly as variable as the variance of $\delta_t P_{it}$ would require.

What are we to make of this? Some have responded by questioning the detrending applied to dividends. The trend in dividends could be spurious. Some have claimed that formal statistical tests should be undertaken to resolve the issue (e.g. Flavin, 1982). To my mind, such tests are not the central issue. There is always going to be uncertainty whether observed variability of dividends is a good measure of their potential variability. Investors could have been worrying about a 'disaster' or 'windfall' with low probability which did not chance to occur in the sample. Suppose the 'disaster' they were concerned with was possible nationalization of stocks. Is any statistical test going to tell us they were or were not right to worry about this?

Imagine that you were asked to write a paper analysing the probability that the stock market in the USA might become worthless. You would probably try to think of scenarios in which this might happen, and what comes to mind might be such unlikely events as foreign domination, damaging wars, and natural disasters, as well as nationalization. Given that these are the most likely scenarios, would it make any sense to give a quantitative analysis by constructing a time-series model for dividends and computing the probability that it crosses zero at some horizon? Those who advocate formal testing of stock market models based on time-series methodology are in effect proposing such a quantitative approach. In fact, we have no reason to think that actual dividends are in fact an autoregressive process or the like. The probabilities produced by such an analysis could not be taken seriously.

Before turning to other models, it is important to understand the relevance of the literature on the distribution of stock returns which has considered the possibility that variances of returns do not exist (for example Fama, 1965). What this literature has actually shown is not that variances do not exist but that distributions of stock returns are 'fat-tailed', i.e. tend to show high sample kurtosis. It has been pointed out that the phenomenon could be the result of a tendency for important infrequent breaks in information which cause occasional very large price movements. Given our model (1) such a tendency could indeed cause returns to have fat-tailed distributions. So long as the variance of dividends exists, however, the variance of price changes will also exist. For any variance of dividends, there is an upper bound on the variance of the innovation in price, found by turning around the inequality (5). A tendency for information to come in big lumps occasionally cannot raise the variance of price above this upper bound. For a given dividend stochastic process, such a tendency may actually serve to lower the variance of the innovation in price by causing price to be stable for long intervals of time between the information breaks.

Another issue concerns the use of the fact that price in (1) is the expected value of a weighted moving average of dividends. Moving averages have the effect of smoothing the series averaged, i.e. of reducing the power in the high frequencies of the spectral density. The conditional expectations operator in (1) means, however, that this point cannot be directly applied so as to imply that price should be smooth in this sense. In fact, the price series could have more power in the highest frequencies than the series D_{it}/r_i. Restrictions on the model in terms of spectral densities are discussed in Shiller (1979). There is in fact a sense in which the moving average in (1) does cause price to behave smoothly.

A CONSUMPTION-BASED ASSET PRICING MODEL

Since changes of prices of corporate stocks cannot be represented as the response to new information about any changes in dividends actually observed over the last century or so, we are inclined to look elsewhere for a story why prices are so variable. Let us return to basics. Apart from the empirical evidence, why has it seemed plausible that expected returns should be constant through time? Recall that the exact constancy of expected returns through time was what gave the result that (1) holds and thus that price movements can be interpreted only in terms of new information about dividends. Recall that with the 'fads' example of an autoregressive process for prices, with autoregressive coefficient close to one, returns are still not *very* forecastable but always *slightly* forecastable. In that example, price movements had nothing whatever to do with information about dividends. Why is this story which fits the data better (in the sense that the volatility inequality tests are not evidence against the model) not more popular? One reason may be that economists may be disinclined to put any irrational behaviour in the models, even though just a little irrational behaviour (in the sense of creating little profit opportunities) might change them a lot.

It is, however, the notion that profit opportunities are created be departures from the model (1) that bothers economists. Certainly, they feel 'unexploited profit opportunities' ought not to exist. But what implausible profit opportunities are created by the 'fads' example? Is the non-constancy through time of the expected return on an asset itself evidence of a profit opportunity? It is if one can reallocate one's consumption or production through time 'profitably' in response to the non-constancy.

Consider the consumption decision. If I am willing to forego consumption when expected returns are high, I can expect to make money doing so. But here is the issue: When do such high expected returns come? Suppose they are high just when consumption is low. In times of recession, let us say, people try to cash in the shares thereby creating a price decline and 'profit opportunity' (in an expected value sense) when prices return to normal level. The expected profit opportunity may not be a genuine opportunity if it tends to come at a bad time.

Consider the case of an additively separable utility function for the representative individual of the constant relative risk aversion variety:

$$U = \frac{1}{1-A} \sum_{k=0}^{\infty} \rho^k c_{t+k}^{1-A} \qquad 0 < \rho < 1, \quad 0 < A. \tag{6}$$

A first-order condition for maximization of this utility function is that

$$E_t(1 + R_{it})M_t^{(1)} = 1 \tag{7}$$

where $M_t^{(1)}$ is the one-period ahead marginal rate of substitution equal to $\rho(c_t/c_{t+1})^A$. By iterating (7) using the definition of R_{it} in (2) we get the expression

$$P_{it} = E_t \sum_{k=0}^{\infty} M_t^{(k+1)} D_{it+k} \tag{8}$$

where $M_t^{(k)} = \rho^k(c_t/c_{t+k})^A$ is the k-period marginal rate of substitution. In Grossman and Shiller (1981) we found that 'perfect foresight' price computed from (8) without the expectations operator fits actual price somewhat for most of the sample if k is around 4. Amazingly, even if people actually knew all future stock price movements and future consumption with certainty there may be no true profit opportunity! The perfect foresight assumption is of course unrealistic. One might however introspect in these terms: Suppose in a recession your consumption was reduced by circumstances to, say, 10 per cent below its long-run value, and you expected prosperity to return in, say, about four years. If you also thought stock prices would climb about 40 per cent, or about 10 per cent a year over this period, would you be inclined to cut your consumption even further to invest more in stock? If you are not sure, then our value of 4 for the coefficient of relative risk aversion is not way off the mark for you. If others are like you, major movements in stock prices in response to consumption movements are plausible.

One problem with this analysis is that consumption in the United States has been very stable in the post World War II period, while asset prices have been quite variable, so that only a very high A would fit the model. Another problem with this story is that the different asset prices shown in figure 2.1 do not show apparent comovements. If the big swings in stock prices are due to big movements in discount factors $M_t^{(k)}$, why then are housing and land prices not moving somewhat similarly? Of course, the real dividend patterns for these assets are quite different from that of stocks. Most notably, the real dividends on bonds has been generally trending downwards due to inflation. Real dividends on housing or land may also show very different patterns. Since housing is a reproducible asset, its price may be driven by its reproduction cost, and rental rates might then show a tendency to respond to the business situation, rather than prices. Still, it would seem that we should see *some* tendency for comovements if stock price movements are due primarily to large discount rate movements.

Various modifications in the model have been discussed which did not seem, on further inspection, to be promising avenues to explain both the disparity across assets in their prices and the high volatility of prices. Heterogeneity of investor information and investor wealth was considered (Grossman and Shiller, 1982). Non-separable preferences have been considered in recent work by Hansen and Singleton.

The above analysis fits neatly into the 'intertemporal substitution' approach to macroeconomics, which assumes that markets clear and that the business cycle can be understood in terms of utility maximizing and profit maximizing behaviour constrained only by a budget constraint (see for example Barro, 1979). Recent work along these lines particularly relevant to our purposes has been done by Lucas (1978) and Breeden (1979). The competing approach to understanding business fluctuations with which the intertemporal substitution school is often contrasted is described in terms of disequilibrium (see for example Bénassy, 1976; Dréze, 1975; Malinvaud, 1977). This approach emphasizes that non-market clearing phenomena are crucial to understanding business fluctuations. Economic agents are limited in the amounts they can buy or sell in certain markets, and prices may not move to clear markets.

Much of the discussions in the disequilibrium literature has considered abstract models which do not lend themselves readily to empirical application. Those who apply disequilibrium theory need first specify how sticky various prices are and why they are sticky. Moreover, they must understand the nature of the rationing mechanism that is used when markets do not clear. It is likely that models which have descriptive power will be very complicated and inelegant. There is not just *one* reason why prices are sticky, not just *one* rationing mechanism. We may be in a situation where the complexity of the simplest model which would seem appropriately descriptive may be far beyond our data to estimate.

One of the appeals of the approach embodied in expressions (7) and (8) is that it does not necessarily require any assumption that markets clear. Thus, if individuals are rationed or if the trading is restricted in markets for certain financial assets, then so long as individuals maximize (6), expressions (7) or (8) still hold for any asset for which the constraint is not binding. Imagine, moreover, that the economy is in what Malinvaud (1977) called a 'Keynesian equilibrium' where producers are constrained in product markets and consumers in labour markets. So long as the marginal utility of consumption is not directly affected by labour fluctuations, then (7) or (8) should still hold. One approach to introducing labour fluctuations directly into the model is to modify the utility function (6) by appending additively separable terms in labour supply. There is then under the assumption that there are no binding restrictions on trades in labour markets an expression analogous to (7) or (8) with labour in place of consumption. Perhaps these alternative expressions seem less promising than those involving consumption, since individuals are less free to choose their labour supply. Expression (7) with labour in place of consumption was tested by Mankiw et al. (1982) (analogous work was done by Altonji, 1982) and found not at all descriptive of the data.

Bewley (1982) has argued that rationing in credit markets may be essential to understanding why long-term asset prices may be so volatile. His story emphasizes not only that borrowing is limited but also that there is uninsured risk causing wealth fluctuations across individuals. Individual consumption paths may be much more variable than aggregate consumption paths. Persons in temporarily adverse circumstances are up against their borrowing constraint and hold no stocks. Those in advantageous circumstances hold stocks to smooth out their consumption. Because of the no-borrowing constraint, the aggregation results of Breeden (1979) and Grossman and Shiller (1982) do not apply. If we had data on consumption of the most wealthy fraction of the population it could still not be used to validate (6) since (6) applies to consumption of individuals. The volatility of stocks might thus possibly be attributed to unobserved fluctuations in consumption of individuals.

CONCLUSION

There were several tentative conclusions that I was led to in the work summarized here. It must be remembered that these 'conclusions' do not have the kind of authority that would follow from a more explicit probabilistic model construction and testing. The reader is reminded of the methodological discussion in the introduction.

The conclusions of the variance bound analysis might be summarized by saying that the frequent large swings in real stock prices were never followed by correspondingly large swings in real dividends. Basically, the present value of real dividends in the USA has just followed a trend over the last century.

The observed variability of stock prices might be attributed to information about potential variability in dividends which did not chance to be observed in the sample. For example, investors may have been concerned about nationalization or some other big event. Whether change in opinions about such an event is plausible or whether we want to attribute price movements to investor fads is a matter of judgement. No data are available which would resolve the matter.

Stock price movements might also be attributed to changes in the rate at which future dividends are discounted into today's price. Such an explanation for the variability of stock prices seems plausible if consumption is sufficiently variable. For the post-war USA, however, aggregate consumption is not very variable. Moreover, prices of other assets, land, housing and bonds, have not moved in tandem with stock prices. The explanation might still be saved if we introduce both disequilibrium notions and investor heterogeneity. People are sometimes unable to borrow. Moreover, they may find it difficult to trade their homes or other land. A well worked-out empirical model explaining asset price volatility along these lines is not yet available.

APPENDIX

Sources of data

The data used in this paper are described in Shiller (1982) and thus only brief descriptions are included here. The only difference in the data in this paper is that the separate housing price series are linked together here using the Boekch construction cost index for 1948–53, to yield a continuous series. Before, there had been a short gap in the series from 1949 to 1952. The quality of the data is discussed in the above reference. The housing and land series may be subject to important errors.

The series plotted in figure 2.1 are all divided by the consumption deflator for non-durables and services 1972 = 1.00, so that all series are measured in 'real' terms.

The stock price series is the Standard and Poor Composite Stock Price Index, and the dividend series is the Standard and Poor Series on dividends per share adjusted to index.

The land price series is the index of average value of farm real estate per acre from the US Department of Agriculture. The bond price series is the price of a 5 per cent coupon 25-year bond whose yield is given by an Aaa bond yield average.

The housing price series is obtained by linking together four different series on the market price of homes and one home construction cost index (for the brief gap noted above).

NOTE

This work was supported by the United States National Science Foundation.

REFERENCES

Altonji, J. G. (1982) 'The Intertemporal Substitution Model of Labor Market Fluctuations: An Empirical Analysis', *Review of Economic Studies*, **49**, 783–824.

Barro, R. J. (1979) 'Developments in the Equilibrium Approach to Business Cycles', mimeographed, University of Rochester.

Bénassy, J. P. (1976) 'The Disequilibrium Approach to Monopolistic Price Setting and General Monopolistic Equilibrium', *Review of Economic Studies*, **43**, 69–81.

Bewley, T. F. (1982) 'Thoughts on Tests of the Intertemporal Asset Pricing Model', mimeographed, Northwestern University.

Breeden, D. (1979) 'An Intertemporal Asset Pricing Model with Stochastic Consumption and Investment Opportunities', *Journal of Financial Economics*, **7**, 265–96 (September).

Dréze, J. (1975) 'Existence of an Equilibrium Under Price Rigidity and Quantity Rationing', *International Economic Review*, **16**, 301–20.

Fama, E. F. (1965) 'The Behaviour of Stock Market Prices', *Journal of Business*, **38**, 34–105 (January).

Flavin, M. (1982) 'Same Sample Bias in Tests of Excess Volatility in the Bond Market', mimeographed, University of Virginia, Charlottesville.

Grossman, S. J. and Shiller, R. J. (1981) 'The Determinants of the Variability of Stock Market Prices', *American Economic Review* (May).

Grossman, S. J. and Shiller, R. J. (1982) 'Consumption Correlatedness and Risk Measurement in Economies with Non-Traded Assets and Heterogeneous Information', *Journal of Financial Economics*, **10**, 195–210.

LeRoy, S. and Porter, R. (1981) 'The Present Value Relation: Tests Based on Implied Variance Bounds', *Econometrica* (March).

Lucas, R. E. (1978) 'Asset Prices in an Exchange Economy', *Econometrica*, **46**, 1429–45 (November).

Malinvaud, E. (1977) *The Theory of Unemployment Reconsidered*, Basil Blackwell, Oxford.

Mankiw, G., Rotemberg, J. and Summers, L. (1982) 'Intertemporal Substitution in Macroeconomics', mimeographed, MIT.

Shiller, R. (1979) 'The Volatility of Long-Term Interest Rates and Expectations Models of the Term Structure', *Journal of Political Economy*, **87**, 1190–219.

Shiller, R. (1981a) 'Do Stock Prices Move Too Much to be Justified by Subsequent Changes in Dividends?' *American Economic Review*, 421–36 (June).

Shiller, R. (1981b) 'The Use of Volatility Measures in Assessing Market Efficiency', *Journal of Finance*, **36**, 291–304 (May).

Shiller, R. (1982) 'Consumption, Asset Prices and Macroeconomic Fluctuations', *Carnegie Rochester Conference Series in Public Policy*, Vol. 17, North-Holland, Amsterdam, pp. 203–38.

Tukey, J. W. (1977) *Exploratory Data Analysis*, Addison-Wesley, Reading, Ma.

Comment

ALAIN MONFORT

Once again, Robert Shiller has provided a very interesting and stimulating paper. The issues discussed are related to various fields and the following comments will be restricted to the probabilistic and statistical problems. Even though these problems are not presented explicitly in this survey, they are the basis of all the arguments and, therefore, seem worth discussing in some detail. We shall first deal with two points which have already been widely discussed in the literature: the solution of a rational expectation model and the regression tests of efficient markets. Then, we shall look at the new tools suggested by the author and, in particular, the variance bounds.

The solutions of rational expectation models such as (2) have been studied in a recent paper by Gourieroux, Laffont and Monfort (*Econometrica*, March 1982). In this paper it is shown, among other things, that the set of solutions of models like model (2) is much larger than one would originally have thought. The 'forward solution' (1) is only one solution among an infinite set of solutions; moreover, the set of 'non-explosive' solutions is still infinite. In other words, it is not possible to say that '(2) is a rational expectation model which, if solved, yields (1)'; in order to make this proposition true, it would be necessary to impose extra conditions leading to the forward solution, but it is not clear that it is possible to find conditions whose interpretation is satisfactory.

The other classical point discussed by the author is the test of efficient markets by means of regression. The regression made, which is not reported in this present paper, is a regression of the annual stock market returns on the lagged price. Some minor remarks could be made about this regression: other variables and other lags could have been introduced in the regression in order to see more precisely the origin for the rejection of the efficient markets theory; on the other hand, the discussion on R^2 is not very useful since, in a simple regression, it provides exactly the same information as the Student statistic. However, a more serious problem with this regression comes from the fact that the price has been detrended. This detrending is particularly questionable in the present case because the stock prices have no clear trend and the choice of a particular detrending is likely to have a strong influence on the result; it would have been interesting to have had some information about this sensitivity problem.

Among the new tools proposed by Robert Shiller, the more attractive is probably the variance bound for dividends. The proof of the result is very interesting and the bound obtained provides a simple test based on estimates of the variances. However, this kind of test has two serious drawbacks. First of all, it is not a genuine statistical test since it only consists of the comparison of two point estimates without any size or power considerations: in fact, as suggested in the paper by LeRoy and Porter (1981), the power is likely to be low and this is relatively intuitive since one is testing a remote consequence of the markets efficiency hypothesis. The other drawback of this test is that the rejection does not indicate in which direction it would be recommended to go; it is only known that at least one of the assumptions made must be abandoned. Let us consider some of these assumptions. First, it is assumed that (1) holds exactly; it would have been natural to introduce, as usual in econometrics, a white noise disturbance term. In (1) it is also implicitly assumed that there is a kind of instantaneous causality since P_t is explained by variables at time t. Stationarity assumptions are also made; in particular (5) is shown under the assumption that dividends are a stationary process, and it is specially unrealistic. All these assumptions cannot be tested because there is no clear probabilistic framework; in fact, in the course of the text, several frameworks are referred to (random walk, univariate autoregressive scheme, disaster model, . . .) but all these frameworks are partial and their links are not clear. There is obviously a need for a global probabilistic framework. In the introduction, the author rules out this possibility and justifies exploratory data analysis because 'it may not be helpful to define a model in an arbitrarily narrow way just to allow formal statistical analysis to proceed'. In fact, such narrow models are proposed in the text: for instance, the 'constant dividends–autoregressive prices' model is so narrow that the conclusions are almost identical to the assumptions. However, it is certainly a good idea to begin with exploratory data analysis, and such analysis is perfectly compatible with a probabilistic framework provided that this framework is sufficiently general.

Such a framework could be the multivariate autoregressive scheme advocated by C. Sims. In this context, the problem of the exactness of (1) reduces to the significance of the variance of the price innovation; the stationarity is related to the roots of the characteristic determinant; the instantaneous causality is readily tested with a Student procedure (using a recursive normalization); the one-sided causalities, which underline several discussions in the paper, are also easily tested with a Fisher procedure; and finally the efficient markets assumption is equivalent to a non-linear constraint on the parameters. This constraint can be tested with one of the three classical procedures: Wald, Lagrange or likelihood ratio tests. In the present context, it seems that the Wald procedure would be the more convenient because it does not necessitate the computation of the constrained estimates, which is more complicated than the unconstrained estimation.

We can think that, with such a general model, it would be possible to identify more precisely the assumptions which are not compatible with the data and, therefore, to go one step further in the very interesting and fruitful analysis proposed by the author.

3

Expectations Formations and Macroeconometric Modelling

M. H. PESARAN

INTRODUCTION

What expectations actually are, how they influence economic behaviour, how they are formed, and whether expectations held by economic agents are susceptible to formal representations are issues of paramount importance in macroeconometric modelling. Amongst the various theories of expectations so far advanced in economics, the hypothesis of rational expectations due to Muth (1961) has presented by far the most formidable challenge for current macroeconometric practice. According to this hypothesis, subjective expectations held by economic agents are equal to or will eventually converge to the corresponding mathematical expectations. There is already a large and growing literature which deals with the various theoretical and empirical implications of the Rational Expectations Hypothesis (REH). Some of these developments have been surveyed critically by Shiller (1978), Buiter (1980) and Tobin (1980) and favourably by McCallum (1980) and Begg (1982). The problems and ambiguities involved in the identification and empirical testing of rational expectations macroeconometric models are also discussed by Wallis (1980), Revankar (1980), Hoffman and Schmidt (1981) and Pesaran (1981, 1982).

Our aim in this paper is to look at the REH from a different and in many ways more fundamental viewpoint. First, we examine whether there exists a basis for the 'rational' formation of expectations in Muth's sense when the uncertainty surrounding the decision-making of economic agents stems mainly from their ignorance of other agents' behaviour. We contrast this type of uncertainty (which we refer to as 'behavioural uncertainty') with the more readily understood type of uncertainty which is for all practical purposes exogenous to agents' decisions and is partly due to man's ignorance of his physical environmental and/or the uncertainty that may be associated with the state of nature itself, such as variations in the weather. We argue that when the decision-making process is dominated by behavioural uncertainty, the necessary basis for a formal representation of the process of expectations formations along the lines suggested by Muth usually does not exist and an institutional and conventional view of the expectations formations process advanced by Keynes (1936: chapter 12) and Simon (1958) would be much more fruitful. In this light we advocate the use of tendency survey data on expectations in the construction of macroeconometric models and emphasize the importance of *direct* measures of expectations for the study of the process of expectations formations in economics. Employing the results of industrial surveys carried out by the Confederation of British Industry (CBI), we consider the practical problems involved in the conversion of qualitative survey results into quantitative measures of expectations and suggest a new method (based on an early work by Anderson (1952)) which does not seem to suffer from some of the shortcomings inherent in the techniques initially proposed by Theil (1952, 1955, 1966) and later by Knöbl (1974) and Carlson and Parkin (1975). Finally, we demonstrate and compare our procedure with the Carlson and Parkin method by constructing alternative series of expected inflation in British manufacturing over the period 1959–81.

SOURCES OF UNCERTAINTY

The need to form expectations primarily (but not exclusively) arises because individuals in deciding which course of action to follow are constantly faced with an uncertain environment. How expectations are actually formed or whether they eventually converge to the mathematical expectations formed on the basis of the objective probability distributions of the events is very much dependent on the source and nature of the uncertainty involved in a particular decision. Uncertainty exists whenever individuals are not completely aware of the potential consequences of their actions.[1] Uncertainty can be due to 'chance' or 'ignorance' or both. The outcome of a toss of a 'fair' coin is uncertain because of the element of pure chance involved; but the uncertainty associated with the potential moves of one's rival in a game of chess is basically due to ignorance. In reality both types of uncertainty are usually present. A simple example due to Dubey and Shubik (1977) can be used to illustrate our point further. Consider two individuals, one with normal eyesight and the other blind, both of whom wish to cross a road where there is a probability p that a truck is approaching silently and a probability $1 - p$ that it is not approaching. Assume now that the one who is blind is told (but not accompanied) by the one who can see whether it is safe to cross the road. In this example the blind man faces two distinct types of uncertainty: the uncertainty associated with the state of nature (i.e. whether the truck approaches or not) and the blind person's uncertainty concerning the motivation and the strategy of the person who can see. The blind person cannot be sure of the sincerity of the advice given to him. We call the former type of uncertainty 'exogenous' uncertainty, and refer to the latter as 'behavioural' uncertainty. Put more formally, when the probability of the occurrence of a given event is invariant to an individual's action, we say (for that individual) the uncertainty which surrounds the occurrence of the event is exogenous; otherwise we say it is 'behavioural' or 'endogenous'.

In the above example, behavioural uncertainty can only exist if there is uncertainty about the state of nature. But in general this need not be the case.[2] The uncertainty involved in the outcome of a chess game can be regarded as purely behavioural. In duopolistic or oligopolistic market conditions where actions by one market participant have a potentially non-negligible impact upon the actions of other participants, behavioural uncertainty will be present even if demand for the industry's output and the individual firm's cost functions happen to be known with certainty. It is the capacity of individuals to adapt and react to one another (in a non-negligible manner) which is the root cause of the existence and prevalence of behavioural uncertainty in economic and social systems.

The degree of behavioural uncertainty associated with a particular circumstance is closely related to the degree to which an individual market participant is potentially capable of influencing the action of others by his own action. At one extreme, perfect competition provides an example of a market structure where behavioural uncertainty is totally absent almost by assumption. All market participants are price-taking profit maximizers and are completely informed about the potential outcome of their actions and make their decisions in the sole pursuit of their own welfare. When conditions of perfect competition prevail, firms will only be faced with uncertainties that are associated with the state of the nature and are exogenous to the functioning of the market mechanism. Perfect competition is, however, an abstraction which should only be taken seriously if its emergence from a given economic background (given endowments, tastes and technology) can be shown rather than assumed. In reality, markets are far from being 'perfectly' competitive and there is no reason to believe that, starting from a given market condition, there would be any tendency towards a perfectly competitive structure. If anything, the reverse seems more likely to be the case. In the words of Joan Robinson (1971: 102) 'where competition is vigorous, there must be a tendency toward monopoly, which is often held up at the stage of oligopoly when a few powerful firms prefer armed neutrality to the final battle for supremacy'. In conditions of oligopoly and imperfect competition, behavioural uncertainty continues to remain an integral part of the market environment, and any study of uncertainty and expectations in economics has to deal with both types of uncertainty.

PROCESS OF EXPECTATIONS FORMATIONS

We now turn our attention to the problems connected with the formation and modelling of expectations both when the uncertainty surrounding future events is exogenous to the decision process and when it is behavioural in the sense discussed above.

By expectations is usually meant the 'attitudes, dispositions or psychological states of mind' that relate to events of which we have no previous experience.[3] In this sense expectations are psychologically held subjective beliefs that may or may not be related to the individual's past experience or his present perception. Whether such subjective beliefs can be represented by probability measures is itself the subject of an old controversy which was considerably revived (in economics) by the appearance of Keynes's *Treatise on Probability* and Shackle's subsequent work on expectations and uncertainty (see for example Shackle, 1949, 1955).[4] The logical impossibility of the probabilistic formalization of 'knowledge' was first emphasized by Hume, who maintained that it is not logically justifiable to infer from *repeated* instances of which we have experience to the *probability* of instances of which we have no experience. While this is true it does not necessarily mean, as is forcefully argued by Popper (1972), that we should abandon all attempts at (empirical) explanations and opt for a system of beliefs and dogmas completely unrelated to past observations and present realities.

The fact that the possibility of learning by mere repetition is rather limited does not, on its own, rule out the possibility of learning by 'understanding' through the method of trial-and-error elimination.[5] In practice this would involve the formulation (or trial) and falsification (or elimination) of theories, which could be carried out either by means of classical statistical methods or by resort to Bayesian techniques. Whether such a learning process would be capable of narrowing down the discrepancy that may exist between subjective beliefs and the 'true' state of the world is very much dependent on the available information and the degree of *a priori* understanding of the functioning of the systems involved. That this is so has been demonstrated by the recent and growing literature on the learning process underlying the formation of (rational) expectations. When agents know the 'true' probability distribution associated with the *stable* data generation process but are uncertain of the true parameter values of the underlying probability distribution, it can be shown that agents' learning process will be 'rational' in the sense that convergence to the rational expectations equilibrium will be ensured (see for example Cyert and DeGroot, 1974; Taylor, 1975; Friedman, 1979; Townsend, 1978). However, the situation is entirely different when agents do not know the 'true' data generation process, and attempt to learn on the basis of misspecified models. In these circumstances there is no guarantee that the learning process will become rational in Muth's sense even if agents are allowed to change the specification of their models when they eventually realize that they are false.[6] In short, whether agents can learn how to form rational expectations crucially depends on their *a priori* understanding of the way the economic system functions. The process of 'trial and error' is helpful as a mechanism of throwing out false theories, but there is no guarantee that it will lead agents to the 'true' data generation process. Learning can only become 'rational' by chance and not by design.

In situations where the source of uncertainty is behavioural, agents face the additional difficulty that the 'true' data generation may not even be stable. In the case of exogenous uncertainty, a probabilistic representation of uncertainty will be invariant to the action of economic agents. Decision by an individual not to carry an umbrella does not alter the probability of rain, but a decision by an oligopolist to increase his price is unlikely to leave the probability of price increases by other oligopolists unchanged. Under behavioural uncertainty, even if we ignore Hume's objection to induction, the knowledge of past evolution of a system may be of little guide to its likely future development. The decision-making process will generally be in the form of a non-cooperative non-zero sum game where mixed strategies and unstable outcomes cannot be ruled out and may even become quite prevalent over certain periods. The breakdown of business confidence, the occurrence of social unrest and revolutionary upheavals are examples that immediately come to mind. The highly interactive nature of decision-making under behavioural uncertainty also initiates and involves changes in economic and social institutions.[7] There is no *stable* data generation process that agents can hope to learn about. The basis for formation of expectations as mathematical expectations derived from economic theory simply does not exist; not necessarily because of Hume's or Keynes's objections to the frequency interpretation of probability and inference, but due to the interactive nature of decision-making under behavioural uncertainty.

The fact that an objective basis for probability representation of behavioural uncertainty may not exist does not, however, mean that agents will not form expectations or that their expectations would necessarily be unstable for all variables at all times. Possible reasons for this have been suggested by Hume, himself an arch critic of the inductive method of inference. According to Hume 'custom and habit' condition individuals to form expectations in which they have great confidence. A similar point of view has also been advanced by Keynes (1936) in chapter 12 of his *General Theory*. Popper (1972) even goes a step further and points to 'the immensely powerful *need for regularity*' which makes individuals seek for regularities. The need for regularities arises because of the individual's desire to solve the recurrent problems that he is constantly facing, which in turn leads to the creation of institutions within which conventions, norms and habits can be exercised with ease. He habitually uses certain rules of thumb in the conduct of his business affairs even if it means not acting in an optimal manner at all times.[8] The fact that erratic changes in business expectations are not usually observed is largely due to the relatively stable nature of our economic and social institutions.

It should, however, be noted that apart from the individual's desire for order and regularity, the source of institutional stability is not very well understood (but see Schotter, 1981). Spurts of institutional instability and periods of collapse of business confidence clearly cannot be ruled out as is often painfully demonstrated at times of social unrest and revolutionary upheavals. 'As if' theorizing of the kind advocated by the rational expectations school that presupposes the existence and continuation of particular market institutions and behaviour (which is only compatible with equilibrium) can only result in unwarranted complacency. In conditions where behavioural uncertainty is predominant, the best that can be hoped for is to detect past patterns of regularity, to attempt to understand such regularities and to watch for possible changes in society's institutions and habits. Within this research strategy, the study of expectations and their possible impact upon economic decisions cannot be meaningfully carried out without *direct* information on expectations.

MEASUREMENT OF EXPECTATIONS

One important source of direct measurement of expectations is the public and professional opinion survey data which are now available for a wide range of variables in most industrialized countries. A pioneering attempt at systematic surveys of businessmen's current perceptions and future outlooks was made by the IFO-Institute of Munich at the beginning of 1950. The results of these surveys, usually referred to as the 'Business Test' data, have been extensively studied, notably by Anderson (1952) and Theil (1952, 1955, 1965). In the case of the USA, surveys of expectations include the Livingstone biannual survey of inflation expectations, the Michigan and Conference Board consumer surveys, the McGraw-Hill and Commerce/SEC investment survey and a host of other surveys concerning wages and interest rates expectations. Livingston's inflation expectations series records specific point forecasts of a small sample of professional economists and has proved to be by far the most popular measure of inflation expectations in the USA. Turnovsky (1970), Turnovsky and Wachter (1972), Pesando (1975), McGuire (1976), Carlson (1977), Mullineaux (1978, 1980), Brown and Maital (1981) and Figlewski and Wachtel (1981) have used the Livingstone series to study the formation of inflationary expectations, and Pyle (1972), Gibson (1972), Lahiri (1976) and Cargil (1976) have used it to study the Fisher effect on nominal interest rates. Survey expectations data on other variables in the USA have been employed by Friedman (1980) in the case of interest rates, by De Leeuw and McKelvey (1981) in the case of price expectations of business firms, and by Leonard (1982) in the case of wage expectations.[9]

The main sources of survey data on expectations in the UK are the monthly Gallup Polls and the CBI's Industrial Trends Surveys. The Gallup Poll qualitative survey results have been used by Carlson and Parkin (1975) to construct a series of the general public's inflation expectations. The method they use to convert the qualitative survey results to quantitative measures of inflation expectations is basically the same as the method first proposed by Theil (1952) in his study of Munich Business Test data. Knöbl (1974), de Menil and Bhalla (1975) and Danes (1975) have used similar methods to derive expected inflation rate series from qualitative surveys in West Germany, USA and Australia respectively.[10] Batchelor (1982) has used a modification of the Carlson and Parkin technique to quantify businessmen's expectations of inflation and output for Belgium, France, Germany and Italy, using monthly surveys of manufacturing enterprises coordinated by the Directorate General for Economic and Social Affairs of the Commission of the European Communities. The use of survey data in the case of Japan, Austria, Norway, Finland and the OECD as a whole has also been reported by Aiginger (1981).

Clearly this resurgence of interest in direct measures of expectations has not come about by accident and can be traced to the advent of rational expectations hypothesis and the ambiguities that surround the indirect tests of the rational expectations hypothesis. The need to embed the REH within a particular economic theory, such as the natural rate hypothesis, creates numerous difficulties and in the last analysis can only allow a joint test of rationality of expectations formation and the validity of the underlying theory. Survey data on expectations are not, however, without their shortcomings: the results of sample surveys can be quite sensitive to sampling errors and the phrasing of questions. Respondents may express opinions that are different from the ones they actually choose to act upon. These drawbacks have led some researchers to seek methods that are based on observed economic behaviour and attempt to measure expectations as manifested in market prices on the assumption that a particular economic theory is valid. Assuming financial markets are efficient and the real rate of interest is fixed, Fama (1975) has suggested the use of the nominal interest rate minus a constant (representing the value of the assumed constant real rate of interest) as a proxy for the measurement of the expected rate of inflation. In the same vein, by relaxing the hypothesis that the real rate of interest is fixed in the short run but maintaining the assumption that it is constant in the long run, Frankel (1982) has also proposed an 'implicit' method of measuring the long-term expectations of the rate of inflation (up to a constant term) from the observed term structure of interest rates.[11] Such 'implicit' methods of the measurement of inflation expectations are, however, only as good as the theory and the auxiliary assumptions that underlie them. They are of little use in empirical testing of the theories that help to generate them and should not be regarded as substitutes for direct survey measurements of expectations. What are needed are better and more robust techniques of measuring expectations from opinion survey data rather than the abandonment of direct methods of measurement in favour of theory-loaded implicit methods.

The above-mentioned objections to the measurement of expectations on the basis of survey data are not, however, applicable with the same force to all surveys. Surveys that require respondents to give point forecasts for the variables in question are more susceptible to sampling and measurement errors than tendency surveys that only question the respondents about the expected direction of change: whether a variable is expected to 'go up', to 'stay the same', or to 'go down'. As is pointed out by Katona (1958: 70), quantitative questions about prospects of, say, prices or profits may suggest that 'business managers ought to have that information, and the information may therefore be given even though substantial uncertainty exists'. Furthermore, to the extent that expectations are 'attitudes or states of mind' of the respondents and are not merely forecasts, methods based on the measurement of ordinal responses seem less likely to be subject to measurement errors than direct attempts at cardinal measurement of expectations.

CONVERSION OF QUALITATIVE RESPONSES TO QUANTITATIVE MEASURES

Ordinal measurements of expectations are, however, of little use in practice and, before they can be used to study the process of expectations formations or be incorporated within a macroeconomic model, their conversion into quantitative measures is clearly needed. A solution to this conversion problem has been given by Theil (1952) and independently rediscovered by Knöbl (1974) and Carlson and Parkin (1975). It is based on the assumption that respondents have a common subjective probability distribution over the future changes in, say, prices. The method also assumes that an expected change will be reported only if respondents expect prices to change by more than some reporting threshold value which is assumed to be identical across the respondents.[12] This approach (which may be referred to as the subjective probability approach) is, however, subject to a number of important drawbacks: the form of the aggregate probability distribution of respondents is usually unknown and, as is pointed out by Batchelor (1981), it may diverge significantly from normality whenever the subjective probability distributions of respondents do not have finite first and second moments.[13] There is no reason why the response thresholds should be symmetric. The assumption that the response thresholds are constant over time can give rise to peculiar problems. If, for example, more than half of the respondents say prices will 'go up', a shift in responses from the 'stay the same' to the 'down' category will cause the expected inflation measured by the Carlson and Parkin approach to increase! This is because the variance of the aggregate distribution must increase to allow for the smaller percentage of respondents who say prices will stay the same. As was initially pointed out by Theil (1952: 111), the subjective probability approach breaks down whenever the percentages of respondents reporting a rise or fall in prices vanish. Finally, the estimation of the response thresholds by Carlson and Parkin assumes expectations are unbiased; and contrary to what Batchelor claims his estimation technique (intended to remedy this shortcoming) also involves assuming some form of rationality of expectations formation.[14] These limitations, some of which are inherent in the subjective probability approach to quantification of qualitative response data, are not easily overcome. However, when surveys question respondents about their perception of the past as well as their expectations of the future, the conversion problem can be solved under assumptions that are testable as well as being far less restrictive than the subjective probability approach of Theil and Carlson and Parkin. The basic idea behind this alternative approach is to use the relationship between realizations (measured by official statistics) and respondents' perception of the past (reported in tendency surveys) as a *yardstick* for quantification of respondents' expectations about the future.

The relationship between actual changes in, say, prices of manufactured goods and respondents qualitative perception of the past can be formalized along the lines suggested by Anderson (1952). Denoting the actual percentage change in average selling prices of the manufacturing sector as a whole by π_t, we can write

$$\pi_t = \sum w_i \pi_{ti} \tag{1}$$

where π_{ti} is the actual percentage change in the average selling prices of the ith firm and w_i is the weight of this firm in total manufacturing. If we now categorize firms according to whether they experienced a 'rise', a 'fall', or 'no change' in their prices, (1) can also be written as

$$\pi_t = \sum w_i^+ \pi_{ti}^+ + \sum w_i^- \pi_{ti}^- \tag{2}$$

where the superscripts + and − denote the firms showing an increase and a decrease in their prices respectively. Clearly, firms with no change in their prices will not appear in (2). Since tendency surveys of firms' perception of past price changes do not give exact quantitative information on π_{ti}^{+} (or π_{ti}^{-}), some assumption concerning the variations of π_{ti} across firms and over time is needed. Anderson implicitly assumed that $\pi_{ti}^{+} = \alpha$ and $\pi_{ti}^{-} = -\beta$ and therefore obtained

$$\pi_t = \alpha \sum w_i^{+} - \beta \sum w_i^{-} + v_t$$

where α and β are both positive unknown parameters and v_t is a residual error term. But the sums $\sum w_i^{+}$ and $\sum w_i^{-}$ are nothing but the percentages of firms (appropriately weighted) that report a 'rise' and a 'fall' in their prices respectively. Under Anderson's assumptions, the relationship between actual price changes and the survey responses will be[15]

$$\pi_t = \alpha R_t - \beta F_t + v_t \tag{3}$$

where R_t and F_t stand for the percentages of firms reporting a price rise and a price fall, respectively. Although Anderson (1952) and Theil (1952) both found strong empirical support for (3) in their analysis of Munich Business Test data, in periods of rising and variable inflation Anderson's assumptions of fixed π_{ti}^{+} and π_{ti}^{-} clearly cannot hold. During periods of generally rising prices, it is more reasonable to expect an asymmetrical relationship between the rate of change of individual firms' prices and the overall rate of inflation depending on whether the firm reports a price fall or a price rise. For our purposes we adopt the following simple hypothesis for π_{ti}^{+}:

$$\pi_{ti}^{+} = \alpha + \lambda \pi_t \qquad \alpha \geq 0, \quad 0 \leq \lambda < 1 \tag{4a}$$

but we shall continue to retain Anderson's implicit assumption concerning π_{ti}^{-}, i.e.

$$\pi_{ti}^{-} = -\beta \qquad \beta \geq 0. \tag{4b}$$

Relation (4a) is intended to capture the uniform effect of rising money wages on manufacturing prices and should be regarded as a first approximation to the complicated relationship that may exist between changes in the prices of individual firms, the overall rate of inflation and other firm-specific factors.[16]

Using relations (4a) and (4b) in (2) yields

$$(1 - \lambda R_t)\pi_t = \alpha R_t - \beta F_t + v_t \tag{5a}$$

or equivalently

$$\pi_t = \frac{\alpha R_t - \beta F_t}{1 - \lambda R_t} + u_t \tag{5b}$$

where

$$u_t = v_t/(1 - \lambda R_t). \tag{6}$$

The unknown parameters α, β and λ can be estimated by means of a non-linear regression of actual price changes against the qualitative test variates R_t and F_t. Depending on their empirical performance, relations (3) or (5) can be used to convert qualitative survey responses to quantitative measures.

In the case of the linear formulation (3), assuming the v_t are non-autocorrelated, the best linear forecast of π_{t+1} formed conditional upon the qualitative test variates observed at time t will be given by

$${}_t\pi^e_{t+1} = \alpha\ {}_tR^e_{t+1} - \beta\ {}_tF^e_{t+1} \tag{7}$$

where ${}_t\pi^e_{t+1}$ stands for a quantitative measure of expectations of price changes for the manufacturing sector as a whole; ${}_tR^e_{t+1}$ is the percentage of firms (appropriately weighted) that at time t *expect* a rise in their prices over the period $t + 1$; and ${}_tF^e_{t+1}$ is the percentage of firms that at time t expect a fall in their prices. For the non-linear formulation (5), the problem of conversion of the qualitative test variates to a quantitative measure of ${}_t\pi^e_{t+1}$ is more complicated and involves knowing the variances as well as the means of the test variates. As the variances of the test variates across the firms are not readily available from the CBI surveys, we adopt the following conversion formula as a first approximation:

$${}_t\pi^e_{t+1} = \frac{\alpha\ {}_tR^e_{t+1} - \beta\ {}_tF^e_{t+1}}{1 - \lambda\ {}_tR^e_{t+1}}. \tag{8}$$

Further adjustments to (7) and (8) are needed whenever the disturbances of their underlying relations are autocorrelated. For example, if the v_t in (5a) follows a first-order autoregressive scheme with parameter ρ, then the correct expression for ${}_t\pi^e_{t+1}$ becomes

$${}_t\pi^e_{t+1} = \frac{\alpha\ {}_tR^e_{t+1} - \beta\ {}_tF^e_{t+1} + \rho[(1 - \lambda R_t)\pi_t - \alpha R_t + \beta F_t]}{1 - \lambda\ {}_tR^e_{t+1}}. \tag{9}$$

This approach to quantification of expectations has a number of advantages over the Carlson and Parkin technique. The procedure does not break down if one of the percentages R_t, F_t, ${}_tR^e_{t+1}$, ${}_tF^e_{t+1}$ vanishes. A shift from the 'same' category to the 'fall' category does not result in an increase in price expectations. The estimation of the unknown scaling parameters (i.e. α, β, λ and ρ) can be carried out independently of whether expectations are unbiased or not. The procedure can be easily extended to surveys with more than three response categories.[17] The underlying assumptions of the approach are, in principle, testable.

INFLATION EXPECTATIONS IN BRITISH MANUFACTURING

In this section we demonstrate our conversion method by applying it to the results of the CBI Industrial Trends Surveys in the case of average selling prices of British firms in the manufacturing sector. The CBI surveys were first introduced in 1958 and were conducted three times a year until 1971 after which they were carried out quarterly. The surveys currently cover over 1700 firms accounting for over three million employees and nearly half of the UK's manufacturing exports.[18] The questions regarding selling prices were asked in the following ways:

> Excluding seasonal variations, what has been the trend over the PAST FOUR MONTHS and what are the expected trends for the NEXT FOUR MONTHS . . .

All replies have been appropriately weighted to take account of the firm's size by employment and net output. The percentages of firms falling in the four categories 'up', 'same', 'down' and 'N/A' are given in table 3.1 for the period 1958–81. In our computations we ignored the 'N/A' category and adjusted the other three categories to sum to one hundred. This is equivalent to assuming 'N/A' responses are distributed independently of the other responses. For data on the actual rate of change of manufacturing prices, we used the monthly price indices of the Wholesale Prices of Manufactured Goods. For each month that the survey was carried out we calculated the percentage change in the index from its level four months previously.[19] This method of computation was followed to ensure that the actual rates of change in prices corresponded to the respondents' timespan of their own price changes. The actual rates of price changes (denoted by π_t) are given in table 3.2.

Choice of the conversion formula

We started our econometric investigations with the Anderson type relationship and estimated (3) by the ordinary least-squares (OLS) method over the period 1959–81. We obtained[20]

$$\pi_t = \underset{(21.38)}{8.64}R_t - \underset{(-2.24)}{3.98}F_t + \hat{v}_t \tag{10}$$

$$LL = -27.33, \quad \bar{R}^2 = 0.7085, \quad DW = 0.72, \quad \hat{\sigma} = 1.43, \quad T = 79.$$

The bracketed figures are ratios of estimated parameters to their (asymptotic) standard errors. LL is the maximized log-likelihood value, $\bar{R}$ is the adjusted multiple correlation coefficient, DW is the Durbin–Watson statistic, $\hat{\sigma}$ is the estimated standard error of v_t, and T is the total number of

TABLE 3.1 Past and expected trends in average selling prices of British manufacturing

	Trend over past four months				Expected trend over next four months			
	Up	Same	Down	N/A	Up	Same	Down	N/A
1958: June	3	66	30	1	2	75	20	3
Oct.	3	66	30	1	7	73	16	4
1959: Feb.	9	62	29	0	3	76	17	4
June	9	64	26	1	7	75	15	3
Oct.	12	67	20	1	10	75	12	3
1960: Feb.	12	70	16	2	14	76	7	3
June	22	66	11	1	12	77	6	5
Oct.	16	71	12	1	13	76	8	3
1961: Feb.	25	64	11	0	21	68	7	4
June	24	64	11	1	15	72	7	6
Oct.	22	64	13	1	11	74	10	5
1962: Feb.	12	70	17	1	13	71	12	4
June	13	66	19	2	13	72	11	4
Oct.	16	66	17	1	11	74	12	3
1963: Feb.	12	68	19	1	11	75	11	3
June	13	69	17	1	11	76	10	3
Oct.	12	75	11	2	13	77	6	4
1964: Feb.	27	63	8	2	28	62	6	4
June	32	58	9	1	14	76	6	4
Oct.	24	63	11	2	25	62	7	6
1965: Feb.	26	67	5	2	32	61	5	2
June	33	58	5	4	23	67	5	5
Oct.	19	72	7	2	16	73	8	3
1966: Feb.	21	70	7	2	29	62	7	2
June	32	60	5	3	30	60	4	6
Oct.	18	67	9	6	5	76	12	7
1967: Feb.	4	78	14	4	8	76	10	6
June	7	75	15	3	14	71	9	6
Oct.	13	69	14	4	18	67	9	6
1968: Feb.	31	58	8	3	45	47	4	4
June	40	51	5	4	25	65	4	6
Oct.	23	69	7	1	20	74	4	2

Continued

TABLE 3.1 (*cont.*)

	Trend over past four months				Expected trend over next four months			
	Up	Same	Down	N/A	Up	Same	Down	N/A
1969: Feb.	32	62	5	1	40	53	3	4
June	37	57	4	2	35	57	3	5
Oct.	41	51	6	2	39	52	4	5
1970: Feb.	47	46	5	2	56	35	4	5
June	59	35	4	2	58	35	2	5
Oct.	60	35	2	3	64	29	2	5
1971: Feb.*	59	34	3	4	58	35	2	5
June	59	33	5	3	52	41	3	4
Sep.	41	50	6	3	26	67	4	3
1972: Jan.	31	58	8	3	39	54	3	4
April	40	50	7	3	49	44	3	4
July	44	49	5	2	53	43	1	3
Oct.	49	45	4	2	55	42	2	1
1973: Jan.	36	61	2	1	31	67	1	1
April	23	74	2	1	43	53	2	2
July	44	53	1	2	53	44	1	2
Oct.	58	39	1	2	55	41	1	3
1974: Jan.	65	32	2	1	72	25	1	2
April	77	22	1	0	77	20	1	2
July	77	17	2	4	70	25	2	3
Oct.	75	22	1	2	73	22	2	3
1975: Jan.	74	20	4	2	73	22	4	1
April	72	22	5	1	64	31	3	2
July	62	29	5	4	64	28	4	4
Oct.	57	35	5	3	63	32	2	3
1976: Jan.	59	37	3	1	65	29	3	3
April	60	34	4	2	66	30	2	2
July	63	33	2	2	69	27	1	3
Oct.	68	27	3	2	73	23	1	3
1977: Jan.	70	26	1	3	76	22	1	1
April	73	22	3	2	69	28	1	2
July	59	36	3	2	63	32	3	2
Oct.	52	42	6	0	54	42	4	0

Continued

TABLE 3.1 (*cont.*)

	Trend over past four months				Expected trend over next four months			
	Up	Same	Down	N/A	Up	Same	Down	N/A
1978: Jan.	43	49	7	1	55	41	3	1
April	48	45	6	1	52	45	2	1
July	44	52	3	1	56	41	2	1
Oct.	44	51	4	1	55	43	1	1
1979: Jan.	47	50	1	2	61	37	1	1
April	59	38	2	1	66	31	1	2
July	67	29	3	1	66	31	1	2
Oct.	62	34	2	2	62	33	2	3
1980: Jan.	58	37	3	2	66	30	1	3
April	61	34	4	1	59	37	3	1
July	46	43	11	0	43	47	10	0
Oct.	29	51	19	1	32	55	12	1
1981: Jan.	25	58	17	0	34	58	8	0
April	27	52	21	0	37	53	9	1
July	28	55	16	1	35	57	7	1
Oct.	30	57	12	1	46	50	4	0

* Estimated.
Source: The Confederation of British Industry's Industrial Trends Survey. The figures refer to the percentage of respondents in the surveys reporting (or expecting) a price change.

observations. The estimated parameters ($\hat{\alpha}$ and $\hat{\beta}$) have the correct signs and are significant at conventional levels, and considering the different types of data that underlie π_t and (R_t, F_t) the fit of the estimated equation is satisfactory. Nevertheless, the equation suffers from highly autocorrelated residuals, which raises doubt as to the significance of the estimated parameters, and the maximum (four-monthly) rate of inflation that can be predicted using (10) is 8.6 per cent which is substantially below the rate of 11.94 per cent actually observed over the sample period. Re-estimating (3) under alternative error specifications yielded[21]

$$\pi_t = \underset{(11.74)}{8.51R_t} - \underset{(-0.77)}{2.14F_t} + \hat{v}_t \tag{11a}$$

$$\hat{v}_t = \underset{(7.4)}{0.64\hat{v}_{t-1}} + \hat{\eta}_t \tag{11b}$$

$$LL = -6.57, \quad \bar{R}^2 = 0.8288, \quad DW = 2.14, \quad \hat{\sigma} = 1.10, \quad T = 79.$$

TABLE 3.2 Actual and expected rates of price changes in British manufacturing (per cent)

	Actual	Expected: Carlson and Parkin method	Expected: The proposed method
1958: June	0.27	—	—
Oct.	0.18	—	—
1959: Feb.	0.36	−0.73	0.36
June	−0.36	−1.21	0.13
Oct.	0.27	−0.64	−0.01
1960: Feb.	0.27	−0.16	0.13
June	1.16	0.57	0.45
Oct.	0.35	0.52	0.52
1961: Feb.	0.88	0.41	0.45
June	1.05	1.10	0.79
Oct.	1.12	0.67	0.58
1962: Feb.	0.85	0.08	0.49
June	0.34	0.08	0.74
Oct.	0.51	0.16	0.57
1963: Feb.	0.50	−0.08	0.34
June	−0.17	0.0	0.42
Oct.	1.34	0.08	0.17
1964: Feb.	0.41	0.59	0.74
June	1.81	1.71	1.32
Oct.	1.29	0.67	0.46
1965: Feb.	1.84	1.43	1.38
June	1.96	2.06	1.99
Oct.	0.46	1.43	1.34
1966: Feb.	0.92	0.63	0.58
June	1.21	1.68	1.34
Oct.	0.37	2.06	1.42
1967: Feb.	0.37	−0.63	−0.07
June	0.00	−0.17	0.32
Oct.	0.82	0.41	0.57
1968: Feb.	2.07	0.72	0.89
June	1.58	3.30	3.25
Oct.	0.52	1.69	1.10

Continued

TABLE 3.2 (*cont.*)

	Actual	Expected: Carlson and Parkin method	Expected: The proposed method
1969: Feb.	1.98	1.29	0.52
June	1.01	2.88	2.39
Oct.	1.34	2.51	1.65
1970: Feb.	2.48	2.77	1.62
June	2.58	4.70	3.80
Oct.	2.44	4.77	3.72
1971: Feb.	2.96	5.67	4.17
June	2.92	4.77	3.36
Sept.	1.65	4.04	2.66
1972: Jan.	0.99	1.71	0.72
April	1.62	2.79	1.82
July	1.87	3.72	2.81
Oct.	2.89	3.99	3.18
1973: Jan.	2.23	4.13	3.53
April	1.69	2.36	1.63
July	3.67	3.10	3.04
Oct.	5.20	3.94	4.46
1974: Jan.	6.59	4.18	4.71
April	11.94	6.28	8.12
July	7.78	7.36	10.82
Oct.	7.19	6.53	7.27
1975: Jan.	8.98	7.24	7.05
April	8.80	7.74	7.61
July	6.91	5.54	6.34
Oct.	4.20	6.00	6.84
1976: Jan.	5.04	5.28	5.76
April	4.92	5.83	6.04
July	5.33	5.65	6.14
Oct.	5.94	5.91	6.82
1977: Jan.	8.11	6.63	7.67
April	7.88	6.93	8.70
July	6.63	5.78	6.97
Oct.	2.76	5.36	6.29

Continued

TABLE 3.2 (*cont.*)

	Actual	Expected: Carlson and Parkin method	Expected: The proposed method
1978: Jan.	2.70	4.05	3.91
April	3.14	4.20	3.82
July	2.53	3.84	3.63
Oct.	2.55	4.25	4.04
1979: Jan.	2.76	4.07	3.85
April	4.55	4.67	4.68
July	7.11	5.35	5.84
Oct.	5.50	5.35	6.40
1980: Jan.	5.78	5.14	5.69
April	7.42	5.45	6.83
July	4.32	4.69	5.93
Oct.	2.14	2.69	3.60
1981: Jan.	2.59	1.58	2.30
April	5.47	1.98	2.64
July	3.30	2.21	4.46
Oct.	3.03	2.14	3.97

Source: Actual figures from *Monthly Digest of Statistics:* Wholesale Price Index of Manufactured Goods adjusted for the effect of reductions in the VAT exclusive prices of alcoholic liquor, tobacco and cigarettes, matches and mechanical lighters which took place in April 1973. The actual rates of change of prices are computed as the percentage change in the Wholesale Price Index of each month over its value four months previously.

This result clearly shows that the significance of the coefficient of F_t in (10) has been spurious and the hypothesis $\beta = 0$ can no longer be rejected. The problem of underprediction of the maximum rate of inflation, however, continues to be present in the case of this relation and seems to be due to the linear forms of (10) and (11). As a possible way of dealing with this problem, we estimated and obtained the following non-linear regression:[22]

$$\pi_t = \frac{\underset{(7.25)}{4.08R_t}}{1 - \underset{(-9.55)}{0.82R_t}} + \hat{u}_t \tag{12a}$$

$$\hat{u}_t = \underset{(5.0)}{0.49}\hat{u}_{t-1} + \hat{\varepsilon}_t \tag{12b}$$

$$LL = 2.89, \quad \bar{R}^2 = 0.8665, \quad DW = 2.16, \quad \hat{\sigma} = 0.97, \quad T = 79.$$

This result is a definite improvement over the Anderson type linear regressions. The maximized value of the log-likelihood function has increased by 9.46. The degree of residual autocorrelation, although still significant, has decreased somewhat. The ML estimate of λ ($=0.82$) falls within its acceptable range of variations. The maximum rate of inflation which can be predicted using (12) (around 23 per cent) is well in excess of the actual rates of inflation observed in the sample period. Nevertheless, the application of White's (1980) test of heteroskedasticity to the residuals of (12) suggests that the hypothesis of equal variances for u_t cannot be maintained.[23] In the light of (6) this is not surprising and follows immediately if the v_t's happen to have a constant variance.

As a way of overcoming this shortcoming and checking to see whether v_t's do in fact possess constant variances, we estimated (5a) and obtained the following result:[24]

$$(1 - 0.85R_t)\pi_t = \underset{(10.69)}{3.78}R_t + \hat{v}_t \tag{13a}$$

$$\hat{v}_t = \underset{(3.39)}{0.42}\hat{v}_{t-1} + \underset{(2.41)}{0.26}\hat{v}_{t-2} + \hat{\eta}_t \tag{13b}$$

$$LL = 14.95, \quad \bar{R}^2 = 0.9609, \quad DW = 2.08, \quad \hat{\sigma} = 0.5245, \quad T = 79.$$

This formulation clearly gives a better fit. The maximized log-likelihood value has increased from 2.89 to 14.95 which is a substantial increase, considering that in going from (12) to (13) only one extra parameter has been estimated. In order to check the effectiveness of our procedure in dealing with the heteroskedasticity problem, we also carried out the following auxiliary regression:

$$\hat{\eta}_t^2 = \underset{(2.00)}{0.415} - \underset{(-1.03)}{0.515}X_t + \underset{(1.17)}{0.264}X_t^2$$

$$R^2 = 0.0187, \quad DW = 1.95, \quad \hat{\sigma} = 0.792$$

where $X_t = R_t/(1 - 0.85R_t)$. This regression suggests that the hypothesis that v_t in (5a) have equal variances cannot be rejected (see White, 1980).[25]

Before relation (13a) can be chosen for quantification of expectations we need to test (13) against other possible explanations of π_t (in terms of the test variates R_t and F_t). As an alternative formulation to (13a) and (13b), we first estimated (by the OLS method) the following dynamic counterpart of (13a):

$$Y_t = \underset{(3.69)}{0.41}Y_{t-1} + \underset{(2.38)}{0.27}Y_{t-2} + \underset{(5.28)}{3.74}R_t - \underset{(-2.45)}{2.71}R_{t-1} + \underset{(0.32)}{0.26}R_{t-2} + \hat{v}_t \tag{14}$$

$$LL = 17.08, \quad \bar{R}^2 = 0.9606, \quad \hat{\sigma} = 0.526, \quad T = 79$$

where $Y_t = (1 - 0.85R_t)\pi_t$. Clearly (14) is nested within (13), and the application of the likelihood ratio test indicates that the imposition of the two common factor restrictions on (14) cannot be rejected and (13) is upheld at conventional levels of significance.[26] The relevant χ^2 statistic for the test of (13) against (14) is equal to $2(17.08 - 14.95) = 4.26$ which is below the 95 per cent critical value of the χ^2 distribution with two degrees of freedom.

A different kind of alternative specification to (13) can be obtained by applying the Carlson and Parkin method to businessmen's perception of their past price changes. According to this method the actual rate of change in prices will be related to

$$d_t = (f_t + r_t)/(f_t - r_t)$$

where f_t and r_t are the abscissa of the frequencies F_t and $1 - R_t$ of the cumulative distribution assumed to represent businessmen's subjective probability distribution of their perception of past price changes. Assuming this cumulative distribution to be normal, the values r_t and f_t can be computed (in terms of R_t and F_t) by solving $\Phi(f_t) = F_t$ and $\Phi(r_t) = 1 - R_t$, where Φ stands for the cumulative distribution function of a standard normal variate. Running regressions of π_t on d_t and d_t^2 we obtained

$$\pi_t = \underset{(2.06)}{0.83} + \underset{(3.24)}{2.00d_t} + \underset{(2.35)}{0.67d_t^2} + \hat{u}_t \qquad (15a)$$

$$\hat{u}_t = \underset{(2.72)}{0.285\hat{u}_{t-1}} + \underset{(3.55)}{0.3712\hat{u}_{t-2}} + \hat{\varepsilon}_t \qquad (15b)$$

$$LL = -1.05, \quad \bar{R}^2 = 0.8491, \quad DW = 2.08, \quad \hat{\sigma} = 1.03, \quad T = 79.$$

Although this result presents a satisfactory alternative to Anderson's linear specification (11), it clearly falls short of providing a viable alternative to either of the non-linear specifications (12) and (13). Despite the larger number of parameters estimated under (15), the value of its maximized log-likelihood function is substantially below that of (12) and (13).[27]

Measures of inflation expectations

In the light of the above econometric investigations, we decided to adopt relation (13) as the basis for the estimation of the expected rate of inflation in British manufacturing over the period 1958–81. Using results of the CBI surveys relating to the expected changes in prices over the next four months (see table 3.1), the following two alternative expressions for the expected rate of inflation (formed at time t for the period $t + 1$) can be written down depending on whether the effect of residual autocorrelation is taken into account or not:

$$ {}_t\pi^{e}_{t+1} = \frac{3.78\ {}_tR^{e}_{t+1} + 0.42\hat{v}_t + 0.26\hat{v}_{t-1}}{1 - 0.85\ {}_tR^{e}_{t+1}} \qquad (16a) $$

$$ {}_t\pi^{e}_{t+1} = \frac{3.78\ {}_tR^{e}_{t+1}}{1 - 0.85\ {}_tR^{e}_{t+1}} \qquad (16b) $$

where

$$ \hat{v}_{t-i} = (1 - 0.85R_{t-i})\pi_{t-i} - 3.78R_{t-i}, \qquad i = 0, 1. $$

The choice between the above two measures is not clearcut, but the measure (16a) which corrects the expectations for previous errors is likely to be a more accurate forecasting equation and we adopt it as our proposed measure of expected inflation expectations in British manufacturing. The results of these computations are given in table 3.2. For purposes of comparison we also computed the expected rate of change in prices according to the Carlson and Parkin method.[28] These results together with the series for the actual rate of price changes are also given in table 3.2. All the three series are plotted in figure 3.1. It is clear that both measures of inflation expectations follow each other quite closely. (The simple correlation coefficient between the two series is 0.943.) Nevertheless, they differ significantly with respect to both their average levels and their cyclical patterns. The proposed measure is closer to the actual series than is the Carlson and Parkin measure. The simple correlation coefficient between the proposed measure and the actual series is 0.903, while the correlation coefficient of the Carlson and Parkin measure and the actual series is 0.846. It is important to note that qualitatively these results hold even if we adopt the measure (16b) which does not adjust expectations for past errors.[29]

CONCLUDING REMARKS

Our emphasis in this paper has been on the importance of having independent measures of expectations for hypothesis testing and econometric modelling. To this end we have suggested a new procedure for converting qualitative response data into quantitative measurements. We have demonstrated the feasibility of this procedure by applying it to the CBI surveys of business expectations of price changes in British manufacturing.

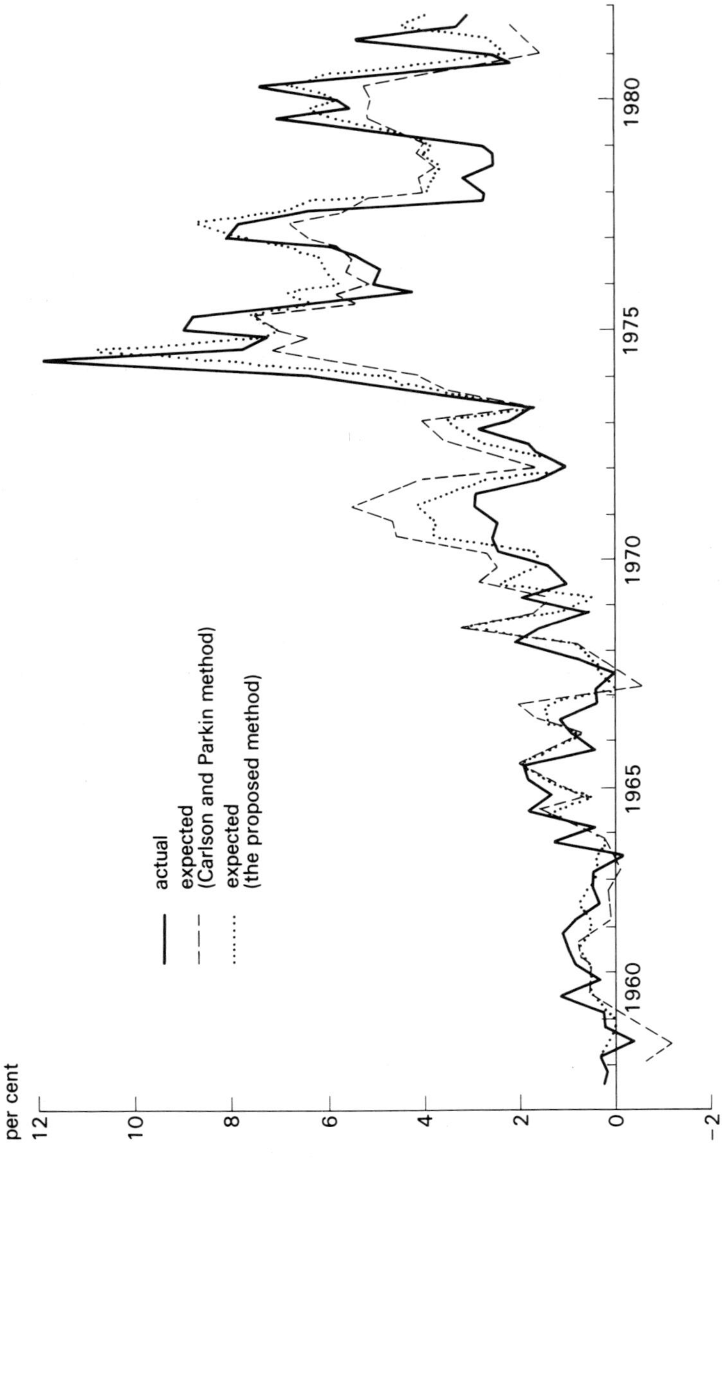

FIGURE 3.1 Actual and expected rates of price changes in British manufacturing (source: table 3.2)

NOTES

The early work on the statistical part of this paper was carried out in collaboration with Mr R. Gulamani, who also personally extracted the data given in table 3.1 from the files of the Industrial Trends and Economic Forecasting Department of the Confederation of British Industry. I am extremely grateful to Mrs Kudla of the CBI for her cooperation and help with the CBI surveys. I have also benefited greatly from comments made on a previous version of this paper by Tony Lawson and Geoff Harcourt and participants in the seminars at Queen's University, University of Western Ontario, Princeton University, University of Massachusetts (Amherst), and at the International Seminar on Recent Developments in Macroeconometric Modelling, Paris, CEPREMAP.

1 Notice that here we use the concept of uncertainty in the sense usually used in statistical literature which should not be confused with the Knightian notion of uncertainty. Knight's (1921) distinction between 'risk' and 'uncertainty' depends on whether an objective basis for the calculation of probabilities exists.

2 The example of a 'beauty contest' given by Keynes (1936: 156) whereby it is required to anticipate 'what average opinion expects the average opinion to be', provides a vivid illustration of the nature and the source of what we have called behavioural uncertainty. However, Keynes under the influence of Marshallian analysis was preoccupied with a distinction between the state of 'short-run' and 'long-run' expectations and did not make an explicit attempt to distinguish between exogenous and behavioural sources of uncertainty.

3 For a discussion of the meaning of expectations from a psychological viewpoint see Katona (1951: 52–3). Also see Ożga (1965: chapters 1 and 2).

4 For recent appraisals of Keynes's views on uncertainty and their implication for macroeconomic theory, see Lawson (1981) and Coddington (1982), from different perspectives. Coddington argues that Keynes's position on uncertainty is 'odd and unhelpful' and suggests that 'Keynes's forays into this area [uncertainty] was an opportunistic but mild flirtation with subjectivism'. Coddington's sweeping dismissal of Keynes's views on uncertainty is not convincing and misses the main points of Keynes's objections to frequency interpretation of probability and uncertainty. We shall have more to say on this matter later on. Lawson's account of Keynes's views on the state of long-term expectations is more balanced but, as acknowledged by Lawson himself, is rather limited in scope.

5 For a psychological account of the importance of 'understanding' in expectations formations, see Katona (1951: 53–7).

6 Papers by Blanchard (1976), Bray (1982) and DeCanio (1979) include examples of learning processes that do not converge to rational expectations solutions. In an interesting paper, Blume and Easley (1982) also show that, even when one of the models considered by agents in their learning process is a correct description of the rational expectations equilibrium, 'the learning process may get stuck at an incorrect model'.

7 See Schotter and Schwödiauer (1980) for a comprehensive survey of game theory in which the importance of endogenization of a theory of institution creation is emphasized. Also see Schotter (1981).

8 For an interesting discussion of the importance of 'habitual' as opposed to 'genuine' decisions or 'programmed' as opposed to 'unprogrammed' decisions see Katona (1951) and Simon (1958).

9 Incidentally, none of these three studies finds any empirical basis for supporting the rational expectations hypothesis.

10 Note, however, that in footnote 5 on page 86 of his article, Knöbl (1974) points out that he developed the conversion method he used in collaboration with two of his Austrian colleagues independently of Carlson and Parkin.

11 In order to derive his inflation expectations series, Frankel (1982) is also forced to make a number of further assumptions involving the adjustment mechanism of the short-term real rate of interest to its long-run value and the relationship between maturity and the liquidity premium. Elsewhere Frankel (1977) has also proposed measurement of inflation expectations based on data from the forward foreign exchange market.

12 The reporting thresholds have been called 'indifference interval' by Theil (1952: 101), 'sensibility interval' by Knöbl (1974: 98) and 'difference limen' by Carlson and Parkin (1975: 125).

13 The possibility of non-normality of respondents' subjective probabilities has been emphasized by Carlson (1975) in relation to Livingston's price expectation series.

14 Batchelor (1982: 5) estimates parameters c_0 and c_1 (see his relation (12)) by the method of ordinary least squares, which is based on the assumption that the disturbances u_t have zero means and are distributed independently of p_t^e. But (12) and (13) together also imply that $p_t = p_t^e + u_t$, and the assumption that u_t has zero mean is equivalent to *assuming* price expectations are unbiased predictors of actual price changes.

15 A probabilistic interpretation of (3) based on a uniform distribution with constant range was subsequently given by Theil (1952). Also see Theil (1955) for other possible rationales of (3).

16 Note that unlike the assumptions underlying the Carlson and Parkin approach, the assumptions concerning the relationship between π_{ti}^+ and π_{ti}^- and the overall rate of inflation can, in principle, be tested directly.

17 Generalization of the Carlson and Parkin method to surveys with more than three response categories is also possible and has been recently carried out by Visco (1981) in the context of the Italian Mondo Economico Surveys.

18 The number of respondents to the survey carried out in the last quarter of 1981 was 1766. The sample size for the early 1960s was less than 1000 firms but exceeded this figure for later years. For a more detailed description of the CBI surveys see Smith (1978) who applies the Carlson and Parkin technique in order to generate time series of firms' price and output expectations in the UK manufacturing sector.

19 The indices were taken from various issues of the *Monthly Digest of Statistics* and were adjusted for the effect of reductions in the VAT exclusive prices of alcoholic liquor, tobacco and cigarettes, matches and mechanical lighters which

took place in April 1973. They are not seasonally adjusted, but no significant pattern of seasonality could be detected in the published data.

20 In estimating the parameters of the various relations reported in this section, R_t and F_t were measured in fractions and π_t in percentages.

21 The relevant computer algorithms for the computation of the ML estimators are set out in Pesaran and Slater (1980). We also estimated (3) subject to a second-order autoregressive process for v_t, including and excluding an intercept, but the results did not show any significant improvement over the first-order autoregressive scheme. Notice that $\hat{\sigma}$, $\bar{R}^2$ and DW are computed on the basis of the adjusted residuals $\hat{\eta}_t$.

22 The estimation is carried out by the ML method, and the reported t ratios are based on the asymptotic standard errors of the ML estimators.

23 The relevant regression result for White's test is given by

$$\begin{aligned} \hat{\varepsilon}_t^2 &= \underset{(2.19)}{1.12} - \underset{(-2.14)}{2.78X_t} + \underset{(3.41)}{2.13X_t^2} \\ \bar{R}^2 &= 0.2395, \quad DW = 1.75, \quad \hat{\sigma} = 1.90 \end{aligned}$$

where $\hat{\varepsilon}_t$ is defined by (12b) and $X_t = R_t/(1 - 0.82R_t)$.

24 The reported values of LL and $\bar{R}^2$ correspond to the inflation rate and not the $(1 - 0.85R_t)\pi_t$ variable. As a result they are directly comparable to the statistics given for relations (10) and (11). The reported t ratios are based on the standard errors computed conditional on the value of $\lambda = 0.85$. The χ^2 statistic pertinent to the test of the hypothesis $\lambda = 0$ is equal to 42.15.

25 The value of $TR^2 = 1.50$ is well below the 95 per cent (or even 90 per cent) critical value of the chi-squared distribution with two degrees of freedom.

26 Strictly speaking, because of the different treatment of the initial values implicit in the estimation of (13) and (14), these two specifications are nested only in large samples.

27 Since (12), (13) and (15) are non-nested, a straightforward application of the classical hypothesis testing procedures to them will not be appropriate.

28 In our notations the Carlson and Parkin measure of inflation expectations is given by

$$_t\pi_{t+1}^e = \hat{c}\ _td_{t+1}^e$$

where

$$\begin{aligned} _td_{t+1}^e &= (_tf_{t+1}^e + {_tr_{t+1}^e})/(_tf_{t+1}^e - {_tr_{t+1}^e}) \\ \Phi(_tf_{t+1}^e) &= {_tF_{t+1}^e} \\ \Phi(_tr_{t+1}^e) &= 1 - {_tR_{t+1}^e} \end{aligned}$$

and

$$\hat{c} = \sum_{t=1}^{79} \pi_t \Big/ \sum_{t=1}^{79} {_{t-1}d_t^e}.$$

29 The simple correlation coefficient of the actual rate of price changes and their expectations based on the conversion formula (16b) is equal to 0.883.

REFERENCES

Aiginger, K. (1981) 'Empirical Evidence on the Rational Expectations Hypothesis Using Reported Expectations', *Empirica*, **1**, 25–72.

Anderson, O., Jr (1952) 'The Business Test of the IFO-Institute for Economic Research, Munich, and its Theoretical Model', *Revue de L'Institut International de Statistique*, **20**, 1–17.

Batchelor, R. A. (1981) 'Aggregate Expectations Under the Stable Laws', *Journal of Econometrics*, **16**, 199–210.

Batchelor, R. A. (1982) 'Expectations, Output and Inflation: The European Experience', *European Economic Review*, **17**, 1–25.

Begg, D. K. H. (1982) *The Rational Expectations Revolution in Macroeconomics*, Philip Allan, Oxford.

Blanchard, O. J. (1976) *The Non-Transition to Rational Expectations*, mimeographed, Massachussetts Institute of Technology.

Blume, L. E. and Easley, D. (1982) 'Learning to be Rational', *Journal of Economic Theory*, **26**, 340–51.

Bray, M. (1982) 'Learning, Estimation, and the Stability of Rational Expectations', *Journal of Economic Theory*, **26**, 318–39.

Brown, B. W. and Maital, S. (1981), 'What do Economists Know? An Empirical Study of Experts' Expectations', *Econometrica*, **49**, 491–504.

Buiter, W. H. (1980) 'The Macroeconomics of Dr Pangloss: A Critical Survey of the New Classical Macroeconomics', *Economic Journal*, **90**, 34–50.

Cargill, T. F. (1976) 'Anticipated Price Changes and Nominal Interest Rates in the 1950s', *Review of Economics and Statistics*, **58**, 364–7.

Carlson, J. A. (1975) 'Are Price Expectations Normally Distributed?', *Journal of the American Statistical Association*, **70**, 749–54.

Carlson, J. A. (1977) 'A Study of Price Forecasts', *Annals of Economic and Social Measurement*, **6**, 27–56.

Carlson, J. A. and Parkin, M. (1975) 'Inflation Expectations', *Economica*, **42**, 123–38.

Coddington, A. (1982) 'Deficient Foresight: A Troublesome Theme in Keynesian Economics', *American Economic Review*, **72**, 480–7.

Cyert, R. M. and DeGroot, M. H. (1974) 'Rational Expectations and Bayesian Analysis', *Journal of Political Economy*, **82**, 521–36.

Danes, M. (1975) 'The Measurement and Explanation of Inflationary Expectations in Australia', *Australian Economic Papers*, **19**, 75–87.

DeCanio, S. (1979) 'Rational Expectations and Learning from Experience', *Quarterly Journal of Economics*, **93**, 47–57.

De Leeuw, F. and McKelvey, M. (1981) 'Price Expectations of Business Firms', *Brookings Papers on Economic Activity*, June, 299–314.

De Menil, G. and Bhalla, S. S. (1975) 'Direct Measurement of Popular Price Expectations', *American Economic Review*, **65**, 169–80.

Dubey, P. and Shubik, M. (1977) 'A Closed Economy with Exogenous Uncertainty, Different Levels of Information, Money, Futures and Spot Markets', *International Journal of Game Theory*, **6**, 231–48.

Fama, E. F. (1975) 'Short-term Interest Rates as Predictors of Inflation', *American Economic Review*, **65**, 269–82.

Figlewski, S. and Wachtel, P. (1981) 'The Formation of Inflationary Expectations', *Review of Economics and Statistics*, **63**, 1–10.

Frankel, J. A. (1977) 'The Forward Exchange Rate, Expectations, and the Demand for Money—The German Hyperinflation', *American Economic Review*, **67**, 653–70.

Frankel, J. A. (1982) 'A Technique for Extracting a Measure of Expected Inflation from the Interest Rate Term Structure', *Review of Economics and Statistics*, **64**, 135–42.

Friedman, B. M. (1979) 'Optimal Expectations and the Extreme Informational Assumptions of Rational Expectations Macromodels', *Journal of Monetary Economics*, **5**, 23–41.

Friedman, B. M. (1980) 'Survey Evidence on the 'Rationality' of Interest Rate Expectations', *Journal of Monetary Economics*, **6**, 453–65.

Gibson, W. E. (1972) 'Interest Rates and Inflationary Expectations: new evidence', *American Economic Review*, **62**, 854–65.

Hoffman, D. L. and Schmidt, P. (1981) 'Testing the Restrictions Implied by the Rational Expectations Hypothesis', *Journal of Econometrics*, **15**, 265–87.

Katona, G. (1951) *Psychological Analysis of Economic Behaviour*, McGraw-Hill, New York.

Katona, G. (1958) 'Business Expectations in the Framework of Psychological Economics (Toward a Theory of Expectations)', in M. J. Bowman (ed.), *Expectations, Uncertainty, and Business Behavior*, Social Science Research Council, New York.

Keynes, J. M. (1936) *The General Theory of Employment Interest and Money*, Macmillan, London.

Knight, F. H. (1921) *Risk, Uncertainty and Profit*, New York.

Knöbl, A. (1974) 'Price Expectations and Actual Price Behaviour in Germany', *International Monetary Fund Staff Papers*, **21**, 83–100.

Lahiri, K. (1976) 'Inflationary Expectations: Their Formation and Interest Rate Effects', *American Economic Review*, **66**, 124–31.

Lawson, T. (1981) 'Keynesian Model Building and the Rational Expectations Critique', *Cambridge Journal of Economics*, **5**, 311–26.

Leonard, J. S. (1982) 'Wage Expectations in the Labour Markets: Survey Evidence on Rationality', *Review of Economics and Statistics*, **64**, 157–61.

McCallum, B. T. (1980) 'Rational Expectations and Macroeconomics Stabilization Policy: An Overview', *Journal of Money, Credit and Banking*, **12**, 716–46.

McGuire, T. W. (1976) 'Price Change Expectations and the Phillips Curve', in K. Brunner and A. Meltzer (eds), *The Economics of Price and Wage Controls*, North-Holland, Amsterdam, pp. 65–114.

Mullineaux, D. J. (1978) 'On Testing for Rationality: Another Look at the Livingston Price Expectations Data', *Journal of Political Economy*, **86**, 329–36.

Mullineaux, D. J. (1980) 'Inflation Expectations and Money Growth in the United States', *American Economic Review*, **70**, 149–61.

Muth, J. F. (1961) 'Rational Expectations and the Theory of Price Movements', *Econometrica*, **29**, 315–35.

Ożga, S. A. (1965) *Expectations in Economic Theory*, Weidenfeld and Nicolson, London.

Pesando, J. E. (1975) 'A Note on the Rationality of the Livingston Price Expectations', *Journal of Political Economy*, **83**, 849–58.

Pesaran, M. H. (1981) 'Identification of Rational Expectations Models', *Journal of Econometrics*, **16**, 375–98.

Pesaran, M. H. (1982) 'A Critique of the Proposed Tests of the Natural Rate–Rational Expectations Hypothesis', *Economic Journal*, **92**, 529–54.

Pesaran, M. H. and Slater, L. J. (1980) *Dynamic Regression: Theory and Algorithms*, Ellis Horwood, Chichester.

Popper, K. R. (1972) *Objective Knowledge: An Evolutionary Approach*, Oxford University Press.

Pyle, D. M. (1972) 'Observed Price Expectations and Interest Rates', *Review of Economics and Statistics*, **54**, 275–80.

Revankar, N. S. (1980) 'Testing of the Rational Expectations Hypothesis', *Econometrica*, **48**, 1347–63.

Robinson, J. (1971) *Economic Heresies*, Macmillan, London.

Schotter, A. (1981) *The Economic Theory of Social Institutions*, Cambridge University Press.

Schotter, A. and Schwödiauer, G. (1980) 'Economics and the Theory of Games: A Survey', *Journal of Economic Literature*, **18**, 479–527.

Shackle, G. L. S. (1949) *Expectations in Economics*, Cambridge University Press.

Shackle, G. L. S. (1955) *Uncertainty in Economics*, Cambridge University Press.

Shiller, R. J. (1978) 'Rational Expectations and the Dynamic Structure of Macroeconomic Models: A Critical Review', *Journal of Monetary Economics*, **4**, 1–44.

Simon, H. A. (1958) 'The Role of Expectations in an Adaptive or Behavioristic Model', in M. J. Bowman (ed.), *Expectations, Uncertainty, and Business Behavior*, Social Science Research Council, New York, pp. 49–58.

Smith, G. W. (1978) 'Producers' Price and Cost Expectations', in M. Parkin and M. T. Sumner (eds), *Inflation in the United Kingdom*, Manchester University Press.

Taylor, J. B. (1975) 'Monetary Policy During the Transition to Rational Expectations', *Journal of Political Economy*, **83**, 1009–21.

Theil, H. (1952) 'On the Time Shape of Economic Microvariables and the Munich Business Test', *Revue de L'institut International de Statistique*, **20**, 105–20.

Theil, H. (1955) 'Recent Experiences with the Munich Business Test: An Expository Article', *Econometrica*, **23**, 184–92.

Theil, H. (1966) *Applied Economic Forecasting*, North-Holland, Amsterdam.

Tobin, J. (1980) *Asset Accumulation and Economic Activity: Reflections on Contemporary Macroeconomic Theory*, Yruo Jahnsson Lectures, Basil Blackwell, Oxford.

Townsend, R. M. (1978) 'Market Anticipations, Rational Expectations, and Bayesian Analysis', *International Economic Review*, **19**, 481–94.

Turnovsky, S. J. (1970) 'Empirical Evidence on the Formation of Price Expectations', *Journal of the American Statistical Association*, **65**, 1441–54.

Turnovsky, S. J. and Wachter, M. L. (1972) 'A Test of the 'Expectations Hypothesis' Using Directly Observed Wage and Price Expectations', *Review of Economics and Statistics*, **54**, 47–54.

Visco, I. (1981) *Measurement, Analysis and Formation of Inflation Expectations*, PhD Dissertation, University of Pennsylvania.
Wallis, K. (1980) 'Econometric Implications of the Rational Expectations Hypothesis', *Econometrica*, **48**, 49–73.
White, H. (1980) 'A Heteroskedasticity-Consistent Covariance Matrix Estimator and a Direct Test for Heteroskedasticity', *Econometrica*, **48**, 817–38.

Comment

C. GOURIEROUX

DIRECT AND INDIRECT APPROACHES

In the econometric literature, the tests of the rational expectations (RE) hypothesis have been performed along two different lines.

The indirect approach

The indirect approach is based on a model which links the endogenous variable with its expectations and the exogenous variables. For instance, such a model may be

$$y_t = a\ {}_t\hat{y}_{t+1} + \mu_t \qquad |a| < 1 \tag{1}$$

where y_t and μ_t are the values of the endogenous and exogenous variables at time t and where ${}_t\hat{y}_{t+1}$ is the expectation at time t of y_{t+1}.

Furthermore, if we assume the RE relationship

$${}_t\hat{y}_{t+1} = E[y_{t+1}/\mathscr{I}_t] \tag{2}$$

where $\mathscr{I}_t$ is the information set available at t, if we specify this set $\mathscr{I}_t$, for instance

$$\mathscr{I}_t = \{y_t, y_{t-1}, y_{t-2}, \ldots\} \tag{3}$$

and if we consider a particular evolution of the exogenous process, for instance

$$\mu_t - m = \rho(\mu_{t-1} - m) + \varepsilon_t \tag{4}$$

(where ε_t is a zero-mean white noise), it is possible to derive a reduced form which gives the evolution of the endogenous y. In the present case, this form is

$$y_t = \frac{a(1-\rho)}{(1-a)(1-a\rho)}\, m + \frac{\mu_t}{1-a\rho}. \tag{5}$$

The test is obtained by comparing the observed evolution of y and μ to the theoretical one given by (4) and (5).

The main advantage of this approach is that it does not necessitate the observation of the predictions $\hat{y}$. However, it has an important drawback: the test based on the reduced form is not really a test of the RE hypothesis (2), but is a simultaneous test of (1), (2) and (3). The reduced form (5) may be rejected when the RE hypothesis is true and the model (1) or the information set are misspecified; on the other hand, the reduced form (5) may be accepted in some cases where (1), (2) and (3) would not be satisfied.

The direct approach

The direct approach is based on a comparison of the variable y_t with the expectations ${}_t\hat{y}_{t+1}$. It can only be performed if simultaneous observations on these two variables are available. In the case of quantitative variables and of linear predictions, the RE hypothesis $\{\forall\, t\; \exists\; \mathscr{I}_t\colon {}_t\hat{y}_{t+1} = E\{y_{t+1}/\mathscr{I}_t]\}$ is equivalent to the conditions:

$$\forall\, t\; E[{}_t\hat{y}_{t+1} - y_{t+1}] = 0$$

$$\forall\, t\; E\; {}_t\hat{y}_{t+1}[{}_t\hat{y}_{t+1} - y_{t+1}] = 0.$$

Then a 'model-free' test can be built from the previous equalities.

This is the latter approach that Pesaran develops in his paper, with the important difference that the variables y_t and ${}_t\hat{y}_{t+1}$ are qualitative.

SOME DIFFICULTIES RELATED TO QUALITATIVE DATA

Measurement error

Qualitative formulations with three alternatives, i.e. 'up', 'equal', 'down', are introduced in opinion surveys to decrease partially the response errors. In particular, it is often considered that a respondent who does not know what answer to give will choose the alternative 'equal'; in such a case the only relevant information is some measure of comparison between the percentage of firms that report 'rise' and that report 'fall', such that the balance is $R_t - F_t$.

Let us consider the implication of this remark on the conversion procedure given by (1), (4) and (5). This procedure is based on the variables R_t and F_t measured without error and equation (5) has to be distinguished from Pesaran's (12) for instance, in which R_t is the variable measured with error. Therefore, in the usual case of errors on the level R_t, F_t (but not on the difference $R_t - F_t$), the estimated formulae such as (10), (11) and (12) have to be considered only as statistical conversion formulae without any particular interpretation.

Qualitative prediction

A different point concerns the definition of RE in a qualitative context. The qualitative variable y is generally associated with a quantitative latent variable z. Let us consider for convenience the dichotomous case 'up', 'down'; the choice of the alternative depends on the sign of the modifications z of a latent variable:

$$y = \text{'up'} \qquad \text{if } z > 0$$

$$y = \text{'down'} \qquad \text{if } z < 0.$$

In such a case the concept of RE may be defined in two different ways.

(a) If the rationality concerns the quantitative part, ${}_t\hat{y}_{t+1}$ will be defined from the conditional expectation of z: ${}_tz^*_{t+1} = E[z_{t+1}/z_t, z_{t-1}, \ldots]$ by

$${}_t\hat{y}_{t+1} = \begin{cases} \text{'up'} & \text{if } {}_tz^*_{t+1} > 0 \\ \text{'down'} & \text{if } {}_tz^*_{t+1} < 0. \end{cases}$$

(b) On the other hand, if the rationality is directly defined for the qualitative part we have to compute the expectation of y_{t+1} given $y_t, y_{t-1}, \ldots$:

$${}_t\hat{y}_{t+1} = {}_ty^*_{t+1} = E[y_{t+1}/y_t, y_{t-1}, \ldots].$$

Since the mapping which associates y to z is nonlinear and since the conditional expectation does not commute with such applications, these two possible definitions are not compatible.

Microeconomic or macroeconomic level

Finally note that from individual data it is intuitively possible to test the RE hypothesis at a microeconomic level. However, since the author chooses a definition of rationality related to the quantitative latent variable, it is necessary to aggregate the available data by means of the conversion formulae and thus the microeconomic aspect is lost.

Comment

JEAN TIROLE

Pesaran's paper investigates the theoretical and empirical validity of the rational expectations hypothesis (REH). At a theoretical level he argues strongly that economic agents cannot have correct expectations (even on average) because their environment is fundamentally unstable. The empirical part builds a series of expected inflation rates for Great Britain, presumably to test whether inflation expectations are formed rationally (indeed in a previous version of the paper the author tested and rejected the hypothesis that inflation expectations in British manufacturing are formed rationally). Since Gourieroux discusses the econometric part in much detail, I will put more emphasis on the theoretical critique of the REH.

The author draws a sharp distinction between two types of uncertainty: 'exogenous uncertainty' and 'behavioural uncertainty'. Roughly speaking, exogenous uncertainty encompasses random variables that are not under the control of some agent of the system (exogenous random variables); behavioural uncertainty refers to the unpredictability of the agents' behaviour. Take the Dubey–Shubik example quoted in the second section: A blind person wishes to cross a road and is told by another person that it is safe to cross the road. The blind person does not know (1) whether a vehicle is coming (exogenous uncertainty), (2) whether the other person is telling the truth (behavioural uncertainty). I would not necessarily describe the uncertainty about the quality of information given by the person who can see as behavioural uncertainty. I would rather say that the latter has preferences as to whether the blind person ought to be run over or not. The blind person typically has *incomplete* information about the other's preferences; therefore from the blind person's point of view, everything is *as if* the other person behaved randomly. But he does not; for example, if he means well, he will not give poor information to the blind person. Admittedly this procedure of interpreting apparent behavioural uncertainty as unknown preferences is pushing the description of uncertainty one step back. But I think it makes an important difference. Under the so-called behavioural uncertainty we have no way (especially when the situation is not repeated) of putting probability on the different events. In this sense behavioural uncertainty can be used to explain any outcome and has no predictive power. On the contrary one may have some assessments of other agents' preferences. For example, one may believe that, with high probability, the person who can see would not want the blind person to be run over. Of course these probabilities are very subjective; by treating any uncertainty as exogenous (except for mixed strategies), they allow us to *identify* (in a probabilistic sense) others' likely behaviour. Note, in passing, that when testing the REH, the econometrician must take into account the fact that his prior probabilities may differ from the agent's.

The second theoretical criticism of the REH concerns the learning process. We know, for example, that when the agent's initial model is misspecified, the system may not converge to a REH even if correct statistical methods are employed. On the other hand, if all events have positive probability, Bayesian updating ensures convergence of beliefs (see the work of Bray and Kreps). Underlying parameters need not be fully revealed even asymptotically; one can view the whole learning process itself as a rational expectation equilibrium. Agents act in their own interest and update beliefs using Bayes's rule. If the criticism that agents are not in a rational expectations equilibrium means that they do not know the underlying parameters or more generally that their beliefs change over time due to updating, the point is well taken. Updating and the corresponding difficulty for an outsider to assess current beliefs makes the econometrician's life hard. However, I do not think that this in any sense contradicts rationality.

The second part of the paper discusses the transformation of qualitative data into quantitative data. With these quantitative measures it is then possible to operate direct tests. Indirect tests are often obscured by the fact that they are testing joint hypotheses, and that there is sometimes serious doubt about the structure of the underlying model. Therefore direct tests have recently become very popular. They clearly also have shortcomings, among them the fact that one is also testing joint hypotheses. Being very much of an outsider in the field, I will content myself with some remarks.

First, firms are asked whether they experienced (forecast) a rise (+), a fall (−), or no change (0) in their prices. Assuming that firms answer honestly (and that they are not confused by inflation), quantitative measures of inflation for each firm are then computed:

$$\pi_{ti} = \begin{cases} \alpha + \lambda\pi_t & \text{if } (+) \\ -\beta & \text{if } (-) \end{cases}$$

where π_t is the aggregate rate of inflation. One may wonder what the status of this transformation is. α, β and λ do not depend on time or on the firm. It would be nice to test this kind of hypothesis directly in order to know if it makes sense. In the absence of such a test, it becomes important to explain where these equations come from. I would like—I may be wrong—to interpret them as behavioural equations. But both the intuition and the preliminary theoretical research on inflation processes do not seem to confirm such behaviour. Maybe these equations are simple statistical relationships, in which case they are hard to explain.

The estimation of α, β and λ is done using much information. Several fits are tried which do not necessarily conform to the model. For example the relation (13), which is adopted, has a different AR form for the residuals and ignores the negative answers (the hypothesis $\beta = 0$ could not be rejected before; however, assuming that $\beta \simeq 0$, it is difficult to know whether this comes from real-world behaviour or the phrasing of the questions, for example).

Lastly, firms are asked whether they forecast a rise, a fall, or no change in their prices. The answers are then used to construct an aggregate expectation of inflation. We thus see that the whole process of constructing 'expected inflation' makes a lot of assumptions and therefore we should be most cautious when using such estimates to test the REH.

4

The Aggregate Labour Market in the United Kingdom: Some Experiments with Rational Expectations Models

S. G. B. HENRY and S. WREN-LEWIS

INTRODUCTION

The justification we offer for undertaking yet another investigation into employment functions involves two considerations. First, since the early 1960s there has been a fairly continuous effort among applied econometricians to identify employment functions which exhibit parameter stability and data coherence. There have also been a number of attempts to provide a rationalization for the well publicized finding of apparent increasing returns to labour in the short run, which generally characterizes estimated employment output relationships. Since we will be looking at some aspects of these questions again, this paper may be viewed in part as a contribution to this continuing endeavour. Here, as we detail below, the effort will concentrate on employment models which postulate a close relationship between expectations and adjustment lags, the implications of which, as Kennan (1979) points out, have received little attention in the literature. The second consideration is a more practical one. Since 1979 extremely large changes have occurred in unemployment and employment in the UK. In particular, employment in manufacturing has fallen by a little over 1.8 million since 1979, or 15.4 per cent. The paper is concerned, therefore, with the usefulness of alternative employment models in explaining these changes. As the empirical tests reported later show, we place particular emphasis on the tracking performance of employment models over the post-1979 period.

Although procyclical movements in output per head have been long recognized as a regular phenomenon for which any employment model worthy of consideration should provide a rationalization, another aspect of the time-series behaviour of output per head is noteworthy. Since the mid-1960s jumps in output per head have occurred at discrete intervals in the UK. Sizeable fluctuations are most noticeable in 1971–75 and 1979–81, and to a lesser extent in 1967 also. Two points may be made about this feature. First, output per head is a (crude) measure of 'labour productivity' and so such jumps have often (mistakenly in our view) been associated with changes in underlying productivity performance in the economy. Secondly, such behaviour is not implied by the familiar lagged employment output relationships, which predict a steady productivity trend, with harmonic movement around this produced by random shocks. Such traditional models, based on a mechanical adjustment of employment to lagged output, may rationalize (or cohere) with one important feature of the time-series behaviour of output and employment—the procyclical movement in output per head.

Viewed as a transfer function such an equation displaces both the phase and the period of the time-series of employment given the behaviour of output. But, as we argue below, the presence of jumps in output per head is suggestive of dynamic adjustment in the presence of revisions to expectations. In what follows, the models described will be based on explicit intertemporal optimizing assumptions and will incorporate explicit forward-looking models for expectation formation. There are strong arguments for adopting the first assumption. A hypothesis based on explicit dynamic analysis provides an *a priori* justification for lagged responses (and rationalizes the presence of planned labour hoarding in employment functions, for example) and is preferable to *ad hoc* formulations. Also, models based on explicit dynamic analyses may provide an explanation of the increasing returns to labour phenomenon (see e.g. Sargent, 1978).

[We might note, however, a related development whereby the largely data-based *error correction mechanism* which has been so successful in time-series modelling may be represented as optimal behaviour by agents in an uncertain environment (see Hendry and von Ungern-Sternberg, 1980).]

The decision to consider forward-looking endogenous models of expectation formation is based on two considerations. First, the phenomenon of discrete movements in labour productivity, as we have already noted, may be explicable as revisions to expectations of sales or factor costs. In a rational expectations framework these could enter as substantial unanticipated shocks. In forward-looking models, where expectations are based on information on the current behaviour of the macroeconomy, substantial revisions, to e.g. expected output, could arise due to changes in announced policy targets. This argument is conjectural of course, but the present examples are aimed at revealing whether there is evidence in support of the conjecture. Secondly, the assumption of intertemporal optimizing subject to static or adaptive expectations (the latter being optimal only under very special conditions) is theoretically unsatisfactory, and an approach incorporating optimal prediction and intertemporal optimization seems preferable.

The layout of this paper will be to provide an assessment and extension of some models of the labour market. The alternative models that we will discuss below are models which emphasize the role of real wages, and those which emphasize expectations of future output movements. Below, we provide short critical accounts of these models, and then proceed to subject them to additional empirical testing before making judgements on their usefulness for appraising the recent events in the UK labour market.

As will be evident in the succeeding sections, the models considered will be highly simplified. They will concern simple optimizing models concentrating on the firm's employment decision, subject to fairly conventional (but not therefore unexceptional) assumptions about labour cost functions. By implication, additional features such as alternative cost structures, pricing policy, optimal stock-building and investment plans are ignored. We do this partly from a wish to concentrate on employment, and partly because it is difficult to derive tractable models for optimal factor demands when extensions, such as we have noted, are introduced. We have explicitly excluded models based on disequilibrium theories of the labour market. The main reason for this is the poor quality of the empirical results reported for models based on disequilibrium concepts (see for example Muellbauer, 1980). We have instead examined models which have already registered good empirical results when applied to UK data.

The plan of the rest of the paper is to provide a short account of some standard background theory, and then to proceed to the account of the models and the further tests on them. Results are noted, and conclusions are then summarized.

SOME BASIC CONCEPTS

This section briefly notes the conceptual framework of optimal decisions, first under certainty, and secondly when explicit modelling of expectations is included. In the main the applications have been directed at factor demand equations, although one example noted later is directed at optimal union behaviour. Apart from this, there is much which is common in the analysis, although individual differences obviously emerge due to assumptions concerning, *inter alia*, specific forms for the production function, levels of disaggregation and cost minimizing or profit maximizing as the firm's objective. These features will not be discussed here, though they will be described, where they matter, in the next section.

Dynamic rules under certainty

The optimizing decision for the cost-minimizing case, involving quadratic adjustment costs on quasi-fixed factors, is a convenient formulation for initiating this outline. For the representative firm, it may be described thus:

$$\underset{\Delta N,\, N}{\text{Min}} \sum_{0}^{\infty} \alpha^t \left(\sum_i w_i(N_i)N_i + \frac{1}{2} \beta \sum_i \Delta N_i^2 \right) \tag{1}$$

$$\text{s.t.} \qquad F_j(N_i, \Delta N_i, Q) = 0, \quad j = 1, \ldots, k \tag{2}$$

where N_i are factors and w_i factor prices. Here we have adopted a particularly simple framework, which could, for example, be the cost-minimizing model of the firm conditional upon (certain) output facing a separable cost function with simple quadratic costs arising from the adjustment of factors.

In the case of a single factor (e.g. labour of one type), single constraint case, the first-order Euler equation is of the general form

$$aN_{t+1} + bN_t + G(N_t, P_t) + cN_{t-1} = d_t \tag{3}$$

where P depends on output and relative factor prices and d is a forcing term.

In order to derive a tractable form for deriving an analytical expression for the dynamic path of employment, it is conventional to invoke linearization of (3) in some form. With a linearized equation, a closed solution for the endogenous variable may then be derived. Tinsley (1971) contains the most explicit derivation of this of which we are aware (Nickell (1981) provides a similar account). Without giving a detailed presentation here, in outline the steps involve the *static* equilibrium of the optimizing problem of (3), itself based on myopic forms for P and the forcing term. Next a linearization of (3) proceeds by defining average values of the static equilibrium N^*, and the relative price (call these $\bar{N}^*$ and $\bar{P}$), so that (3) may be written in a general fashion as

$$aN_{t+1} + [b + G_n(\bar{N}^*, \bar{P})]N_t + cN_{t-1} \simeq [G_n(\bar{N}^*, \bar{P})]\bar{N}_t^*$$

or

$$a_1 N_{t+1} + a_2 N_t + a_3 N_{t-1} = a_4 N_t^*.$$

This may be written in lag operator notation as

$$(a_1 L^{-1} + a_2 + a_3 L)N_t = a_4 N_t^*$$

or

$$A(L)N_t = a_4 N_t^*. \tag{4}$$

$A(L)$ may be factorized, and a decision rule for N is obtained of the form

$$N_t = \lambda_1 N_{t-1} - \frac{a_4}{a_3} \lambda_1 \sum_{i=0}^{\infty} \left(\frac{a_1}{a_3} \lambda_1 \right)^i N_{t+i}^* \tag{5}$$

where λ_1 is the stable root of (4) (compare Wickens, 1974; Nickell, 1981; Sargent, 1978; Tinsley, 1971).

To proceed to estimation, an analytical expression is needed for the forward convolution in (5). This generally means explicit expectations hypotheses. The next section discusses some procedures when it is assumed that expectations are formed rationally.

Expectations

We now turn to the role of the REH in designing a form for (5) which may be estimated, and outline some potential problems in identifying dynamic models under the REH.

Full implementation of the REH necessitates the solution of quite formidable problems, even though the models discussed here are single equations types. Considerable simplification is achieved if the right-hand variables in the objective function are exogenous. We describe this case first.

Exogenous regressors

The RHS variable may be postulated to be *strongly* exogenous with respect to the endogenous variable (see Engle et al. (1981) for definitions and discussion of this term). Sargent (1978), for example, argues that the real wage is not 'caused' (i.e. Granger caused) by employment and so may be treated as exogenous. The basic structure of the optimal decisions which this postulate implies is clearly laid out in Sargent, and it is used in other applications reported in the present paper. For this reason we first describe this model which relates employment to the real wage.

The model is based on the maximization of present value, which depends on the *variable of concern* to the agent—the real wage (w)—but uncontrollable by him, and productivity shocks equated with a random variable (a), perceived by the agent.

The firm maximizes present value, dependent on labour costs which arise from straight time (N_1) and overtime labour (N_2). There is a premium p on overtime, and each labour component incurs adjustment cost approximated by simple quadratics with parameters d, c respectively for N_1 and N_2. The production function is also quadratic in the two labour types, i.e.

$$\begin{aligned} f(N_1,) &= (f_0 + a_1)N_1 - (f_1/2)N_1^2 \\ f(N_2,) &= (f_0 + a_2)N_2 - (f_1/2)N_2^2 \end{aligned} \tag{6}$$

where a_i are the productivity shocks. The solutions for the two labour types which are given by the usual first-order conditions (see above) are

$$\begin{aligned} N_{1t} &= \delta_1 N_{1t-1} - (\delta_1 h_i/d) \sum_0^\infty \left(\frac{1}{\delta_2}\right)^i [w_{t+i} - a_{1t+i}] \\ N_{2t} &= \mu_1 N_{2t-1} - (\mu_1 h_i/e) \sum_0^\infty \left(\frac{1}{\mu_2}\right)^i [pw_{t+i} - a_{2t+i}] \end{aligned} \tag{7}$$

where constants have been ignored for simplicity, h_i are hours worked by each labour type, and δ_i and μ_i are the roots of the system. If w_t is assumed to follow the $AR(n)$ process

$$w_t = v_0 + v_1 w_{t-1} + \cdots + v_n w_{t-n} + e_t \tag{8}$$

then, written as a first-order $(n + 1)$ vector, it is

$$\mathbf{X}_t = \mathbf{A}\mathbf{X}_{t-1} + \mathbf{e}_t \tag{9}$$

$$\mathbf{X}_t = (w_t, w_{t-1}, \ldots, w_{t-n+1}, 1)^T$$

$$\mathbf{A} = \begin{pmatrix} v_1 & v_2 & v_n & v_0 \\ 1 & 0 & 0 & 0 \\ 0 & 1 & \cdot & \cdot \\ 0 & \cdot & 0 & 1 \end{pmatrix}$$

$$\mathbf{e}_t = (e_{3t}, 0, \ldots, 0)^T$$

Expectations for $\mathbf{X}$ are then given by the optimal forecasting rules

$$\hat{\mathbf{X}}_{t+1} = \mathbf{A}\mathbf{X}_t \tag{10}$$

$$\hat{\mathbf{X}}_{t+j} = \mathbf{A}^j\mathbf{X}_t$$

since

$${}_tE\mathbf{e}_{t+j} = 0, \qquad j > 0.$$

Assuming the a's follow a simple autoregressive scheme of the form

$$a_{it} = \rho_i a_{it-1} + \varepsilon_{it}, \qquad i = 1, 2 \tag{11}$$

then substituting (10) and (11) in (7) gives a solution for $N_i (i = 1, 2)$ in terms of lagged real wages. In particular for N_1, ignoring constants, etc.,

$$(1 - \rho_1 L)N_{1t} = (1 - \rho_1 L)[\delta_1 N_{1t-1} + \alpha_1 w_{t-1} + \alpha_2 w_{t-2} + \cdots + \alpha_n w_{t-n} + \alpha_{n+1} w_{t-n-1}] + n_{1t} \tag{12}$$

where α_i are combinations of v_i, and n_1 is an error term.

Then the estimation proceeds by estimating two equations for employment of the form given in (12), and the autoregressive model for real wages in (8), subject to the restrictions embodied in factorizing the optimal equations and the definition of the v's contained in the matrix $\mathbf{A}$.

The importance of this closed-form solution for the dynamic adjustment of employment with expectations formed rationally is that estimating agents' decision rules jointly with models of the stochastic environment they inhabit, in principle, can identify the parameters of the stochastic processes and the parameters of agents' objectives functions (Hansen and Sargent, 1980). It is possible then to calculate how decision rules change as the stochastic environment changes, proceeding a good way to meeting the invariance property described by Lucas (1976) (see Pesaran (1980) for an extensive discussion of identification and the invariance property).

The central question to consider is that of the exogeneity of real wages in the employment decision. First, this property must be established *prior* to estimation, since, if it does not hold, clearly the relatively simple form of the optimal employment rule described above must be abandoned. Secondly, as Sims (1972) shows, a necessary condition of strong exogeneity is Granger (non-) causality of real wages by employment. So we may proceed to check this assumption by taking evidence from the UK, using the same procedures as reported in Sargent, for Granger causality. The results are given in table 4.1.

TABLE 4.1 Vector autoregression of employment and real wages (manufacturing sector) 1965(01)–1979(04)

	ln N	ln W
$N(-1)$	1.36 (8.4)	0.71 (1.0)
(-2)	−0.04 (0.2)	−0.65 (0.5)
(-3)	−0.35 (1.3)	−0.07 (0.1)
(-4)	−0.40 (1.5)	−0.23 (0.2)
(-5)	0.36 (1.4)	1.05 (0.9)
(-6)	−0.04 (0.2)	−0.39 (0.3)
(-7)	−0.05 (0.2)	0.45 (1.2)
(-8)	0.05 (0.3)	−0.41 (0.6)
$W(-1)$	−0.00 (0.0)	0.94 (5.8)
(-2)	−0.01 (0.2)	−0.03 (0.1)
(-3)	0.02 (0.4)	−0.06 (0.3)
(-4)	0.04 (0.8)	0.10 (0.5)
(-5)	−0.04 (0.8)	−0.18 (0.8)
(-6)	−0.03 (0.6)	0.21 (0.9)
(-7)	0.02 (0.5)	−0.23 (1.0)
(-8)		0.15 (0.2)
$F(8,39)$	0.35	0.88
s.e.	0.0041	0.0176
$\chi^2_2(8)$	121	52
$\chi^2_1(8)$	3.8	2.5
$LM(4)$	12.6	7.0

t values are in brackets. All equations include a constant, trend and seasonal dummies, $\chi^2_2(.)$ tests for one-step forecasting accuracy, $\chi^2_1(.)$ is the Box Pierce statistic, and LM is the Lagrange multiplier test for residual autocorrelation.

The *F* statistic in either case tests whether the independent variable Granger causes the dependent variable. The interesting result is that employment is more likely to cause real wages than vice versa! Actually this is being slightly unfair to real wage to employment causation. As the *LM* test indicates there is serial correlation in the first equation. This can be removed by adding another *three* lags on real wages, whence the *F* statistic rises to 0.65. What is abundantly clear is that we cannot conclude that in the UK there is unidirectional causality from real wages to employment; bidirectional causality seems much more likely. (In contrast for US data, Sargent reports *F* statistics of 0.9 and 0.1 respectively.)

Further testing on this is desirable, but is not pursued here. In an extensive study of the two-way relationship between real wages and employment, one finding reported by Drobney (1982) is that the assumption that real wages are not Granger caused by employment is not upheld in the UK.

Non-exogenous regressors

If the RHS variables are not strongly exogenous then the full implementation of the REH requires the substitution of restricted reduced-form equations for these regression variables in terms of realization functions of exogenous processes. If these variables are part of a macromodel of any reasonable size, this task is computationally formidable.

A number of more limited estimation techniques for rational expectation models have been proposed, and indeed used. These generally employ two-stage or instrumental variable (*IV*) methods, as in Kennan (1979) for example. (An alternative procedure has been used in the context of employment functions by Muellbauer (1980). This involves transformations which, although producing a more manageable deterministic structure to the model, do so at the cost of further complication in error models.) Instrumental variable methods which implant *unrestricted* reduced-form equations for exogenous variables in structural equations may achieve consistency, but since the full model restrictions are not used in estimation, the resulting estimates are neither fully rational, nor will they be efficient.

Related procedures have recently been advocated by Hansen and Sargent (1980) based on exploiting orthogonality conditions between endogenous variables and a reduced information set, though again the procedures are only claimed to be consistent.

The examples reported below will explore the properties of models estimated by *IV* methods.

EMPLOYMENT MODELS

Each of the models to be described and estimated in this section is based to a greater or lesser degree on the preceding dynamic analysis. The policy implications of the different models are, however, profoundly different in some cases. All of the results, with one exception, will be based on reduced-form (*IV*) methods of implementing the REH, so neither efficiency nor policy invariance properties can be realized in any of these examples. These features are also true of the one exception, which estimates an unrestricted version of the Sargent employment–real wage relationship. In the other examples, the method proceeds by deriving a submodel for the regression variable(s), and predictions from these are entered as data in the employment equation, which can then be estimated using standard estimators.

Employment and real wages

In order to implement this model, a submodel for real wages is needed. How this may be specified is discussed more fully below. First, however, a preliminary investigation of the data is provided by estimating an unrestricted version of the Sargent employment–real wage model. This builds on an *AR*(3) time-series model for the real wage, which is a moderately good and parsimonious representation for the data. The autoregression is shown below:

$$\ln w_t = \underset{(9.689)}{1.223} \ln w_{t-1} + \underset{(0.352)}{0.069} \ln w_{t-2} - \underset{(1.487)}{0.291} \ln w_{t-3}$$

$$\text{s.e.} = 0.016, \quad \chi_1^2(16) = 15.06, \quad \chi_2^2(8) = 26.449$$

sample 196401–197904

(Note: This equation was run with seasonals and a constant, which are not reported.) Although we might readily reparametrize this equation (for example, a dynamic equation in Δw_t is indicated by these results), we have not undertaken such an exercise, since the level of the real wage seems well enough represented by the equation. The result indicates that the level of the real wage should enter the employment equation with up to four lags (see equation (12)). The result of estimating such an employment equation is shown in table 4.2.

TABLE 4.2 Unrestricted employment–lagged real wage model

Dependent variable $\ln N_t$

$\ln N_{t-1}$	$\ln N_{t-2}$	$\ln w_{t-1}$	$\ln w_{t-2}$	$\ln w_{t-3}$	$\ln w_{t-4}$
1.581	−0.706	−0.007	−0.061	0.0477	0.008
(18.998)	(8.52)	(0.265)	(1.392)	(1.078)	(0.273)
const.	s.e.	$\chi_1^2(16)$	$\chi_2^2(8)$	sample	
1.116	0.0036	22.772	137.4	196401	
(4.209)	(0.0036)			197904	

Two findings emerge from these results: First, the real wage effect on employment does not appear well founded, since none of the lagged effects appear significant. Secondly, the forecasting performance of the model is very poor, with the $\chi_2^2(8)$ statistic for one-step predictions being 137.4.

To move to the two-stage version of the real wage–employment model, the first stage is to estimate a submodel suggested by complete labour market models. To do this we have based the model on two examples, both recently estimated on British data, and for which the reported results have been favourable. In Beenstock and Warburton (1982) an 'error-correction' equation for the real wage is postulated as part of a real wage–employment model. Variables which appear as regressors in the real wage equation include the working population, the level of real benefits, and tax variables affecting demand and supply decisions. A similar labour market model is proposed by Minford (1981), though here the theory is avowedly based on the assumption of rational expectations (although see Henry and Trinder (1982) for a critical assessment of this model). Apart from the variables already noted, this model allows for possible effects of the percentage of the labour force unionized on the real wage.[1] So in our strategy to model real wages, we have derived a submodel for the real wage dependent upon this set of variables, and have included these variables and determined the order of their lags by a process of deriving a data-coherent specification for the real wage. In estimating this model we have tested for the presence of any interrelationships between all the independent variables. However, in practice, it turns out that only in one case can we reject the proposition that the non-wage variables are strongly exogenous, and can therefore be predicted using a simple time-series model.

Our starting point for estimating the real wage expectations system is therefore a vector autoregression in real labour costs (the real wage price), real benefits (B), the rate of unionization (u) and the working population (P). (For a detailed definition of these variables see the appendix.) Up to eight lags were allowed for on each variable and a constant, seasonal dummies and a time trend were included in each equation. All four variables were logged, and the real benefits variable was a four-quarter moving average, thereby eliminating the 'saw-tooth' character of the original series arising from the annual uprating of nominal benefits. The estimation period was 1965 to 1979, and post-sample stability tests were carried out over 1980 and 1981.

Taking the real labour cost equation first, theory suggests a negative influence from increases in population, but a positive effect (if anything) from both real benefits and unionization. The data were consistent with all three effects. In the equation reported in table 4.3 we have eliminated insignificant lags to increase efficiency.

TABLE 4.3

Dependent variable w					
w_{t-1}	w_{t-5}	Δu_{t-2}	Δu_{t-4}	u_{t-8}	
0.76	−0.18	+1.20	+0.63	+0.61	
(10.4)	(2.9)	(2.9)	(2.4)	(3.9)	
ΔP_{t-1}	P_{t-4}	ΔP_{t-5}	B_{t-5}	B_{t-6}	
+1.71	−1.48	−1.37	+0.36	−0.17	
(3.0)	(4.4)	(2.3)	(3.0)	(1.5)	
B_{t-7}	Q_1	Q_2	Q_3	T	
+0.10	−0.004	−0.007	+0.002	+0.0039	+11.19
(2.1)	(0.6)	(0.9)	(0.4)	(0.4)	(3.9)
Sample	s.e.	$\chi_2^2(8)$	$\chi_1^2(16)$	$LM(8)$	
1965–79	0.0128	41.0	33.0	14	
$F(19, 23)$	Chow(16, 28)				
0.46	1.35				

As all the equations estimated in this system are reduced forms, theory tells us little about dynamics, and so the dynamics in each of the equations estimated here are largely data based. Although the level of real benefits does have a positive impact on labour costs, it is worth noting that in our most general equation we could not reject the hypothesis that real benefits had no direct influence on real labour costs (with $F(8,23) = 0.56$), while the other two variables had a more powerful influence. Another interesting result is that in the short run an increase in the working population also raises labour costs, and any attempt to exclude this short-run influence is data rejected. In the long run, however, an increase in the working population does reduce real labour costs to a significant extent. As the Chow test indicates, the equation remains stable when estimated over the subperiods 1965–71 and 1972–79. (The F test shows that this is a data acceptable restriction of the maintained hypothesis.)

There is no *a priori* reason for expecting either real labour costs, real benefits or population to have any particular impact on the level of unionization. The estimated maintained hypothesis did not suggest any powerful long- or short-run influences of this kind, and the data did not reject the hypothesis that unionization was independent of lagged values of these other variables ($F(24, 23) = 0.96$). Further data-based simplification suggested the simple time-series model in table 4.4 for the unionization variable.

The equation passes a Chow test, but fails the post-sample stability test, the reason being that within the sample period the dependent variable is a

TABLE 4.4

Dependent variable u			
u_{t-1}	u_{t-2}	t	
1.557	−0.636	+0.00044	+0.287
(15.8)	(6.7)	(3.3)	(3.1)
sample	s.e.	$\chi_2^2(8)$	$\chi_1^2(16)$
1965–79	0.0037	50.0	9
$LM(8)$	$F(33, 23)$	Chow (4, 52)	
5.5	0.79	0.77	

fairly continuous upward trend, whereas in 1981 the level of unionization actually declines.

We could also accept the hypothesis that the working population was a simple time-series model ($F(24, 23) = 0.72$). Further simplification gave the equation in table 4.5.

At the 5 per cent level the equation fails the Chow test, although it passes at a 1 per cent significance level.

It could be argued that the level of real benefits might be positively related to real wages, and hence to real labour costs. However, the proposition that real benefits were independent of lagged real labour costs was easily accepted in our maintained hypothesis ($F(8, 23) = 0.34$), and its long-run coefficient in this equation was actually negative. There seems to be no *a priori* reason why benefits should be related to lagged values of population or unionization, but in both cases these variables could *not* be eliminated.

(For example when comparing a general equation excluding both labour costs and population with one excluding labour costs alone, an F test gave

TABLE 4.5

Dependent variable P				
P_{t-1}	P_{t-3}	P_{t-6}	Q_1	Q_2
0.84	+0.31	−0.24	−0.0019	+0.0017
(9.3)	(2.6)	(2.9)	(1.6)	(1.0)
Q_3	t			
+0.0043	+0.00007	+0.916		
(2.8)	(2.1)	(2.1)		
sample	s.e.	$\chi_2^2(8)$	$\chi_1^2(16)$	$LM(8)$
1965–79	0.0032	14.0	13.5	10.4
$F(29, 23)$	Chow (8, 44)			
0.64	2.47			

TABLE 4.6

Dependent variable B

B_{t-1}	B_{t-2}	ΔB_{t-4}	B_{t-6}	ΔP_{t-6}	Δu_{t-6}
1.22	−0.355	0.65	−0.156	+0.83	−0.76
(14.7)	(3.9)	(5.3)	(4.8)	(2.2)	(2.8)
Q_1	Q_2	Q_3	t		
−0.007	−0.002	−0.000	+0.00082	−0.577	
(2.0)	(0.4)	(0.0)	(4.1)	(4.7)	
sample	s.e.	$\chi_1^2(16)$	$LM(8)$	$F(26, 32)$	Chow (11, 28)
1965–79	0.0093	17	5.6	0.84	1.5

$F(8, 31) = 2.5$ compared to a critical 5 per cent value of 2.3.) As the equation in table 4.6 indicated, movements in the level of both variables influence benefits only temporarily, and although these influences are difficult to explain their impact on the properties of the system as a whole is unlikely to be large.

These four equations represent a system for generating expectations about future real labour cost movements. These expectations depend directly on past values of all four variables in the system. We used this system to generate series for expected real labour costs from one period ahead ($WE(0)$, the expected level of real labour costs in the current period formed in the period (-1)) up to eight periods ahead ($WE(8)$, again formed in period (-1)). We then included each variable in an employment equation which also included three lagged dependent variables, seasonal dummies and a time trend. This is a procedure which is adopted for all subsequent regression models.

Our justification for third-order lags, as opposed to first-order as suggested for example for one type of labour in equation (11), is largely empirical. Theory suggests higher-order lags arise due to, for example, the aggregation over different labour types to derive total employment (Sargent, 1979, Nickell, 1981, illustrate this), or because the assumption of simple quadratic adjustment cost functions is inadequate. In our tests we attempt to meet these points by including higher terms in lagged employment. Generally, there is support for the inclusion of up to three lags.

The results of our general employment–real wage model is shown next.

$$N = \sum_{+1}^{+3} a_i N(-i) + \sum_{0}^{8} b_i WE(i) - \underset{(2.7)}{0.0008T} - \underset{(0.5)}{0.001Q_1} - \underset{(0.7)}{0.001Q_2}$$

$$-\underset{(0.6)}{0.002Q_3} + \underset{(3.6)}{1.88}$$

a_i: 1.29, −0.20, −0.30 sum = 0.79
(8.9) (0.8) (2.1)

b_i: −0.01, 0.04, −0.10, 0.01, 0.13, −0.22, 0.35, −0.14, −0.05
(0.2) (0.3) (0.7) (0.1) (0.6) (0.6) (0.8) (0.3) (0.2)

sum = 0.01
sample 1965–79, s.e. = 0.0040, $\chi_2^2(8) = 203.0$, $\chi_1^2(8) = 5.6$,
$LM(4) = 6$

The results are extremely poor. None of the expectations series are significant, and we can easily reject their combined presence in the equation ($F(8, 43) = 0.88$). As in the model based on lagged labour costs alone, there appears to be no long-run effect from the level of expected real labour costs on employment. Eliminating insignificant terms does not alter the results, and an equation estimated from 1972 is just as bad. Finally we should note the appalling forecasting performance in 1980–81. These two experiments suggest that employment models based on expected real wages do not perform well in the UK. Of course, this evidence is not enough to dismiss models based on real factor prices altogether. In particular, we have looked at models in which employment decisions depend on movements in real labour costs, whereas a more complete model would include other factor prices such as the cost of capital (see Symons, 1982, for example.) Nevertheless the results above suggest that the recent sharp fall in manufacturing employment is not simply explained by the proposition that real wages were too high.

A model of employment and output

This section is inspired by the recent results reported by Nickell (1981) for employment models based on expected output. One feature of the theoretical model is that it assumes two labour types N_1 and N_2 as does Sargent, though here they could relate to different skill types. Labour enters a production function of the form

$$Y(t) = F(N_1(t)^{1/\varepsilon}h_1(t),\ N_2(t)^{1/\varepsilon}h_2(t))A(\bar{k}(t),\ \bar{M}(t))e^{Bt} \tag{13}$$

where h_i is hours worked by the ith labour type, and $\bar{k}$ and $\bar{M}$ are average capital–labour ratios and materials plus energy–labour ratios. Minimizing the discounted cost functional subject to this and an expected output constraint produces an equation for aggregate employment (N) dependent upon forward movements in expected output, i.e.

$$N_t = a_0 + a_1 N_{t-1} + a_2 N_{t-2} + a_3 Y_t + a_4 t + a_5 A(\bar{k}, \bar{M}) + \sum \alpha_i \, \Delta Y(t+s) \tag{14}$$

where we have dropped underlying parameters for convenience (they are not utilized in the estimation). Formally the estimation problem posed by this model is similar to the case described earlier, but where output expectations now replaces real wage expectations. A submodel of output is therefore required, and a set of variables postulated which determine output movements. First, we consider the performance of this approach with the specification for the output submodel originally suggested by Nickell which used the growth rate in the nominal money supply (M) and real share prices (S). Later in the section, results are provided based on an alternative model. One important detail remains. The cost-minimizing model implies a dependence of output upon relative prices as well as expected output. We reconsider this below in the fourth subsection.

Nickell's model shows a remarkable degree of success in ex-ante forecasting for the period 197403–197904 (see Nickell, 1981: 29). To assess the usefulness of the model over more recent times, we need to re-estimate and conduct further stability tests. We have used a sample of 196501–197904 to fit our version of this model, and saved the eight quarters of 1980–81 for post fitting stability tests, though it should be stressed that we have *not* used these stability tests as part of the general specification testing in deriving the preferred model. Again, all variables are logged, and a within-sample data coherent version of the model for output (Y), dropping all insignificant variables, is shown in table 4.7.[2] (Seasonal dummies are not reported.)

Some of the detailed dynamics in this equation differ from that in the original, due partly to our decisions to use variables in logs, but also because we have concentrated on within-sample fit in deriving this preferred form, whereas stability and forecasting performance appear to have entered as criteria in the original. In terms of data coherence—significance of individual parameters, absence of serial correlation, etc.—this equation is fairly good. Its performance in providing a statistical explanation of 1980–81,

TABLE 4.7

Dependent variable Y

Y_{t-1}	Y_{t-4}	Y_{t-7}	S_{t-3}	M_{t-2}	ΔM_{t-7}
0.702	−.21	−0.258	0.045	0.422	−0.402
(11.2)	(2.1)	(2.8)	(4.4)	(3.5)	(3.5)
t	s.e.	$\chi_1^2(8)$	$\chi_2^2(8)$	Chow (11, 38)	
0.0017	0.014	1.8	235.0	0.9	
sample 196501–197904					

TABLE 4.8

Dependent variable M						
M_{t-1}	M_{t-4}	$\Delta_2 Y_{t-3}$	ΔS_{t-1}	t	$\chi_1^2(8)$	$\chi_2^2(8)$
0.459	0.314	−0.122	0.052	0.000	5.3	14.3
(3.8)	(2.2)	(1.7)	(2.5)	(0.1)		
Dependent variable S						
S_{t-1}	S_{t-2}	ΔS_{t-3}	M_{t-2}	M_{t-3}	Y_{t-3}	ΔY_{t-7}
1.236	−0.38	0.08	1.257	−2.45	0.28	−1.94
(10.7)	(3.1)	(0.6)	(1.6)	(3.0)	(0.8)	(3.4)
t	$\chi_1^2(8)$	$\chi_2^2(8)$				
−0.005	5.4	10.2				
(2.3)						
sample 196501–197904						

however, is abysmal. The $\chi_2^2(8)$ statistic is extremely large, reflecting the systematic overprediction of one-step forecasts from the equation. Moreover, the reason for this is quite simple, and is due to the behaviour of the driving variables over this period. Neither S nor M fall significantly either immediately before or during 1980–81. This does not augur well for the forecasting performance of the employment equation over the same period, but for the present we complete the estimation of that model, and return to this feature later.

Equations for the money supply and share-price index are in table 4.8.

Proceeding therefore to use these equations and that for output, to provide forward movements in output, a model of employment based on these is shown in table 4.9.

TABLE 4.9

Dependent variable N_t					
N_{t-1}	N_{t-2}	N_{t-3}	$\Delta\hat{Y}(t+8)$	$\hat{Y}(t+5)$	t
1.212	0.19	−0.62	0.289	0.137	−0.001
(11.0)	(1.0)	(5.3)	(3.2)	(5.7)	(7.9)
s.e.	$\chi_1^2(8)$	$\chi_2^2(8)$			
0.0031	5.5	185.0			
sample 196501–197904					

This equation is a simplified version of a maintained hypothesis which included expected output series ranging from one step ahead to nine steps ahead ($\hat{Y}(t)$ to $\hat{Y}(t + 8)$). In contrast to the models based on real wages, the *level* of expected output is significant over the estimation period. However, the most serious result for this experiment is the poor forecasting performance of the model. This was anticipated in reporting the same sort of failure for the output model, and one piece of information yielded by these regressions is the decomposition of the failure of the employment model. Evidently it is the failure to forecast the output variable which contributes substantially to the problems here. The results in the fourth subsection and in Nickell (1981) suggest that a more comprehensive examination of this model should involve terms in factor prices.

Apart from the problems noted above, the submodel for output is open to criticism on its underlying *a priori* basis, and these criticisms may indicate potential respecification. The terms M and higher orders may be viewed as proxies for unanticipated movements in the money supply which, according to equilibrium theories of output, given misperceptions of absolute and relative magnitudes could produce temporary real-nominal interactions. However, this model, as the author notes, implies that steady-state output is an increasing function of steady-state growth in the money supply, contradicting long-run neutrality. The use of real share prices, which are introduced to proxy variables observed by agents but not by the investigator (Nickell, 1981: 16), is interesting but also problematic. Consequently, other variables may do better in accounting for output movements, and we move on to a suggestion for one set of alternatives next.

An alternative model of output and employment

In Nickell's model the impact of actual changes in policy are only captured directly insofar as they alter the growth rate of nominal $M3$. In the alternative model estimated below we attempt to provide some differentiation between the impact of fiscal and monetary policy on output. Our summary measure of fiscal policy is the 'cyclically adjusted, weighted real budget deficit' as constructed by Price (1978) and Savage (1982). All such measures inevitably involve important simplifications which may detract from their usefulness in estimation, but this particular measure avoids some of the more obvious shortcomings. A measure of monetary policy is equally problematic. Real or nominal UK interest rates would be obvious candidates, but recent analysis stemming from Dornbusch (1976) has focused on the role of international interest rate differentials coupled with rational expectations in the foreign exchange markets in influencing the real exchange rate. Given sticky domestic prices, real exchange rate movements will influence output both through international trade and also perhaps through profit-

TABLE 4.10

Dependent variable Y					
Y_{t-1}	Y_{t-4}	ΔC_{t-1}	C_{t-3}	C_{t-6}	F_{t-1}
0.43	−0.716	−0.18	−0.22	−0.49	4.9
(3.1)	(4.2)	(1.5)	(2.3)	(2.8)	(2.5)
F_{t-4}	F_{t-5}	t	s.e.	$\chi_1^2(8)$	$\chi_2^2(8)$
13.4	−9.0	0.003	0.017	14.8	34.4
(4.6)	(3.6)	(3.1)			

ability (see Buiter and Miller, 1981). The authorities can of course influence exchange rates through direct intervention in the foreign exchange market. This analysis suggests including a measure of the real exchange rate as our second explanatory variable influencing expected output.

Clearly neither fiscal policy nor the real exchange rate can be considered as strongly exogenous, and so in deriving series for expected output we will need to estimate equations for these other variables as well. Nor is it sensible to assume that this model will remain stable over the period before and after the move to a floating exchange rate regime, and so our estimation period in this case begins in 1972.[3]

We begin with a simplified version of the output equation based on competitiveness (C) and the adjusted budget deficit (F), shown in table 4.10.

Before discussing this result we note the equations for F and C, estimated again from 1972–79, and given in table 4.11.

TABLE 4.11

Dependent variable F					
F_{t-1}	F_{t-2}	Y_{t-1}	C_{t-2}	C_{t-4}	t
1.01	−0.469	0.031	0.019	0.011	−0.0002
(1.6)	(3.9)	(3.3)	(3.2)	(1.3)	(4.2)
s.e.	$\chi_1^2(8)$	$\chi_2^2(8)$			
0.0012	6.1	8.7			
Dependent variable C					
C_{t-1}	$\Delta\Delta C_{t-3}$	Y_{t-1}	ΔY_{t-4}		
0.89	0.22	−0.24	0.44		
(10.2)	(1.4)	(1.4)	(1.7)		
F_{t-4}	t	s.e.	$\chi_1^2(8)$	$\chi_2^2(8)$	
4.34	0.001	0.029	10.1	21.5	
(1.5)	(3.0)				

TABLE 4.12 Output forecasts (1975 = 100)

		Actual	One-quarter prediction*		Six-quarter prediction*	
			A	B	A	B
1980	1	100	106	102	109	97
	2	98	104	94	108	98
	3	94	100	96	108	97
	4	88	99	91	106	95
1981	1	87	93	88	108	100
	2	88	98	92	103	98
	3	90	94	92	107	98
	4	90	99	96	102	99
1982	1				109	98
	2				107	98
	3				107	98
	4				107	96
1983	1				108	97

* Period refers to quarter predicted.

Reverting to the output equation, its one-step forecasting performance is a big improvement on the previous model, though it is not entirely satisfactory. (The problem is largely due to the failure of the equation to capture 198104 output.) However, the equation does not reveal systematic over-prediction as does the previous example. Further detail in the equations forecasting performance compared with the previous model is shown in table 4.12, on a current and six-step basis. Model A is the first output model above, model B is the second version in this section.

Whilst this new model for output is not perfect, it is clearly a considerable improvement on the earlier model. Moreover, it suggests that firms anticipated the recession to some extent, whereas in the earlier model firms are taken completely by surprise, continuing to believe the recession to be temporary.

Estimating an employment output equation based on this second output submodel might therefore be expected to provide a rather better account of the recent movements in employment. Unfortunately this does not appear to be the case, as shown in table 4.13.

Although the within-sample properties of this equation are fairly good, the irony is that its forecasting performance is no improvement on the earlier model. One feature contributing to this is the change in the dynamics of the equation compared with the previous one. There, the

TABLE 4.13

Dependent variable N				
N_{t-1}	N_{t-2}	N_{t-3}	$\hat{Y}_t$	$\hat{Y}_{t+2}$
0.86	0.25	−0.35	0.05	0.12
(4.6)	(0.9)	(2.3)	(1.4)	(3.3)
$\Delta_2 \hat{Y}_{t+6}$	t	s.e.	$\chi_1^2(8)$	$\chi_2^2(8)$
0.06	−0.0000	0.00307	9.8	242.0
(1.7)	(4.4)			

dynamic responses were sharper, and the present model—though based on an apparently more realistic output forecast—with more sluggish responses to falls in actual employment, has an equally poor one step forecasting record.

Employment, output and relative prices

The last employment equation considered here takes the model produced by combining expected output using the output model from above and certain factor prices in the intertemporal cost-minimizing decision. Comparable results for the myopic case are given in Henry (1980), a two-stage version is reported by Nickell (1981) and a related model is reported by Muellbauer (1980).

Whereas it is evident that relative factor prices enter as a determinant of factor demands in a cost-minimizing model, the precise form in which these enter is not unambiguous in recent examples. Nickell for example proxies factor ratios by factor price ratios. Muellbauer proposes an *ad hoc* set of variables to represent both demand shift and raw material price terms. Finally in Henry the short-run substitution between average hours worked and numbers employed was emphasized, depending on the relative cost of adjusting average hours compared with the discounted cost of adjusting numbers employed.

In this section we use a collection of relative factor price terms to add to the expected output model of employment. One major problem encountered in this extension is that of deriving precise measures of the relevant costs. The problems in obtaining a realistic cost of capital series are fairly well known, though we have attempted to overcome the obvious ones with our measure. There are also severe limitations in UK wage data, so that meaningful separation of labour cost into hours and numbers employed components is well nigh impossible. The hours variable for example is for operatives only, and basic wage series are incomplete and cover only manual workers. Mainly for these reasons, a 'portmanteau' approach to the modelling of relative price influences seems advisable. Hence we have incorporated:

(a) the ratio of labour to cost of capital variable (*REA*);
(b) the ratio of labour to material and other input cost variable (*REB*); and
(c) a proxy for changes in the relative costs of employment versus hours at the margin, given by the level of overtime hours ($H - H_N$), where H_N is standard or normal hours.[4]

Again, the reported versions of the employment model were derived without extensive search over the lag structure on the various relative price terms. What appeared a regular feature of the experiments however was that the wage relative to the cost of capital variable (*REA*) was always incorrectly signed. Hence this variable was dropped. Of the remaining additional factors, both tended to be correctly signed, but not significant. A typical result of this is shown in table 4.14.

On the face of this, the evidence is not particularly favourable to the presence of important relative price effects at work here. What should not be ignored in the assessment of this equation however is that the forecasting performance has improved considerably compared to earlier examples. Some further experimentation with this form of the equation seems advisable.

On the basis of this result, there is a very marginal preference for the relative price term over the hours variable. One general factor at work here though may be a degree of intercorrelation between the variables. (Increasing hours tending to increase measured labour cost.) Hence we decided to try each variable separately, and the results are shown in table 4.15, as equations (1) and (2).

The version of the equation using the hours variable appears to perform better, both in terms of individual significance and forecasting performance. This equation is now virtually consistent with the behaviour of employment in 1980–81 on a single-step basis, and on this criterion seems preferred to the other models discussed here.

TABLE 4.14

Dependent variable N

N_{t-1}	N_{t-2}	N_{t-3}	$\hat{Y}_{t+1}$	$\hat{Y}_{t+2}$	$\hat{Y}_{t+4}$	$\hat{Y}_{t+6}$
1.039	0.277	−0.416	0.017	0.183	−0.058	0.123
(4.803)	(0.819)	(2.540)	(0.463)	(4.318)	(1.613)	(3.525)
$\hat{Y}_{t+7}$	ΔREB_{t-1}	$\Delta_2(H - H_N)_{t-1}$	s.e.	$\chi_1^2(8)$	$\chi_2^2(8)$	
0.060	−0.018	−0.023	0.0029	12.28	20.313	
(1.797)	(1.163)	(0.839)				

TABLE 4.15

Dependent variable N

	N_{t-1}	N_{t-2}	N_{t-3}	$\hat{Y}_{t+1}$	$\hat{Y}_{t+2}$	$\hat{Y}_{t+4}$	$\hat{Y}_{t+6}$
(1)	1.114	0.161	−0.375	0.037	0.166	−0.047	0.124
	(5.247)	(0.484)	(2.27)	(1.005)	(4.312)	(1.303)	(3.659)
(2)	0.971	0.373	−0.442	0.01	0.192	−0.067	0.121
	(4.88)	(1.182)	(2.769)	(0.273)	(4.72)	(1.993)	(3.496)

	$\hat{Y}_{t+7}$	ΔREB_{t-1}	$\Delta_2(H - H_N)_{t-1}$	s.e.	$\chi_1^2(8)$	$\chi_2^2(8)$
(1)	0.049		−0.051	0.00302	8.744	15.66
	(1.472)		(2.240)			
(2)	0.061	−0.025		0.0029	9.168	29.01
	(1.826)	(1.871)				

Several notes of caution are required, however. The problem of increasing returns to scale noted earlier (and evident in earlier sections) has been transformed into one of sharply diminishing returns. The long-run coefficient on expected output in this equation is a lot larger than unity. This transformation has been produced solely by adding relative price terms which are somewhat *ad hoc*. Finally, although this equation predicts the dramatic events of 1980–81 fairly successfully, we do not know whether it would remain stable before 1972.

CONCLUSION

This paper has considered various models of manufacturing employment based on explicit forward-looking expectations. In particular, we have focused on the ability of these models to explain recent changes in employment. Given the size of these changes it is perhaps not surprising, but at the same time rather disturbing, that most of these models fail to account for (i.e. remain structurally stable over) this period. However, despite this general failure, it is evident that models based on expectations about the real wage appear to be distinctly less satisfactory than those based on cost minimization given expected output.

APPENDIX

N = Employment in manufacturing, logged
Y = Manufacturing output, logged
C = UK manufacturing whosesale prices (home sales)/world manufacturing export prices in sterling, logged

F = Real weighted full employment budget deficit
S = F.T. Share Price Index/GDP deflator, logged
M = $\Delta \ln M3$
H = Average operative hours in manufacturing
H_N = Normal hours in manufacturing
$REA = W/[g(0.005 + V) - \Delta g]$, in logs
$REB = W/$(index of raw material and energy inputs to manufacturing), in logs
W = Total labour cost including national insurance and other contributions/total employment in manufacturing
g = Implicit deflator of capital goods
V = Local authority rate of interest
u = Proportion of workforce unionized, logged
P = Working population, logged
B = Benefit entitlement of single unemployed man with no children/ retail price index, logged

NOTES

This is a revised version of the invited paper given at the 1982 International Seminar on Recent Development in Macroeconomic Modelling in Paris. Thanks are extended to Stephen Hall and Stephen Nickell for constructive suggestions.

1 Both models allow for output effects also. We defer a consideration of models based on expected output until the next section.
2 We have used a log version for consistency with the practice in the previous section. Nickell reports a levels model for output and he found a logarithmic version inferior (Nickell, 1981: 26).
3 The equation for output below fails a Chow test ($F(16, 28) = 2.5$, compared to a 5 per cent critical value of around 2) when estimated from 1965. Equivalent equations for the pre-1972 period are considered in Wren-Lewis and Henry (1982).
4 Implicit in this is an optimal rule for hours (see Henry, 1980).

REFERENCES

Beenstock, M. and Warburton, P. (1982) 'An Aggregative Model of the UK Labour Market', *Oxford Economic Papers.*

Buiter, W. and Miller, M. (1981) *The Thatcher Experiment: An Interim Report*, Discussion Paper No. 106, Centre for Labour Economics, LSE (also forthcoming in Brookings Papers).

Dornbusch, R. (1976) 'Expectations and Exchange Rate Dynamics', *Journal of Political Economy.*

Drobney, A. (1982) *Causality and the Equilibrium Theory of Employment Fluctuations: Results from the UK*, Working Paper, QMC (London).

Engle, R. F., Hendry, D. F. and Richard, J. F. (1981) *Exogeneity*, Discussion Paper No. 162, University of Warwick.

Hansen, L. and Sargent, T. (1980) 'Formulating and Estimating Dynamic Linear Rational Expectations Models', *Journal of Economic Dynamics and Control.*

Hendry, D. F. and von Ungern-Sternberg, T. (1980) 'Liquidity and Inflation Effects on Consumers Expenditure' in *Essays in the Theory and Measurement of Consumer Behaviour*, ed. A. S. Deaton.

Henry, S. G. B. (1980) 'Forecasting Employment and Unemployment', in *The Economics of the Labour Market*, eds Hornstein, Grice and Webb, HMSO.

Henry, S. G. B. and Trinder, C. (1982) *Unemployment and Real Wages: The Role of Real Benefits and Unionisation*, mimeographed.

Kennan, J. (1979) 'The Estimation of Partial Adjustment Models with Rational Expectations', *Econometrica.*

Lucas, (1976) 'Econometric Policy Evaluation; A Critique', in *The Phillips Curve and Labour Markets*, eds K. Brunner and A. Meltzer.

Minford, P. (1981) *Labour Market Equilibrium in an Open Economy*, Discussion Paper No. 8103, Economics Department, University of Liverpool.

Muellbauer, (1980) *Are Employment Decisions Based on Rational Expectations?* Discussion Paper, No. 74, Birkbeck College, London.

Nickell, S. (1981) *An Investigation of the Determinants of Manufacturing Employment in the UK*, Discussion Paper No. 105, Centre for Labour Economics, LSE.

Pesaran, M. H. (1980) *Identification of Rational Expectations Models*, mimeographed, Trinity College, Cambridge.

Price, R. (1978) 'Budgetary Policy' in *British Economic Policy*, ed. Blackaby, Cambridge University Press.

Sargent, T. (1978) 'Estimation of Dynamic Labour Demand Schedules Under Rational Expectations', *Journal of Political Economy.*

Savage, D. (1982) 'Fiscal Policy, 1974/5–1980/1: Description and Measurement', *National Institute Economic Review*, no. 99.

Sims, C. (1972) 'Money, Income and Causality', *American Economic Review.*

Symons, J. (1982) *Relative Prices and the Demand for Labour in British Manufacturing*, Discussion Paper No. 137, Centre of Labour Economics, LSE.

Tinsley, P. (1971) 'A Variable Adjustment Model of Labour Demand', *International Economic Review.*

Wickens, M. (1974) 'Towards a Theory of the Labour Market', *Economica.*

Wren-Lewis, S. and Henry, S. G. B. (1983) *Employment and Expected Output*, mimeographed.

Comment

JEAN WAELBROECK

Large models are the dominant type of econometric system today. They are popular in part because they seem complete; there is no part of the economy which is absent, or which could not be added readily. The large models of today are generally estimated by unsophisticated methods: almost always least squares. The specifications of equations tend to be simple, and are robust enough to permit frequent re-estimation. Experience does suggest that this frequent re-estimation is useful, to the point of casting some doubt on the stability of the relations estimated. Prediction with the large models tends to lean significantly on the judgement of the forecaster, with fairly extensive use of intercept adjustment and other fine tuning devices.

This approach meets the 'market test': users are willing to pay for these forecasts and for the right to use these models. New ones are built all the time, and it would be an awesome task to list all those in existence.

As often, this success has entailed a certain loss of scientific curiosity and methodological purity. One is reminded somehow of the history of the Christian Church, losing some of its idealism as it became successful in the worldly sense. What gives the 'big modellers' a clear conscience is awareness of the fact that at the time when their approach was at the experimental stage, the sophisticated techniques of the day–notably simultaneous equations estimation—were experimented with extensively, and were not found to help predictive performance appreciably.

As in Church history, the somewhat unimaginative complacency that has come to characterize most 'big modelling' work has engendered the desire for a return to the more stirring purity of the original econometric gospel. It is probably in England that the reaction was most marked, fostered by an interesting and varied group of econometricians, most of whom have studied or still do study or work in London. Names such as those of Sargent, Hendry, Mizon, Wallis, Beenstock and of course Henry and Wren-Lewis readily come to mind. Like any true school, they are separated by disagreements about aspects of the methodology to be followed and their investigations move in different directions, which does not prevent the group from making a coherent and very interesting contribution to today's econometric research.

From what does the unity stem? First—this is the return to the original gospel—there is a strong belief in the merits of careful specification of the stochastic model which generates the data, implying the use of a sophisticated statistical approach. There is also a keen interest in the dynamic specification of equations—reasonable indeed if the goal is prediction. Finally, there is a strong 'small is beautiful' feeling: the sense that small models can forecast as well or probably better than their giant brothers. Is this making a virtue out of necessity? Certainly, it is hardly thinkable to use the intelligence—intensive and time-consuming procedures advocated by the members of the school to all the equations of a large econometric model.

What have been the achievements of the 'small models' so far? Their advocates claim that they produce excellent forecasts; the examples that I know of suggest that the claim is exaggerated. What is true is that the approach has brought back some of the fun and joy of model building, by restoring the sense of excitement that goes with deep and thorough analysis of specific aspects of the economic system.

The Henry and Wren-Lewis paper tackles a relation which is one of the hardest to estimate, that which predicts movements of employment. The relation is dynamic because there are significant costs to changing the level of employment. A rational employer should predict the future level of demand, and adjust the number of workers in advance of the expected changes of demand or of other relevant variables.

It is future output (or profitability) which is the driving variable, but of course the expected values of variables are not observed. It is necessary to generate them. This the authors do by means of autoregressive schemes. Using the expected values thus calculated, it is then possible to estimate and construct the prediction equation for employment. The 1980–81 data are set aside to be used to assess the predictive ability of the equation.

This is a hard—and not altogether fair—test. The Thatcher government came to power in mid-1979, and implemented policies which differed sharply from those of its predecessors. Of greatest importance for the employment decisions of firms was perhaps the clear indication given by the Thatcher administration that the fight against inflation would henceforth take precedence over full employment as an objective of economic policy. The theory of rational expectations invoked by the authors emphasizes the impact on behaviour of the announcement of shifts in policy patterns. If agents are rational, they will immediately adapt their behaviour to the new information. The stochastic process which generates economic variables should of course reflect agents' new behaviour.

This means that it is inappropriate to use regressions based on pre-1980 behaviour to generate expectations for the subsequent period. Whether a particular equation predicts 1980–81 developments is not a fair test of the corresponding theory.

The other problem is more a practical than a fundamental one. It is hard to capture in the regression which generates the assumed expectations of agents all the factors which they may have in mind, because this would raise problems of multicollinearity and of lack of degrees of freedom. For example, the authors use in various regressions variables such as the rate of unionization, social benefits, the money stock, stock market prices, the full employment budget surplus, and various indicators of the ratio of selling prices to costs; of course, these are never all used simultaneously. Many would argue that the full list of variables which should be considered is far wider. The 'big modellers' would point with pride to the far broader range of factors encompassed by their systems (the fact that 'everything is included' of course does not mean that each factor is given its right weight and place).

These arguments—especially the first—argue for caution in evaluating the results obtained. Henry and Wren-Lewis are quite successful on the whole in fitting specifications to pre-1980 data, but the different models predict subsequent developments poorly. Perhaps this only suggests that the change in policies made the autoregressive patterns estimated for the earlier period irrelevant in predicting subsequent behaviour. Would the results have been better if the policy pattern had not suddenly changed—e.g. if Labour had won the election, or if Mr Heath had prevailed over Mrs Thatcher in the struggle for leadership of the Tories?

The authors' conclusion is prudent. Would another interpretation of their results be that—as pointed out by Lucas—changes of policies change the coefficients of the equations which link variables together? This would be a discouraging finding for all modellers, whether of the 'big' or of the 'small' variety.

PART TWO

Exchange Rate Models

5

Real Exchange Rates and Structural Transformations

M. AGLIETTA and G. OUDIZ

The experience of the last 20 years clearly demonstrates the inadequacy of the theories derived from purchasing power parity as explanations of exchange rate movements. Very important deviations from PPP have persisted not only in the short term but also in the medium to long term among all the major currencies, as is clearly shown by the consistent real depreciation of the dollar during the 1970s.

Most of the recent literature on exchange rates, though improving greatly our understanding of short-term fluctuations of nominal parities, has however neglected the importance of real exchange rate movements. The necessity of deriving simple models and the emphasis on short-term evolutions has generally led the various authors to rely on simple PPP assumptions in the long run.

In this paper we do not take into account the short-term aspects of exchange rate determination but rather focus on the medium- to long-term analysis of the real exchange rate. The purpose of the study is to support our basic view that 'deviations' from PPP are not due to exceptional short-term distortions among nominal parities but are on the contrary fundamentally related to structural differences in income distribution, international specialization, capital accumulation and growth which exist among countries.

In the first part of this paper we review briefly the main parity theories of exchange rate. Then we discuss how the Ricardian theory of international trade leads to a different conception of the exchange rate. Finally we derive from these considerations a theoretical model of the real exchange rate.

In the second part of the paper we discuss an econometric analysis of the exchange rates of the ten leading industrial countries over the years 1960–79. In the first section we discuss the nature of the data and the econometric methodology adapted to pooled country cross sections which is used for our estimates. In the second section we discuss the adequacy of equilibrium parity models and in the third section we present estimates of various models of the real exchange rate derived from our theoretical discussion.

THE EXCHANGE RATE IN THE LONG RUN: SOME THEORETICAL CONSIDERATIONS

Two basic conceptions of international economic relations can be opposed in the literature. On the one hand, stress is put on market forces, the world economy being apprehended as an interdependent system of market equilibriums, national heterogeneities playing only a minor role. On the other hand, the crucial importance of structural differences among nations is stressed. This implies that the analysis no longer assumes homogeneous markets and equilibrium price determination but more fundamentally takes into account the nature of production conditions, relative price systems and domestic demand within nations.

To these two conceptions of the world economy correspond two approaches to the long-term determination of exchange rates. The first approach can be defined as a *parity theory*. The nominal exchange rate results from the unicity of equilibrium prices. The real exchange rate is then either equal to unity or identical to the relative price of non-traded and traded goods when product differentiation is taken into account. The second approach does not associate the long-term exchange rate to a *price equilibrium* but to a *flow equilibrium*. It is the global equivalence of the values of the quantities of labour exchanged between nations which then defines the real exchange rate.

The parity theories of exchange rate

We shall only outline here the well known assumptions of these theories in order to note the main differences with our approach of the real exchange rate (for an extensive discussion see Aglietta, 1978).

Purchasing power parity

PPP is based on the assumption of the long-term neutrality of money, the nominal exchange rate being considered as a strictly monetary variable independent of the terms of trade. The law of one price is applied to the 'market' of money holdings. Money is only a particular good, the utility of which is its purchasing power on all other goods. The purchasing power is the inverse of the price which balances nominal supply and real demand of money in each country:

$$P = \frac{M}{L(r, y)}, \qquad P^* = \frac{M^*}{L^*(r^*, y^*)}$$

where P, M, r, Y and L represent respectively the price of output, the supply of money, the interest rate, the volume of output and the real money demand function, an asterisk denoting the foreign country variables. PPP then determines the nominal exchange rate with the assumption of a homogeneous world money market:

$$e = \frac{P}{P^*} = \frac{M}{M^*}\frac{L^*}{L}$$

where e is the national currency price of foreign exchange.

PPP allows for an influence of real variables on the equilibrium exchange rate only through the determination of real money demands. From this 'absolute' PPP relationship, a 'relative' PPP relationship can be derived by log-linear differentiation:

$$\dot{e} = (\dot{M} - \dot{M}^*) - k(\dot{y} - \dot{y}^*) + h(r - r^*)$$

where a dot indicates the growth rate of a variable. The above equation yields the following well known results. A rise in domestic money supply leads to an equiproportional currency depreciation. An increase in the growth rate of output arises the real demand for money which induces a slowdown in domestic prices and eventually an appreciation of the exchange rate. Finally an increase in the domestic interest rate relative to the foreign interest rate leads to a fall of the real demand for money which, all things equal, causes a rise in domestic inflation compensated by a depreciation of the national currency.

The law of one price

Here the homogeneous market assumption applies only to internationally traded goods whereas domestic, or non-traded goods are not submitted to international competition. The law of one price leads to the following equilibrium equation:

$$e = \frac{P_1}{P_1^*}$$

where P_1 is the price of traded goods. This determination of the nominal exchange rate is then related to the purchasing power of money by introducing the price of non-traded goods relative to traded goods, also called the domestic terms of trade:

$$q = \frac{P_2}{P_1}$$

where P_2 is the price of non-traded goods. The price of output is then defined by

$$P = P_1^{\alpha} P_2^{1-\alpha}$$

where α is the share of traded goods in output. The equilibrium conditions for money markets then lead to

$$e = \frac{M}{M^*}\frac{L^*}{L}\frac{(q^*)^{1-\alpha^*}}{(q)^{1-\alpha}}$$

and by log-linear differentiation to

$$\dot{e} = (\dot{M} - \dot{M}^*) - k(\dot{Y} - \dot{Y}^*) + h(r - r^*) - (1 - \alpha)\dot{q} + (1 - \alpha^*)\dot{q}^*.$$

The equilibrium exchange rate is determined first by PPP trends, the first three right-hand terms of the previous equation, and then by a deviation from PPP which depends on the relative price of traded goods.

The long-term evolution of the real exchange rate is here a function of the domestic terms of trade. This theory thus allows for some link between structural differences among countries, which condition the formation of relative prices, and the exchange rate. A devaluation of the domestic currency, for example, induces a rise in the price of traded goods.[1] This in turn leads to a fall of domestic absorption, or equivalently to an increase of money demand in the home country. Symmetrically, foreign absorption rises and at the new equilibrium the home country runs a current account surplus, i.e. domestic supply of traded goods is in excess of domestic demand. Simultaneously the fall of domestic demand for non-traded goods causes their relative price to diminish in order to bring back market equilibrium for these goods.

Exchange rate determination and structural differences among countries

A structural determination of the real exchange rate

The second type of approach to the determination of exchange rates does no longer consider the process of market equilibrium but grants a major role to the specialization of each country. National differences are considered from a three-fold point of view: production techniques, income distribution and the structure of final demand.

This approach is based on a Ricardian conception of international trade which focuses on the exchange of quantities of labour. Production techniques and income distribution determine simultaneously the specialization pattern of each country and the unit values of the exchangeable national quantities of labour. The accumulation of capital in the long run results from full employment output. Consumption and capital accumulation together determine the amount and structure of international trade. The real exchange rate is then defined by the equilibrium condition of the current account. This condition implies that no country will indefinitely accumulate foreign assets or liabilities.

The key variables in explaining the real value of the exchange rate in the long run are the factors which explain structural differences among countries: specialization, growth and income distribution. The real exchange rate is thus defined independently of any price equilibrium condition. Moreover, the assumption of a homogeneous world market for a single theoretical traded good is irrelevant here. Two countries may be perfectly totally specialized and produce and export a different good, making the law of one price meaningless. It is here no longer the concept of money as a purchasing power on all goods which prevails but more fundamentally the concept of labour as the source of value of goods.

These considerations explain why the empirical measure of the real exchange rate which we shall use in the subsequent empirical analysis is not based on relative GNP deflators or on relative wholesale prices but rather takes into account unit labour costs. More precisely we shall study here the real exchange rate as measured by the ratio of nominal exchange rate adjusted relative unit labour costs in manufacturing industries which constitute the best proxy to the theoretical traded goods sector.

A simple model of the real exchange rate

In order to derive an empirically testable model of the real exchange rate we have specified a simple theoretical model of two growing industrial economies. The basic country model is largely derived from Henry (1979). Our two-country model mostly adds a formalization of international trade, consumption structure and the current account equilibrium condition. The model is presented in table 5.1.

Each country produces a traded good which it consumes, uses for domestic capital formation or sells abroad for consumption; and a non-traded good which is used solely for domestic consumption. Home and foreign traded goods and home non-traded goods are imperfect substitutes for the domestic consumer. Under standard choice assumptions one can derive the three demand equations (7), (8) and (9) which simply imply constant budget shares for each good.

Price equations (5) and (6) describe income distribution with the traded good taken as a numéraire. The wage rate and the profit rate are here implicity equalized by the intersectoral mobility of labour.

The consumption equation, (10), assumes a single savings rate for profits and wage income.

At each period full employment output for traded or non-traded good is determined by equations (1) and (2) as functions of the stock of capital (K) and of the supply of labour (N). Equations (3) to (10) then determine consumption of domestically produced goods, imports of foreign traded goods, the price of non-traded goods relative to traded goods, the wage rate, the profit rate, and investment in terms of capital stock and of the labour

TABLE 5.1 A two-country model

(1) $K = v_1 Y_1 + v_2 Y_2$	(1′) $K^* = v_1^* Y_1^* + v_2^* Y_2^*$
(2) $N = l_1 Y_1 + l_2 Y_2$	(2′) $N^* = l_1^* Y_1^* + l_2^* Y_2^*$
(3) $Y_1 = CD_1 + CM_1^* + I + \delta K$	(3′) $Y_1^* = CD_1^* + CM_1 + I^* + \delta^* K^*$
(4) $Y_2 = CD_2$	(4′) $Y_2^* = CD_2^*$
(5) $1 = l_1 w + v_1(r + \delta)$	(5′) $1 = l_1^* w^* + v_1^*(r^* + \delta^*)$
(6) $p = l_2 w + v_2(r + \delta)$	(6′) $p^* = l_2^* w^* + v_2^*(r^* + \delta^*)$
(7) $CD_1 = \gamma_D C$	(7′) $CD_1^* = \gamma_D^* C^*$
(8) $CM_1 = q\gamma_M C$	(8′) $qCM_1^* = \gamma_M^* C^*$
(9) $pCD_2 = (1 - \gamma_D - \gamma_M)C$	(9′) $p^* CD_2^* = (1 - \gamma_D^* - \gamma_M^*)C^*$
(10) $C = (1 - s)[wL + (r + \delta)K]$	(10′) $C^* = (1 - s^*)[w^* L^* + (r^* + \delta^*)K^*]$
(11) $K_{+1} = K + I$	(11′) $K_{+1}^* = K^* + I^*$
(12) $L_{+1} = L(1 + n)$	(12′) $L_{+1}^* = L^*(1 + n^*)$
(13) $qCM_1^* = CM_1$	

Notation: 1 denotes the traded goods sector, 2 denotes the non-traded goods sector, an asterisk indicates the foreign country, and subscript +1 indicates the value of variables at the subsequent period.

The traded good is chosen as numéraire in each country, real variables are thus expressed in terms of traded good.

List of variables and parameters

Y_i = Real output of sector i
v_i = Capital-output ratio of sector i
l_i = Labour-output ratio of sector i
K = Real stock of capital
N = Labour supply
p = Price of non-traded good in terms of traded good
CD_i = Domestic consumption of good i
CM_1 = Domestic consumption of foreign traded good
C = Aggregate domestic consumption
I = Real net capital formation
w = Real wage rate
r = Real profit rate
δ = Depreciation rate of capital
s = Saving rate
γ_D, γ_M = Propensities to consume domestic and foreign traded goods
n = Labour supply growth rate
q = Nominal exchange rate adjusted price of home traded good relative to foreign traded good (term of trade)

supply. Finally the dynamics of the system are defined by equations (11) and (12) which yield the values of K and N for the following period.

We shall not discuss here the long-term implications of the basic country model. Henry (1979) showed that, in a bisectoral closed economy model of this type, with fixed technical conditions and where quantities determine prices (and not the reverse), the Rybczynski path determines the intertemporal evolution of the structure and level of production which, in turn, determine prices along Sraffa's frontier.

The last equation, (13), is the current account equilibrium condition which can be used to derive the long-run value of the real exchange rate.

Substituting (8) and (8′) in (13) yields

$$q = \frac{\gamma_M^*}{\gamma_M}\frac{C^*}{C}.$$

Then (10), (10′) and equations (1), (2), (5) and (6) yield

$$q = \frac{\gamma_M^*}{\gamma_M}\frac{1 - s^*}{1 - s}\frac{Y^*}{Y}$$

where $Y = Y_1 + pY_2$ and $Y^* = Y_1^* + pY_2^*$.

The real exchange rate as we chose to define it, i.e. the nominal exchange rate adjusted unit labour costs for traded goods, is

$$e_r = \frac{qwl_1}{w^*l_1^*} = \frac{wl_1}{w^*l_1^*}\frac{\gamma_M^*}{\gamma_M}\frac{1 - s^*}{1 - s}\frac{Y^*}{Y}.$$

The partial derivatives of the real exchange rate with respect to each of its determinants are straightforward:

$$\frac{\partial e_r}{\partial(wl_1/w^*l_1^*)} > 0, \qquad \frac{\partial e_r}{\partial(\gamma_M/\gamma_M^*)} < 0$$

$$\frac{\partial e_r}{\partial([1 - s]/[1 - s^*])} < 0, \qquad \frac{\partial e_r}{\partial(Y/Y^*)} < 0$$

A country where the share of wages in the manufacturing sector is higher than abroad will have a structurally lower real exchange rate. Similarly a country whose dependence on foreign imports is more important than abroad or whose saving rate is lower than in the foreign country will in the long run experience a depreciated real exchange rate. Finally the last partial derivative shows that a higher relative growth of output is associated with a lower real exchange rate.

The real exchange rate of the home currency relative to the foreign currency thus appears to be a function of structural differences between the two countries:

(a) differences in income distribution measured by the share of labour in the value added of the traded goods sector,
(b) differences in national specialization measured by the share of imports in domestic consumption and the savings rate, and
(c) differences in growth measured by the ratio of total national and foreign outputs.

In the appendix to this paper we derive relationships between the real exchange rate and other structural indicators: the level of output (or employment) of the traded goods sector relative to the non-traded goods sector, the relative price of the two goods and the rate of profit. Under the assumption that the traded goods sector is more capital intensive than the non-traded goods sector, we show that a higher level of the real exchange rate is associated with a higher relative output of the traded goods sector, a lower price of traded goods relative to non-traded goods and a lower rate of profit.

AN ECONOMETRIC ANALYSIS OF THE REAL EXCHANGE RATE OF THE TEN LEADING INDUSTRIAL COUNTRIES, 1960–79

In the first part of this paper we have reviewed the main theories of exchange rate determination over the long run. As we have seen there are basically two trends among these: the first trend considers that some kind of market equilibrium exchange rate will prevail eventually leading to a real exchange rate equal to one in terms of traded good prices ('law of one price') or in terms of GDP prices (PPP) whereas the second trend, following the Ricardian approach to international trade, explicitly takes into account the structural determinants of real exchange rate distorsions.

In this second part we shall try and discuss how well these theories apply to the analysis of real exchange rate evolutions among the ten leading industrial countries over the last 20 years. Our study will be divided in two sections. In the first section we shall present the importance of the real exchange rate deviations from parity theories, PPP or 'law of one price', and the inadequacy of models predicting the long-run stability of real exchange rates. In the second section we shall discuss the relationships between real exchange rates and structural transformations within and among the countries included in our sample. Finally we shall present estimates of a few models of the real exchange rate derived from the Ricardian approach discussed at the end of the first part of this paper.

Data and methodology

Definition of variables

Let s_{nt} denote the number of dollars per unit of the currency of country n in period t, 0 be the base period, x_{nt} a price index in period t relative to period 0 for country n, y_{nt} an economic indicator for country n (which can be either an index number relative to period 0 or a measure of variable y in period t), and s be the index of the standard country. The dollar exchange rate index S_{nt}, the standard currency exchange rate index R^{s}_{nt}, the standard relative price index X^s_{nt} and the standard relative economic indicator Y^s_{nt} are defined as follows:

$$S_{nt} = \frac{s_{nt}}{s_{n0}}, \qquad R^s_{nt} = \frac{S_{nt}}{S_{st}}$$

$$X^s_{nt} = \frac{x_{nt}}{x_{st}}, \qquad Y^s_{nt} = \frac{y_{nt}}{y_{st}}.$$

Let P be the GDP price index, P_1 be the value added deflator index of manufacturing industries and ULC be the unit labour cost index of manufacturing industries. Then the purchasing power parity in its relative form (see Officer, 1976) implies

$$R^s_{nt} = (P^s_{nt})^{-1}.$$

In the same way the law of one price implies

$$R^s_{nt} = (P^s_{1\,nt})^{-1}.$$

Finally the real exchange rate will be defined by the product of X^s_{nt} and R^s_{nt}. In terms of GDP prices, manufactured goods prices and unit labour costs, the real exchange rates will thus be equal to, respectively

$$P^s_{nt} R^s_{nt}, \qquad P^s_{1\,nt} R^s_{nt}, \qquad ULC^s_{nt} R^s_{nt}.$$

Sample and data

We have gathered data for the following eleven countries,[2] for the years 1960 to 1979:

1	USA	7	West Germany
2	Canada	8	Italy
3	Japan	9	Netherlands
4	Belgium	10	Sweden
5	Denmark[3]	11	United Kingdom.
6	France		

The variables include the dollar exchange rate, s, the GDP at constant prices, Y, the GDP deflator index, P, the manufacturing value-added, Y_1, the manufacturing value added deflator index, P_1, the manufacturing unit labour costs index, ULC, the employment in the whole economy, N, and in manufacturing industries, N_1, and the investment in manufacturing industries at constant prices I_1:[4]

The base period for all indexes is 1963 and the choice of the base period for the study of PPP relationships is a crucial one. Officer (1980) provides quite convincing evidence that 1963 was a year of exchange rate stability close to equilibrium.

We have considered three standard countries: the United States, West Germany (for regressions involving only European countries) and a basket of the main currencies ('the world') weighted by the share of each country in the world trade of manufactured goods in 1970.

Let 0 be the index of the 'world' standard. Then

$$S_{0t} = \prod_n (S_{nt})^{W_n}$$

for $n = 1, 2, 3, 4, 6, 7, 8, 9, 11$; and

$$\begin{aligned} W_1 &= 0.206 & W_7 &= 0.197 \\ W_2 &= 0.069 & W_8 &= 0.075 \\ W_3 &= 0.114 & W_9 &= 0.060 \\ W_4 &= 0.066 & W_{11} &= 0.117. \\ W_6 &= 0.096 \end{aligned}$$

In the same way,

$$X_{0t} = \prod_n (X_{nt})^{W_n} \qquad \text{and} \qquad Y_{0t} = \prod_n (Y_{nt})^{W_n}.$$

In the rest of this paper we shall refer to the exchange rate against the world currency as the effective exchange rate. The following notations will be used:

$$EX_{nt} = X^0_{nt} R^0_{nt}$$

$$EY_{nt} = Y^0_{nt}$$

$$RX_{nt} = X^1_{nt} R^1_{nt}$$

$$RY_{nt} = Y^1_{nt}.$$

Thus $EULC_{nt}$ will be the real effective exchange rate in terms of ULC, and $RULC_{nt}$ will be the real dollar exchange rate in terms of ULC.[5]

Econometric methodology

Econometric analysis of panel data such as the one we are dealing with allows a variety of regressions. These can help to take into account the double dimension, country and time, of the available information.

We have followed here a methodology first applied by Eisner (1967, 1978) to the study of the investment behaviour of a panel of industrial firms. The basic principle of this methodology is that different structurings of the data should modify the proportion of transitory and permanent variance in the variables and thus allow one to distinguish between different transitory and permanent effects.

Let Z_{nt} be the value of variable Z for country n in period t, N the number of countries and T the number of periods. Then

$$Z_{n.} = \frac{1}{T} \sum_{t} Z_{nt} \quad \text{is the average of } Z \text{ for country } n$$

$$Z_{.t} = \frac{1}{N} \sum_{n} Z_{nt} \quad \text{is the average of } Z \text{ at date } t$$

$$Z_{..} = \frac{1}{NT} \sum_{n,t} Z_{nt} \quad \text{is the overall average of } Z.$$

The various structurings of the data which we used for our estimates are

Z_{nt}, for overall regressions

$Z_{nt} - Z_{n.} + Z_{..}$, for country times series

$Z_{nt} - Z_{.t} + Z_{..}$, for country cross sections.

Variations over time of one variable for a single country involve a larger proportion of transitory variance than cross-sectional differences among countries in just the same way as Friedman's permanent income effect on consumption is better taken into account through cross-sectional analysis than with time series. The cross-sectional variance relates more to structural differences among countries, which implies that regressions on country cross sections ($Z_{nt} - Z_{.t} + Z_{..}$) should yield more significant estimates for those variables the 'permanent' level of which affect the 'permanent' level of the real exchange rate. On the contrary, variables which alter the real exchange rate of a country through their transitory variations will be better taken into account through time series regressions ($Z_{nt} - Z_{n.} + Z_{..}$). It is of course conceivable that a variable should affect the real exchange rate both through permanent and transitory effects, the sign and magnitude of which may then be different.

The evolution of real exchange rates over the 1960s and 1970s

Real exchange rate distortions

Table 5.2, 5.3 and 5.4 present computations of the real exchange rates (in terms of unit labour costs) for the years 1970, 1975 and 1979 relative to the base period, 1963. They illustrate the basic distortions which have taken place over the past 20 years.

Tables 5.2 and 5.3 confirm the well known depreciation of the dollar in real terms against all the other major currencies, which took place in the 1970s and led by 1975 to an undervaluation of the dollar of close to 40 per

TABLE 5.2 Deviation from cost parity in manufacturing relative to the USA*. Base period 1963; in per cent

Country	1970	1975	1979
Canada	−1.73	12.99	2.14
Japan	−4.91	50.49	53.41
Belgium	−2.46	50.72	58.64
France	−19.20	32.77	37.70
W. Germany	7.78	59.76	77.20
Italy	0.04	49.29	46.73
Netherlands	6.06	64.50	71.58
Sweden	−2.77	45.82	50.92
United Kingdom	−9.63	28.81	48.64
Mean	−2.98	43.90	49.66
Standard deviation	8.06	16.22	21.64

* Measured by 100 × ln($RULC_{nt}$).

cent. On the other hand computations of real exchange rates relative to the Deutsche mark show the regular real appreciation of this currency which amounted to 23.9 per cent in 1975 and close to 35 per cent in 1979. The means of real effective exchange rates deviations computed in table 5.3 show that the world currency we have considered is close to cost parity. In other words this basket is neither overvalued nor undervalued on average.

TABLE 5.3 Deviation from cost parity in manufacturing relative to the world average.* Base period 1963; in per cent

Country	1970	1975	1979
USA	1.91	−35.85	−42.42
Canada	0.18	−22.86	−40.29
Japan	−3.00	14.63	10.98
Belgium	−0.54	14.86	16.21
France	−17.29	−3.09	−4.72
West Germany	9.69	23.90	34.77
Italy	1.95	13.44	4.30
Netherlands	7.97	28.64	29.15
Sweden	−0.85	9.96	8.49
United Kingdom	−7.72	−7.04	6.22
Mean	−0.77	3.66	2.27
Standard deviation	7.66	20.66	25.75

* Measured by 100 × In($EULC_{nt}$).

TABLE 5.4 Deviation from cost parity in manufacturing relative to West Germany*—European countries (base period 1963; in per cent)

Country	1970	1975	1979
France	−26.98	−26.99	−39.49
Belgium	−10.23	−9.04	−18.56
Italy	−7.74	−10.47	−30.47
Netherlands	−1.72	4.74	−5.62
Sweden	−10.54	−13.94	−26.28
United Kingdom	−17.41	−30.95	−28.55
Mean	−12.44	−14.44	−24.83
Standard deviation	8.74	12.99	11.58

* Measured by 100 × In($ULC^{7}_{nt}\, R^{7}_{nt}$).

This is obviously the result of the evolutions of the two main currencies considered in the basket.

The standard deviations presented in table 5.3 illustrate the large range of national situations. Some countries like West Germany or the Netherlands have faced a marked overvaluation of their currencies (i.e. an increase of their real exchange rates) where as others like France or Sweden have had a relatively stable real exchange rate and the United States or Canada have had a depreciating real exchange rate.

It is also clear from tables 5.2, 5.3 and 5.4 that the period of floating exchange rates has corresponded to increased exchange rate deviations from 'equilibrium' parities. The standard deviation of the deviation from cost parity relative to the world average has increased from 7.66 to 25.75 per cent over the 1970s.

A detailed examination of the three real exchange rate measures considered here (*ULC*, GDP deflator and manufacturing value added deflator) shows that the main countries faced rather stable trends of appreciation or depreciation. Table 5.5 presents estimates of these trends for the period under study. It shows how the gap has widened during the 1970s between the two major currencies: the dollar and the Deutsche mark. The comparison of the computed trends for the various measures of the real exchange rate outlines the structural differences between the various price indexes, especially between manufacturing prices (*ULC*, P_1) and GDP deflators. The distortion is particularly striking for Japan which has had, on average, a stable real exchange rate in terms of *ULC* or manufactured goods price and a real exchange rate in terms of GDP price rising at close to 3 per cent per year.

We shall not discuss here the crucial role of these real exchange rate trends in explaining the 'virtuous circles' of appreciation, low inflation,

TABLE 5.5 Average trend of the real effective exchange rate 1960–79* (in per cent)

Country	1960–71			1971–79			1960–79		
	EULC	EP_1	*EP*	*EULC*	EP_1	*EP*	*EULC*	EP_1	*EP*
USA	−1.0	−0.6	−0.8	−3.9	−3.0	−3.6	−2.8	−2.1	−2.3
Japan	0.4	0.5	1.4	0.2	−0.2	2.8	1.4	0.4	2.1
France	−1.2	−1.4	−0.6	1.3	1.3	1.0	−0.4	−0.6	−0.2
W. Germany	1.3	1.5	0.6	2.1	2.3	1.6	2.3	2.4	1.6
United Kingdom	−1.1	−1.0	−1.2	0.7	0.4	−0.6	−0.7	−0.6	−1.3

* Measured by the regression of the logarithm of the corresponding real exchange rate index on time.

moderate growth and external surplus and the 'vicious circles' of devaluation, inflation and trade deficit which the main industrial countries, especially in Europe, have faced over the last ten years (see Aglietta et al. 1981, 1982). However this role must be taken into account when analysing the determinant of real exchange rate movements as we shall see further.

Exchange rates and relative prices

Another way of discussing the inadequacy of the various parity theories (PPP, law of one price, cost parity) of the exchange rate is to estimate models relating nominal exchange rates and relative prices. This has been done by many authors (see for example Roll and Solnick, 1978; Frenkel, 1981) on a bilateral time-series basis.

We have estimated such models in an overall regression framework (i.e. by pooling cross section observations) for all the countries in our sample.

Table 5.6 summarizes the main results of our estimates. It shows that none of the parity laws hold when the standard currency is the dollar. Even the regression involving the price of manufactured goods, which is a close measure of the price of traded goods, yields a coefficient of −4.8 which is far from the theoretical −1.0. The fact that the absolute value of the estimated coefficient is smaller than one illustrates once more the real depreciation of the dollar. On the other hand estimates of similar models with the 'world' as standard country yielded much more satisfactory results with a coefficient very close to unity when the price of manufactured goods was used. However R^2 computations show that a large part of the variance of the exchange rates remains unexplained. Estimates carried out on a subsample of European countries with the Deutsche mark as standard currency show surprisingly significant coefficients and very high R^2. This result is consistent with previous studies (see Frenkel, 1981) which emphasized the stability of real exchange rates among European countries due to the

TABLE 5.6 Exchange rates and relative prices, 1960–79

Standard country	ULC			P_1			P			Number of countries
	b	R^2	d.f.	b	R^2	d.f.	b	R^2	d.f.	
USA	−0.11 (1.6)*	0.01	198	−0.48 (5.4)	0.14	175	−0.14 (1.6)	0.01	175	10
West Germany	−1.36 (21.0)	0.76	138	−1.41 (18.3)	0.75	115	−1.29 (19.9)	0.74	115	7 (Europe)
World	−0.72 (10.3)	0.33	218	−0.92 (13.1)	0.47	195	−0.71 (8.3)	0.24	195	11

Coefficients estimated from the overall regression of the basic equation

$$\ln R^s_{nt} = a + b \ln X^s_{nt}$$

where R^s_{nt} is the index of the number of units of the currency, s, per unit of currency n in period t, relative to period 0, and χ^s_{nt} is the ratio of the price index in country n relative to the standard country.

* t ratios in parentheses.

various formal agreements which existed during the 1970s (snakes, EMS, . . .) and to the intra-European trade.

The real appreciation of the Deutsche mark which we have discussed earlier accounts for the larger than unity absolute values of the coefficients. It is basically this European phenomenon which explains the improvement of the estimates observed when the standard country is changed from the USA to the world.[6]

It thus appears that these latter regressions cannot be considered as an empirical confirmation of any equilibrium parity law. The various empirical evidence presented here is more consistent with a heterogeneous world monetary system involving countries like the USA or West Germany which have faced very noticeable bilateral real exchange rate distortions and countries like the members of the EEC which have had rather stable real interparities.

These different movements of real exchange rates, not taken into account by equilibrium theories, remain, then, to be explained. As we have seen in the first part of this paper a number of structural factors which differ from country to country should be taken into account in modelling real exchange rate changes.

Real exchange rates and structural transformations

In this section we shall present a number of estimates which attempt to relate changes in real exchange rates to structural transformations and differences within and among countries. We shall first discuss the link between real exchange rates and the relative position of the manufacturing sector within national economies and then we shall present estimates of real exchange rate models derived from the last section of the first part of this paper.

The real exchange rate and the manufacturing sector

Exchange rate movements are primarily important for the manufacturing sector which constitutes the bulk of the traded goods sectors for developed economies. On the one hand the evolution of the exchange rate conditions the external competitivity of manufactured goods and its profitability through both growth and internal relative price changes. On the other hand the quality of the international specialization of the economy, the heart of which lies in manufacturing industries, is the condition for a higher relative real exchange rate (see first part).

On average during the 1960s most of the countries of our sample have faced similar evolutions as far as the manufacturing sector was concerned (table 5.7):

(a) an increase in the share of manufacturing in total value added at constant prices; and
(b) a constant deterioration of the relative price of manufactured goods.

TABLE 5.7 The relative position of the manufacturing sector—structural indicators (1963 = 1.00)

Country	Share in total employment, N_1/N			Share in value added at constant prices, Y_1/Y			Relative value added price, P_1/P			Investment rate, I_1/Y_1		
	1970	1975	1979	1970	1975	1979	1970	1975	1979	1970	1975	1979
USA	0.98	0.86	0.86	1.00	0.95	1.01	0.91	0.87	0.84	1.14	2.21	1.27
Canada	0.93	0.85	0.80	1.04	0.98	1.00	0.85	0.82	0.84			
Japan	1.07	1.12	1.00	1.19	1.38	1.50	0.85	0.70	0.57	1.13	0.92	0.59
Belgium	0.98	0.92	0.79	1.13	1.14	1.15	0.92	0.78	0.74			
France	1.00	1.02	0.95	1.19	1.20	1.21	0.83	0.79	0.77	1.01	0.78	0.76
W. Germany	1.08	1.02	0.97	1.09	1.04	1.04	0.95	0.91	0.91	1.15	0.77	0.78
Italy	1.12	1.16	1.12	1.14	1.13	1.22	0.88	0.91	0.88			
Netherlands	0.94	0.85	0.75	1.04	0.98	0.98	0.84	0.75	0.65			
Sweden	0.96	0.91	0.83	1.10	1.09	1.03	0.89	0.93	0.85			
United Kingdom	1.00	0.92	0.92	1.05	0.97	0.85	0.90	0.90	0.88	1.12	0.93	1.00
World*	1.02	0.96	0.91	1.10	1.06	1.09	0.89	0.83	0.80	1.13	0.91	0.89
Mean	1.01	0.96	0.90	1.10	1.09	1.10	0.88	0.84	0.79	1.11	0.92	0.88
Standard deviation	0.06	0.11	0.11	0.06	0.13	0.18	0.04	0.08	0.11	0.06	0.18	0.26

* The world investment rate is a weighted average of the five countries for which data were available.

Of course these movements have differed both in their importance and in their timing. For example, in the USA, the share of industry in value added started declining as early as 1966, whereas in France it grew until the first years of the 1970s.

The second part of the period under study, the 1970s, has been characterized by the inversion of these evolutions. The generalized 'deindustrialization' movement among the leading economies has been very marked for the UK, relatively more moderate for the USA, and has amounted to a mere stabilization of the share of industry in France. In the same time the relative price of manufactured goods has stabilized itself within the acceleration of global inflation which took place after the first oil shock. Japan is a striking exception to these general trends for it has faced neither a decrease of the share of manufacturing in total value added, which reached an index level of 1.50 by 1979, nor a slowdown of the decline of the relative price of manufactured goods.

A closer country-by-country study shows that these evolutions have been closely linked to different exchange rates configurations (see Aglietta et al., 1981, 1982).

The discussion of the theoretical model presented in the first part of this paper has shown that a higher real exchange rate should be associated with a larger share of traded goods in total output and employment and a lower relative price of traded goods.

In order to evaluate empirically the significance of these links, we have estimated three simple linear equations relating the real exchange rate of the ten countries in our sample to three structural indicators.

All these variables significantly affect, with the expected signs, the real exchange rate as can be seen from the overall regressions in table 5.8. The negative sign of the relative price variable implies that in countries which have had an increasing real exchange rate the manufacturing sector has faced less satisfactory profitability conditions than in the standard country and reciprocally that the decline in real exchange rates in countries like the USA or France has allowed an improvement of manufacturing profits.

The time-series and cross-sectional regressions do not yield significantly different results except for the estimates involving employment and value added shares for the period 1971–79. As we have seen above, the differences in national configurations have greatly widened during the 1970s leading to marked structural gaps between countries. It is not surprising, then, that a permanent positive effect of these measures of industrialization should dominate. The coefficient of $\ln(EN_1/EN)$ (0.38) is significant and positive, implying that countries which have had a permanent share of the manufacturing sector in total employment (relative to the base period) higher than in the standard country have experienced a higher real exchange rate. The conclusion is similar for (EY_1/EY). The coefficients obtained in the country

TABLE 5.8 Real effective exchange rate: regression on structural variables, 1960–79; ten countries

Period	Type of regression*	$\ln(EN_1/EN)$	d.f.	R^2	$\ln(EY_1/EY)$	d.f.	R^2	$\ln(EP_1/EP)$	d.f.	R^2
1960–79	(1)	0.35	198	0.03	0.36	195	0.04	−0.34	195	0.03
		(2.6)†			(2.9)			(2.6)		
	(2)	0.58	198	0.08	0.50	195	0.06	−0.42	195	0.04
		(4.2)			(3.5)			(2.9)		
	(3)	0.36	198	0.04	0.36	195	0.04	−0.34	195	0.03
		(2.8)			(2.9)			(2.6)		
1971–79	(1)	0.38	88	0.04	0.46	88	0.07	−0.42	88	0.05
		(1.9)			(2.5)			(2.2)		
	(2)	−0.16	88	0.00	−0.34	88	0.01	−0.45	88	0.06
		(0.4)			(1.1)			(2.4)		
	(3)	0.38	88	0.04	0.46	88	0.07	−0.43	88	0.05
		(1.9)			(2.5)			(2.3)		

Coefficients estimated from the basic equation:

$$\ln EULC = a + b \ln X$$

where a is a constant and X is the explanatory variable.

* (1): Overall regression (Y_{nt})
(2): Country time series ($Y_{nt} - Y_{n.} + Y_{..}$)
(3): Country cross sections ($Y_{nt} - Y_{.t} + Y_{..}$)

† t ratios in parentheses.

time-series regression for $\ln(EN_1/EN)$ and $\ln(EY_1/EY)$, though not significant, have a negative sign which is not incompatible with past experience. They imply that transitory increases of the real exchange rate have been associated with transitory declines of the importance of industry in the economy.

Table 5.9 presents similar estimates for real dollar exchange rates. The conclusions are essentially similar. The coefficients of the explanatory variable are however more significant, with higher R^2, for the overall estimates over the years 1960–79 and not significant though yielding correct signs for the years 1971–79. In the same way the opposition between the signs of permanent and transitory effects appear with non-significant t ratios.

On the whole these estimates are consistent with a significant link between real exchange rates and structural variables of the countries in our sample. These regressions, however, explain only a very small amount of the total variance of real exchange rates and it is clear that more complete models must be studied in order to discuss medium-term evolutions.

Models of the real exchange rate

In the first part of this paper we have derived a relation between the real exchange rate and its structural determinants, the relative share of wages in the value added of the traded goods sector, the relative level of specialization and the relative growth of total output. The discussion of partial derivatives has shown that the real exchange rate is positively correlated to the first two variables and negatively correlated to the latter one.

As we have seen we shall consider manufacturing industries as the empirical counterpart of the theoretical traded goods sector and measure the real exchange rate by the nominal exchange rate adjusted unit labour costs in manufacturing in the country under study relative to the standard country.

We give the precise definition and sources of the variables in the appendix to this paper. Some explanations are needed however for the measure of specialization used here. Lafay (1976, 1980) has built a series of international specialization indicators for the leading industrial countries by grading the performance of these countries, measured by the ratio of production to domestic demand, at a very disaggregated product level. The performance is considered positive if production is increased for products with fast rising demand and decreased for products with declining demand. The improvement of a country's international specialization is all the more important that it implies a marked inversion of previous trends. Based on these two principles the notation of Lafay yields global specialization indicators presented in table 5.10. We have used the first set of indicators (1964–72) for the years 1960–72 and the second set (1970–77) for the years 1973–79.

TABLE 5.9 Real dollar exchange rate: regression on structural variables, 1960–79; nine countries

Period	Type of regression*	$\ln(RN_1/RN)$	d.f.	R^2	$\ln(RY_1/RY)$	d.f.	R^2	$\ln(RP_1/RP)$	d.f.	R^2
1960–79	(1)	1.11	178	0.16	0.90	175	0.12	−0.70	175	0.05
		(5.9)†			(5.0)			(3.2)		
	(2)	1.65	178	0.27	1.38	175	0.21	−1.19	175	0.10
		(8.2)			(6.8)			(4.4)		
	(3)	0.19	178	0.01	0.13	175	0.01	−0.20	175	0.02
		(1.6)			(1.1)			(1.7)		
1971–79	(1)	0.15	79	0.01	0.13	79	0.00	−0.40	79	0.04
		(0.7)			(0.6)			(1.9)		
	(2)	−0.36	79	0.01	−0.71	79	0.03	−1.03	79	0.11
		(0.7)			(1.5)			(3.2)		
	(3)	0.19	79	0.01	0.19	79	0.02	−0.27	79	0.03
		(1.1)			(1.1)			(1.6)		

Coefficients estimated from the basic equation:

$$\ln RULC = a + b \ln X$$

where a is a constant and X is the explanatory variable.

* Type of regression: see note to table 5.8.
† ratios in parentheses.

TABLE 5.10 International specialization indicators; five countries

Country	1964–72	1970–77
USA	−3.9	−3.8
France	−0.2	+16.7
W. Germany	+7.7	+5.4
UK	−10.1	−10.1
Japan	+39.3	+24.2

Source: Lafay (1980).

Three models of the real exchange rate have been estimated for the whole period (1960–79) and one subperiod (1971–79) corresponding to the regime of floating exchange rates, with two standard countries: the world and the USA. For the world as a standard country the models are the following:

(1) $\ln EULC_{nt} = a + b \ln EWL_{nt} + c\ SP_{nt} + d \ln EG_{nt}$

(2) $\ln EULC_{nt} = a + b \ln EWL_{nt} + c\ SP_{nt}$

(3) $\ln EULC_{nt} = a + b\ SP_{nt} + c \ln EG_{nt}$

The estimates presented in table 5.11 show that on the whole all the explanatory variables have significant coefficients with the expected signs and that the regressions are much more satisfactory in terms of R^2.

TABLE 5.11 Overall regression of the real effective exchange rate on explanatory variables; five countries

Period	Constant	ln *EWL*	*SP*	ln *EG*	d.f.	*MSE*	R^2
1961–79	−0.037	1.056	0.303×10^{-2}	−1.525	91	0.016	0.27
	(2.47)*	(3.71)	(2.18)	(1.78)			
1960–79	−0.027	1.280	0.092×10^{-2}		97	0.016	0.25
	(1.99)	(4.94)	(1.08)				
1961–79	−0.044		0.549×10^{-2}	−2.63	92	0.019	0.16
	(2.73)		(4.21)	(3.07)			
1971–79	−0.058	10.010	0.524×10^{-2}	−3.222	41	0.032	0.32
	(1.88)	(2.03)	(1.80)	(1.48)			
1971–79	−0.048	1.055	0.324×10^{-2}		42	0.033	0.28
	(1.56)	(2.09)	(1.24)				
1971–79	−0.070		0.888×10^{-2}	−3.492	42	0.034	0.25
	(2.24)		(3.73)	(1.58)			

Dependent variable: ln *EULC*.

* *t* ratios in parentheses.

The variety of conditions which national manufacturing industries face when setting their prices, as measured by *EWL*, appear to be a very significant variable in explaining the real exchange rate. The coefficient of ln *EWL* is significantly positive, which is consistent with the theoretical model presented in the first part of this paper. The fact that this coefficient is generally close to one implies that the explanatory variables included in our models would appear with similar coefficients in estimates of deviations from the 'law of one price', i.e. real exchange rates in terms of manufactured goods trade.

The measure of international specialization (*SP*) appears also with satisfactory coefficients. In most estimates the real exchange rate is positively correlated with *SP* and the coefficients vary between 0.003 and 0.009.[7]

Finally the relative growth rate yields a negative coefficient consistent with our basic model. A rate of growth higher than in the standard country leads to a lower real exchange rate. In other words, the terms of trade of national labour tend to worsen in order to achieve a relatively higher growth.

The estimates for the subperiod 1971–79 are similar. The coefficients of *SP* and ln *EG* are, however, globally larger in absolute values. During this period both real exchange rates and the structural indicators used in the models have known quite important distortions which should account for this result.[8]

Table 5.12 presents estimates of the same four models over two periods with the USA as standard country. The fit is also very good for the larger

TABLE 5.12 Overall regression of the real dollar exchange rate on explanatory variables; four countries

Period	Constant	ln *RWL*	*SP*	ln *RG*	d.f.	*MSE*	R^2
1961–79	0.060	2.010	$+0.059 \times 10^{-2}$	-0.764	72	0.031	0.50
	(2.34)*	(6.92)	(0.34)	(0.85)			
1960–79	0.050	2.188	-0.050×10^{-2}		77	0.030	0.54
	(2.18)	(9.43)	(0.42)				
1961–79	0.138		0.606×10^{-2}	-3.848	73	0.051	0.18
	(4.64)		(3.07)	(3.82)			
1971–79	0.231	0.942	0.212×10^{-2}	-1.485	32	0.045	0.16
	(3.91)	(1.78)	(0.65)	(0.68)			
1971–79	0.233	0.970	0.109×10^{-2}		33	0.044	0.15
	(4.00)	(1.85)	(0.38)				
1971–79	0.303		0.492×10^{-2}	-1.778	33	0.048	0.08
	(6.89)		(1.67)	(0.80)			

Dependent variable: ln *RULC*.

* *t* ratios in parentheses.

period when the relative share of wages variable is included (models 1 and 2). This last variable has significantly positive coefficients for all estimates except one (model 4, 1971–79) which is, as previously, consistent with our theoretical hypothesis. The coefficients are however close to one only for the period 1971–79. Over the period 1960–79 it appears that changes in profit–wage distribution within the manufacturing sector have altered both the real exchange rate in terms of *ULC* and in terms of manufactured goods prices.

The specialization variable performs rather poorly except for model 3. Its coefficient has however in most cases the proper positive sign. Finally the relative growth variable *RG* has negative coefficients consistent with the theoretical model but not significantly different from zero except in one case (model 3, 1961–79).

On the whole these estimates, though similar to those considering the world as the standard country, tend to grant a much stronger role to inter-country differences in profit–wage distributions.

In order to try to distinguish between permanent and transitory effects of explanatory variables, we have estimated cross section and time series regressions of our four models. The results for models 1 and 4 are given in tables 5.13 and 5.14.

In the case where the world is taken as the standard country (table 5.13), two structural variables *SP* and *EG* appear to have a noticeably stronger importance in country cross sections ($Y_{nt} - Y_{.t} + Y_{..}$) than in country time series ($Y_{nt} - Y_{n.} + Y_{..}$). This implies that the permanent level of the real exchange rate is related to the permanent level of these variables. In other

TABLE 5.13 Permanent and transitory effects of explanatory variables in models of the real effective exchange rate; five countries

Period	Type of regression*	ln *EWL*	*SP*	ln *EG*	d.f.	R^2
1961–79	(1)	1.638	-0.148×10^{-2}	0.227	91	0.37
		(5.47)†	(0.70)	(0.32)		
	(2)	1.066	0.316×10^{-2}	−1.653	91	0.28
		(3.72)	(2.26)	(1.91)		
1971–79	(1)	1.095	0.130×10^{-2}	−0.492	41	0.23
		(3.21)	(0.51)	(0.54)		
	(2)	1.047	0.541×10^{-2}	−3.753	41	0.33
		(2.09)	(1.86)	(1.65)		

Dependent variable: ln *EULC*.

(1): Country time series ($Y_{nt} - Y_{n.} + Y_{..}$)
(2): Country cross sections ($Y_{nt} - Y_{.t} + Y_{..}$)
† ratios in parentheses.

TABLE 5.14 Permanent and transitory effects of explanatory variables in models of the real dollar exchange rate; four countries

Period	Type of regression*	ln *RWL*	*SP*	ln *RG*	d.f.	R^2
1961–79	(1)	−2.703	$+0.151 \times 10^{-2}$	0.982	72	0.67
		(10.41)†	(0.50)	(1.30)		
	(2)	0.032	0.347×10^{-2}	−1.619	72	0.10
		(0.10)	(2.58)	(1.89)		
1971–79	(1)	−1.876	0.349×10^{-2}	0.312	32	0.41
		(4.67)	(0.74)	(0.23)		
	(2)	0.286	0.603×10^{-2}	−2.334	32	0.15
		(0.51)	(2.24)	(1.04)		

Dependent variable: ln *RULC*.
* Type of regression: see note table 5.13.
† *t* ratios in parentheses.

words, structural differences among countries explain a structural hierarchy of real exchange rates. This is particularly clear for the specialization indicator (*SP*) and for the relative growth (*EG*). The coefficients of *SP* and *EG* are not significant and sometimes appear with inverted signs in country time series regressions for both periods whereas they have proper signs and are significant, or close to significant, for country cross sections. For example in model 1, for the period 1961–79 the coefficient of ln *SP* is −0.00148 for the country time series regression with a *t* ratio of 0.70 and 0.00316 with a *t* ratio of 2.26 for country cross-section estimate.

Finally *EWL* which measures the differences in profit shares among countries and over time, yields for both models 1 and 4 and for both periods coefficients which are larger in absolute value and more significant for country time series regressions. The country cross-section estimates yield coefficients of *EWL* which are significant and have a proper positive sign in most cases. In this case both permanent differences among countries and short-term variations of profit shares appear to influence the real exchange rate; the latter effect is however stronger.

If we turn now to table 5.14 which presents the same regressions in the case where the USA is taken as the standard country, the conclusions are essentially the same. The specialization indicator and the relative growth variable have significant permanent effects with a correct sign except in one case (*EG* in model 1, 1971–79).

The coefficients of the relative share of wages are in three cases out of four significant with a positive sign in country time series, but in all cases they are not significantly different from zero in country cross sections.

TABLE 5.15 Share of wages in the value added of manufacturing industries (1963 = 1.00)

Country	1970	1975	1979
USA	1.07	1.02	1.04
Canada	1.07	1.02	0.97
Japan	1.02	1.39	1.30
Belgium	0.99	1.22	1.14
France	1.04	1.19	1.11
W. Germany	1.02	1.11	1.07
Italy	1.07	1.27	1.12
Netherlands	1.05	1.20	1.19
Sweden	1.00	1.01	1.04
United Kingdom	1.06	1.15	1.15
World	1.04	1.15	1.11

This would tend to support the idea that, when the dollar is taken as the standard currency, structural differences in profit shares are not relevant in explaining the permanent levels of real exchange rates. The values given in table 5.15 shows that in the United States (and in Canada) the share of wages has been stable with an index value of 1.04 in 1979 whereas it has very noticeably risen in the four other countries considered for these estimates, particularly for Japan and in the United Kingdom where it amounted to 1.30 and 1.15 respectively, in 1979.

It thus appears that the permanent variance of *WL* among countries in our sample (except the USA) is greatly reduced, which should partly explain the reason why this variable does not have significant coefficients in the country cross sections estimates in table 5.14.

On the whole these estimates are consistent with our previous discussion of the real exchange rate. Structural variables measuring constraints weighing on manufacturing price formation (*WL*), the international specialization (*SP*) and growth (*G*), play an important role in explaining the permanent level of real exchange rates, especially when the United States is not singled out as a standard country.

Given these structural differences among countries it also appears that short-term transitory fluctuations in price setting conditions and consequently in profits and investment are linked to fluctuations in real exchange rates.

SUMMARY AND CONCLUSIONS

A rapid review of the theory of real exchange rates has shown that two different approaches have been adopted in the literature. A first approach includes the market equilibrium parity theories, PPP, law of one price or cost parity, which postulate that the nominal exchange rate will somehow tend to move in order to correct price differences finally leading to a level of the real exchange rate equal to one (absolute PPP, LOP or CP theories) or to an index of the real exchange rate (relative to an adequate base period), equal to one ('relative' PPP, LOP or CP theories). A second approach which was followed in this paper tries to discuss the evolution of the real exchange rate without referring to any kind of market equilibrium parity. On the contrary it insists on the importance of structural differences among countries in explaining real exchange rates.

In the second part of this paper we have presented the results of an empirical analysis based on a sample of ten leading industrial countries over the years 1960–79. A simple description of the data shows clearly that during this period nominal exchange rates have in no way moved in accordance with any equilibrium parity theory. On the contrary it appears that real exchange rates have had very different evolutions for the main countries. On the one hand the dollar has been consistently depreciating in real terms over the 1970s whereas on the other hand the European countries have had much more stable real interparities.

We have then presented some econometric estimates attempting to relate real exchange rate movements, relative to a world currency basket or to the dollar, to structural differences among countries. A first set of estimates shows that structural variables measuring the relative position of the manufacturing sector in national economies are significantly related to real exchange rates.

A second set of estimates consists of models of the real exchange rate derived from our theoretical discussion in the first part of this paper. The real exchange rate is related to a set of three variables measuring manufacturing price-setting conditions, international specialization and GDP growth relative to the standard country.

The estimates are consistent with our *a priori* statements. 'Permanent' differences in the levels of these structural variables do appear to affect significantly the 'permanent' level of the real exchange rate. It also appears that given these structural differences, transitory fluctuations in the constraints weighing on manufacturing price setting are related to real exchange rate short-term fluctuations.

On the whole this limited empirical evidence, though still insufficient to yield complete models of the real exchange rates, clearly emphasizes, in our view, the necessity to consider the real exchange rate not through its 'derivations' from an equilibrium parity theory but rather as a fully autonomous economic variable dependent on structural national differences.

APPENDIX 1

List and sources of variables

All indexes are relative to the base period 1963.

s = Dollar exchange rate, IFS supplement on exchange rates, supplement series no. 1, 1981

P = GDP deflator index, OECD national accounts

P_1 = Manufacturing industries value added deflator index, OECD national accounts and EEC unpublished data

ULC = Unit labour costs in manufacturing index, US Department of Labor, Bureau of Labor Statistics, Office of Productivity and Technology, December 1981

N_1 = Employment in manufacturing index, US Department of Labor, BLS

N = Total employment, OECD labour force statistics

Y = GDP at constant prices index, OECD national accounts

Y_1 = Value added in manufacturing industries at constant prices index, OECD and EEC

I_1 = Gross investment of manufacturing industries at constant prices index, national accounts

SP = International specialization indicator, Lafay (1976, 1980)

IN = I/Y = Investment rate in manufacturing industries

W_1 = ULC/P_1 = Share of wages in the value added of manufacturing industries

g = $\dfrac{Y_t - Y_{t-1}}{Y_{t-1}}$ = Growth rate of GDP at constant prices

APPENDIX 2

Resolution of the two-country model

Equations (1) and (2) yield

$$\frac{Y_1}{N} = \Delta^{-1} l_2(k - k_2)$$

$$\frac{Y_2}{N} = \Delta^{-1} l_1(k - k_1)$$

where

$$\Delta = l_1 l_2(k_1 - k_2), \qquad k = \frac{K}{L}, \qquad k_1 = \frac{v_1}{l_1}, \qquad k_2 = \frac{v_2}{l_2}.$$

Equations (1), (2), (5), (6) and (10) yield:

$$C = (1 - s)(Y_1 + pY_2)$$

Substituting (3) and (4) in the above yields

$$pY_2 = (1 - \gamma_D - \gamma_M)(1 - s)(Y_1 + pY_2)$$

$$C = \frac{(1 - s)}{1 - (1 - s)(1 - \gamma_D - \gamma_M)} Y_1$$

and

$$p = \frac{(1 - s)(1 - \gamma_D - \gamma_M)}{1 - (1 - s)(1 - \gamma_D - \gamma_M)} \frac{Y_1}{Y_2}.$$

Finally (5) and (6) yield

$$w = \Delta^{-1} v_1 \left(p - \frac{v_2}{v_1}\right)$$

$$r = \delta - \Delta^{-1} l_1 \left(p - \frac{l_2}{l_1}\right).$$

The sign of Δ is of crucial importance.

We shall assume here that Δ is positive. This implies that the traded goods sector is more capital intensive. In this case, we have the following results:

$$\frac{\partial(Y_1/L)}{\partial k} > 0, \qquad \frac{\partial(Y_2/L)}{\partial k} < 0.$$

The increase in overall capital intensity is associated with a rising Y_1/Y_2 ratio, i.e. an increase in 'industrialization':

$$\frac{\partial p}{\partial k} < 0, \qquad \frac{\partial w}{\partial k} < 0, \qquad \frac{\partial r}{\partial k} > 0.$$

Along a path of rising k the relative price of non-traded goods falls, so does the wage rate expressed in terms of traded goods. Consequently the rate of profit rises.

If we consider now the real exchange rate relation derived in the paper it is possible to calculate some other partial derivatives:

$$e_r = \frac{wl_1}{w^* l_1^*} \frac{\gamma_M^*}{\gamma_M} \frac{1 - s^*}{1 - s} \frac{Y^*}{Y}.$$

The equations for p, w and r yield:

$$\frac{\partial w}{\partial p} > 0, \qquad \frac{\partial w}{\partial r} < 0, \qquad \frac{\partial w}{\partial(Y_1/Y_2)} > 0$$

thus

$$\frac{\partial e_r}{\partial p} > 0, \qquad \frac{\partial e_r}{\partial r} < 0, \qquad \frac{\partial e_r}{\partial(Y_1/Y_2)} > 0.$$

An increase in the real exchange is associated in the long run with:

(a) a fall of the price of traded goods relative to non-traded goods;
(b) a fall of the rate of profit; and
(c) an increase of the share of traded goods in total output or employment.

NOTES

We are grateful to Pierre Sicsic for his very helpful research assistance.

1 Dornbusch (1973) shows in a very simple framework that the rise in P_1 is less than proportional to the devaluation.
2 The numbers refer to the country indexes *n* used in our formulae.
3 For this country, data concerning manufacturing value added deflator were not available. They have consequently been excluded from many of our regressions.
4 Available only for France, Japan, Germany, USA and UK.
5 Unless otherwise specified, we shall always refer to this measure of the real exchange rate.
6 European countries account for 61 per cent of the world basket considered here.
7 The level of the coefficient is due to the difference in magnitude of the dependent variable (overall mean of ln $EULC = -0.012$) and of the explanatory variable (overall mean of $SP = 6.5$).
8 The investment rate index (1963 = 1.0), for example, varies between 0.98 (France) and 1.14 (W. Germany) in 1971 and between 1.27 (USA) and 0.59 (Japan) in 1979.

REFERENCES

Aglietta, M. (1978) *La parité des Pouvoirs d'Achat et ses Ambiguités*, Note du Service des Programmes, INSEE, Paris.

Aglietta, M., Ewenczyk, P. and Oudiz, G. (1982) 'L'Europe dans l'Affrontement International des Années 80', Paper presented at the Conference organized by the 'Cambridge Journal of Economics', *Western Europe in the 1980's*, Cambridge, July; Document de Travail, CEPII.

Aglietta, M., Orléan, A. and Oudiz, G. (1980) 'Contraintes de Change et Régulations Macroéconomiques Nationales', *Recherches Economiques de Louvain*, **46**, No. 3, September.

Aglietta, M., Orléan, A. and Oudiz, G. (1981) 'Des Adaptations Différenciées aux Contraintes Internationales', *Revue Economique*, **32**, No. 4, July.

CEPII (1980) 'Le Taux de Change Est Redevenu une Arme Économique', *La Lettre du CEPII*, September.

Dornbusch, R. (1973) 'Devaluation, Money and Non-traded Goods', *American Economic Review*, December.

Eisner, R. (1967) 'A Permanent Income Theory for Investment: Some Empirical Explorations', *American Economic Review*, June.

Eisner, R. (1978) *Factors in Business Investment*, NBER, General Series No. 102, Ballinger, Cambridge, Ma.

Frenkel, J. (1981) The Collapse of the Purchasing Power Parities during the 1970's', *European Economic Review*, **16**, No. 1, May.

Henry, J. (1979) *Les Gains de l'Échange Dans un Modèle Post-Keynésien*, Research Paper No. 7909, Department of Economics, University of Ottawa, November.

Lafay, G. (1976) 'Compétitivité, Spécialisation et Demande Mondiale', *Economie et Statistique*, No. 80, August–September.

Lafay, G. (1980) 'La Nouvelle Spécialisation des Grands Pays Industriels', *Economie Prospective Internationale*, No. 1, January.

Officer, L. (1976) 'The Purchasing Power Parity Theory of Exchange Rates', *International Monetary Fund Staff Papers*, **23**, 1–61.

Officer, L. (1980) 'Effective Exchange Rates and Price Ratios: A Test of the Purchasing Power-Parity Theory', *Canadian Journal of Economics*, **XIII**, No. 2, May.

Roll, R. and Solnick, B. (1978) 'Système Monétaire International et Risque de Change', *Economica*, Paris.

Comment

VIVIEN LEVY-GARBOUA

Anyone who has addressed himself to empirical work on exchange rates has probably come out of this experience with greater wisdom and modesty, and surely with a renewed interest in new theories. In this respect, the paper by Aglietta and Oudiz is welcome. It gives a theoretical explanation of the real exchange rate and attempts a first empirical test. I shall limit my comments to the theoretical part, and consider first various versions of the PPP, before I deal with the real exchange rate.

THE PPP AND SUCCESSIVE VERSIONS OF IT

The usual version of PPP is, strictly speaking, only valid for an open economy producing traded goods and too small to influence the world price of these goods. It is the famous 'law of one price'. It leads to the monetary theory of the nominal exchange rate provided you assume that (i) real money demand is a stable function of income and the interest rate, and (ii) the money supply is exogenous and well under control. Unfortunately neither of these assumptions is true and the theory does not fit the facts in this simple form.

A more elaborate version divides the economy into two sectors, a traded goods sector and a non-traded goods sector. The law of one price applies to the former, not to the latter. The terms of trade are constant, and the relative price of the two goods, *the real exchange rate* governs the allocation of supply and demand between the two sectors and becomes the key variable.

Clearly, Aglietta and Oudiz are more interested in explaining the real exchange rate. But, instead of making the distinction between traded an non-traded goods, they seem to prefer to distinguish between 'homogeneous' and 'specific' sectors. The distinction, which seems to overlap that between industry and services, is not clear to me, and no theoretical justification is given for it.

Aglietta and Oudiz then go on to present three distinct versions of the PPP, in which (1) unit costs of production; (2) prices of production; and (3) market prices are equalized across countries.

In fact they consider:

$$\left(\frac{p}{ep^*}\right)_1 = \frac{w}{w^*} \cdot \frac{q^*}{q}$$

$$\left(\frac{p}{ep^*}\right)_2 = \frac{w}{w^*} \cdot \frac{q^*}{q} \cdot \frac{m}{m^*}$$

$$\left(\frac{p}{ep^*}\right)_3 = \frac{w}{w^*} \cdot \frac{q^*}{q} \cdot \frac{m}{m^*} \cdot \frac{x}{x^*}$$

where w, q, m and x are the wage rate, labour productivity, a markup rate, and the export margin (i.e. the ratio of the export price on the production price) respectively (and the starred letters are the corresponding magnitudes for the foreign country).

Two things remain unclear in these versions of the PPP: how unit costs of production or prices of production can be equalized across countries; and how an export margin can appear on top of the 'normal' profit which is already included in the prices of production.

THE REAL EXCHANGE RATE

Aglietta and Oudiz base their theory on two propositions:

(1) Prices are production prices in a Leontief–Sraffa technology
(2) The real exchange rate is not the result of any market equilibrium, but of the trade balance equilibrium: the *value* of exports must equal the value of imports

This, of course, is not intended to be a short-term description of the determinants of the real exchange rate. Rather it is a long term view. Let me restate this in a slightly different form, which is more in line with the usual analysis of real exchange rates. (The model presented here is adapted from Levy-Garboua et al. (1978).)

First I shall consider prices. In the usual macro-models of the open economy, the consumption price level is a weighed average of internal prices and import prices (world prices). Internal prices are derived from unit costs plus a markup (possibly depending on the level of activity). And the nominal wage rate is (more or less) indexed on the price level. Two versions appear here: one is the Phillips curve hypothesis, according to which the growth of nominal wage responds to the *level* of activity; another, documented by Gordon (1975) in the United States, links the *level* of nominal

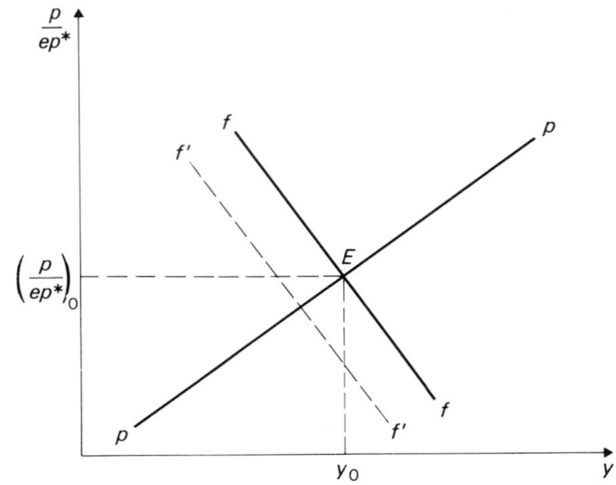

FIGURE 1

wage to the *level* of GNP. Of course, the first hypothesis brings us back to PPP. The latter gives a positive link between the real exchange rate and GNP: curve (*pp*) on figure 1.

Secondly, the stock-flow equilibrium relationship links the market for foreign assets to the trade balance, through the equation:

$$F = B + (1 + r^*)\frac{e}{e_{-1}}F_{-1}$$

where F = Net holdings by residents of foreign assets (in domestic currency)
B = Balance of current account
e = Nominal exchange rate
r^* = Foreign interest rate.

(e_{-1} and F_{-1} are lagged variables).

Assume that net holdings of foreign asset are derived from a portfolio choice:

$$F = \left[a + b\left(r^* - r + \frac{\tilde{e} - e}{e}\right)\right]p \cdot y$$

that is, the interest rate parity is not necessarily satisfied (it would be if $b = \infty$).

Then, in the long run

$$(f - r^* - \varepsilon)[a + b(r^* - r + \tilde{\varepsilon})]py = B$$

if we call ε the depreciation of the exchange rate ($\tilde{\varepsilon}$ the expected depreciation) and f the growth rate of nominal income. If we define the long run as a steady state with no technical progress and population growth, then f is the domestic inflation rate (π) and $\varepsilon = \pi - \pi^* = \tilde{\varepsilon}$, i.e. the relative version of PPP must be satisfied. Hence:

$$B = -(r^* - \pi^*)[a + b((r^* - \pi^*) - (r - \pi))]p \cdot y$$

One can see from this relationship that $B = 0$ is *not* a long run equilibrium condition. Since B is a function of the real exchange rate and income, one can derive a second long-run relationship between p/ep^* and y (given r^*, π^*, r and π). The slope of the curve (ff) is negative, and intersects (pp) on figure 1, at a point E, determining both the real exchange rate and equilibrium output.

In this model, the rate of inflation is determined by monetary policy (if the money supply is controlled), and the interest rate by the *IS* relationship.

As an exercise, one can derive from this model the effect of a rise in the foreign real interest rate ($r^* - \pi^*$). The (ff) curve is shifted to ($f'f'$): there should both be a decrease in income, and a depreciation of real exchange rate.

REFERENCES

Gordon, R. J. (1975) 'The Effect of Aggregate Demand on Process', *Brookings Papers on Economic Activity*, **6**, 613–62.

Levy-Garboua, V., Oudiz, G., Sterdyniak, H., and Villa, P. (1978) 'Change, Inflation, Intérêt: un Modèle', *Revue Economique*, 25, 866–926.

Comment

UWE WESTPHAL

One main subject of the theory of international economics has been the overshooting of exchange rates. Looking into the literature, one gets the impression that the theory itself seems not to be immune against overshooting.

At the time when the Marshall–Lerner condition was being discussed, the current account was considered as the dominant factor influencing exchange rate. During the era of the Mundell–Fleming model, monetary and real factors including the current account and the exchange rate were conceived as an interdependent system. The current account as determinant of exchange rates disappeared in the first stages of the portfolio balance approach. It was not rediscovered until the second half of the 1970s: Dornbusch's survey article (1980) has nourished the hope that exchange rate theory would develop towards an eclectic and more realistic integration of monetary and real factors and of the current account. The paper presented by Aglietta and Oudiz, however, is not in line with this tendency: it stresses the current account (and the factors behind it) as the sole determinant of exchange rates, negating the influence of all factors of the economy's monetary side.

The authors start with the notion that exchange rates deviate persistently and considerably from purchasing power parity. In the second section a lot of evidence against the PPP theory is presented. These results are in line with empirical research of other economists (e.g. Dornbusch, 1980; Frenkel, 1981). Aglietta and Oudiz conclude that a theory of exchange rates should not be based on the PPP assumption, which is obviously contrary to reality. I think that there should be no disagreement with this conclusion.

The empirical analysis is based on a theoretical two-country two-sector model. In each period capital stock and labour supply are given by past investment and by the exogenous demographic factors. Despite a constant capital output ratio and a constant labour productivity, it is assumed that in each economy all factors of production are fully employed: real capital and labour seem to be perfectly mobile between traded and non-traded goods sectors within each country. Output of the domestic non-traded goods sector is fully absorbed by domestic private households. They also buy domestic and foreign traded goods; demand for both commodity groups depends on the full employment income. Output of the traded goods sector not being demanded by consumers is absorbed by investment (a residuum). There is no financial sector in the model, no international capital movement. The equilibrium exchange rate therefore is determined by equating exports and imports. Thus the level of the exchange rate depends on the level of full employment output in both countries, on the marginal propensities to consume, and on the marginal propensities to spend on foreign goods.

I do not see any reason not to test this hypothesis directly. The authors, however, regress real exchange rates on the difference between growth rates of actual GNP, a measure of specialization and the relative share of wages in the value added of the traded goods sector. The relation between the hypothesis derived from the theoretical model and the estimated equation is not very clear.

To summarize, the authors avoid the PPP assumption, which is contrary to the facts. Instead they assume full employment, an always balanced current account and the absence of international capital movements. I am not convinced that it is reasonable to substitute one unrealistic assumption by three.

REFERENCES

Dornbusch, R. (1980) 'Exchange Rate Economics: Where Do We Stand', Brookings Papers on Economic Activity, 1.

Frenkel, J. (1981) 'The Collapse of the Purchasing Power Parities during the 1970's', *European Economic Review*, **16**, No. 1, May.

6

A Model of Exchange Rate Determination With Policy Reaction: Evidence From Monthly Data

WILLIAM H. BRANSON

INTRODUCTION AND SUMMARY

During the 1970s an extensive theoretical literature has developed analysing market determination of freely floating exchange rates. At the same time, there has been extensive and continuous intervention in the market by central banks. Exchange rates have not been floating freely; they have been managed, or manipulated, by central banks. However, most of the description of exchange rate policy, as actually practised has been informal, or 'literary', not integrated with the formal theoretical literature. Recent examples are the surveys in Branson (1981) and Mussa (1981).

In this paper I integrate exchange rate policy into a model of exchange rate behaviour, and examine the monthly data from the 1970s econometrically, to infer hypotheses about policy behaviour. I focus on four major currencies, the US dollar, the Deutsche mark, sterlin and the Japanese yen, and analyse movements in their effective (weighted) exchange rates as calculated by the IMF.

In the second section a model of market determination of a floating exchange rate is laid out. It is a rational expectations version of the model in Branson (1977) and it draws on the model of Kouri (1978). It is the same as the model in Branson (1984). The model shows how unanticipated movements in money, the current account and relative price levels will cause first a jump in the exchange rate, and then a movement along a 'saddle path' to the new long-run equilibrium. Here the role of 'news' in moving the exchange rate, as recently emphasized by Dornbusch (1980) and Frenkel (1981), is clear. The model emphasizes imperfect substitutability between domestic and foreign bonds, in order to prepare for the analysis of intervention policy in the third section.

Exchange rate policy is introduced in the third section. We analyse the options available to the central bank that wants to reduce the jump in the exchange rate following a real or monetary disturbance—'news' about the current account, relative prices, or money. This is the policy characterized as 'leaning against the wind' in Branson (1976). The distinction is made between monetary policy and sterilized intervention.

We next turn to the monthly data. The quarterly data were analysed in Branson (1984). Systems of vector autoregressions (*VAR*s) are estimated for each of the countries, and the correlations among their residuals are studied. These represent the 'innovations', or 'news' in the time series. A clear pattern emerges in these correlations, in which policy in the US and Japan drives exchange rates, and policy in Germany and the UK reacts by moving interest rates, and by sterilized intervention. This is essentially the same result that appeared in the quarterly data in Branson (1984). Thus the analyses tend to reinforce each other; both data sets tell basically the same story.

AN ASSET MARKET MODEL WITH RATIONAL EXPECTATIONS

Introduction

The purpose of this section is to lay out a simple asset market model of exchange rate determination within which, in the next section, monetary policy reaction to movements in the exchange rate can be analysed. The literature of the 1970s has identified three principal macroeconomic variables that influence movements in exchange rates. These are money supplies, relative price levels and current account balances. Here I develop a representative model that explicitly includes all three elements. The model is an extension of the asset market model sketched in Branson (1975), and developed in full in Branson (1977). It is a close relative of Kouri (1978). In the early versions of this model the focus was on the roles of relative prices and asset markets, and static expectations were assumed. Here the model is extended to study the effects of underlying 'real' disturbances influencing the current account and to include explicitly policy intervention in a rational expectations framework.

Asset market specification

To make the analysis manageable, let us consider one country in a many-country world. We can aggregate the assets available in this country into a domestic money stock M, which is a non-earning asset, holdings of domestically issued assets B, which are denominated in home currency, and net holdings of foreign-issued assets F, which are denominated in foreign exchange.[1] B^p (for bonds) is government debt held by the private sector, and B^c is government debt held by the central bank. Total government debt is

$$B = B^p + B^c.$$

F^p (for foreign assets) is the net claims on foreigners held by the domestic private sector and R is central bank foreign reserves. Total national net claims on foreigners

$$F = F^p + R.$$

The money stock M is equal to $R + B^c$, with a 100 per cent reserve system. I assume the initial exchange rate is indexed to unity, and that the central bank does not permit capital gains or losses in R to influence M. The current account in the balance of payments gives the rate of accumulation of F over time. The rate of accumulation of B is the government deficit. M is controlled by central bank purchases (or sales) of B or F from (or to) the domestic private sector.

The rate of return on F is given by $\bar{r}$, fixed in the world capital market, plus the expected rate of increase in the exchange rate, $\hat{e}$. The rate of return on B is the domestic interest rate r, to be determined in domestic financial markets. Total private sector wealth, at any point in time, is given by

$$W = M + B^p + eF^p$$

so here the exchange rate e, in home currency per unit of foreign exchange (e.g. \$0.50 per DM), translates the foreign exchange value of F into home currency.

The total supplies of B and F to the national economy are given at each point in time. Each can be accumulated only over time through foreign or domestic investment.[2] Given the existing stocks of B and F at any point in time, the central bank can make discrete changes in M by swapping either B or F with the domestic private sector; these are open-market operations in government debt or foreign assets.

The demand for each asset by the private sector depends on wealth,

$$W = M + B^p + eF^p$$

and both rates of return, r and $\bar{r} + \hat{e}$. As wealth rises, demands for all three assets increase. The demands for B and F depend positively on their own rates of return and negatively on those of the other assets. The demand for money depends negatively on both r and $\bar{r} + \hat{e}$; as either rises, asset holders attempt to shift from money into the asset whose return has gone up.

These asset market equilibrium conditions are summarized in equations (1)–(6):

$$M \equiv R + B^c = m(r, \bar{r} + \hat{e})W \tag{1}$$

$$B^p = b(r, \bar{r} + \hat{e})W \tag{2}$$

$$eF^p = f(r, \bar{r} + \hat{e})W \tag{3}$$

$$W = M + B^p + eF^p \tag{4}$$

$$B^c + B^p = \bar{B} \tag{5}$$

$$F^p + R = F. \tag{6}$$

Equation (4) is the balance sheet constraint, which ensures that

$$m + b + f = 1.$$

The three demand functions give the desired distribution of the domestic wealth portfolio W into the three assets. Specifying the asset demand functions as homogeneous in wealth eliminates the price level from the asset market equilibrium conditions. Given the balance sheet constraint (4), and gross substitutability of the three assets, we have the constraints on partial derivatives of the distribution functions:

$$m_r + f_r = -b_r < 0, \qquad m_{\bar{r}} + b_{\bar{r}} = -f_{\bar{r}} < 0.$$

Here a subscript denotes a partial derivative. The three market equilibrium conditions (1)–(3) contain two independent equations given the balance sheet constraint (4). In equation (5) the bar over B indicates that the total supply of government debt is fixed.

Asset accumulation and the current account

Equations (1)–(6) provide the specification of asset markets in the model. The other main building block of the model is the current account equation. The balance-of-payments accounts provide the identity

$$\dot{F} \equiv \dot{F}^p + \dot{R} \equiv X + \bar{r}(F^p + R) \equiv X + \bar{r}F$$

where X is net exports of goods and non-capital services in terms of foreign exchange. Net exports depend on the *real exchange rate* e/p, private sector wealth W (given by equation (4) above), and an exogenous shift factor z which represents real events such as changes in tastes in technology, oil discoveries, etc., which increase net exports for given values of e/p and W. Thus we can write

$$X = X(e/P, W, z), \qquad X_e > 0, \quad X_W < 0, \quad X_z > 0.$$

The sign of X_e assumes the Marshall–Lerner condition holds; X_W reflects wealth effects on import demand.

Substitution of the function for net exports into the balance-of-payments identity gives us the equation for accumulation of national net foreign assets:

$$\dot{F} = X(e/p, W, z) + \bar{r}F. \tag{7}$$

It is important to note that open-market swaps between the central bank and the domestic private sector have no direct effect on W *or* F in (7). And the effect of accumulation of *national* net foreign assets through a current account surplus ($\dot{F} > 0$) on W *and* F is the same regardless of the distribution of $\dot{F}$ between $\dot{F}^{\mathrm{p}}$ and $\dot{R}$. Since an increase in R, *ceteris paribus*, increases the money stock, which is part of W, any increase in F will raise W by $\mathrm{d}F$ independently of the split between $\dot{F}^{\mathrm{p}}$ and $\dot{R}$. Thus the central bank's intervention policy will have no effect on how a current account balance moves F and W in (7).

The effect of an increase in F on $\dot{F}$ in (7) is unclear:

$$\frac{\partial \dot{F}}{\partial F} = X_W + \bar{r}$$

with $X_W < 0$ and $\bar{r} > 0$. Below we will conveniently assume that $\partial \dot{F}/\partial F = 0$; it will quickly become apparent why this is convenient. In Branson (1981) the case where $\partial \dot{F}/\partial F < 0$ is analysed.

Equations (1)–(7) plus the assumption of rational expectations (or, more precisely, perfect foresight in this non-stochastic model) give us a complete dynamic model in $\dot{F}$ and $\hat{e}$. Price dynamics are suppressed, but we will discuss below exogenous price movements as delayed response to monetary shocks.

Solution of the model

Solution of the model proceeds as follows. First, the rational expectations assumption is that $\hat{e}$ is the rate of change of e. Then two equations of (1)–(3), with wealth substituted from (4), can be used to solve for r and $\hat{e}$ as functions of M, W and eF^{p}. The $\hat{e}$ and $\dot{F}$ equations then are two dynamic equations in e and F that can be solved for the movement in these two variables.

Divide equations (1) and (3) by W and differentiate totally, holding $\bar{r}$ constant:

$$\begin{aligned} \mathrm{d}(M/W) &= m_r\,\mathrm{d}r + m_{\hat{e}}\,\mathrm{d}\hat{e} \\ \mathrm{d}(eF^{\mathrm{p}}/W) &= f_r\,\mathrm{d}r + f_{\hat{e}}\,\mathrm{d}\hat{e}. \end{aligned} \tag{8}$$

These can be solved in matrix form as

$$\begin{pmatrix} \mathrm{d}r \\ \mathrm{d}\hat{e} \end{pmatrix} = \frac{1}{(m_r f_{\hat{e}} - f_r m_{\hat{e}})} \begin{bmatrix} f_{\hat{e}} & -m_{\hat{e}} \\ -f_r & m_r \end{bmatrix} \begin{pmatrix} \mathrm{d}(eF^{\mathrm{p}}/W) \\ \mathrm{d}(M/W) \end{pmatrix}. \tag{9}$$

The solution for $\mathrm{d}\hat{e}$ is then

$$\mathrm{d}\hat{e} = \frac{1}{m_r f_{\hat{e}} - f_r m_{\hat{e}}} [-f_r\,\mathrm{d}(M/W) + m_r\,\mathrm{d}(eF^{\mathrm{p}}/W)]. \tag{10}$$

The coefficients of eF^p/W and M/W are the partial derivatives of the $\hat{e}$ adjustment function,

$$\hat{e} = \phi\left(\frac{eF^p}{W}, \frac{M}{W}\right), \qquad \phi_1 > 0, \quad \phi_2 < 0. \tag{11}$$

This is the dynamic equation to be solved along with (7) for $\dot{F}$ to obtain equilibrium e and F^p.

In the e, F^p space of figure 6.1, the $\hat{e} = 0$ locus is a rectangular hyperbola. This can be seen by observing that in ϕ, e and F^p enter multiplicatively (in W as well as the numerator eF^p), so changes in e and F^p that hold the product eF^p constant will hold $\hat{e}$ constant. Combinations of e and F^p off the locus move e away from it, as the arrows show. For example, since $\phi_1 > 0$ an increase in e or F^p from a point on the locus makes $\hat{e} > 0$.

An increase in M/W, holding eF^p/W constant, would shift the $\hat{e} = 0$ locus in figure 6.1 up. This would be the result of an expansionary open-market operation in the government debt market with $dB^c = dM > 0$, and no change in F^c or F^p. An increase in eF^p/W, holding M/W constant, will shift $\hat{e} = 0$ down; this could result from an open-market swap between F and B. An expansionary open-market operation in the foreign asset market, with the central bank exchanging M for F with the private sector, would shift $\hat{e} = 0$ up both by increasing M/W and reducing eF^p/W. This will provide the difference between intervention in the bond or foreign asset markets in the model.

For given values of z and p in the $\dot{F}$ equation (7), the $\dot{F} = 0$ locus in e, F^p space is a horizontal line at the e value where $X = -\bar{r}F$. This is shown in figure 6.2. If e is above this value, the current account is in surplus and

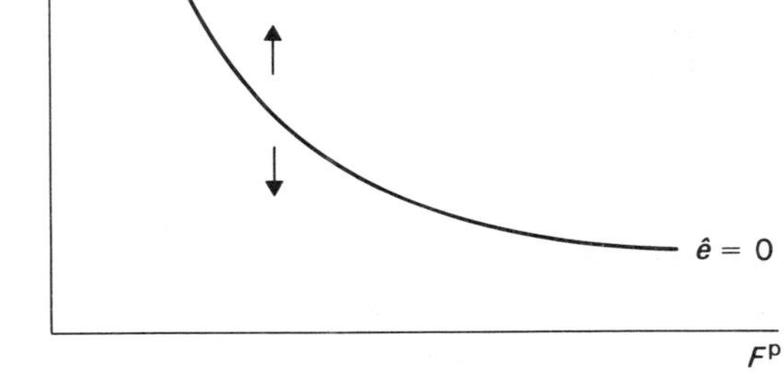

FIGURE 6.1 Locus where $\hat{e} = 0$

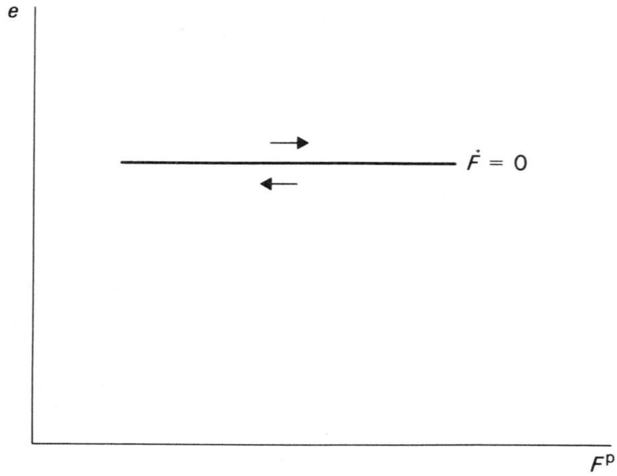

FIGURE 6.2 Locus where $\dot{F} = 0$

$\dot{F} > 0$. In the third section we will introduce a 'leaning-against-the-wind' exchange rate policy in which the authorities attempt to reduce the extent of jumps in the exchange rate, but not to reverse them. Thus we rule out here the possibility that the monetary authority 'over-intervenes', and assume that the sign of $\dot{F}^p$ is the same as the sign of $\dot{F}$; this is the same as assuming $|\dot{R}| < |\dot{F}^p|$. This essentially assumes that the authorities permit the market to guide the system towards its long-run equilibrium, but perhaps slow the movement. The assumption gives the arrows showing movement in figure 6.2; above $\dot{F} = 0$, $\dot{F}^p > 0$, below it is negative.

An increase in z in (7) will shift the $\dot{F} = 0$ locus down. Given the assumption that $X_W + \bar{r} = 0$, the extent of the shift is simply given by the effect of a change in e on X:

$$\left.\frac{de}{dz}\right|_{\dot{F}=0} = -\frac{1}{X_e}.$$

If z rises, increasing X and giving a current account surplus, e must fall (currency appreciate) enough to restore the original value of X. An increase in P will shift $\dot{F} = 0$ up, with

$$\left.\frac{de}{dp}\right|_{\dot{F}=0} = 1.$$

Equilibrium of the system is shown in figure 6.3. There is one saddle path into the equilibrium shown by the broken line. For a given value of F^p, it is assumed that following a disturbance, the market will pick the value for e that puts the system on the saddle path towards equilibrium. The system

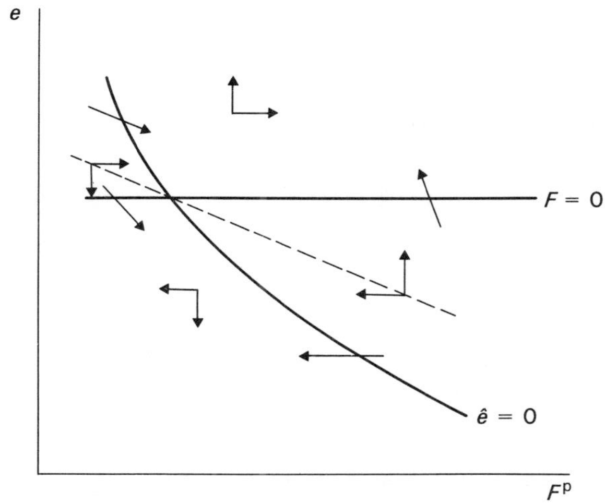

FIGURE 6.3 Equilibrium path for e, F^p

would have quite different properties under a policy regime of 'over-intervention' that reversed the pattern of movement in the horizontal direction.

Reaction to exogenous shocks

Monetary disturbance

Consider an (unanticipated) expansionary open-market operation in government debt. This initially leaves W and F^p unchanged. There are two extreme assumptions on price adjustment to consider: no change in P, or $dP/P = dM/M$ immediately.

With no change in P as M increases, the $\dot{F} = 0$ locus in figure 6.4 does not shift, but $\hat{e} = 0$ shifts up. With F^p initially given, the exchange rate jumps (currency depreciates) from initial equilibrium E_0 to E_1 on the new saddle path. This establishes $\hat{e} < 0$ as needed for asset holders to hold the existing stock of F^p given the lower interest rate. The rise in e/P generates a current account surplus, and F^p rises with e falling towards E_2. This is an extreme form of 'overshooting'.

Suppose the domestic price level immediately reacts by rising by the same proportion as the money stock. Then $\dot{F} = 0$ also shifts up by that same proportion. The extent of the upward shift in $\hat{e} = 0$ depends on initial portfolio distribution and the degree of substitutability among F, M and B. One borderline case would be $M = eF^p$ and $m_r = f_r$. It can be seen in the expression for $d\hat{e}$ in equation (10) that in this case a proportional increase in e will maintain $\hat{e} = 0$. To the extent that $M > eF^p$ or $|f_r| > |m_r|$, the $\hat{e} = 0$ curve

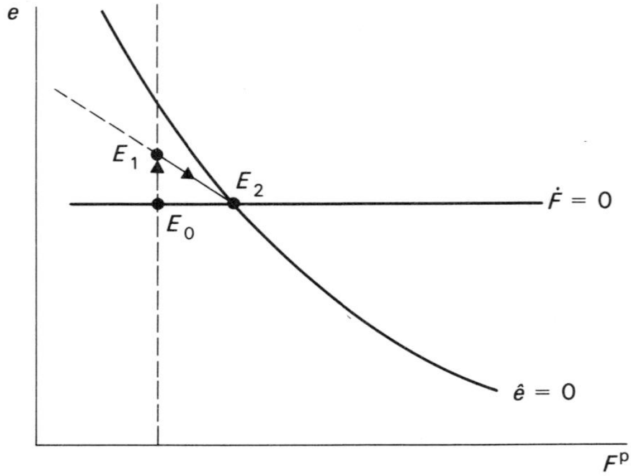

FIGURE 6.4 Open-market operation in B, no change in F^p

would shift up more than $\dot{F} = 0$, requiring 'overshooting' and $\hat{e} < 0$, $\dot{F}^p > 0$ moving to equilibrium. The reverse initial conditions would yield 'undershooting' with $\hat{e} > 0$, $\dot{F}^p < 0$ in the movement to equilibrium.

Real disturbance

The effect of an unanticipated fall in z (or an increase in P) is shown in figure 6.5. The decrease in competitiveness shifts $\dot{F} = 0$ up from its initial intersection with $\hat{e} = 0$ at E_0. The exchange rate jumps (currency

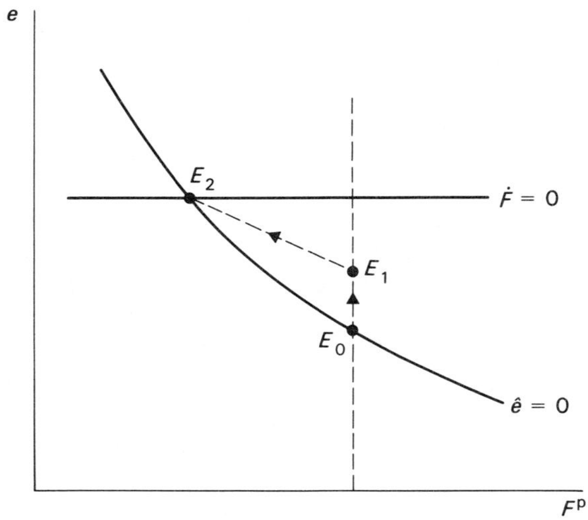

FIGURE 6.5 Deterioration in competitiveness

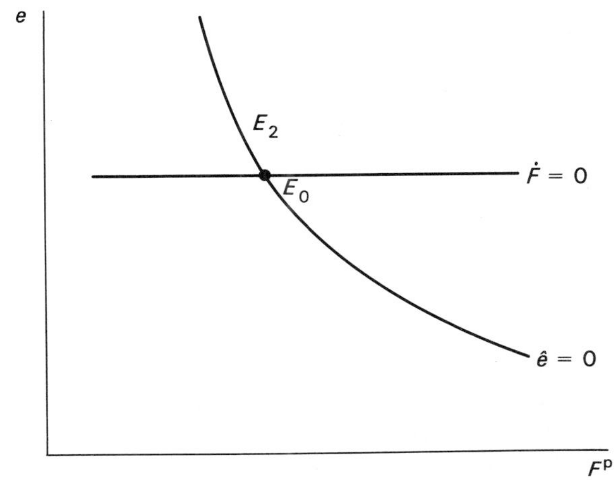

FIGURE 6.6 Sluggish price adjustment

depreciates) from E_0 to E_1, and then gradually rises to E_2 as F^p falls. The depreciation of the currency restores current account balance ($\dot{F} = 0$). The model 'undershoots' in response to real disturbances.

Sluggish price adjustment

A limiting case of sluggish price adjustment could be modelled as a combination of figures 6.4 and 6.5. Expansionary monetary policy would begin this process illustrated in figure 6.4. The delayed price response would then resemble figure 6.5. To the extent that the price response is lagged and unanticipated, the e, F^p point would follow a path illustrated in figure 6.6. Quicker price response or anticipation would straighten the path to E_2, which may be to the right or left of E_0 depending on initial portfolio distribution and substitutability.

Conclusions and empirical implications

It is convenient to summarize here the basic conclusions from the analysis so far.

(1) Unanticipated changes in money, the price level, or underlying real conditions should cause a jump in the exchange rate towards the new rational expectations saddle path.

(2) Thus we should expect to see correlation between unanticipated movements in e and M, X and P in the data. Evidence on quarterly data was presented in Branson (1984); monthly data are presented below.

(3) Movement of the exchange rate following a real disturbance is likely to be monotonic, while monetary disturbances are likely to produce 'overshooting'. Lagged price adjustment makes 'multiple overshooting' possible. This can be seen in a combination of figures 6.4 and 6.6.

'LEANING AGAINST THE WIND' AS EXCHANGE RATE POLICY

Introduction

There is already ample evidence that monetary authorities have generally tried to slow the movement of exchange rates. This type of intervention has long been characteristic of US domestic montary policy; in Branson (1976) I labelled this 'leaning against the wind' as exchange rate policy. Artus (1976) and Branson et al. (1977) presented evidence that German monetary policy responded to movements in the exchange rate in this fashion. Branson et al. (1977) estimated a reaction function of the form

$$\Delta M = \alpha \Delta e + \cdots$$

with $\alpha < 0$ for Germany. As the exchange rate rose (DM depreciated), the money supply was reduced (relative to its trend). Amano (1979) describes Japanese monetary policy as attempting to stabilize the exchange rate similarly. UK exchange rate policy was discussed briefly in OECD (1977), where a regression of the form

$$\Delta r_{\mathrm{m}} = \beta \Delta e + \cdots$$

with r_{m} the minimum lending rate (MLR) and $\beta > 0$ is reported. This suggests that when sterling depreciated (e rose), the MLR was increased as a policy reaction. More recently, Mussa (1981) has presented a thorough review of exchange rate intervention which is consistent with a 'leaning-against-the-wind' model.

The purpose of this section of the paper is to characterize policy intervention in terms of the model of the previous section, to prepare for interpretation of the empirical results in the following section. The objective is not to evaluate policy; it is to describe it. The main difference from the previous models is the description of intervention as instantaneous and discrete changes in asset stocks via open-market operations to reduce the size of discontinuous jumps in exchange rates. This type of policy behaviour is discernable in the 'innovation' correlations in the section below.

We will begin with the description of monetary policy reaction to real disturbances via open-market operations in government debt or foreign assets. Then we study sterilized intervention in the foreign asset market.

Monetary policy

Consider a real disturbance to the current account that shifts $\dot{F} = 0$ up (rise in e) to restore equilibrium. This is illustrated in figure 6.7, where in the absence of policy intervention, the exchange rate would jump from the initial equilibrium E_0 to E_1 and then depreciate further to E_2. If the central bank tightened money by selling bonds to the public, holding F^p initially constant, the $\hat{e} = 0$ curve in figure 6.7 would shift down as shown by the broken $\hat{e} = 0$. This would shift the saddle path down to the path running to E'_2, and reduce the exchange rate jump to E'_1. Thus instantaneous intervention would reduce the initial jump in e. This would be an unexpected change in M, since the originating shift in z and X was unexpected. So this type of intervention could reduce the variability of e over time.

If the open-market operation were done in the foreign asset market, a smaller quantitative intervention would give the same shift in $\hat{e} = 0$ and in the saddle path in figure 6.7, because eF^p/W in equation (8) would rise. In addition, since F^p would rise, the initial jump would be to a point on the new saddle path below E'_1. Thus intervention on the foreign asset market would, in a sense, be more efficient than open-market operations in the bond market. This is essentially the same result that is obtained by Branson (1977) and Kenen (1982) under static expectations.

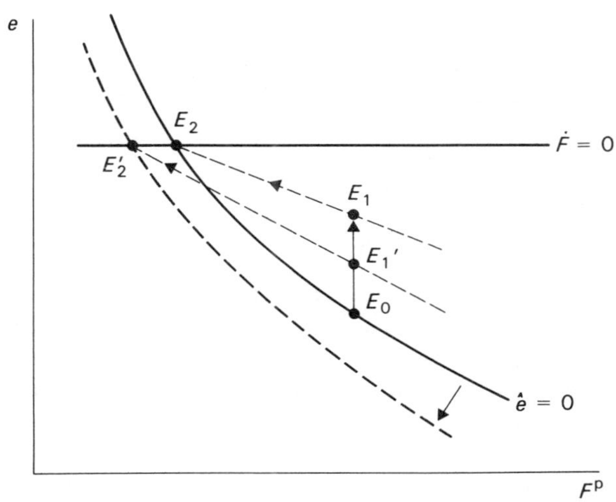

FIGURE 6.7 Monetary policy reaction

Sterilized intervention

There is by now ample evidence that central banks intervene in the foreign exchange markets but attempt to prevent the intervention from changing the path of M. The literature was cited in Whitman (1975); more recent results are discussed in Obstfeld (1980, 1982). In terms of the model of the previous section, this is an open-market exchange of foreign assets for bonds by the central bank, with

$$\Delta B^p = -e\Delta F^p$$

initially. The result is again a downward shift in $\hat{e} = 0$, as in figure 6.7, plus an outward shift in F^p. Thus the jump in the exchange rate is to a point below E_1, since F^p increases. This presents the possibility for intervention that does not move the path of the money supply.

Empirical implications

The principal empirical implication of the present model of policy intervention is that we should observe the intervention in the correlation of unexpected movements or 'innovations' in exchange rates with innovations in money and/or reserves. Monetary intervention would give a negative correlation between exchange rate and money innovations. Intervention with interest rate control would give a positive correlation between exchange rate and interest rate innovations. If the monetary intervention is done in the foreign asset market, a positive correlation between exchange rate innovations and reserves would result. Sterilized intervention would give the reserve–exchange rate correlation without a money–exchange rate correlation. Thus we can study the correlation matrix of innovations in the following section to infer hypotheses about policy behaviour.

EMPIRICAL RESULTS USING VECTOR AUTOREGRESSION

Introduction

A useful technique for studying the relationships between the innovations in money, the current account balance, relative price levels, interest rates, reserves, industrial production and the exchange rate is vector autoregression (VAR). Here each variable of a system is regressed against the lagged values of all variables (including itself) in the system, to extract any information existing in the movements of these variables. The residuals from these 'vector autoregressions' are the innovations—the unanticipated movements—in the variables. We can study the correlations of the residuals to see if they are consistent with the hypotheses implied by the theory of earlier sections. The vector autoregression technique is introduced and justified by Sims (1980). A clear exposition is presented in Sargent (1979). Interesting and instructive applications are discussed in Taylor (1980), Ashenfelter and Card (1981) and Fischer (1981).

Here I estimate systems of *VAR*s on monthly data for each of the four countries, the US, the UK, Germany and Japan. The data are described in table 6.1. Two systems were estimated for each country. Both include the effective exchange rate *e*, the current account balance *CAB*, and the effective relative price $P/\bar{P}$, the interest rate *IS*, industrial production *Y*, reserves *R*; the difference between the two is that one includes M_1 and the other M_3. Industrial production is added to control for business cycle effects on the demand for money.

The lengths of the lags in the *VAR*s were chosen by a series of preliminary univariate autogressions for each variable. The lag length in the *VAR* for each variable was set at the maximum number of significant lags in the univariate autoregression for that variable. The procedure is described in some detail in Branson (1984). The one exception is Japan, where the current account balance has significant lags at one month and five months. Separate *VAR* systems were estimated for Japan using one and five lags on *CAB*. The results were essentially the same, so only the one-lag system is reported here. The lag lengths and details of specification are summarized in table 6.2.

The *VAR*s, then, are a system of regressions of the current value of each of the variables listed in table 6.2 on the indicated lags on all the variables, with the same set of regressors for each equation. A separate system is estimated for each country. The residuals from the *VAR*s are denoted by a ~ over the dependent variable.

After the *VAR* systems are estimated, we correlate their residuals to study the relationship among inovations. The correlations are given for the systems with M_1 for the US, Germany and Japan, and both M_1 and M_3 for the UK in tables 6.3–6.7 below. The two sets of correlations are sufficiently similar in the cases of the US, Germany and Japan that separate discussions of them are unnecessary. Each table includes the correlation coefficients among the *VAR* 'innovations' and in parentheses the probability of that correlation occurring under the null hypothesis that the true correlation is zero. In discussing the correlations, we will focus on the correlations particularly relevant for analysing exchange rate determination and policy. Detailed discussion of all the results would be far too tedious.

United States

The correlations of *VAR* innovations for the US M_1 system are shown in table 6.3. Remember that the effective nominal exchange rate is defined in

TABLE 6.1 Variable definitions and data

I *Variable name*

e	Effective nominal exchange rate, in units of domestic currency per unit of foreign currency as computed by the IMF
$P/\bar{P}$	Relative wholesale prices (ratio of home to competitors indices)
M_1	Narrow money, as defined by the IMF in the *International Financial Statistics* (*IFS*)
M_3	Broad money, as defined by the IMF (M_1 plus quasi-money) in the *IFS*
CAB	Current account balance
IS	Short-term interest rate
R	Reserves
Y	Industrial production

II *Countries*

United States
United Kingdom
Federal Republic of Germany
Japan

III *Data*

(1) All data are monthly, and cover 1971:1 to 1980:12 unless otherwise noted

(2) *Exchange rates*: e_t is the log of the average effective exchange rate during month t. The units are domestic currency per unit of foreign currency. The index is based on a geometrically weighted average of bilateral rates between the home and 13 other industrial countries. The weights are the same as those used to calculated $P/\bar{P}$. Base: 1975 = 100. Source: IMF. Note that these are not the *MERM* rates published in *IFS*

(3) *Relative prices:* The index is a log of the ratio of home to foreign monthly wholesale price indices. P is a composite and uses the same weights as does e (see above). Base = 1975. Source: IMF. This index is not the same as that published in the *IFS*. Our data are based on indices in local (not a common) currency. Series length: 1971:7 to 1980:12

(4) *Money stocks:* This is the log of the monthly money stock. German and Japanese data are end-of-the period money stocks from *IFS*, 'money' for M_1 and 'money + quasi-money' for M_3. UK data are from OECD, *Main Economic Indicators*, various issues. Series length: 1971:10–1980:12. US data are monthly averages from Citibank Economic Data Base

(5) *Current account:* This is the dollar value of the flow during the month (not measured in logs). German data are from Deutsche Bundesbank, *Monthly Report*, various issues converted to US dollars using line rf of *IFS*. Japanese data are from Bank of Japan, *Economic Statistics Monthly*, various issues. US and UK monthly data are quarterly data from *IFS* (described in Branson, 1983), interpolated following the monthly trade balance from *IFS* converted to dollars using line rf in the case of the UK. The interpolation was performed using the procedure of Chow and Lin (1971)

TABLE 6.1 (*cont.*)

(6) *Short-term interest rate:* Data are taken from *IFS* as indicated in the table on 'Money Market and Euro Dollar Rates'. Source: *IFS* country pages
(7) *Reserves:* These are the dollar value of reserves measured at end of period. Source: *IFS*. These series did not vary significantly from the series adjusted for valuation changes provided by the IMF
(8) *Industrial production:* This is the log of the monthly index of industrial production. Source: *IFS*

units of home currency per unit of foreign exchange. So an increase in e is a depreciation.

The first row of table 6.3 gives the correlations of exchange rate innovations with those in the other variables. The positive sign for M_1 and the negative sign for the short-term interest rate IS are consistent with monetary policy driving the exchange rate. The negative correlation of $\tilde{e}$ and $\tilde{R}$, and the positive correlation of $\tilde{CAB}$ and $\tilde{R}$ are both consistent with 'leaning-against-the-wind' intervention in the exchange markets. An unanticipated increase in the current account surplus or appreciation of the dollar (a negative $\tilde{e}$) is significantly associated with an increase in US reserves. The reserve and M_1 innovations have an insignificant negative correlation, indicating that exchange market intervention is sterilized. The M_3 *VAR* innovations for the US have the same pattern.

TABLE 6.2 Variables included in vector autoregression systems

Variable	Length of lag			
	US	Germany	UK	Japan
ln e	2	2	2	2
ln $P/\bar{P}$	2	2	2	2
ln M	2	3	1	2
R	2	1	2	2
IS	3	2	2	2
CAB	3	2	2	1
ln Y	2	1	1	1

All *VAR*s included 11 monthly dummies and an intercept.
Regressions estimated in monthly data 1973:7 to 1980:12.
Two *VAR* systems were estimated for each country, one with M_1, the other with M_3.

TABLE 6.3 Correlations of innovations from US monthly vector autoregression system with M_1

	$\tilde{e}$	$\tilde{P}/\bar{P}$	$\tilde{M}_1$	$\tilde{R}$	$I\tilde{S}$	$C\tilde{A}B$	$\tilde{Y}$
$\tilde{e}$	1.00	−0.00	0.18	−0.24	−0.48	−0.08	0.11
		(0.99)	(0.10)	(0.02)	(0.00)	(0.43)	(0.29)
$\tilde{P}/\bar{P}$		1.00	−0.12	0.01	0.27	−0.19	−0.07
			(0.25)	(0.93)	(0.01)	(0.08)	(0.49)
$\tilde{M}_1$			1.00	−0.17	−0.05	0.06	−0.02
				(0.11)	(0.67)	(0.57)	(0.85)
$\tilde{R}$				1.00	−0.08	0.21	0.02
					(0.48)	(0.06)	(0.85)
$I\tilde{S}$					1.00	0.06	−0.02
						(0.58)	(0.85)
$C\tilde{A}B$						1.00	−0.04
							(0.74)
$\tilde{Y}$							1.000

CAB is the monthly interpolation of the quarterly current account using the monthly trade data and the Chow–Lin interpolation procedure.

The hypotheses that I would infer from the US data are as follows. On a monthly timescale money and interest rates move the exchange rate, with little role for relative prices. Monetary policy is essentially oriented towards domestic targets; movement in the exchange rate is a side effect. The US monetary authorities intervene and sterilize, but do not follow a tight rule. This shows up in the strong correlation between $\tilde{R}$ and $C\tilde{A}B$, and in the correlation between $\tilde{R}$ and $\tilde{e}$.

Germany

The innovation correlations of the M_1 system for Germany are shown in table 6.4. In the first row we see a very strong positive correlation between exchange rate and relative price innovations. This could come from exchange rates causing prices or vice versa, but through innovations and market expectations rather than a tight PPP relationship. The correlation of exchange rate innovations with reserves must reflect leaning-against-the-wind policy in terms of exchange market intervention. The lack of correlation between money and reserves or exchange rates indicates that intervention is sterilized. The negative correlation between money and industrial production could indicate that monetary policy attempts to stabilize real output. The German M_3 *VAR* correlations show essentially the same pattern.

TABLE 6.4 Correlations of innovations from German monthly vector autoregression system with M_1

	$\tilde{e}$	$\tilde{P}/\bar{P}$	$\tilde{M}_1$	$\tilde{R}$	$\tilde{IS}$	$\tilde{CAB}$	$\tilde{Y}$
$\tilde{e}$	1.00	0.22	−0.05	−0.33	0.14	0.16	−0.01
		(0.04)	(0.64)	(0.00)	(0.21)	(0.14)	(0.96)
$\tilde{P}/\bar{P}$		1.00	−0.00	0.13	0.07	0.16	0.03
			(0.97)	(0.23)	(0.52)	(0.15)	(0.78)
$\tilde{M}_1$			1.00	0.03	−0.17	0.11	−0.24
				(0.81)	(0.12)	(0.32)	(0.02)
$\tilde{R}$				1.00	−0.08	0.02	0.08
					(0.46)	(0.84)	(0.48)
$\tilde{IS}$					1.00	0.04	−0.09
						(0.69)	(0.41)
$\tilde{CAB}$						1.00	−0.06
							(0.58)
$\tilde{Y}$							1.00

CAB are the monthly data from *Monthly Report* of the Deutsche Bundesbank.

Thus the German data suggest fairly strongly a situation in which (a) price and exchange rate innovations go together, and (b) the authorities react to exchange rate movements through sterilized intervention. This is consistent with the earlier results of Branson et al. (1977) and of Herring and Marston (1977) for the fixed-rate regime.

United Kingdom

The UK correlations are shown in tables 6.5 and 6.6 for the M_1 and M_3 systems, respectively. Comparison of the correlations between exchange rate and money innovations suggests that news about M_3, but not M_1, moves the exchange rate. The monthly correlation between innovations in relative prices and the exchange rate is virtually zero. In both tables we see correlations between exchange rate innovations and those in reserves and short-term interest rates that are a strong indication of leaning-against-the-wind intervention and interest rate policy. The negative correlations between reserve and money innovations suggest that exchange market intervention is over-sterilized; unanticipated increases in reserves go along with *decreases* in both M_1 and M_3 on a monthly basis. Thus the UK data show a strong policy reaction to exchange rate changes, with some independent effect of M_3 on the exchange rate.

TABLE 6.5 Correlations of innovations from UK monthly vector autoregression system with M_1

	$\tilde{e}$	$\tilde{P}/\bar{P}$	$\tilde{M}_1$	$\tilde{R}$	$I\tilde{S}$	$C\tilde{A}B$	$\tilde{Y}$
$\tilde{e}$	1.00	−0.02	−0.08	−0.36	0.30	−0.05	−0.07
		(0.83)	(0.47)	(0.00)	(0.00)	(0.65)	(0.52)
$\tilde{P}/\bar{P}$		1.00	0.03	0.18	−0.05	−0.11	0.09
			(0.80)	(0.10)	(0.63)	(0.31)	(0.41)
$\tilde{M}_1$			1.00	−0.23	−0.25	−0.09	−0.13
				(0.03)	(0.02)	(0.39)	(0.24)
$\tilde{R}$				1.00	−0.09	−0.27	0.27
					(0.41)	(0.01)	(0.01)
$I\tilde{S}$					1.00	−0.06	−0.14
						(0.55)	(0.19)
$C\tilde{A}B$						1.00	−0.14
							(0.19)
$\tilde{Y}$							1.00

CAB is interpolated quarterly data as in US case.

TABLE 6.6 Correlations of innovations from UK monthly vector autoregression system with M_3

	$\tilde{e}$	$\tilde{P}/\bar{P}$	$\tilde{M}_3$	$\tilde{R}$	$I\tilde{S}$	$C\tilde{A}B$	$\tilde{Y}$
$\tilde{e}$	1.00	−0.07	0.25	−0.42	0.35	−.05	−0.03
		(0.52)	(0.02)	(0.00)	(0.00)	(0.66)	(0.76)
$\tilde{P}/\bar{P}$		1.00	−0.19	0.28	−0.17	−0.09	0.02
			(0.08)	(0.01)	(0.12)	(0.42)	(0.83)
$\tilde{M}_3$			1.00	−0.36	0.16	0.25	−0.17
				(0.00)	(0.15)	(0.02)	(0.11)
$\tilde{R}$				1.00	−0.25	−0.17	0.12
					(0.02)	(0.12)	(0.27)
$I\tilde{S}$					1.00	−0.12	−0.02
						(0.29)	(0.85)
$C\tilde{A}B$						1.00	−0.14
							(0.20)
$\tilde{Y}$							1.00

Japan

The results from the M_1 system for Japan are shown in table 6.7. The results from the M_3 system are essentially the same. The correlations of exchange rate innovations with those in M_1 and *CAB* indicate that both of those variables drive the exchange rate, consistent with the theory of the

TABLE 6.7 Correlations of innovations from Japan monthly vector autoregression system with M_1

	$\tilde{e}$	$\tilde{P}/\bar{P}$	$\tilde{M}_1$	$\tilde{R}$	$\tilde{IS}$	$C\tilde{A}B$	$\tilde{Y}$
$\tilde{e}$	1.00	0.31	0.21	−0.42	0.16	−0.26	0.05
		(0.00)	(0.06)	(0.00)	(0.13)	(0.02)	(0.64)
$\tilde{P}/\bar{P}$		1.00	0.23	−0.16	0.23	−0.27	0.05
			(0.03)	(0.15)	(0.03)	(0.01)	(0.63)
$\tilde{M}_1$			1.00	−0.10	0.29	−0.11	−0.34
				(0.35)	(0.01)	(0.31)	(0.00)
$\tilde{R}$				1.00	−0.11	0.31	0.08
					(0.33)	(0.00)	(0.49)
$\tilde{IS}$					1.00	−0.11	0.06
						(0.30)	(060)
$C\tilde{A}B$						1.00	−0.09
							(0.43)
$\tilde{Y}$							1.00

CAB are monthly data from Bank of Japan, *Economic Statistics Monthly.*

second section. There is also a strong positive correlation between exchange rate and relative price innovations.

The reserve correlations with the exchange rate and $C\tilde{A}B$ strongly suggest 'leaning-against-the-wind' intervention, with the central bank absorbing part of the *CAB* innovations to reduce movement in the exchange rate. The lack of correlation of $\tilde{M}_1$ with reserves or the exchange rate indicates sterilization. The negative correlation of $\tilde{M}_1$ with industrial production suggests that, as in Germany, monetary policy is aimed at stabilizing real output.

An interesting story emerges from the Japanese correlations. They suggest that monetary policy is oriented towards domestic objectives, and moves the exchange rate, as in the second section. The authorities intervene to neutralize this effect, and they also attempt to sterilize M_1 from the intervention.

Summary of VAR results on policy

An interesting view of how the monetary system and interdependence have worked in the 1970s emerges from the *VAR* innovation correlations. My interpretation, or inferred set of hypotheses, is as follows. The US sets monetary policy, largely by controlling quantities, with domestic objectives foremost. On a monthly basis the market looks to innovations in money and interest rates to set the US exchange rate. The US or foreign monetary authorities attempt sterilized intervention occasionally.

In Japan, monetary policy is also set according to domestic objectives. As in the US, this moves the exchange rate, but a stronger attempt is made to neutralize this effect through sterilized intervention in Japan than in the US.

Movements in the US and Japanese effective rates, caused partly by fundamentals and partly by policy, are mirrored instantaneously in the UK and German effective rates, and their policy reacts. The reaction appears as 'defensive' interest rate movements sensitive to exchange rate innovations, and largely sterilized intervention in the foreign exchange market. Thus a story in which domestically oriented policy in the US and Japan is transmitted to the UK and Germany is consistent with the *VAR* innovation results. This is a familiar story in Europe.

NOTES

1 Since the analysis here applies to any single country in the international financial system, I use the terms 'home' and 'foreign' to denote the country being discussed and the rest of the system, respectively. At the level of generality of this discussion no damage would be done if the reader substituted 'US' for 'home country', 'dollar' for 'home currency' and 'Fed' for 'central bank'.

2 Since F is home claims on foreigners less home liabilities to foreigners, an asset swap which exchanges a claim and a liability with a foreign asset holder is a transaction within F, changing claims and liabilities by the same amount. This transaction would leave F and B unchanged. The reason for using this particular aggregation will become clear when we study dynamic adjustment below. Basically, we want to define net foreign assets consistently with the balance of payments and national income and product accounts, which record the capital account balance as the change in US private holdings of net foreign assets. The assumptions outlined above make M and B non-traded assets. This implies that the total stocks of M, B and F in domestic portfolios are given at any point in time.

REFERENCES

Amano, A. (1979) *Flexible Exchange Rates and Macroeconomic Management: A Study of the Japanese Experience in 1973–1978*, Kobe University, mimeographed.

Artus, J. (1976) 'Exchange Rate Stability and Managed Floating: The Experience of the Federal Republic of Germany', *International Monetary Fund Staff Papers*, **23**, July, 312–333.

Ashenfelter, O. and Card, D. (1981) *Time-Series Representations of Economic Variables and Alternative Models of the Labor Market*, University of Bristol, Working Paper.

Branson, W. H. (1975) 'Comment on M.v.N. Whitman: Global Monetarism and the Monetary Approach to the Balance of Payments', *Brookings Papers on Economic Activity*, **6**, No. 3, 537–542.

Branson, W. H. (1976) 'Leaning Against the Wind as Exchange Rate Policy', Paper presented at Graduate Institute of International Studies, Geneva, revised 1981 for book publication by the Institute.

Branson, W. H. (1977) 'Asset Markets and Relative Prices in Exchange Rate Determination', *Sozialwissenschaftliche Annalen*, **1**, 69–89.

Branson, W. H., Halttunen, H. and Masson, P. (1977) 'Exchange Rates in the Short Run: The Dollar–Deutschemark Rate', *European Economic Review*, **10**, December, 303–324.

Branson, W. H. (1980) 'Monetary and Fiscal Policy With Adjustable Exchange Rates', in US Congress, Joint Economic Committee, *The International Economy: US Role in a World Market*, Government Printing Office, Washington, pp. 459–500.

Branson, W. H. (1981) *Macroeconomic Determinants of Real Exchange Rates*, NBER Working Paper No. 801, November.

Branson, W. H. (1984) 'Exchange Rate Policy After a Decade of 'Floating', in J. F. O. Bilson and R. C. Marston (eds), *Exchange Rate Theory and Practice*, University of Chicago Press.

Chow, G. C. and Lin, A. (1971) 'Best Linear Unbiased Interpolation, Distribution and Extrapolation of Time Series by Related Series', *Review of Economics and Statistics*, **53**, 372–375.

Dornbusch, R. (1980) 'Exchange Rate Economics: Where Do We Stand?', *Brookings Papers on Economic Activity*, **11**, No. 1, 143–186.

Fischer, S. (1981) 'Relative Shocks, Relative Price Variability and Inflation', *Brookings Papers on Economic Activity*, **12**, No. 2.

Frenkel, J. (1981) 'Flexible Exchange Rates, Prices and the Role of 'News': Lessons from the 1970s', *Journal of Political Economy*, **89**, August, 665–705.

Herring, R. J. and Marston, R. C. (1977) *National Monetary Policies and International Financial Markets*, North-Holland, Amsterdam.

Kenen, P. B. (1982) 'Effects of Intervention and Sterilization in the Short Run and the Long Run', in R. N. Cooper, P. B. Kenen, J. B. de Macedo and J. van Ypersele (eds), *The International Monetary System under Flexible Exchange Rates: Essays in Honour of Robert Triffin*, Ballinger, Cambridge, MA, pp. 51–68.

Kouri, P. J. K. (1978) *Balance of Payments and the Foreign Exchange Market: A Dynamic Partial Equilibrium Model*, Yale University, Cowles Foundation Discussion Paper No. 510.

Mussa, M. (1981) *The Role of Official Intervention*, Occasional Paper No. 6, New York, Group of 30.

Obstfeld, M. (1980) *Portfolio Balance, Monetary Policy, and the Dollar–Deutschemark Exchange Rate*, Columbia University Economics Dept, Discussion Paper No. 62, March 1982.

Obstfeld, M. (1982) 'Can We Sterilize? Theory and Evidence', *American Economic Review*, May 1982.

OECD Interfutures (1977) *Long Term Aspects of the Monetary System*, OECD Paris, mimeographed.

Sargent, T. (1979) 'Estimating Vector Autoregressions Using Methods Not Based on Explicit Economic Theories', *Federal Reserve Bank of Minneapolis Quarterly Review*, Summer, 8–15.

Sims, C. (1980) 'Macroeconomics and Reality', *Econometrica*, **48**, January, 1–48.

Taylor, J. (1980) 'Output and Price Stability: An International Comparison', *Journal of Economic Dynamics and Control*, **2**, February, 109–132.

Whitman, M.v.N. (1975) 'Global Monetarism and the Monetary Approach to the Balance of Payments', *Brookings Paper on Economic Activity*, **3**, 471–536.

Comment

RAYMOND COURBIS

Quite often, macroeconometric models consider economic or monetary policy tools to be exogenous. Such a simplification is quite understandable for models built for governments if one emphasizes simulations that precisely enlighten how the policy tools are to be managed by the government (and central banks). But one has to bear in mind two points:

(a) using a macroeconometric model for *forecasts* requires one to make explicit assumptions on economic and monetary policy and, consequently, to analyse, at least in a informal way, the behaviour of government and central banks; and
(b) considering economic and monetary policy tools as exogenous can, if one solves the model by an iterative process, have an impact on the *convergence properties* of the system.

Independently of its theoretical interest, Branson's model of exchange rate determination is interesting for a modeller in two ways.

First, it appears that if 'leaning against the wind', the reaction of the central bank can reduce the jumps in exchange rates which would follow a real or monetary disturbance. If introduced in a macroeconometric model, such a mechanism could have stabilizing effects and would improve the convergence of the iterative process used for solving the model.

Secondly, Branson's empirical results clearly indicate how the behaviour of the central banks works practically for the US, Japan, West Germany and the UK. It appears in particular that, for the US and Japan, monetary policy is oriented towards domestic objectives and moves the exchange rate. For the US, movement in the dollar exchange rate is a side effect and the jump of the dollar value since 1980 illustrates clearly the US behaviour as described by the Branson model. For Germany, on the contrary, it appears that monetary policy attempts to stabilize real output and the authorities react to exchange rate movements through sterilized intervention. For the UK, data show a strong policy reaction to exchange rate changes and to unanticipated increases or decreases in reserves; it appears that the UK authorities react by moving interest rates.

It is interesting here to see that for France the behaviour of the central bank looks like that described for the UK by Branson. In the MOGLI model that we built at GAMA for the French economy,[1] the interest rate on the monetary market is considered to be determined by interventions by and the behaviour of the Banque de France (the central bank): it depends on exchange rate movements of the French franc, the increase or decrease in official reserves and the external trade surplus (and also, at the same time, on the values of interest rates in the US and in West Germany—a direct linkage with US and German policies and also the result of the impact, in a reduced-form approach, of foreign opportunities to hold assets in French money). The behaviour of the Banque de France as described in the MOGLI econometric equation looks like a 'leaning-against-the-wind' reaction in the Branson approach. The simulations made with the MOGLI model have well illustrated the interest one had, as emphasized in the Branson model, to describe endogenously the reactions of authorities.

The empirical results demonstrated in the Branson model also point out the asymmetry of the US (and partly Japan) vis-à-vis the other countries. The actual interest in Branson's results is to enlighten why the dollar value is increasing since 1980: it is the consequence of the high value of US interest rates which are only managed for domestic objectives and without any regard to the impact of such a policy in other countries.

Branson's paper appears quite stimulating; it clearly demonstrates that an analysis of the behaviour of public authorities is not only useful but feasible.

NOTE

1 MOGLI is an annual dynamic pluri-sectoral model (built for short-term and medium-term simulations and forecasts), where we have tried to endogenize, as much as possible, the behaviour of government and central bank. Public demand (public consumption and public investment, employment in administrations), and partly taxation, is endogenous, as is also the Banque de France behaviour on the monetary market. For the MOGLI model, see Courbis, R., Fonteneau, A., Le Van, C. and Voisin, P. (1980) 'Le modèle MOGLI', *Prévision et Analyse économique* (*Cahiers du GAMA*), **1**, No. 2–3.

Comment

PAUL de GRAUWE

In the first, theoretical part of his paper Branson develops a portfolio balance model determining the exchange rate. Needless to say that Branson pioneered the use of portfolio balance models to explain the exchange rate. In this paper he adds two features to his model. One is the rational expectations (perfect foresight) assumption; the other is official intervention in the foreign exchange market. In the second part of the paper there is an attempt at empirical verification of the model.

In my comment I first want to concentrate on the theoretical part. Next, I will dwell upon some empirical issues.

The model presented here is attractive both because of its elegance and because of its power to understand how exchange rates behave. The least successful aspect, in my opinion, is the one which deals with the role of official intervention in the exchange market. The prevalent mode of official intervention has been the 'leaning-against-the-wind' intervention. Yet, all the Branson model does is to analyse unexpected discretionary sales or purchases of currencies in the foreign exchange market. It fails to integrate into the model the predictable intervention rules which have been used. These rules, as they become known, should affect the structure of the model. They do not in Branson's model.

Another weak link in the way Branson models foreign exchange market intervention is that no distinction is made between sterilized and non-sterilized intervention, although this distinction could easily be incorporated into the model. As will be remembered, sterilized intervention leaves the domestic money stock unchanged, and only affects the relative supplies of privately held foreign and domestic bonds. Non-sterilized intervention changes the domestic money stock. One would expect, therefore, that these two types of intervention would affect the terminal values of the exchange rate. Yet as far as I can see this does not happen in the analysis of Branson. Take, for example, a real disturbance to the current account (analysed in the third section) which shifts the $\dot{F} = 0$ line up (see Branson's figure 6.7;

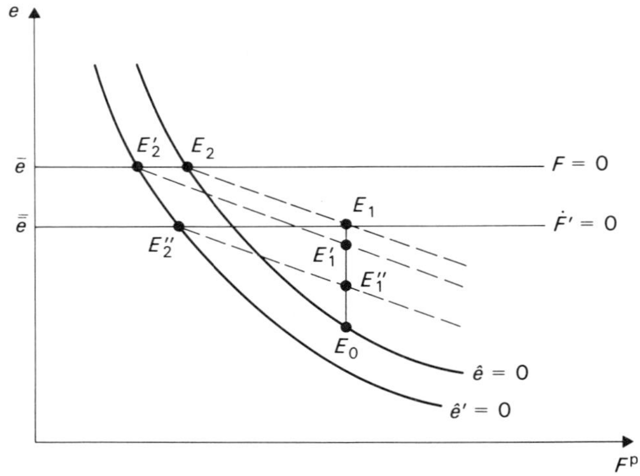

FIGURE 1 Sterilized and non-sterilized intervention in Branson's model

figure 1 in this comment). The intervention in the exchange market shifts the $\hat{e} = 0$ line downwards thereby reducing the initial jump in the exchange rate, from $E_0 - E_1$ to $E_0 - E_1'$. After this jump, however, the exchange rate moves to its long-run equilibrium level $\bar{e}$.

This is the long-run equilibrium exchange rate also obtained when there is no intervention in the foreign exchange market. Thus, it appears that Branson analyses sterilized intervention. Non-sterilized intervention, by reducing the domestic money stock, would also reduce the long-run equilibrium exchange rate $\bar{e}$. Thus, under non-sterilized intervention the $\dot{F} = 0$ line would shift downwards. As a result, the initial jump will be reduced relative to the sterilized intervention. The economy now jumps from E_0 to E_1''. In addition, as the long-run equilibrium exchange rate is reduced to $\bar{\bar{e}}$, the domestic currency has to depreciate less when moving to E_2'' than in the case of sterilized intervention. The conclusion from this analysis is that the distinction between the two types of intervention is important as it changes the whole dynamic path of the exchange rate.

In the empirical part, Branson attempts, among other things, to verify whether the predictions of the model are borne out by the facts. One of these predictions is that unexpected monetary shocks (innovations) lead to unexpected jumps (innovation) in the exchange rate. Another is that, when the monetary authorities intervene, the causality runs the other way, i.e. exchange rate innovations then lead to monetary innovations.

A first general comment I have is that not only the portfolio balance model but also monetarist models, with perfect foresight, produce the same theoretical predictions. As a result, the broad consistency of the facts with these theoretical predictions cannot be interpreted as evidence that the portfolio balance model is the true underlying model. More elaborate testing will be necessary to discriminate between these different models. It is worth pointing out here that the empirical tests by Meese and Rogoff (1983) do not seem to be very favourable for either the monetarist or the portfolio balance model.

As a second comment, I would like to suggest that using the *VAR* methodology, Branson could have gone a little further in testing his theory. One of the conclusions Branson arrives at is that monetary surprises in the US drive the exchange rate. In turn, this triggers intervention in Germany, changing the money stock there. (Incidentally, this conclusion is broadly consistent with the recent findings of McKinnon (1982).) A direct test of this proposition could be done by correlating the US and the German monetary innovations. A positive correlation could then be interpreted as additional evidence supporting this proposition.

A final comment on the empirical part concerns the use of effective exchange rates. This may pose some problems with a country like Germany where the effective exchange rate has changed because of realignments within the EMS (or in earlier days the 'Snake'). In general, a change in the effective exchange rate due to such a realignment has different implications for intervention policies than a change in the dollar/DM rate. Let me illustrate this. When the dollar rate declines, the Bundesbank shows a tendency to buy dollars, and thus to expand the German money stock (if the intervention is non-sterilized). When the French franc is devalued within the EMS, this also produces an increase in the German effective exchange rate. However, it is unclear what the implications are for intervention and, therefore, for the German money stock. It is not unusual that after such a realignment, French francs are sold and Deutsche marks are *bought* in the exchange market, because of the reversal of speculative capital movements. The empirical test of Branson does not allow one to discriminate between these two sources of changes in the effective exchange rate of the DM. It might be useful, therefore, to do some testing using the dollar/DM exchange rate.

To conclude, I wish to stress that Branson's paper is a novel and original piece of research. In my criticism I have concentrated on suggestions to refine the model and to increase the power of the empirical tests.

REFERENCES

McKinnon, R. (1982) 'Currency Substitution and Instability in the World Dollar Market', *American Economic Review*, June, 320–333.

Meese, R. and Rogoff, K. (1983) 'Empirical Exchange Rate Models of the Seventies: Do They Fit Out of Sample?', *Journal of International Economics*, February, 3–24.

7

Exchange Market Intervention in a Small Open Economy: An Expository Model

STEPHEN J. TURNOVSKY

INTRODUCTION

Traditionally, the international macroeconomic literature has been concerned almost exclusively with analysing perfectly fixed or perfectly flexible exchange rate systems. Yet both of these regimes represent polar forms of intervention policy. In the former, the domestic monetary authorities continually intervene in the foreign exchange market so as to maintain the exchange rate at some given target level. In the latter case, the domestic monetary authorities abstain from any active intervention, allowing the exchange rate to fluctuate freely in response to market forces. Intermediate between these two extremes is that of a 'managed float' in which the monetary authorities intervene partly to offset movements in the exchange rate, so that the adjustments to changes in market pressure are met by a combination of both movements in the exchange rate and the accumulation or decumulation of foreign reserves. The intensity with which the domestic monetary authorities intervene in the foreign exchange market is a policy decision. In this paper we analyse how the stability of a small open economy is affected by the degree of exchange market intervention and also derive optimal intervention policies for particular cases.

The question of optimal exchange market intervention has begun to receive attention in the literature. Boyer (1978) and Roper and Turnovsky (1980) analyse the problem by extending the framework developed by Poole (1970) in his well known analysis of the monetary instrument problem. These analyses are based on the assumption that the price of domestic output remains fixed. While this assumption may be convenient for pedagogic purposes, it obviously needs to be relaxed if the analysis is to be at all relevant for current conditions in which the price mechanism is one key channel through which the international transmission of disturbances takes place. Another recent paper is by Buiter (1979) who analyses intervention policy in terms of discrete time control theory. Casting the intervention rule in terms of a feedback control law is restrictive, however, because current intervention is related only to past rather than present market data.[1] Some market data, such as the exchange rate and the quantity of central bank liabilities outstanding, are observable on a fairly current basis. As Kareken et al. (1973) have shown in their work on optimal monetary strategy for a closed economy, currently observable data provided information about the sources of random shocks to the economy, the exploitation of which allows a greater degree of stability to be achieved in the economy.[2]

The present paper analyses exchange market intervention policy in a small open economy in which the domestic price level, as well as domestic real output, is endogenously determined. Particular attention is devoted to exchange rate expectations and price expectations, both of which are assumed to be formed rationally. Also, the approach taken in this paper assumes that the intervention policy exploits information contained in current observable market data. The analysis draws heavily on a recent paper by Turnovsky (1983), and the purpose of the present paper is primarily expository. The previous paper devoted a lot of attention to the technical details of the solution of the model and the general derivation of the optimal exchange intervention policy. These are deleted from our present analysis and our focus is much more on trying to present a simple graphical and intuitive explanation of the optimal policies in a number of special instances.

The remainder of the paper is structured as follows. The following section outlines the simple model underlying the analysis. The next section reports the solution given that expectations are formed rationally. It is shown how the short-run solution depends upon the degree of exchange market intervention and the responses of the system to changes in this parameter are briefly discussed. The derivation of the optimal intervention policy turns out to be a tedious exercise and in the fourth section we consider the optimal intervention policy corresponding to the separate disturbances taken individually in turn. We do this graphically making use of the notion of exchange market pressure introduced by Girton and Roper (1977) and utilized by Roper and Turnovsky (1980). It is seen that the optimal intervention may vary quite dramatically, both in quantitative magnitude and qualitatively, depending upon the sources of the stochastic disturbances impinging on the economy. The main body of the analysis is based on the assumption of perfect capital mobility, so that uncovered interest parity holds. Some brief comments on the extension of the model to imperfect capital mobility are given in the fifth section, while the main conclusions are summarized in the final section.

A SMALL OPEN ECONOMY

In order to keep the technical details to a minimum, we shall base our analysis on the simplest model. Specifically we shall assume that there is one traded commodity whose price in terms of foreign currency is given. Also, there is a single traded bond, with the domestic bond market perfectly integrated with that in the rest of the world. Thus purchasing power parity (PPP) and uncovered interest rate parity (UIP) hold throughout.

The model can be summarized as follows:[3]

$$P_t = Q_t + E_t \tag{1a}$$

$$M_t - P_t = \alpha_1 Y_t - \alpha_2 r_t + u_{1t} \tag{1b}$$

$$r_t = \Omega_t + E^*_{t+1,t} - E_t \tag{1c}$$

$$M_t = \bar{M} - \mu(E_t - \bar{E}) \tag{1d}$$

$$Y_t - \hat{Y} = \gamma(P_t - P^*_{t,t-1}) + u_{2t} \tag{1e}$$

while for any variable, X say,

$$X^*_{s,t} = \mathscr{E}_t(X_s) \tag{1f}$$

where $\mathscr{E}_t$ = conditional expectations operator, conditional on information at time t; P_t = domestic price of the traded good at time t, expressed in logarithms; Q_t = world price of the traded good at time t, expressed in logarithms; E_t = current exchange rate (measured in units of the domestic currency per unit of foreign currency), expressed in logarithms; $\bar{E}$ = equilibrium (steady-state) level of E, endogenously determined; M_t = domestic nominal money supply, expressed in logarithms; Y_t = real domestic output at time t, expressed in logarithms; $\hat{Y}$ = full employment level of Y; r_t = domestic nominal interest rate at time t; Ω_t = foreign nominal interest rate at time t; $\bar{M}$ = fixed exogenous component of the domestic nominal supply; $E^*_{t+s,t}$ = expectation of E for time $t+s$, held at time t, $s = 1, 2, \ldots,$ all t; $P^*_{t+s,t}$ = expectation of P for time $t+s$, held at time t, $s = 1, 2, \ldots,$ all t; u_{1t} = stochastic disturbance in demand of domestic money; and u_{2t} = stochastic disturbance in domestic output supply.

The equations of the model are in the main fairly standard. Given purchasing power parity, the domestic price of a freely traded commodity equals the price abroad multiplied by the exchange rate. Equation (1a) is just the logarithmic version of this relationship. The domestic monetary sector is summarized by equations (1b)–(1d). The first of these equations describe the domestic *LM* curve, making the usual assumption that all domestic money is held by domestic residents, who also hold no foreign currency.[4] The assumption of perfect capital market integration is embodied in the interest rate parity condition (1c). The intervention policy is described by (1d), which describes the degree of intervention by the authority as a function of the observed deviation of the exchange rate from its long-run equilibrium level and which the authorities are assumed to know. The limiting cases $\mu = \infty$, $\mu = 0$, correspond to fixed and flexible regimes, respectively, while any finite, non-zero value of μ describes a managed float. A policy of setting $\mu > 0$ implies that, if the current exchange rate is above its long-run level, the monetary authorities should introduce a monetary contraction (set M below $\bar{M}$), thereby reducing the pressure on the exchange rate. Differentiating (1d) with respect to t, implies

$$\dot{M} = -\mu\dot{E}$$

that is, the domestic money supply is decreased at a rate which is proportional to the rate of exchange depreciation. Such a policy is often described as 'leaning against the wind'. If $\mu < 0$, the monetary authorities react to a devaluating exchange rate by adopting an expansionary policy, thereby adding to the pressure on the exchange rate. This may be referred to as 'leaning with the wind'. The optimal intervention policy is to choose μ to optimize an objective, yet to be specified, and as we shall demonstrate, an optimal policy may involve either $\mu > 0$ or $\mu < 0$, depending upon the primary source of the stochastic disturbances. Note that the reaction function (1d) is expressed in terms of current values of M and E, which are therefore assumed to be instantly observable.[5]

The supply of domestic output is specified by (1e). This relationship postulates the deviation in output from its full employment level to depend upon the unanticipated component of the current domestic price of output. This formulation resembles a Lucas (1973) supply function, although as Flood (1979) has argued with both international and intranational trading, this rationale is inappropriate. Rather it may be justified in terms of the wage determination model of Gray (1976) and Fischer (1977). Finally, equation (1f) describes the rationality of expectations.

The two domestic stochastic disturbances, u_{1t}, u_{2t}, are assumed to have zero means, and finite second moments satisfying

$$\mathscr{E}(u_{1t}) = \mathscr{E}(u_{2t}) = 0 \tag{2a}$$

$$\mathscr{E}(u_{1t}^2) = \sigma_1^2, \qquad \mathscr{E}(u_{2t}^2) = \sigma_2^2, \qquad \mathscr{E}(u_{1t}u_{2t}) = \sigma_1\sigma_2\rho \tag{2b}$$

where ρ is the correlation coefficient between the two variables. While we have written u_{1t} as reflecting a stochastic disturbance in demand, it can equally well be interpreted (with sign change) as being a stochastic disturbance in supply. The two foreign variables in the system Ω_t, Q_t are also assumed to be random, being described by

$$Q_t = \bar{Q} + q_t \tag{3a}$$

$$\Omega_t = \bar{\Omega} + \omega_t \tag{3b}$$

where $\bar{Q}$, $\bar{\Omega}$ are constant (see appendix) and

$$\mathscr{E}(q_t) = \mathscr{E}(\omega_t) = 0 \tag{4a}$$

$$\mathscr{E}(q_t^2) = \sigma_q^2, \qquad \mathscr{E}(\omega_t^2) = \sigma_\omega^2, \qquad \mathscr{E}(q_t \omega_t) = \sigma_q \sigma_\omega \eta \tag{4b}$$

while η denotes the corresponding correlation coefficient. In addition, all random variables are assumed to be independently distributed over time and for simplicity we assume that domestic and foreign variables are uncorrelated. This enables us to distinguish quite clearly between domestic and foreign stochastic influences.

But whereas q_t, ω_t are exogenous to the small country, they are themselves endogenously determined in the rest of the world, reflecting the various stochastic influences occurring abroad. To solve for these variables it is reasonable, given the small country assumption of the domestic economy, to treat the rest of the world as a large closed economy, unaffected by the domestic economy. One can then solve for the q_t, ω_t as functions of the random variables occurring abroad. It thus is evident that these variables will almost certainly be correlated, although the sign of the correlation will depend upon the sources of the disturbances abroad. For example, an increase in demand abroad will cause both q_t and ω_t to rise, while a monetary expansion will cause q_t to rise but ω_t to fall. A foreign supply shock will cause q_t to fall, while the interest rate may either rise or fall depending upon relevant demand elasticities abroad (see Turnovsky, 1983). For expositional convenience we shall focus primarily on the disturbances q_t and ω_t separately, recognizing that any real-world disturbance will be some composite of the two effects.

In order to simplify notation it is convenient to consider an initial equilibrium defined by assuming that all expectations are realized and setting all random variables to zero. We may then express the system in deviation form about this equilibrium as

$$p_t = q_t + e_t \tag{5a}$$

$$m_t - p_t = \alpha_1 y_t - \alpha_2[e^*_{t+1,t} - e_t] + u_{1t} - \alpha_2 \omega_t \tag{5b}$$

$$m_t = -\mu e_t \tag{5c}$$

$$y_t = \gamma(p_t - p^*_{t,t-1}) + u_{2t} \tag{5d}$$

where lower-case letters denote variables measured in deviation form and for convenience r_t has been eliminated. Equations (5a)–(5d) yield four stochastic difference equations in domestic output y_t, the price of domestic output p_t and its expectations, the exchange rate e_t and its expectation, and the domestic nominal money supply.

SOLUTION OF SYSTEM

Various procedures exist for solving the system (5). In Turnovsky (1983) we adopted the method of undetermined coefficients. This involves first expressing (5) in terms of the following equation in e_t and its expectations:

$$(1 + \alpha_2 + \mu + \alpha_1\gamma)e_t = \alpha_2 e^*_{t+1,t} + \alpha_1\gamma e^*_{t,t-1} + \varepsilon_t \tag{6}$$

where

$$\varepsilon_t \equiv -u_{1t} - \alpha_1 u_{2t} + \alpha_2 \omega_t - (1 + \alpha_1\gamma)q_t \tag{7}$$

and then proposing a solution for e_t of the form

$$e_t = \delta_0 \varepsilon_t + \delta_1\varepsilon_{t-1} + \delta_2 \varepsilon_{t-2} + \cdots. \tag{8}$$

The coefficients δ_i are determined by substituting (8) and the corresponding expressions for expectations, $e^*_{t+1,t}$, $e^*_{t,t-1}$, into (6) and equating coefficients. This leads to the solution

$$e_t = \left(\frac{1 + \alpha_2 \delta_1}{1 + \alpha_2 + \mu + \alpha_1\gamma}\right)\varepsilon_t + \delta_1[\varepsilon_{t-1} + \theta\varepsilon_{t-2} + \theta^2\varepsilon_{t-3} + \cdots] \tag{9}$$

where $\theta \equiv [1 + \alpha_2 + \mu]/\alpha_2$ and δ_1 is still to be determined.

The solution (9) embodies the non-uniqueness characteristic of rational expectations solutions and to complete the solution it is necessary to choose δ_1. This is typically done by imposing some stability condition on e_t. From (9) it is seen that the required condition depends upon whether $|\theta| \gtrless 1$, which in turn depends upon the degree of exchange market intervention μ. If $\mu > -1$ or $\mu < -(1 + 2\alpha_2)$ then $|\theta| > 1$ and the solution for e_t will be unstable in the sense of having an infinite asymptotic variance, unless we choose $\delta_1 = 0$, a condition which is therefore imposed. However, if $-(1 + 2\alpha_2) < \mu < -1$, so that $|\theta| < 1$, the asymptotic variance of e_t will be finite for any arbitrary value of δ_1. The indeterminacy remaining can be resolved by choosing δ_1 to minimize the (finite) variance. This procedure, originally suggested by Taylor (1977), was adopted in the previous paper. However, this procedure is essentially arbitrary since there is no obvious market mechanism to ensure that the variance will be minimized in this way.[6]

In the present analysis we adopt a simpler (but equally arbitrary) argument to determine δ_1. We shall simply assume that irrespective of whether $|\theta| \gtrless 1$, the rational expectations generate a solution for e_t which is based on the minimum amount of information. It is clear that if $\delta_1 \neq 0$, e_t is based on an infinite amount of past information, as embodied in the ε_{t-i}. Applying the minimum information argument allows us to set $\delta_1 = 0$ for all θ, in which case e_t depends only upon current disturbances. This approach has the advantage of ensuring continuity of the optimal policy about the point where $|\theta| = 1$, and avoiding some of the complications associated with the minimum variance criterion encountered in the previous paper and noted in note 6.

Thus setting $\delta_1 = 0$, so that exchange rate and the price level depend only upon current disturbances, it follows that

$$e^*_{t,t-1} = p^*_{t,t-1} = 0. \tag{10}$$

That is, given the stationarity of the system, expectations are static. Both the exchange rate and the price level are always expected to equal their long-run equilibrium values.

The solutions for y_t, p_t and e_t are thus obtained by setting all expectations to zero in (5), yielding the expressions:

$$y_t = \frac{\gamma(\alpha_2 + \mu)q_t + (1 + \alpha_2 + \mu)u_{2t} + \gamma(\alpha_2\omega_t - u_{1t})}{1 + \alpha_2 + \mu + \alpha_1\gamma} \tag{11a}$$

$$p_t = \frac{(\alpha_2 + \mu)q_t - \alpha_1 u_{2t} + \alpha_2\omega_t - u_{1t}}{1 + \alpha_2 + \mu + \alpha_1\gamma} \tag{11b}$$

$$e_t = \frac{-(1 + \alpha_1\gamma)q_t - \alpha_1 u_{2t} + \alpha_2\omega_t - u_{1t}}{1 + \alpha_2 + \mu + \alpha_1\gamma}. \tag{11c}$$

Thus y_t, p_t and e_t all fluctuate statically in response to the domestic random variables (u_{1t}, u_{2t}) as well as the random variables of foreign origin (q_t, ω_t). Note also that the intervention parameter μ affects the response of all three endogenous variables to all four exogenous random shocks.

Differentiating (11) with respect to μ, we can show that an increase in the degree of exchange market intervention, taking the form of more intensive leaning against the wind, has the following effects on the domestic economy. It reduces the impact of disturbances in the domestic monetary sector or in the foreign nominal interest rate on all three variables y_t, p_t and e_t. An increase in μ raises the effect of a domestic supply shock u_{2t} on output, while lowering the effects on the domestic price level and the exchange rate. Finally, an increase in μ raises the effect of a positive foreign price disturbance on y_t and p_t, but reduces the appreciation of the domestic currency.

The following intuitive explanation for the domestic disturbances may be given. An increase in the domestic demand for money tends to raise the domestic interest rate, leading to an appreciation of the domestic currency, which in turn leads to a fall in the domestic price level and a contraction in domestic output. If the monetary authority responds to the appreciating domestic exchange rate by a monetary expansion, this will generate an offsetting expansionary effect, thereby reducing the fall in y_t, p_t and e_t. A positive supply disturbance raises income, lowering the domestic price level, causing the domestic currency to appreciate. If the monetary authority responds by increasing the money supply, output will increase further, thereby reducing the fall in the domestic price level. The foreign disturbance effects can be discussed similarly.

OPTIMAL EXCHANGE MARKET INTERVENTION

The typical approach to the question of the optimal degree of intervention is to choose μ so as to minimize some objective function expressed in terms of the asymptotic variances of relevant endogenous variables in the economy. In Turnovsky (1983) the objective was specified to be a weighted average of the variances of domestic real output and the domestic price level. Even for this simple model the determination of the optimal intervention μ turns out to be extremely complicated. However, two general conclusions can be established. First, the optimal intervention parameter, $\hat{\mu}$, does not in general equal ∞ or 0, so that neither fixed nor flexible rates, which correspond to these extreme values, are generally optimal. Secondly, the optimal policy may involve either leaning against the wind ($\mu > 0$) or leaning with the wind ($\mu < 0$).

Because of the intractability of the general expression for the optimum, we find it convenient to focus on the optimal intervention policy corresponding to the separate individual random disturbances, taken one at a time, when our analysis can be conducted graphically. To do this it is helpful to rewrite (5) in terms of the following four equations, where in accordance with (10) expectations have been set to zero:

EMP:

$$m_t = (1 + \alpha_2 + \alpha_1\gamma)e_t + u_{1t} + \alpha_1 u_{2t} + (1 + \alpha_1\gamma)q_t - \alpha_2\,\omega_t \tag{12a}$$

OP:

$$m_t = -\mu e_t \tag{12b}$$

SS:

$$y_t = \gamma e_t + u_{2t} + \gamma q_t \tag{13a}$$

LM:

$$m_t = \alpha_1 y_t + (1 + \alpha_2)e_t + u_{1t} + q_t - \alpha_2\,\omega_t. \tag{13b}$$

Equation (12a), obtained by combining equations (5a), (5b) and (5d), describes a locus between m_t and e_t, i.e. it describes the trade-off faced by the domestic monetary authority between exchange rate movements (e_t) and movements in international reserves, which are reflected in the domestic money supply (m_t). The coefficient of e_t in this relationship is positive, reflecting the fact that the monetary authorities can appreciate the value of the currency (reduce e_t) only by selling foreign reserves against domestic currency (reducing m_t). This relationship between m_t and e_t reflects the degree of exchange market pressure (EMP), a concept introduced by Girton and Roper (1977) and also used by Roper and Turnovsky (1980). For zero values of the disturbance terms, the EMP line goes through the origin—there is no pressure on the exchange market. Positive exchange market pressure is represented by schedules having negative intercepts. For instance, if there is an increase in u_{1t} (demand for domestic money), the EMP curve will shift to the left. An increase in the foreign interest rate (increase in ω_t) causes downward pressure in the market and a rightward shift of the schedule. Such shifts are illustrated in figures 7.1–7.5.

Given the current values of the random terms, the EMP schedule indicates the volume of intervention necessary to achieve any desired exchange rate target. If the domestic authority pursues a fixed exchange rate policy, the necessary intervention will be given by the intersection of the EMP schedule with the horizontal axis. If the authority pursues a clean float, the exchange rate will be the market clearing rate given by the intersection of the EMP line with the vertical axis. If the authority absorbs part of the market pressure in the rate and part through intervention, a point on the EMP schedule between these two points of intervention will be chosen. The range of such policy options is indicated by equation (12b), which we denote the OP line. This is negatively sloped for a policy of leaning against the wind and positively sloped otherwise.

The next equation, (13a), is just the domestic supply function, which we call the SS curve, while the final equation is the LM curve. In both cases, the domestic price level has been eliminated by using the PPP condition, so that both these equations are expressed in terms of relationships between domestic output y_t and the exchange rate e_t.

These four equations enable us to consider the effects of exchange market intervention and optimal intervention by focusing on: (i) domestic ouput, (ii) the exchange rate, (iii) the domestic money supply. We shall consider the stabilization of domestic output as being the prime objective, although possible conflicts of this with other objectives may be noted. We shall deal with the domestic and foreign disturbances in turn.

Domestic disturbances

Domestic monetary disturbance u_{1t}

From the solution (11a)–(11b) it is seen that the perfectly fixed rate regime, $\mu = \infty$, has the property of stabilizing y_t, p_t perfectly. The economic explanation for this is straightforward. Given that the domestic price level is determined by PPP, it follows that if e_t is fixed, and there are no disturbances in q_t, then p_t must be fixed as well. It then follows from the domestic output supply function that if p_t is fixed and if in addition (i) price expectations are static (as (10) implies), and (ii) there are no disturbances in domestic supply, then domestic output itself must also remain fixed.

The perfect stability of y_t and p_t can also be viewed as an example of the following general characteristic. The current observability of certain market variables implies information on the sources of the random shocks in the economy. More specifically, the observability of m_t and e_t is equivalent to the observability of the linear combination of random variables $u_{1t} + \alpha_1 u_{2t} + (1 + \alpha_1 \gamma)q_t - \alpha_2 \omega_t$; see (12a). When only one random variable is present, it follows that the observability of this linear combination of disturbances reduces to the observability of the random variable itself, which may therefore be appropriately offset, thereby maintaining perfect stability of at least one endogenous variable of the system. The result that both y_t and p_t can be stabilized perfectly follows directly from the fact that for this particular disturbance they move proportionately; see (13a).

The same result can be shown graphically in figure 7.1, using the EMP curve. Suppose that initially u_{1t} (and all other random variables) are zero, so that the EMP, OP, SS and LM curves all pass through the origin. A positive disturbance in the domestic demand for money produces positive exchange market pressure. This is indicated in the left-hand graph of figure 7.1 by the EMP curve having the negative intercept. The LM curve, drawn in the right-hand graph, is also shifted down by the monetary disturbance to LM_f while the SS curve remains unchanged.

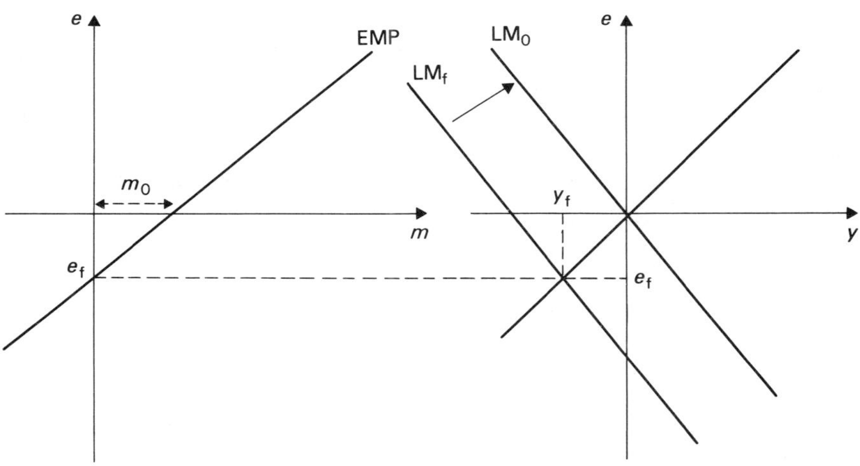

FIGURE 7.1 Domestic monetary disturbance

We now consider the various responses of the increase in exchange market pressure. If the domestic monetary authority follows a pure float and keeps the money supply constant ($m_t = 0$), then the exchange rate falls to the market clearing rate, e_f, and domestic output falls correspondingly to y_f. If the monetary authority maintains a fixed rate by creating domestic money of the amount m_0 (shown in the left-hand graph), the LM curve will shift back to LM_0 and both income and the exchange rate (and the domestic price level) will be stabilized at their original levels.

Domestic supply disturbance u_{2t}

Referring to (11a)–(11c), it is seen that while the fixed rate $\mu = \infty$ will stabilize the domestic price level exactly, this will maximize the instability of domestic real income. On the other hand, income will be stabilized perfectly by adopting the policy of leaning with the wind in accordance with the rule $\mu = -(1 + \alpha_2)$. It is thus impossible to stabilize both p_t and y_t exactly in the face of domestic supply disturbances and a trade-off between the stability of the two variables must be made.

Most discussions of intervention policy limit their attention to parameters which characterize leaning against the wind. The intuitive idea is that such a policy will alleviate fluctuations in the exchange rate, thereby increasing the stability within the economy. The fact that an optimal policy may involve exacerbating swings in the exchange rate is therefore of interest and merits further comment. When the only disturbance is in u_{2t}, equations (12b), (13a) and (13b) may be combined to yield

$$-\mu e_t = (1 + \alpha_2)e_t + \alpha_1 y_t \tag{12b$'$}$$

$$y_t = \gamma e_t + u_{2t}. \tag{13a$'$}$$

It is evident from (12b′) that a policy of leaning with the wind ($\mu < 0$) will tend to provide greater insulation for y_t from the random disturbance u_{2t}, forcing it to be absorbed more fully by the exchange rate. Thus if, for instance, the exchange rate tends to appreciate, the domestic interest rate must take on higher values and m_t must be contracted to keep y_t from rising. If the objective function puts most of the weight on the stabilization of output, this strategy is clearly appropriate.

A graphical illustration of this case is given in figure 7.2. The positive supply shock u_{2t} creates positive exchange market pressure, shifting the EMP curve downwards by an amount $\alpha_1/(1 + \alpha_2 + \alpha_1\gamma)$. At the same time the SS curve is shifted downwards by the greater quantity $1/\gamma$. With a perfectly flexible rate, the exchange rate will appreciate to e_f, corresponding to which output is increased (through the supply shock) to y_f. If the monetary authority now responds to the appreciation in the exchange rate by contracting the money supply by an amount m_0, the LM curve will shift down-

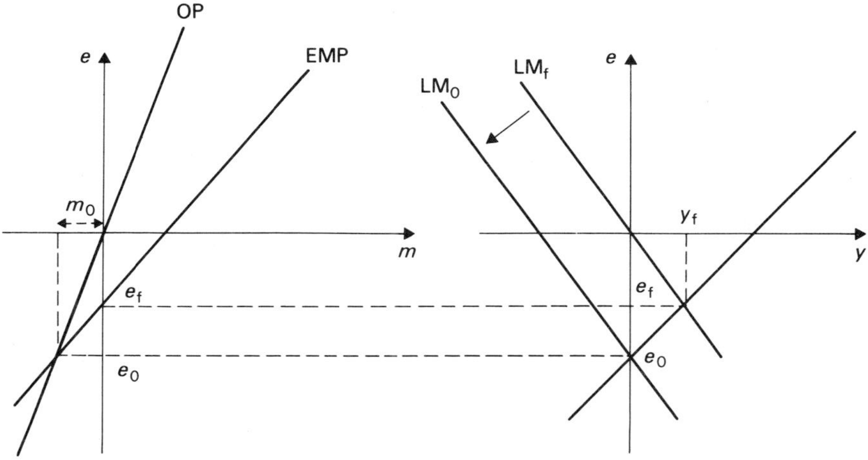

FIGURE 7.2 Domestic output supply disturbance

wards to LM_0. The intersection of that curve and the SS curve ensures that output is stabilized at its original level, while the appreciation of the exchange rate is increased to e_0. The OP line, drawn in the left-hand figure, has positive slope, reflecting the fact that the policy is one of leaning with the wind.

Foreign disturbances

We now turn our attention to the foreign disturbances, which impinge on the economy through q_t and ω_t. Initially we shall treat both of these in turn, although, as noted earlier, they are in fact endogenous, reflecting more fundamental disturbances abroad. To illustrate this, we shall also consider the case of a foreign monetary disturbance, when q_t and ω_t will be disturbed in opposite ways.

Foreign price disturbance

From the solutions (11a)–(11c) it is seen that the leaning-with-the-wind policy $\mu = -\alpha_2$ will stabilize both income and the domestic price level perfectly. This case is illustrated in figure 7.3. The positive disturbance in the foreign price level creates positive exchange market pressure, causing the EMP curve to shift down. Both the LM curve and the SS curve are also shifted down, the former by a lesser amount, the latter by a larger amount than the downward shift in the EMP curve. With a perfectly flexible rate, the exchange rate appreciates to the market clearing rate e_f, with output increased to y_f. If in response to the appreciating exchange rate, the monetary authority engage in a monetary contraction of m_0, the LM curve will

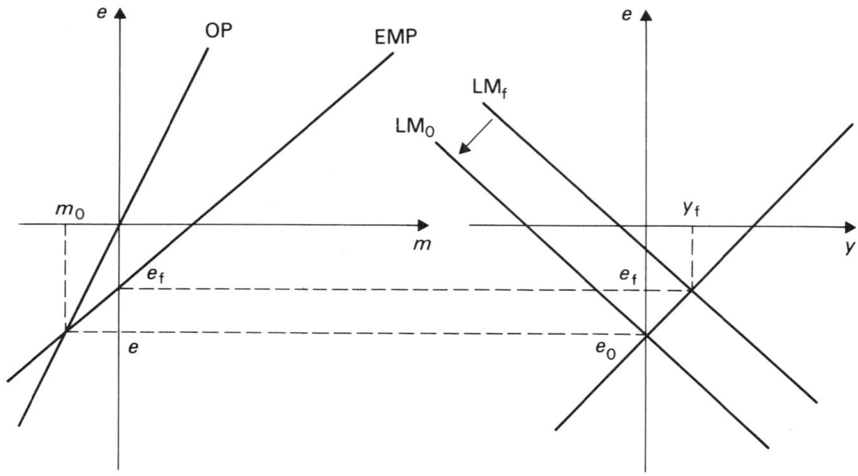

FIGURE 7.3 Foreign price disturbance

shift down to LM_0 and output will be stabilized perfectly at its original level. Corresponding to this policy response, the exchange rate will appreciate further to e_0, which again involves a policy of leaning with the wind.

Foreign interest rate disturbances

This case is equivalent to a stochastic fall in the demand for money and, as in that case, perfect stability can be achieved by adopting a perfectly fixed exchange rate. The policy response is illustrated in figure 7.4, which is just the reverse of figure 7.1 and is therefore self-explanatory.

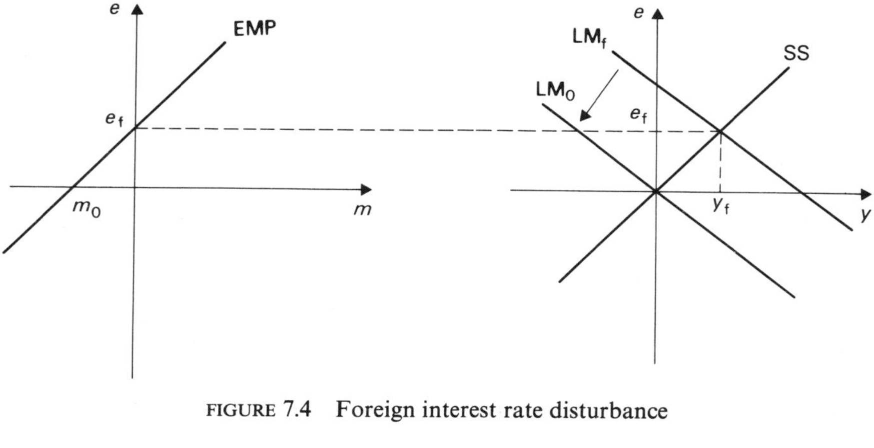

FIGURE 7.4 Foreign interest rate disturbance

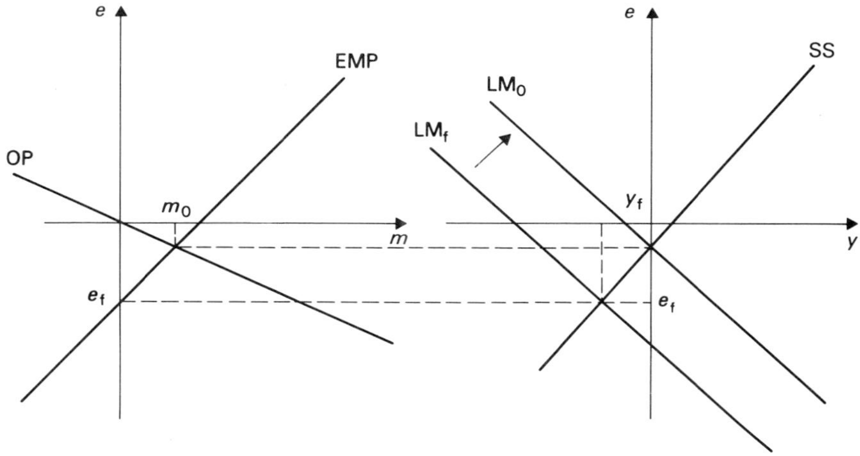

FIGURE 7.5 Foreign monetary expansion

Foreign monetary disturbance

Finally, we shall combine (i) and (ii) to illustrate the effect of a random foreign monetary expansion, which simultaneously raises q_t and lowers ω_t, leading to downward shifts in the EMP, SS and LM curves. From the underlying model for the rest of the world it can be established that the downward shift in the LM curve exceeds that of the EMP curve, which in turn exceeds that of the SS curve. This is illustrated in figure 7.5. With a perfectly flexible rate, the exchange rate appreciates to the market clearing level e_f, while output falls to y_f. If the monetary authority responds to this appreciating exchange rate and expands the domestic money supply by an amount of m_0, the LM curve shifts back up to LM_0 and output is stabilized perfectly at its original level. In this case, the OP curve is negatively sloping, reflecting the fact that the optimal policy is now one of leaning against the wind.

IMPERFECT CAPITAL MOBILITY

An important implication of the assumptions of perfect capital mobility and the time independence of all stochastic disturbances, adopted in the previous sections, is that all expectations are static. In particular, the exchange rate is always expected to equal its long-run equilibrium rate, and hence exchange rate expectations turn out to play a minimal role in the adjustment of the economy to various disturbances. As a consequence, the stable solution is one in which the economy fluctuates about a stationary equilibrium. While this turns out to be very convenient for expositional purposes, it is not particularly realistic. In this section, we briefly indicate some of the issues which are raised when the analysis is extended to allow for the possibility that capital is only imperfectly mobile internationally. This case turns out to be considerably more complicated computationally. We should emphasize that the comments we shall make are only preliminary and that we intend to pursue some of the issues raised in more detail in subsequent work.

The critical relationship which must now be taken into account is the foreign exchange market. This is described by

$$\frac{E'_t \Delta F_t}{P'_t} + \frac{E'_t \Delta B_t}{P'_t} = \frac{\Delta F_t}{Q'_t} + \frac{\Delta B_t}{Q'_t} = C_t \tag{14}$$

where F_t = level of foreign reserves denominated in foreign currency and measured in natural units; B_t = net position of the domestic economy in foreign bonds, measured in natural units; C_t = current account balance, measured in natural units; and E', P', Q' denote the exchange rate, the domestic price level and the foreign price level, all measured in natural units. Because of PPP, $P' = Q'E'$, use of which has been made in (14).

It is convenient to specify the domestic economy's net position in foreign bonds to be proportional to the uncovered interest differential in accordance with

$$B_t/Q_t = \eta(e^*_{t+1,t} - e_t + \omega_t - r_t), \qquad \eta > 0. \tag{15}$$

The coefficient η parametrizes the degree of capital mobility. The limiting case of perfect capital mobility, analysed in previous sections, is obtained by letting $\eta \rightarrow \infty$, when (15) reduces to the uncovered interest rate parity condition. Otherwise, for a finite degree of capital mobility, the gradual accumulation of foreign assets described by (14) imposes a sluggish adjustment process on the economy.[7]

An important consequence of this is that the stable rational expectations solution to the system involves a first-order adjustment, so that exchange rate expectations formed at time t, say, depend upon the state of the economy at that time. The stationarity characteristic of the solution under perfect capital mobility is lost. Thus one can contrast the effects of disturbances on both the short-run and long-run (asymptotic) stability of the system and generally both will be influenced by the degree of exchange market intervention, as will be the dynamic speed of adjustment.

The relaxation of the assumption of perfect capital mobility introduces other issues which are important. First, with investors being risk averse (an assumption implicit in the rejection of uncovered interest parity), there is a genuine role for a forward market and for forward market intervention. This raises the question of fixed versus forward market intervention and the scope for each. These issues are taken up at some length by Eaton and Turnovsky (1984).

Secondly, there is the endogeneity of the parameter η and its dependence upon the intervention parameter μ. At issue here is the following. While the specification of the bond demand function (15) is *ad hoc*, formulations of this form can be derived from two-period mean–variance optimization. In this case, the elasticity of speculation η is inversely related to the coefficient of relative risk aversion, R say, and the one-period variance in the spot exchange rate, $\sigma_e^2(1)$, i.e.

$$\eta \simeq \frac{1}{R\sigma_e^2(1)}.$$

As long as the one-period variance remains fixed, η can quite legitimately be treated as parametric. However, exchange market intervention will in general influence the stability of the exchange rate, so that through $\sigma_e^2(1)$, η becomes a function of μ. Thus, for example, intervention by the monetary authority which stabilizes the spot rate (reduces $\sigma_e^2(1)$) will encourage private speculation. This interaction between the behaviour of the private and public sector needs to be taken into account, particularly in the determination of optimal intervention policy. In fact, when one allows for the endogeneity of the parameters, the rational expectations model becomes inherently non-linear. This immediately raises questions of the possible non-existence of equilibrium, an issue which arises in other contexts and may occur here as well (see McCafferty and Driskill, 1980).

CONCLUDING REMARKS

This paper has analysed the question of exchange market intervention for a small open economy. In order to keep the exposition as simple as possible, the model has been kept as simple as possible. However, even for such a simple model, no strong conclusions emerge. In general, it is seen that the optimal policy may require the monetary authorities to lean with the wind or to lean against the wind, depending upon the source of the random disturbance impinging on the domestic economy. Most policy discussions of intervention policy have been expressed in terms of the domestic monetary authorities responding to downward exchange market pressure by adopting a contractionary policy. The fact that precisely the opposite may in fact be appropriate for maximizing domestic stability is quite significant.

A second general conclusion to be drawn, and to some degree a corollary of the first, is that the case for a perfectly flexible exchange rate is not very great, at least not from the viewpoint of domestic stability. Whereas, under appropriate circumstances—e.g. if the disturbances originate in the domestic monetary sector—a fixed exchange rate may be optimal, this is not the case for flexible rates, unless appropriate coefficients take on extreme values.[8] Furthermore, a fixed exchange rate may provide greater stability in circumstances where traditionally flexible rates may be thought to be superior. For example, abstracting from capital gains resulting from the effects of exchange rate changes on the components of wealth denominated in different currencies—an issue not addressed in the present analysis—it is sometimes argued that flexible rates will provide perfect insulation in the face of foreign monetary disturbances. Using the present model it can be shown that this is not so. On the contrary, it can be shown that a fixed exchange rate may be superior, even in this case. This will be so if, e.g., the domestic interest elasticity of the demand for money is sufficiently high (see Turnovsky, 1983).

Obviously it is difficult to extrapolate the implications of a simple model such as this to provide reliable guidance to real-world intervention policies. But the conclusions of our analysis do suggest that the appropriate choice of policy is an extremely difficult one, being highly sensitive to relevant parameters in the domestic economy and the rest of the world, as well as the relative importance of the various sources of the random disturbances impinging on the economy. Clearly, reliable information on these empirical issues is a necessary ingredient for the implementation of appropriate intervention policies.

NOTES

1 It is, of course, possible to formulate control laws in terms of current data, as well as past data, provided that the current data are immediately observable. Indeed, this is what is proposed here.

2 Other recent contributions to intervention policy which should be mentioned include Henderson (1979) and Cox (1980).

3 For simplicity we abstract from all issues pertaining to wealth accumulation.

4 We therefore abstract from the possibility of 'currency substitution' an issue which is receiving increasing attention in the international monetary literature.

5 In deriving the optimal intervention policy, it is important to distinguish between those variables that the authority can in effect currently observe, and those that are, at least in the short run, unobservable. Given that data on exchange rates and the money supply are available with much greater frequency than income figures, we shall assume that E_t and M_t are observable and that Y_t is unobservable (at time t). This is one of the reasons why in general policy makers cannot stabilize income perfectly. The period of time for which this assumption is most applicable would be something like a month since income is usually observed only quarterly and weekly money figures have considerable noise.

6 This procedure turns out to make the subsequent determination of the optimal intervention policy rather complicated. Essentially one has to consider the two cases (i) $|\theta| > 1$, (ii) $|\theta| < 1$ separately, and ensure that the optimal policy in each case is consistent with the restrictions applicable to that case. The overall

optimum is obtained by taking the superior of these two cases and also involves a consideration of the boundary cases.

7 This, together with the unstable cost generated through the forward-looking expectations, means that the rational expectations solution is characterized by saddle-point behaviour.

8 For example, a flexible rate will be optimal in the face of foreign disturbances (from all sources) if $\alpha_2 = 0$.

REFERENCES

Boyer, R. (1978) 'Optimal Foreign Exchange Market Intervention', *Journal of Political Economy*, **86**, 1045–1056.

Buiter, W. (1979) 'Optimal Foreign Exchange Market Intervention with Rational Expectations', in J. Martin and A. Smith (eds), *Trade and Payments Adjustment under Flexible Exchange Rates*, Macmillan, London.

Cox, W. M. (1980) 'Unanticipated Money, Output, and Prices in the Small Economy', *Journal of Monetary Economics*, **6**, 359–384.

Eaton, J. and Turnovsky, S. J. (1984) 'The Forward Exchange Market, Speculation, and Exchange Market Intervention', *Quarterly Journal of Economics*, **99**.

Fischer, S. (1977) 'Wage Indexation and Macroeconomic Stability', in K. Brunner and A. Meltzer (eds), *Stabilization of the Domestic and International Economy*, North-Holland, Amsterdam.

Flood, R. (1979) 'Capital Mobility and the Choice of Exchange Rate System', *International Economic Review*, **20**, 405–16.

Girton, L. and Roper, D. E. (1977) 'A Monetary Model of Exchange Market Pressure Applied to the Postwar Canadian Experience', *American Economic Review*, **67**, 537–548.

Gray, J. (1976) 'Wage Indexation: A Macroeconomic Approach', *Journal of Monetary Economics*, **2**, 221–235.

Henderson, D. W. (1979) 'Financial Policies in Open Economics', *American Economic Review, Papers and Proceedings*, **69**, 232–239.

Kareken, J. H., Muench, T. and Wallace, N. (1973) 'Optimal Open Market Strategy: The Use of Information Variables', *American Economic Review*, **63**, 156–172.

Lucas, R. E., Jr (1973) 'Some International Evidence on Output–Inflation Tradeoffs', *American Economic Review*, **63**, 326–334.

McCafferty, S. and Driskill, R. (1980) 'Problems of Existence and Uniqueness in Nonlinear Rational Expectations Models', *Econometrica*, **48**, 1313–1317.

Poole, W. (1970) 'Optimal Choice of Monetary Policy Instruments in a Simple Stochastic Macro Model', *Quarterly Journal of Economics*, **84**, 197–216.

Roper, D. E. and Turnovsky, S. J. (1980) 'Optimal Exchange Market Intervention in a Simple Stochastic Macro Model', *Canadian Journal of Economics*, **13**, 296–309.

Taylor, J. (1977) 'Conditions for Unique Solutions in Stochastic Macroeconomic Models with Rational Expectations', *Econometrica*, **45**, 1377–1385.

Turnovsky, S. J. (1983) 'Exchange Market Intervention in a Small Open Economy', in J. Bhandari and B. Putnam (eds), *The International Transmission of Economic Disturbances*, MIT Press, Cambridge, MA.

Comment

JEAN-PIERRE LAFFARGUE

This paper has the usual qualities of other works by Turnovsky: it is clear, rigorous and interesting. Its interest is first methodological, and secondly is to be found in the conclusions, which are far from trivial. All this made my work as a commentator easy and pleasant and I am grateful to the author for that. My comment will be based around two questions:

(1) Does the model really investigate the effects of exchange market intervention policy?
(2) Are all the conclusions of the paper realistic?

(1) My answer to the first question is: No, the model investigates the effects of monetary policy, and under its particular assumptions, exchange market intervention policy plays almost no role in the economy. Let us examine this point in the model of the second section, corrected by assuming an imperfect capital mobility (equation (15) of the paper).

Equations

Purchasing power parity

$$P_t = Q_t E_t \tag{1}$$

Equilibrium on the money market

$$M_t/P_t = A_1 Y_t^{\alpha_1} r_t^{-\alpha_2} \exp(U_{1t}) \tag{2}$$

Demand of foreign bonds

$$B_t/Q_t = A_2[(1 + \Omega_t)E^*_{t+1,t} - (1 + r_t)E_t]^\eta \tag{3}$$

Supply of domestic output

$$Y_t/\hat{Y} = A_3(P_t/P^*_{t,t-1})^\gamma \exp(U_{2t}) \tag{4}$$

Equality between the quantity of money and its counterparts

$$M_t = F_t/\bar{E} + D_t \tag{5}$$

Equilibrium of the balance of payments

$$C_t(\ \ ) \equiv (B_t - B_{t-1})/Q_t + (F_t - F_{t-1})/Q_t. \tag{6}$$

Endogenous variables

B_t = net position of the domestic economy in foreign bonds, measured in foreign currency units
D_t = credits to the private sector and to the government, measured in domestic currency units
E_t = current exchange rate
P_t = price of the traded good expressed in domestic currency units
r_t = domestic nominal interest rate
Y_t = real domestic output

Exogenous variables

Ω_t = foreign nominal interest rate
Q_t = price of the traded good expressed in foreign currency units

Domestic economic policy variables

M_t = domestic money supply
F_t = level of foreign reserves expressed in foreign currency units

Variables which are either predetermined or rationally expected

$$B_{t-1},\ E^*_{t+1,t},\ P^*_{t,t-1},\ F_{t-1}$$

C_t represents the surplus of the current account balance measured in units of traded good. It depends on various variables of the model in a way that there is no point in mentioning here. In equation (5) I have substituted an accounting exchange rate $\bar{E}$ which is fixed by the domestic central bank, for the current exchange rate E_t: the gains (losses) of capital on foreign reserves, resulting from variations of the exchange rates, have no effect on the domestic money supply, because these gains are sterilized by the central bank. Domestic authorities control two economic policy variables: (1) M_t which defines monetary policy (some may prefer to substitute D_t or r_t for it); (2) F_t which defines exchange market intervention policy (some may prefer to substitute E_t for it).

Now most of the paper makes the particular assumption of perfect capital mobility. This case corresponds to $\eta = \infty$, and (3) becomes

Uncovered interest parity

$$(1 + \Omega_t)E^*_{t+1,t} = (1 + r_t)E_t. \tag{3'}$$

Under this particular assumption the model becomes block recursive. The first block is made up of equations (1) to (4) and determines the dynamic paths of the endogenous variables E_t, P_t, r_t and Y_t when the paths of the exogenous variables Ω_t, Q_t *and only the first* economic policy variable M_t are known. The second block is made up of equation (6): let us assume that the first block determines all the variables of the function $C_t(\ \ )$, i.e. the surplus of the current account balance; then the second economic policy variable F_t allocates this surplus between an increase in the level of foreign reserves, and an increase in the net position of the domestic economy in foreign bonds. The third block is independent of both other blocks: economic policy variables M_t and F_t, and the accounting identity (5), determine the last endogenous variable D_t.

Nothing would have to be changed in these results if instead of having assumed predetermined paths for M_t and F_t, I had assumed the policy reaction functions:

Monetary policy reaction function

$$M_t = \bar{M}(E_t/\bar{E})^{\mu 1}(P_t/\bar{P})^{\mu 2}(r_t/\bar{r})^{\mu 3}(Y_t/\hat{Y})^{\mu 4} \tag{7}$$

Exchange market intervention reaction function

$$F_t = \bar{F}(E_t/\bar{E})^{\mu 1'}(P_t/\bar{P})^{\mu 2'}(r_t/\bar{r})^{\mu 3'}(Y_t/\hat{Y})^{\mu 4'} \tag{8}$$

The first function plays an essential role in the dynamics of the model (which the paper investigates in the particular case where $\mu_2 = \mu_3 = \mu_4 = 0$). The second function plays almost no role, in particular in the determination of the exchange rate, which seems in contradiction with reality. Of course M_t changes may be accompanied by no variation of F_t (if $\mu'_1 = \cdots = \mu'_4 = 0$), i.e. by no official intervention on the exchange market. In this case the fluctuations of D_t (credits to the private sector and the government) follows those of M_t.

(2) Solving the model gives results which at the same time are very simple and non-trivial. One of them is that both the exchange rate and the price level are always expected to equal their long-run equilibria values:

$$e^*_{t+1,t} = p^*_{t+1,t} = 0. \tag{9}$$

Now empirical studies show that the logarithm of the *spot* exchange rate almost follows a martingale:

$$e^*_{t+1,t} \simeq e_t \tag{10}$$

which may differ a lot from zero. This empirical result is in strong contradiction with equation (9). Another way of seeing that this equation is unrealistic is that, under the reasonable assumption of covered interest parity, it implies

$$e^*_{t+1,t} = e_t + r_t = e^{\mathrm{f}}_t = 0 \tag{11}$$

where e_t^f is the forward exchange rate applying to forward exchange contracts of 1 period length. A related point is that (10) implies that the asymptotic variance of e_t is infinite, which contradicts an assumption made in the paper. However, the asymptotic variance of $e_t - e_{t-1}$ is finite and this fact suggests another approach for solving the model.

Comment

JACQUES MELITZ

In this paper, Turnovsky proposes a simple model in which two propositions follow:

(1) A managed float is superior to either a perfect float or a system of fixed rates except as a limiting case.
(2) In the case of a managed float, it may be better to 'lean with the wind' rather than 'against' it.

If the author merely wanted to show that these two propositions could be derived in a fairly simple manner, then he succeeds very nicely. If he wanted to show, however, that both propositions are empirically significant, then I believe that his success is not so great. He picks a subordinate argument for the first proposition, while he defends the second one in a context where the major arguments in favour of 'leaning against the wind' are absent.

Much of the problem lies in Turnovsky's use of a stationary model where the sole source of movement is some white noise. It is very difficult to do justice to the arguments for a managed float, or to the preoccupations of the advocates of 'leaning against the wind', in such a context. In Turnovsky's framework, regardless of fixed, floating, or managed exchange rates, on average, output, prices and exchange rates will be the same. The only issue is one of variances. I take it, however, that the basic argument against a fixed exchange rate is that it means accepting a rate of inflation which is decided by the rest of the world. Of course, this argument does not even make any sense if the rate of inflation will be the same in any case. Similarly, the basic argument against a perfectly floating exchange rate is that exchange rate changes affect relative prices and competitivity, especially during episodes of essential appreciation or depreciation. This means that following any large economic shock there may be important exchange rate effects on the international distribution of output and employment (to say nothing of secondary effects on the world level of output). What Turnovsky effectively does is abstract away from all this and consider what is left as an argument for a managed exchange rate.

What is left is a question of signal extraction. Based on official knowledge of the stochastic structure of the economy, in addition to the deterministic one, the authorities could reduce the asymptotic variance of their target variable(s) by intervening on the foreign exchange market. If they do not act this way, then in Turnovsky's terms they float. This is right in his context, but it is worth noting that it would not be so generally. In a non-stationary world, news can affect the mean values of the monetary instruments that are required simply in order to hit the desired target(s) on average. Thus, even if the authorities do not adopt a feedback rule in order to reduce the variance of their target variable(s), they may still engage in a managed float, as the preceding paragraph suggests.

I have wider objections to Turnovky's treatment of 'leaning against the wind'. Suppose we ask ourselves why the authorities try to reduce rather than to accentuate movements in the parity of their currency on a day-to-day basis in the absence of any basic shifts in policy. There are two important reasons, I believe. One is overshooting. Overshooting is a phenomenon that we have observed significantly in the past 12 years: for example, following the two major oil shocks and some shifts in monetary–fiscal policy in the OECD countries. It usually lasts one, two, or three years. The phenomenon then must be understood in the context of an adjustment to a new equilibrium where, as a result of the adjustment, there is the adoption of a new set of targets. Can we really make a convincing case for the view that monetary authorities may be wrong to 'lean against the wind' if we stick to a model where none of these developments can happen?

Furthermore, 'learning against the wind' is a way to buy time while sorting out information about shifts in the direction of the 'fundamental' winds. Obviously, this too is an impossible argument if 'fundamental' winds are never able to shift. The argument very significantly requires something more that Turnovsky does not allow for: the capacity of the authorities to move faster than households and firms do in their output and price behaviour (i.e. in their actions concerning the target variables). Unless the authorities can move thus faster, they really have no time to sort out things anyhow. But if we allow them the presence of 'fundamental' winds of change and the required time to crystallize their views, then we can make sense of the argument.

To 'lean against the wind' is sometimes to interfere with socially wrong decisions, sometimes with socially right ones. In the case of overshooting, it will be to interfere with wrong decisions. By the very nature of overshooting, some of these decisions, however, as a result, will never happen. In case of undershooting, the action will be to interfere with socially right decisions. However, if only the authorities move fast enough, all of these decisions will still happen after recognition that they should not be interfered with. In one case then, the policy cuts down on harmful choices, while in the other, it merely defers right ones, and the argument would be that the benefits outweigh the costs. What if there is neither over- nor undershooting, but only white noise? This is then the limited case where Turnovsky's argument applies. I conclude that his argument is insufficient to raise any fundamental doubt about the wisdom of 'leaning against the wind'.

I also have one criticism of the exposition and formal analysis. The fourth section of the paper can be understood as saying that, depending upon the individual source of a change in the exchange rate, the authorities ought to respond differently. As Turnovsky is very well aware, however, this is rather misleading. In the problem at hand, the authorities are not supposed to be able to tell the source of a change in the exchange rate. Consequently, they must respond to every movement in the rate in a uniform way. Sometimes this will mean exacerbating the impact on the target variable(s). But over a large number of trials, it will mean the opposite on the whole. We know this since the official action reduces the *asymptotic* variance of the target variable around the target mean. This fourth section therefore should have been framed in terms of optimal official responses (values of μ) under different stochastic structures of the economy rather than in terms of optimal responses to different individual disturbances. That is, the section should have treated alternative values of σ^2_{u1}, σ^2_{u2}, σ^2_q and σ^2_ω, rather than alternative values of u_1, u_2, q and ω.

There is a further, related problem since two of the disturbances in Turnovsky's analysis can be observed directly: namely, the two foreign ones, q and ω. q can be seen through Q, the price of the world traded good, ω through Ω, the foreign interest rate. (Turnovsky could have avoided this problem in the case of Q by assuming a lag in the observation of this price, but he could hardly have done the same in the case of Ω.) Consequently, the authorities should never respond to q and ω based on information extracted from E, the exchange rate. Rather the exchange rate should serve them only as a signal about u_1 and u_2. More exactly, Turnovsky's reaction function, or supply of money, should be written

$$M_t = \bar{M} + \mu_1(E - \bar{E}) + \mu_2(Q - \bar{Q}) + \mu_3(\Omega - \bar{\Omega})$$

where

$$\mu_1 \gtrless 0, \qquad \mu_2 > 0, \qquad \mu_3 < 0$$

rather than as $M_t = \bar{M} - \mu(E - \bar{E})$, or his equation (1d). If we think about it, there is no reason why the world security price should not be as much a source of information as the exchange rate in a model where both home and foreign disturbances are present. This is a problem also affecting Turnovsky's recent paper with Roper in the May 1980 *Canadian Journal of Economics*.

PART THREE

New Approaches to Macroeconomic Modelling

8

Monetary, Fiscal and Exchange Rate Policy in a Continuous-Time Econometric Model of the United Kingdom

A. R. BERGSTROM

> It is only if we have complete confidence in our ability to control economic pressures, whatever their strength (and to control them at the precise time when they need to be controlled), that the sort of understanding given by Keynes is enough. Otherwise we must know something about the longer-run consequences of policies; we must have an assurance that policies adopted, to deal with a momentary emergency, will not set up, in the longer run, pressures which are greater than we can hope to withstand. (Hicks, *The Trade Cycle*)

INTRODUCTION

Although the above warning statement was written by Hicks (1950) over 30 years ago, and may seem obvious today, I believe that it has been insufficiently heeded by economists and that some of the econometric models being used as a guide to policy can be very misleading with regard to the longer-run effects of these policies. Perhaps the main reason for this is that those structural parameters whose values influence mainly the long-run behaviour of the system are much more difficult to estimate than the parameters whose values have an important effect on its short-run behaviour; and, consequently, important long-run feedbacks are left out of some models. Another reason is that the long-run behaviour of most large econometric models can be studied only by simulation on a computer. Such simulations have shown that some of these models are incapable of generating plausible long-run behaviour except for special paths of the exogenous variables (see the articles contained in Hickman, 1972). But, since they are not amenable to mathematical analysis, it is difficult to determine which structural features of the model are responsible for this.

The model that will be used in this paper (see Bergstrom and Wymer, 1976) was constructed primarily in order to demonstrate the feasibility of methods of estimating the structural parameters of continuous-time dynamic models (see Bergstrom, 1976; and Gandolfo, 1981). But, in addition to being a continuous-time model, it has other features which distinguish it from most earlier econometric models of complete economies. One is that it is a closely integrated system that makes intensive use of economic theory in order to obtain cross equation restrictions on the parameters. This has resulted in very low asymptotic standard errors for the parameter estimates, particularly for those parameters that have an important influence on the long-run behaviour of the system. Another feature is its amenability to mathematical analysis. In particular, the steady-state solution and the conditions for its asymptotic stability can be expressed explicitly in terms of the structural parameters. These features of the model are very advantageous for the purpose for which the model will be used in this paper; that is, for the study of the long-run effects of introducing various policy feedbacks.

The model does contain an estimated monetary feedback relation which shows the response of the money supply (M_1) to variations in the balance of payments and is capable of ensuring external balance, in the steady state, with a fixed exchange rate. It was not possible to obtain reliable estimates of the independent influence on the money supply of other variables such as employment and output. But the effects of allowing employment or output (in addition to the balance of payments) to influence the money supply were studied in a subsequent article (Bergstrom, 1978). In this paper we shall extend the results given in that article by comparing the effects of several alternative policy rules involving three distinct policy variables: (1) the money supply, (2) the exchange rate, and (3) a fiscal policy variable, which will be precisely defined later.

These policy variables are best regarded as target control variables rather than instruments over which the government and the Bank of England have direct control. An extended version of the Bergstrom–Wymer model was produced later by Knight and Wymer (1978) who introduced variables which would be more directly controllable. But, in this paper, we shall work with the original model, the fact that the policy variables are only indirectly controllable being recognized by allowing these variables to adjust only gradually, rather than instantaneously, in response to changes in output and the balance of payments. A detailed discussion of the extent to which the three policy variables can be independently controlled is beyond the scope of this paper. But it should be observed that the Public Sector Borrowing Requirement (PSBR) can be financed in three distinct ways: (1) by domestic credit creation, (2) by selling bonds on the domestic market, and (3) by foreign borrowing (which is partly a reflection of official intervention in the foreign exchange markets). The division of the financing of the PSBR between these three ways provides two degrees of freedom. A third degree of freedom is provided by variations in the size of the PSBR. There are, therefore, three degrees of freedom altogether, and these should permit some independent control over the three policy variables.

The following section will be devoted to a brief description of the Bergstrom–Wymer model and its steady-state and stability properties. A full discussion of the properties of the model, the method of estimating its parameters and its predictive performance is given in Bergstrom and Wymer (1976). The results obtained in the later article (Bergstrom, 1978) for the effects of policy feedbacks from employment or output to the money supply will be reproduced in the third section of this paper. The new results which relate to the effects of feedbacks involving a fiscal policy variable and the exchange rate will be presented in the fourth and fifth sections and some conclusions drawn in the final section.

THE ESTIMATED MODEL

The model of Bergstrom and Wymer (1976) is a closed system of 13 first-order differential equations based on a prototype cyclical growth model discussed in Bergstrom (1967: chapter 5). It is highly aggregative being, formally, a model of a single sector economy whose product can be used for consumption (private and public), capital formation (private or public) or export. Estimates were obtained, from 1955–66 quarterly data, by first linearizing the differential equations about the sample means and then estimating the equivalent exact discrete model taking full account of the complicated non-linear, cross equation restrictions on the latter model implied by the structure of the continuous-time model. The estimated equations (with t values in parentheses) are as follows:

$$\frac{\mathrm{D}C}{C} = \underset{(5.71)}{0.2454} \log \left[\frac{\overset{(215.18)}{0.9206}\, Y}{C} \right] \tag{1}$$

$$\frac{\mathrm{D}L}{L} = \underset{(4.08)}{0.0990} \log \left[\frac{\overset{(108.04)}{0.0037} \exp(-\overset{(17.29)}{0.0058}t)\,(Y^{-1} - \overset{(24.07)}{1.2180} K^{-1})^{-1}}{L} \right] \tag{2}$$

$$\mathrm{D}k = \underset{(3.36)}{0.0886} \left\{ \underset{(3.87)}{1.1492} \left[\underset{(24.07)}{1.12180} \right] \left(\frac{Y}{K}\right)^2 - r + \frac{\mathrm{D}p}{p} + \underset{(1.52)}{0.0042} - k \right\} \tag{3}$$

$$\mathrm{D}Y = \underset{(5.25)}{0.6437} \left[(1 - \underset{(76.46)}{0.1632})(C + \mathrm{D}K + E) - Y \right] \tag{4}$$

$$\mathrm{D}I = \underset{(3.51)}{0.3486}\,[\underset{(75.46)}{0.1632}(C + \mathrm{D}K + E) - I] + \underset{(7.72)}{0.0448}\,[\underset{(66.15)}{1.5263}(C + \mathrm{D}K + E) - S] \tag{5}$$

$$\frac{\mathrm{D}E}{E} = \underset{(4.18)}{0.2926} \log\left[\frac{\overset{(62.11)}{1365}p^{-1} \exp(\overset{(13.49)}{0.0113}t)}{E}\right] \tag{6}$$

$$\frac{\mathrm{D}p}{p} = \underset{(3.40)}{0.1312} \log\left[\frac{\overset{(108.04)}{0.0037}\, w \exp(\overset{(17.29)}{-0.0058}t)\,[1 - \overset{(24.07)}{1.2180}(Y/K)]^{-2}}{p}\right] \tag{7}$$

$$\frac{\mathrm{D}w}{w} = \underset{(2.85)}{0.1047} \log\left[\frac{\overset{(108.04)}{0.0037}\ \exp(\overset{(17.29)}{-0.0058}t)\,(Y^{-1} - \overset{(24.07)}{1.2180}\,K^{-1})^{-1}}{\underset{(34.57)}{22.1379} \exp(\underset{(0.85)}{0.0008}t)}\right] \tag{8}$$

$$\frac{\mathrm{D}r}{r} = \underset{(1.33)}{0.1990} \log\left[\frac{\overset{(0.62)}{0.0537}p\ Yr^{\overset{(2.08)}{-0.8289}}}{M}\right] \tag{9}$$

$$\mathrm{D}m = \underset{(2.69)}{0.0422} \log\left(\frac{E}{I}\right) + \underset{(4.68)}{0.1562}\, \mathrm{D} \log\left(\frac{E}{I}\right) \tag{10}$$

$$\mathrm{D}S = Y + I - C - \mathrm{D}K - E \tag{11}$$

$$\frac{\mathrm{D}K}{K} = k \tag{12}$$

$$\frac{\mathrm{D}M}{M} = m \tag{13}$$

where C = real consumption, Y = real net income or output, K = amount of fixed capital, E = real exports, I = real expenditure on imports, S = stocks, L = employment, M = volume of money, r = interest rate, p = price level, w = wage rate, k = proportional rate of increase in amount of fixed capital, m = proportional rate of increase in volume of money, t = time, and $\mathrm{D} = \mathrm{d}/\mathrm{d}t$.

Equation (1) is a form of consumption function in which consumption adjusts gradually, rather than instantaneously, to a change in income. Corresponding to any level of income Y there is a partial equilibrium level of consumption $0.9206Y$, and, at each point of time, the proportional rate of increase in consumption is an increasing function of the proportional excess of partial equilibrium consumption over actual consumption. The equation implies that the logarithm of consumption depends, with an exponentially distributed time lag, on the logarithm of income, the mean of the time lag distribution being the reciprocal of the speed of adjustment parameter 0.2454, or about 12 months. It should be noted that, since C includes both private and public consumption, the parameter 0.9206 reflects not only the private propensity to save but also the taxation rate and the government propensity to spend during the sample period. The equation implies, therefore, that fiscal policy was, in a certain sense, neutral over the sample period. This assumption will be relaxed in the fourth section.

It is necessary, before discussing the next few equations, to say something about the underlying assumptions about firm behaviour. It is assumed that the economy is made up of a large number of monopolistic competitors with identical production functions and uniformly differentiated products. In a position of static equilibrium each firm would be employing labour and capital in proportions which make the marginal technical rate of substitution equal to the ratio of the real wage rate to the real interest rate, setting the price of its product equal to marginal cost plus a margin depending on the own-price elasticity of the partial demand function and producing the amount demanded at that price. Since the prices charged by the different firms are equal the economy can be treated as a single product economy, and it tends to a perfectly competitive economy as the degree of differentiation between the products tends to zero, i.e. as the elasticity of the partial demand function for each firm's product tends to minus infinity. (When the model was estimated we were unable to reject this limiting case.)

In order to obtain the dynamic behaviour of the firms we should, ideally, introduce adjustment costs into the production function and derive factor demand and output adjustment equations simultaneously by solving a dynamic optimization problem. Instead we assume that the firm follows simpler rules which implicitly recognize the fact that output can be adjusted more easily (in the short run) than the number of persons employed, because of the possibility of overtime working, and the number of persons employed can be adjusted more easily than the amount of capital. We assume, therefore, that output adjusts in response to sales, that the number of persons employed adjusts in response to output (with the stock of capital taken as given) and that the stock of capital adjusts in response to the difference between the marginal product of capital and the real interest rate. These rules together with the pricing rule are consistent with the static equilibrium condition described in the previous paragraph.

The employment equation (2) is of the same general form as (1). The partial equilibrium level of employment is related to output and the stock of fixed capital by a form of production function in which there is an assumed constant elasticity of substitution 0.5 between labour and capital and Harrod neutral technical progress. The capital intensity parameter

1.218 implies that the average elasticity of output with respect to capital, over the sample period, was 0.13. The technical progress parameter 0.0058 implies that there is a decrease at the instantaneous rate 2.3 per cent per annum in the amount of labour required to produce a given output with a given amount of capital. The speed of adjustment parameter 0.0990 implies a mean time lag of about $2\frac{1}{2}$ years for the adjustment of employment to a change in output. The high degree of precision with which all of these parameters are estimated is a result of the fact that they occur in equations (2), (3), (7) and (8), and the method of estimation makes full use of all cross equation restrictions.

Equation (3) is a second-order differential equation in K and implies, therefore, that the stock of fixed capital depends with a rather complicated distributed time lag on output Y and the real interest rate $r - \mathrm{D}p/p$. Corresponding to any real interest rate and capital output ratio, there is a partial equilibrium proportional rate of increase in the stock of fixed capital, and, at each point of time, the actual rate of increase in capital is increasing at a rate proportional to the excess of the partial equilibrium rate over the actual rate. The partial equilibrium rate of increase in capital is a linear function of the excess of the marginal product of capital 1.2180 $(Y/K)^2$ over the real interest rate. The parameter 0.0042, which reflects entrepreneurs' growth expectations and willingness to take risks, implies that when the marginal product of capital equals the real interest rate the partial equilibrium rate of increase in capital is about 1.6 per cent per annum. The parameter 1.1492 implies that an increase in the real interest rate from, say, 4 per cent per annum to 5 per cent per annum will reduce the partial equilibrium rate of increase in capital from, say 4.5 per cent per annum to 3.35 per cent per annum, or by 25 per cent. The parameter 0.0886 implies a mean time lag of about 3 years for the adjustment of investment to a change in the real interest rate or the marginal product of capital.

Equations (4) and (5) are the production and import adjustment equations and are closely related. The term $C + \mathrm{D}K + E$ equals total sales for consumption, capital formation and export. The parameters 0.1632 and 1.5262 are the partial equilibrium ratios of imports and stocks respectively to sales. Equation (4) implies, therefore, that the increase in output depends on the excess demand for home-produced goods to meet current sales, while equation (5) implies that the rate of increase in imports depends on the excess demand for imports to meet current sales and excess stocks. The coefficient 0.6437 implies a mean time lag of $4\frac{1}{2}$ months for the adjustment of output to a change in sales, while the coefficient 0.3486 implies a mean time lag of 9 months for the adjustment of imports to a change in sales. It was not possible to obtain reliable estimates of the independent influence of excess stocks on the rate of increase in output (the estimated adjustment coefficient being insignificant with the wrong sign). But the parameter 0.0448 measuring the influence of excess stocks on imports is very significant. Since the variable I, like all other real variables in the model, is obtained by deflating the value at current prices by the implicit price deflator of the gross domestic product, equation (5) implies that the elasticity of substitution between imports and home-produced goods is -1.0 and not 0 as it would do if I represented the volume of imports.

Equation (6) is essentially a demand equation for exports. The partial equilibrium level of exports depends on the domestic price level with an assumed elasticity -1.0, and a trend term which allows for the gradual increase in income and prices in the rest of the world. The trend coefficient 0.0113 implies a growth rate of 4.5 per cent per annum. The coefficient 0.2926 implies a mean time lag of 10 months for the adjustment of exports to a change in the domestic price level (or a change in the exchange rate). The parameter 1365 reflects the exchange rate during the sample period and was adjusted to allow for the 1967 devaluation when testing the post-sample predictive performance of the model. It will be treated as a variable in the fifth section when we consider a flexible exchange rate policy.

In the price adjustment equation (7) the partial equilibrium price level equals marginal cost $w(\partial L/\partial Y)$ where the partial derivative $\partial L/\partial Y$ is obtained from the production function in equation (2). The mark-up for imperfect competition was restricted to zero since a preliminary estimate of this parameter was negative and insignificant. The coefficient 0.1312 implies a mean time lag of 2 years for the adjustment of the price level to a change in marginal cost.

In the wage rate adjustment equation (8) the proportional rate of increase in the money wage rate is an increasing function of the proportional excess demand for labour, where the demand for labour is identified with the partial equilibrium level of employment in equation (2) and the supply of labour is represented by a trend term. The trend coefficient implies a rate of growth of the labour supply of 0.3 per cent per annum, while the adjustment parameter 0.1047 implies that a 1 per cent increase in the demand for labour increases the proportional rate of increase in the wage rate by 0.4 per cent per annum (e.g. from 5 per cent per annum to 5.4 per cent per annum). Although the model provides a satisfactory explanation of variations in the inflation rate over the sample period 1955–66 and in the post-sample forecasts up to 1970, it could not, with this wage adjustment equation, explain the large fluctuations in the inflation rate that have occurred during the last decade. The wage adjustment equation should be modified to take account of expectations (possibly rational expectations of the sort that are associated with a unique constant inflation rate level of employment). For this purpose it should be a second-order differential equation. Such a modification would not affect the steady-state solution of the model, although it would affect its stability. But I do not think that it would affect the main qualitative conclusions of this paper.

The interest rate adjustment equation (9) is a dynamic representation of the Keynesian liquidity preference theory of interest rate determination. At each point of time the proportional rate of increase in the interest rate is an increasing function of the proportional excess demand for money, the real demand for money depending on income and the interest rate. The income elasticity of demand for money is assumed to be 1.0, and the estimated interest elasticity of demand for money is -0.8289. The mean time lag for the adjustment of the interest rate in response to a change in the money supply or income is about $1\frac{1}{2}$ years.

Equation (10) represents the influence of the balance of payments on the money supply, this influence being partly automatic and partly a reflection of policy. The rate of increase in the proportional rate of increase in the money supply depends on both the ratio of exports to imports and the proportional rate of change in this ratio. The equation implies that if, for example, the money supply were increasing at 1 per cent per quarter, exports being equal to imports, then a once for all 1 per cent increase in the ratio of exports to imports would cause the money supply to increase by approximately 1.04 per cent next quarter, 1.08 per cent the following quarter and so on. But if the ratio of exports to imports started to increase by 1 per cent per quarter, then the money supply would increase by 1.20 per cent next quarter, 1.44 per cent the following quarter and so on.

The remaining equations in the model are definitional. Although equations (3) and (10) are, essentially, second-order differential equations in K and M respectively, it is mathematically convenient to define k and m by (12) and (13) respectively in order to express the complete model as a system of 13 first-order differential equations.

The system has a steady-state solution in which each variable grows at a constant proportional rate (which is zero for some variables). Introducing the notation

$$\mathbf{x}' = [x_1, \ldots, x_{13}] = [C, L, k, Y, I, E, p, w, r, m, S, K, M]$$

this solution can be written

$$x_i(t) = x_i^* \mathrm{e}^{\rho_i t} \qquad i = 1, \ldots, 13.$$

The steady-state levels $x_1^*, \ldots, x_{13}^*$ and growth rates $\rho_1, \ldots, \rho_{13}$ can all be expressed as explicit functions of the structural parameters of the model, and these formulae are given in Bergstrom and Wymer (1976). The steady-state solution is, essentially, neo-classical; employment grows at the same rate as the labour supply, output and other real variables grow at a rate equal to the rate of technical progress plus the rate of growth of the labour supply, the price level increases at a rate equal to the rate of increase in the money supply minus the rate of growth of output, and the rate of interest is constant. The steady-state rate of increase in the money supply is so related to the rate of increase in prices and income in the rest of the world as to keep the balance of payments in equilibrium at a fixed exchange rate.

A full analysis of the influence of various structural parameters on the steady-state solution is given in Bergstrom and Wymer (1976). It is shown, for example, that the steady-state interest rate is higher the lower is propensity to save and the more capital intensive the production function and that it is unaffected by the liquidity preference parameters in equation (9). The explanation of the latter result is that, in the steady state, the money wage rate is so adjusted to other monetary phenomena in the system that their effect is neutralized and the interest rate is determined by real phenomena. Monetary phenomena do, nevertheless, play an important role in the mechanism generating the transient paths of the real variables. A Keynesian type mechanism involving the liquidity preference relation, the investment function and the wage and price adjustment relations ensures that, provided certain stability conditions are satisfied, output will oscillate about a path that approximately follows the neo-classical full employment path over a long period. The way in which this mechanism works is described in Bergstrom and Wymer (1976: 284–6).

An important property of the model, which greatly facilitates the asymptotic stability analysis, is that the logarithms of the ratios of the variables to their steady-state values satisfy a system of non-linear differential equations which does not involve t, i.e.

$$Dy(t) = \mathbf{f}[y(t)] \tag{14}$$

where

$$y(t) = [y_1(t), \ldots, y_{13}(t)]$$

$\mathbf{f}$ is a vector of functions whose exact form is given in Bergstrom and Wymer (1976: 287) and

$$y_i(t) = \log\left[\frac{x_i(t)}{x_i^* \, e^{\rho_i t}}\right] \qquad i = 1, \ldots, 13.$$

It then follows from Taylor's theorem and a theorem of Perron (see Coddington and Levinson, 1955: 314) that if

$$\mathbf{A} = \left(\frac{\partial \mathbf{f}(y)}{\partial y'}\right)_{y=0} \tag{15}$$

then $y(t) \to 0$ as $t \to \infty$ provided that the eigenvalues of $\mathbf{A}$ have negative real parts and the elements of $y(0)$ are sufficiently small. This means that if the eigenvalues of $\mathbf{A}$ have negative real parts then the proportional deviations of the variables $C(t), \ldots, M(t)$ from their steady-state values will tend to zero provided that the initial proportional deviations from the steady state are

TABLE 8.1 Eigenvalues for linear approximation about the steady state

Real part	t value	Imaginary part	t value
−0.8605	6.65		
−0.2946	4.13		
−0.1707	2.51		
−0.0990	4.08		
−0.0061	7.79		
−0.1791	5.30	±0.1425	3.92
−0.1826	4.52	±0.0599	2.10
−0.0179	5.23	±0.0514	4.55
0.0782	6.16	±0.0742	3.59

sufficiency small. In this case we say that the system is asymptotically stable. It should be noted that the stability analysis would be much more complicated if the functions f_i in (14) included t as a separate argument. For then we should have to verify the second condition of Perron's theorem, i.e. that as $|y|$ (the norm of y) tends to zero $1/|y| \{\mathbf{f}(y, t) - \mathbf{A}y\}$ tends to zero, not only for each value of t (as Taylor's theorem ensures), but also uniformly in t. This point is often overlooked in the economic literature.

The estimated eigenvalues of **A** and their t values are shown in table 8.1.

There are five real eigenvalues, all of which are negative, and four pairs of complex eigenvalues, including three pairs with negative real parts and one pair with a positive real part. The t value associated with the real part of the last pair of complex eigenvalues indicates that the hypothesis that the steady state is asymptotically stable must be rejected at the 1 per cent level of significance. But the model can, nevertheless, produce plausible long-run behaviour if it is modified to take account of the sort of non-linearity introduced by Hicks (1950) in his theory of the trade cycle.

The equation that requires modification is the investment equation (3). Here it has been assumed that the partial equilibrium proportional rate of increase in the amount of fixed capital is a linear function of the excess of the marginal product of capital over the real interest rate. But, since gross investment cannot be negative, it is realistic to assume that k is bounded from below by $-\delta$ where δ is the rate of depreciation. It is realistic to assume, therefore, that the partial equilibrium proportional rate of capital formation $\hat{k}$ is related to the excess of the marginal product of capital over the real interest rate by a non-linear relation

$$\hat{k} = g\left(\frac{\partial Y}{\partial K} - r + \frac{\mathrm{D}p}{p}\right)$$

where the function g is bounded from below by $-\delta$ and is approximated in the neighbourhood of the steady-state value of

$$\frac{\partial Y}{\partial K} - r + \frac{\mathrm{D}p}{p}$$

by

$$1.1492\left(\frac{\partial Y}{\partial K} - r + \frac{\mathrm{D}p}{p}\right) + 0.0042.$$

With this modification the model can be expected to produce a limit cycle if undisturbed. The period of the explosive cycle generated by the approximate linear model is about 21 years. But the constraint imposed by the non-linearity in the investment function is likely to reduce this period.

The fact that the real eigenvalues are negative is important, for it ensures that the system will produce oscillations about the steady state rather than convergence to a permanent state of depression or inflation. If there is a change in the rate of technical progress or the rate of increase in the labour supply there will be a change in the steady-state growth rate. But the internal mechanism of the model (see Bergstrom and Wymer, 1976) will ensure that, over a long period, demand follows supply so that the path of output will converge to a limit cycle about the new steady state.

ALTERNATIVE MONETARY POLICIES

Equation (10) plays an essential role in the model, for it ensures that, over a long period, the change in the domestic price level is so related to changes in income and prices in the rest of the world as to preserve balance-of-payments equilibrium with a fixed exchange rate. In a more general version of the model discussed in Bergstrom and Wymer (1976) the money supply adjustment equation takes the form

$$\mathrm{D}m = \gamma_1 \log\left(\frac{E}{I}\right) + \gamma_2 \mathrm{D} \log\left(\frac{E}{I}\right) + \gamma_3 \log\left(\frac{L}{\beta \mathrm{e}^{\lambda t}}\right) + \gamma_4 \mathrm{D} \log\left(\frac{L}{\beta \mathrm{e}^{\lambda t}}\right) \tag{16}$$

where $\beta \mathrm{e}^{\lambda t}$ can be interpreted as the level of employment aimed at by the policy makers and λ is assumed to be equal to the rate of increase in the labour supply. Although it seems likely that, over the sample period, the level of employment did have some influence on monetary policy, it was not possible to obtain reliable estimates of γ_3 and γ_4, and in the estimated model these parameters were restricted to zero.

It was shown in Bergstrom and Wymer (1976) that the introduction of the last two terms in (16) has no effect on the steady-state level of employment. Moreover, balance-of-payments equilibrium will not be attained in the steady state unless either $\gamma_3 = 0$ or the level of employment aimed at is that which necessarily occurs in the steady state. The inclusion of the last two terms in equation (16) can have a beneficial effect, therefore, only if these terms have a stabilizing influence.

Experience with the prototype model in Bergstrom (1967: chapter 6) suggests that a negative value of γ_3 is likely to be destabilizing, whereas the effect on stability of a negative value of γ_4 is less certain, being fairly sensitive to the values of the other parameters of the model. The following analysis is confined, therefore, to the effect on stability of variations in γ_4 when $\gamma_3 = 0$ and all other parameters of the model have their estimated values. It is concerned, that is to say, with the stability of the system of equations obtained by replacing equation (10) in the estimated model by

$$\mathrm{D}m = 0.0422 \log\left(\frac{E}{I}\right) + 0.1562\,\mathrm{D} \log\left(\frac{E}{I}\right) + \gamma_4(\mathrm{D} \log L - 0.0008) \tag{17}$$

in which the last term is the excess of the rate of increase in employment over the rate of increase in the labour supply.

A negative value of γ_4 implies that the rate of increase in the proportional rate of increase in the money supply is greater the lower is the proportional rate of increase in employment. Suppose, for example, that $\gamma_4 = -1.0$ and that employment is initially constant while the money supply is growing at 1 per cent per quarter. Then, if employment starts to decrease by 1 per cent per quarter the money supply will be increased by approximately 2 per cent next quarter, 3 per cent the following quarter, and so on, provided that the ratio of exports to imports is constant.

Although a variation in γ_4 has no effect on the steady state of the system, it does affect the vector $\mathbf{f}$ of functions in equation (14) and hence the matrix $\mathbf{A}$ defined by (15). The effect of a variation in γ_4 on the stability of the system depends on its effect on the eigenvalues of $\mathbf{A}$. The eigenvalues of $\mathbf{A}$ when $\gamma_4 = -1.0$ are shown in table 8.2. A comparison with table 8.1, which shows the corresponding eigenvalues when $\gamma_4 = 0$, shows that the negative feedback from employment to the money supply makes the system slightly more unstable. The pair of complex eigenvalues that dominates the steady-state behaviour changes from $0.0782 \pm 0.0742i$ to $0.0833 \pm 0.0858i$ so that the system generates a more explosive cycle with a shorter period.

The eigenvalues were calculated for various other values of γ_4 in the range -0.1 to -10.0. But in each case there was one pair of complex eigenvalues with a positive real part and in no case was the positive real part less

TABLE 8.2 Eigenvalues for linear approximation about the steady state when $\gamma_4 = -1.0$

Real part	Imaginary part
−0.8608	0.0000
−0.2946	0.0000
−0.1914	0.0000
−0.1124	0.0000
−0.0061	0.0000
−0.1798	±0.1459
−0.1756	±0.0743
−0.0121	±0.0415
0.0833	±0.0858

than when $\gamma_4 = 0$. The eigenvalues with positive real parts for various values of γ_4 are shown in table 8.3.

We conclude, therefore, that a negative feedback from employment to the money supply of the type considered has a destabilizing influence on the estimated model. This result is undoubtedly explained by the long time lags in the causal chain of relations through which this type of feedback influences the behaviour of the system. We recall that there are mean time lags of $1\frac{1}{2}$ years for the adjustment of the interest rate to the money supply, 3 years for the adjustment of investment to the interest rate, 12 months for the adjustment of consumption to income, $4\frac{1}{4}$ months for the adjustment of output to sales and $2\frac{1}{2}$ years for the adjustment of employment to output.

The last of these lags could be eliminated from the causal chain through which monetary policy works by using a feedback directly from the output

TABLE 8.3 Eigenvalues with positive real parts for selected values of γ_4

γ_4	Real part	Imaginary part
−0.10	0.0786	±0.0755
−0.50	0.0806	±0.0804
−1.00	0.0833	±0.0858
−5.00	0.1025	±0.1129
−10.00	0.1195	±0.1317

to the money supply. We shall consider, therefore, the effect of replacing (17) by the relation

$$\mathrm{D}m = 0.0422 \log\left(\frac{E}{I}\right) + 0.1562\ \mathrm{D}\log\left(\frac{E}{I}\right) + \gamma_5(\mathrm{D}\log Y - 0.0066) \tag{18}$$

in which the last term is the excess of the proportional rate of growth of output over the steady-state growth rate. A negative value of γ_5 implies that the rate of increase in the proportional rate of increase in the money supply is greater the lower is the proportional rate of increase in output.

The eigenvalues of **A** when equation (18) replaces equation (10) in the system of equations (1) to (13) and $\gamma_5 = -1.0$ are shown in table 8.4. A comparison with table 8.1 shows that the negative feedback on output also makes the system slightly more unstable. The pair of complex eigenvalues that dominate the behaviour of the system changes from $0.0782 \pm 0.0742i$ to $0.0798 \pm 0.0981i$, so that it generates a slightly more explosive cycle with a shorter period as compared with the cycle generated when there is no direct feedback from either employment or output to the money supply.

The eigenvalues were calculated for various values of γ_5 in the range -0.1 to -10.0. Again there was, in each case, one pair of complex eigenvalues with a positive real part. The eigenvalues with positive real parts are shown in table 8.5. Only in the case where $\gamma_5 = -0.1$ is the positive real part less than when $\gamma_5 = 0.0$. But, in this case, the effect of the feedback is negligible, the change in the positive real part being from 0.782 when $\gamma_5 =$ 0.0 to 0.781 when $\gamma_5 = -0.1$. We conclude, therefore, that a negative feedback from output to the money supply of the type considered has a destabi-

TABLE 8.4 Eigenvalues for linear approximation about the steady state when $\gamma_5 = -1.0$

Real part	Imaginary part
−0.8582	0.0000
−0.2946	0.0000
−0.1557	0.0000
−0.0990	0.0000
−0.0059	0.0000
−0.1825	±0.1395
−0.1980	±0.0611
−0.0094	±0.0446
0.0798	±0.0981

TABLE 8.5 Eigenvalues with positive real parts for selected values of γ_5

γ_5	Real part	Imaginary part
−0.10	0.0781	±0.0768
−0.50	0.0783	±0.0867
−1.00	0.0798	±0.0981
−5.00	0.1022	±0.1557
−10.00	0.1253	±0.1943

lizing influence when applied with sufficient force to have a significant effect on the behaviour of the system.

In the above analysis we have not considered the effect of policy feedbacks in which the second derivative of the money supply depends on the second- or higher-order derivatives of employment or output. Such policies could, perhaps, have a stabilizing influence. But, since they assume that the money supply can be adjusted instantaneously in response to variations in the level of employment or output, they are rather impracticable.

COMBINED MONETARY AND FISCAL POLICY

In the previous section we implicitly assumed that fiscal policy was, in a certain sense, neutral and that variations in monetary policy were achieved through open market operations. In this section we shall introduce a fiscal policy feedback relation in which taxation rates and government expenditure vary in response to deviations of output from its steady-state path. Although there are no taxation and government expenditure variables in the estimated model they can be allowed for, in a mathematically convenient way, by introducing a fiscal policy variable T defined by

$$T = \frac{0.9206}{g + (0.9206)(1 - \tau)}$$

where g = partial equilibrium ratio of government current expenditure to national income (i.e. gY = partial equilibrium level of public consumption) and τ = taxation rate (i.e. $(1 - \tau)Y$ = real private disposable income).

We then replace equation (1) in the estimated model by

$$\frac{DC}{C} = 0.2454 \log\left[\frac{0.9206Y}{TC}\right] \tag{19}$$

which, using the definition of T, can be written in the form

$$\frac{DC}{C} = 0.2454 \log\left[\frac{gY + (0.9206)(1-\tau)Y}{C}\right].$$

The expression $gY + (0.9206)(1-\tau)Y$ can then be interpreted as the partial equilibrium level of aggregate consumption, which is the sum of gY, the partial equilibrium level of public consumption, and $(0.9206)(1-\tau)Y$, the partial equilibrium level of private consumption. Neutral fiscal policy can be defined as a policy in which $T = 1$, in which case (19) reduces to the estimated equation (1).

We shall now consider the effect of introducing into the model the fiscal policy feedback relation

$$\frac{DT}{T} = \gamma\left[\beta \log\left(\frac{Y}{6.056\exp(0.0066t)}\right) - \log T\right] \tag{20}$$

in which β and γ are policy parameters and the term $6.056\exp(0.0066t)$ is the steady-state growth path of output implied by the estimated parameters of the model (the steady-state growth rate being 0.66 per cent per quarter or about 2.6 per cent per annum). Equation (20) implies that $\log T$ depends with an exponentially distributed time lag on the logarithm of the ratio of output to its steady-state level. It implies, for example, that if g is constant then the taxation rate will be converging to a level which is higher the greater is the proportional excess of output over its steady-state level, while if τ is constant then the government propensity to spend will be converging to a level which is lower the greater is the proportional excess of output over its steady-state level. The parameter β measures the strength of the feedback while γ is a speed of adjustment parameter whose reciprocal is the mean of the distributed time lag with which $\log T$ responds to a change in $\log[Y/6.056\exp(0.0066t)]$. The distributed time lag allows for the time taken for the government to adjust taxation rates and its expenditure plans, and for the lag with which information on output becomes available.

We shall consider the behaviour of the solution of the system comprising the 14 equations (2), (3), ..., (13), (19), (20) for various combinations of the fiscal policy parameters β and γ. In this system we have two policy feedbacks: (i) the feedback from the balance of payments to the money supply represented by equation (10), and (ii) the feedback from output to the fiscal variable represented by equation (20). We shall hold the parameters of the former relation at their estimated levels.

It is obvious from the forms of equations (19) and (20) that the steady-state solution of the system does not depend on the values of β and γ; in the steady state we have $T = 1$ and all other variables following the same paths as in the steady-state solution of the estimated system (1) to (13). The matrix of the linear approximation about the steady state is a 14×14 matrix whose leading 13×13 minor is identical with the matrix $\mathbf{A}$, defined by (15), for the estimated system. The eigenvalues of this 14×14 matrix were computed for the various combinations of values of β and γ shown in table 8.6. The values $\gamma = 1.0$ and $\gamma = 0.5$ imply mean time lags of 3 months and 6 months respectively for the adjustment of taxation rates and government expenditure in response to a change of output. In judging the plausibility (political feasibility) of the assumed values of β it should be noted that if $\beta > 1$ then an increase in output will cause the government to increase the taxation rate and (or) reduce its planned expenditure to such an extent that the partial equilibrium level of aggregate consumption will be less than it would have been if output had not increased. It seems unrealistic, therefore, to assume a value of β much greater than 1.

For each assumed combination of values of β and γ there is one, and only one, pair of complex eigenvalues with a positive real part, while all the real eigenvalues are negative. The values of the complex eigenvalues with positive real parts are shown in table 8.6. In each case the real part of this dominant pair of eigenvalues is less than 0.0782 (the real part of the dominant pair of eigenvalues in the estimated model), indicating that the policy does have a stabilizing effect. Moreover the real part of the dominant pair of eigenvalues is smaller the greater is each of the parameters β and γ, indicating that, over the range of parameter values considered, the system will be more stable the greater is the strength of the policy feedback and the greater the speed of adjustment of the control variables. The complete set of eigenvalues for the pair of parameter values $\beta = 2.0$, $\gamma = 0.5$ is shown in table 8.7.

We may conclude from these results that, under the assumptions of the model, a fiscal policy feedback of the type represented by equation (20) has a mild stabilizing effect. But it should be noted that there is an important

TABLE 8.6 Eigenvalues with positive real parts for selected values of β and γ

		Eigenvalues	
β	γ	Real part	Imaginary part
0.2	1.0	0.0723	± 0.0763
0.5	1.0	0.0637	± 0.0781
1.0	1.0	0.0506	± 0.0783
0.4	0.5	0.0674	± 0.0782
1.0	0.5	0.0518	± 0.0800
2.0	0.5	0.0313	± 0.0744

TABLE 8.7 Eigenvalues for $\beta = 2.0, \gamma = 0.5$

Real part	Imaginary part
−1.0660	0.0000
−0.2920	0.0000
−0.1741	0.0000
−0.1491	0.0000
−0.0990	0.0000
−0.0046	0.0000
−0.1907	±0.1179
−0.1905	±0.3098
−0.0291	±0.0565
0.0313	±0.0744

implicit assumption in equation (19) and the definition of T. This is that the response of consumption to a change in real disposable income resulting from a change in the taxation rate is the same as it is for a change in real disposable income resulting from a change in output. It should be noted also that the model takes no account of the effect of taxation on the labour supply (i.e. an incentive to work).

The fact that a feedback from output to the fiscal policy variable is stabilizing whereas a feedback from output to the money supply (when fiscal policy is neutral) is destabilizing is not very surprising in view of the greater speed with which the fiscal policy variable affects the real variables in the system. It is, perhaps, more surprising that the stabilizing effect of the fiscal policy is not stronger. But it should be remembered that a change in the fiscal policy variable T has an indirect effect through the interest rate. The initial increase in income induced by a fall in T will cause an increase in the interest rate (equation (9)) which will tend to decrease the rate of investment (equation (3)) and hence output (equation (4)). The fiscal policy is stabilizing only because this indirect effect, though the interest rate, is slower and more diffused over time than the direct income effect.

In this model, neither monetary nor fiscal policy can have any permanent effect on employment. The only permanent real effect of a once for all decrease in T is to divert resources from capital formation to consumption (private or public) and hence decrease the steady-state ratio of capital to output and the steady-state level of output. And the only permanent effect of a once for all increase in the money supply (offset by a corresponding change in the exchange rate) is to increase the nominal wage rate and the price level. The relative effects of monetary and fiscal policy in a prototype, closed economy, version of the model are fully discussed in Bergstrom (1967: chapter 6).

EXCHANGE RATE POLICY

We have assumed, so far, that the exchange rate is fixed (as it was over the sample period). Under this assumption the model generates plausible long-run behaviour only if the money supply is allowed to adjust in such a way as to preserve balance-of-payments equilibrium over a long period. This is the function of equation (10) in the estimated model. We shall now relax the assumption of a fixed exchange rate and introduce an exchange rate adjustment relation which will play the same role as equation (10) does in the estimated model. At the same time we shall assume that the money supply is increased at an arbitrary constant rate.

Our aim is to compare the effects of two alternative policies. Under the first policy the exchange rate is fixed and long-run balance-of-payments equilibrium is achieved through adjustments in the money supply, while under the second policy the rate of growth of the money supply is fixed and long-run balance-of-payments equilibrium is achieved through variations in the exchange rate. The real long-run effects of the two policies are identical. The only difference between their long-run effects is that under the former policy the long-run inflation rate is tied to that in the rest of the world while under the latter policy it is determined domestically. But the effects of the two policies on the stability of the system can be very different.

In order to introduce the exchange rate as a variable we replace equation (6) by

$$\frac{\mathrm{D}E}{E} = 0.2926 \log \left[\frac{1365(Qp)^{-1} \exp(0.0113t)}{E}\right] \tag{21}$$

where Q = index of price of sterling in terms of foreign currency with $Q = 1$ over the sample period. When $Q = 1$ equation (21) is identical to the estimated equation (6).

The assumption that the money supply grows at a constant rate is introduced by replacing equation (9) by

$$\frac{\mathrm{D}r}{r} = 0.1990 \log \left[\frac{0.0537p\ Y\ r^{-0.8289}}{M^* \mathrm{e}^{m^* t}}\right] \tag{22}$$

where M^* and m^* are constant, m^* being the assumed growth rate of the money supply. Equation (22) is obtained by substituting $M = M^*\ \mathrm{e}^{m^* t}$ into the estimated equation (9).

Finally we replace equations (10) and (13) by equations (23) and (24) respectively:

$$\mathrm{D}q = \gamma_1 \log \left(\frac{E}{I}\right) + \gamma_2\ \mathrm{D} \log \left(\frac{E}{I}\right) \tag{23}$$

$$\frac{DQ}{Q} = q. \tag{24}$$

Equation (23) is the exchange rate adjustment equation while equation (24) defines q. The policy parameters γ_1 and γ_2 can be interpreted similarly to the estimated parameters 0.0422 and 0.1562 in equation (10) except that the policy variable is now the exchange rate rather than the money supply.

We shall consider the behaviour of the system of equations obtained by replacing equations (6), (9), (10) and (13) in the estimated model by (21), (22), (23) and (24) respectively.[1] It is easy to see that this system has a steady state in which Q changes at a constant proportional rate depending on m^* and that the steady state does not depend on γ_1 or γ_2. It is of particular interest to consider the case in which M^* and m^* are chosen so that $M^* e^{m^*t}$ is identical with the steady-state path of the money supply for the estimated model. In this case we have $Q = 1$ in the steady state while the steady-state paths of all other variables are the same as they are for the estimated model. If m^* is increased by a constant c, then the steady-state rate of increase in the wage rate w, the price level p and the price of foreign currency $1/Q$, and the steady-state level of the interest rate r will all increase by c, while the steady-state paths of all real variables will be unaffected.

The eigenvalues of the matrix of linear approximations about the steady state were computed for the six combinations of the policy parameters γ_1 and γ_2 shown in table 8.8. In each case two of the real eigenvalues are

TABLE 8.8 Eigenvalues with positive real parts for selected values of γ_1 and γ_2

		Eigenvalues	
γ_1	γ_2	Real part	Imaginary part
0.05	0.10	0.1071	
		0.0113	
0.05	0.20	0.1088	
		0.0113	
0.05	0.50	0.1125	
		0.0113	
0.10	0.10	0.1128	
		0.0113	
		0.0064	± 0.2621
0.10	0.20	0.1136	
		0.0113	
0.10	0.50	0.1155	
		0.0113	

positive and, except in one case, the real values of all the complex eigenvalues are negative. The positive eigenvalues and the complex eigenvalues with positive real parts are shown in table 8.8, and the complete set of eigenvalues for the case $\gamma_1 = 0.05$, $\gamma_2 = 1.0$ are shown in table 8.9. These results suggest that, from a stability point of view, the policy of increasing the money supply at a constant proportional rate and relying on adjustments of the exchange rate to preserve long-run balance-of-payments equilibrium is inferior to a policy of keeping the exchange rate fixed and relying on adjustments in the rate of growth of the money supply to preserve long-run balance-of-payments equilibrium. The fact that, in all cases, the dominant eigenvalue is real and positive implies that the economy can fall into a permanent state of depression under the former policy.

This difference between the effects of the two policies on the stability of the system might, at first sight, seem surprising. But there is a simple intuitive explanation. It is known (see Bergstrom, 1967: chapter 3) that the introduction of a foreign trade sector will normally have a stabilizing effect on simple models of the trade cycle. This is because of the damping effect provided by the appearance of a balance-of-payments deficit in the boom and a balance-of-payments surplus in the depression. Or, more technically, it is because of the damping effect on the multiplier–accelerator mechanism of replacing the domestic multiplier by the smaller foreign trade multiplier. Conversely, if these cyclical fluctuations in the balance of payments are reduced through exchange rate variations then the fluctuations in output become more explosive. A similar effect is evidently taking place in the more complicated model being discussed in this paper. The money supply adjustment relation (10) in the estimated model also has a mild destabilizing effect (as indicated by unpublished computations of the eigenvalues for various assumed values of the parameters). But, because the effects of a

TABLE 8.9 Eigenvalues for $\gamma_1 = 0.05$, $\gamma_2 = 0.10$

Real part	Imaginary part
−0.8608	0.0000
−0.3466	0.0000
−0.1786	0.0000
−0.0990	0.0000
−.0061	0.0000
0.0113	0.0000
0.1071	0.0000
−0.1765	±0.0565
−0.1343	±0.1492
−0.0197	±0.1943

change in the money supply are much more diffused over time than the effects of a change in the exchange rate, the money supply adjustment relation (10) is less destabilizing than the exchange rate adjustment equation (23). It is sufficient to ensure that, over a long period, the domestic price level is so adjusted to conditions in the rest of the world as to preserve long-run balance-of-payments equilibrium. But it does not effect the economy with sufficient speed and concentration to reduce significantly the stabilizing effect of internally generated fluctuations in the balance of payments.

CONCLUSIONS

We have been concerned, in this paper, with the effects of introducing into an econometric model of the United Kingdom simple policy feedback rules which might be suggested intuitively, and which appear to represent approximately actual or declared government policies during certain periods. We have followed an approach inspired by the pioneer work of Phillips (1954) who was the first economist to respond seriously to Hicks's warning statement quoted at the beginning of the paper. A more modern and sophisticated approach would be to use optimal control theory. A linear feedback rule could be obtained by assuming a quadratic criterion function and solving the Ricatti equation (see Aoki, 1976: 164), treating the linear approximation about the steady state as if it were the true model. But such a rule would comprise a set of feedback relations in which each policy variable would depend on all other variables in the model, and it would be difficult to interpret these relations intuitively or make any judgement about the likely effects of a particular misspecification in the model.

Subject to qualifications concerning the specification of the model, the results obtained suggest the use of a simple policy rule in which the rate of growth of the money supply is adjusted in response to changes in the balance of payments in such a way as to preserve long-run balance-of-payments equilibrium with a fixed exchange rate, and fiscal variables (taxation and government expenditure) are adjusted in response to changes in output in such a way as to dampen fluctuations in output about the steady-state path. But it is important that the adjustment of the fiscal variables should not be allowed to affect the application of the money supply adjustment rule, for the effects of changes in the money supply are distributed over such a long period, and in such a way, that a policy of accelerating the expansion of the money supply during depressions and decelerating during booms amplifies the fluctuations in output. If fiscal adjustments are not allowed to affect the money supply they do, of course, affect interest rates. But the model does take account of this effect, and it is, presumably, because of the negative feedback through the interest rate that the fiscal policy has only a mild stabilizing effect and, for the range of parameter values that seems feasible, is unable to prevent the occasional deep recession whose end is partly dependent on the non-linearities in the system.

The results suggest also that a policy in which the exchange rate is fixed and long-run external balance is achieved through adjustments in the rate of growth of the money supply is preferable, from a stability point of view, to one in which the rate of growth of the money supply is fixed and external balance is achieved through adjustments in the exchange rate. This is, evidently , because the effects of a change in the money supply are much more diffused over time than the effects of a change in the exchange rate and hence adjustments in the rate of growth of the money supply can preserve long-run external balance without greatly reducing the stabilizing effects on output of internally generated fluctuations in the balance of payments.

A final qualification is that we have, implicitly, treated income and prices in the rest of the world as exogenous trends. If all countries were to adopt the sort of monetary feedback rule incorporated in our model there would be nothing to stop the world inflation rate from drifting, gradually, upwards. This could be avoided by international agreement on bounds (say 0 and 10 per cent per annum) between which the rate of growth of the money supply of each country should be restricted. Each country would then adjust the rate of growth of its money supply in response to changes in its balance of payments subject to the condition that the rate of growth of its money supply is restricted to the agreed range. An investigation of the way in which the international economy would behave under such a policy would, of course, require a linking of models of the economies of the different countries.

NOTE

1 Because of the implicit assumption that the price elasticity of demand for imports is -1.0, equation (5) is unchanged.

REFERENCES

Aoki, M. (1976) *Optimal Control and Systems Theory in Dynamic Economic Analysis*, North-Holland, Amsterdam.

Bergstrom, A. R. (1967) *The Construction and Use of Economic Models*, English Universities Press, London.

Bergstrom, A. R. (ed.) (1976) *Statistical Inference in Continuous Time Economic Models*, North-Holland, Amsterdam.

Bergstrom, A. R. (1978) 'Monetary Policy in a Model of the United Kingdom', in Bergstrom, A. R., Catt, A. J. L., Preston, M. H. and Silverstone, B. D. J. (eds), *Stability and Inflation*, Wiley, New York, pp. 89–102.

Bergstrom, A. R. and Wymer, C. R. (1976) 'A Model of Disequilibrium Neoclassical Growth and its Application to the United Kingdom', in Bergstrom A. R. (ed.) *Statistical Inference in Continuous Time Economic Models*, North-Holland, Amsterdam, pp. 267–327.

Coddington, E. A. and Levinson, N. (1955) *Ordinary Differential Equations*, McGraw Hill, New York.

Gandolfo, G. (1981) *Qualitative Analysis and Econometric Estimation of Continuous Time Dynamic Models*, North-Holland, Amsterdam.

Hickman, B. G. (ed.) (1972) *Econometric Models of Cyclical Behaviour*, Columbia University Press.

Hicks, J. R. (1950) *The Trade Cycle*, Oxford University Press.

Knight, M. D. and Wymer, C. R. (1978) 'A Macroeconomic Model of the United Kingdom', *IMF Staff Papers*, **25**, 742-778.

Phillips, A. W. (1954) 'Stabilization Policy in a Closed Economy', *Economic Journal*, **64**, 290–323.

Comment

JEAN-MICHEL CHARPIN

It has become very frequent to hear specialists of small models criticize the content and use of large models. My remarks will, in this respect, be less common since a specialist of large models has been asked to comment on the use of a small model. Another peculiarity is that this small model is used to establish conclusions relative to real and crucial economic policy issues, and not only for pedagogical purposes.

My comments will concentrate on two points only, a particular one—the treatment of the exchange rate, which illustrates the problems which may be encountered when using small models—and a general one—of methodological nature.

THE TREATMENT OF THE EXCHANGE RATE

Before going into this question, one should notice that Bergstrom and Wymer's model presents the peculiarity of dealing with only one price. The list of variables after equation (13) includes a unique price variable, called p. Therefore the problems of relative prices are not dealt with. It is said that the model describes a single sector economy whose product can be used for consumption, capital formation or export. All variables presented as real variables are indeed obtained by deflating the value at current prices by this unique price variable, which is practically the implicit price deflator of the gross domestic product. However what is written about equations (4) and (5) indicates that the import price, which is not explicitly introduced, may differ from the GDP price. Equation (5) may be read as an equation explaining the volume of imports, with a price elasticity exactly equal to -1, even though the volume of imports is not explicitly introduced and no econometric estimation of the price elasticity of imports has been performed. Then, at the equilibrium, the import price has no influence on the ratio of imports to any other variable, because of this unitary elasticity.

All this is perfectly consistent. But the adopted assumptions clearly make the model unfit for studying the consequences of relative price modifications; the important question now is to know whether the model can deal correctly with the particular case of relative price modification which results from a modification of the exchange rate.

In this respect, the two following remarks may be made:

(i) *The assumption of a unitary price elasticity of imports is absolutely crucial.* If this elasticity were to equal to 0.5, 0.9 or 1.1, not only would the sensitivity of imports to prices be modified, but the whole expression of the static equilibrium would be questioned. At equilibrium, according to equations (4), (5) and (11),

$$Y = (1 - 0.1632)(C + \mathrm{DK} + E)$$

$$I = (C + \mathrm{DK} + E) - Y = 0.1632(C + \mathrm{DK} + E)$$

$$S = 1.5263(C + \mathrm{DK} + E).$$

Such equations, which imply that the ratio $I/(C + \mathrm{DK} + E)$ is constant at equilibrium, can only hold if the price elasticity is one; in the opposite case, this ratio would be a function of the relative price of imports.

Incidentally, it is for this reason that an econometric estimation of the price elasticity would have no justification in the framework of the model. Its structure is consistent only with a unitary value of the elasticity.

(ii) *The export price is assumed to be identical to the GDP price.* This assumption must be maintained even when the exchange rate is modified. In the opposite case, that is if competitors' prices on foreign markets were supposed to have some influence on export prices, once again the whole expression of the model would be questioned. For example, if one supposes that the export prices remain constant in foreign currencies after a change in the exchange rate, then the volume of exports has no reason to be modified and the movements of the exports E would result only from price modifications. In this case the model would directly generate changes in output and employment which have no reason to take place.

To sum up, the model is able to describe the consequences of a modification of the exchange rate only under the two following assumptions:

(a) the price elasticity of imports is unitary;
(b) the export prices in national currency are not directly dependent on the exchange rate.

It is indeed normal that a small model must be based on such assumptions. Otherwise, for example if prices for each demand category were introduced, its size would increase very rapidly. Now it is clear, first, that the results obtained in the section on Exchange Rate Policy and the conclusions drawn from them are likely to be valid only under these two assumptions and, secondly, that these assumptions are strong; consequently the validity of the results can be questioned.

METHODOLOGICAL REMARKS

The method adopted in Bergstrom's paper consists of starting from a model, analysing it carefully and finally drawing economic policy conclusions, presented as having general validity. All this would be perfectly all right if enough attention were paid to the question of the capacity of the model to describe the reality under study.

Unfortunately, in this case, the attention paid to the verification is weak. This is fairly paradoxical. A criticism often made of large models is that their size forbids frequent tests and re-estimations. One might have thought that these operations were easier to perform with a small model. But, the present model, and considering the use made of it in the paper, presents evident major drawbacks. Even setting aside the problem of the treatment of the exchange rate, two other problems can be raised:

(i) *The estimation period.* The model has been estimated from quarterly data covering the 1955–66 period. This feature, which did not create any difficulty as long as the only aim of the model remained the original one, i.e. exploring methodological questions, raises a major problem when economic policy conclusions for the present period are aimed at. Both the trend coefficients and the lag coefficients are estimated over the 1955–66 period and supposed to be still valid today, even when this is obviously no longer true and even when it was relatively easy to obtain less obsolete estimations. I guess there would not have been major difficulties in updating the estimations. But the important point, from a methodological point of view, is to notice that the author has not done it.

(ii) *The wage equation.* Equation (8), which explains wages, raises a serious problem which the author indeed admits. The explained variable is the increase in money wages; the only explanatory variable is the proportional excess supply for labour. No nominal variable is present on the right-hand side of the equation. In spite of the very special characteristics of wage formation in the United Kingdom, it is clear that such an equation has obviously no chance of reproducing correctly the recent past since the wage increases it generates can only be less than those of the estimation period. What is important is not so much to notice this, which is obvious, than to notice that once again the author has not changed the wage equation, which would not have raised dramatic problems, before making his analysis.

In short, and paradoxically, the question of the adequacy of this small model to reality is considered, if not with detachment, at least as a minor problem. My opinion is that, when economic policy conclusions are aimed at, it is mandatory that time and great care be devoted to testing the capacity of the model to describe correctly the complex and changing reality of the economy under study.

Comment

GIANCARLO GANDOLFO

Let me first state that I completely agree with Bergstrom's opinion as to the nature of econometric models to be used as a guide to policy. Everyone knows that in econometric model building for a long time now there has been a tendency towards gigantism, in which one of the recommendations for a model was its size (measured by the number of equations). This tendency still continues but the careful observer will now have realized that another idea has been gaining ground, namely that macrodynamic medium-term econometric models, small in size (from one to three dozen equations) and embodying considerably more economic theory than is usually possible, are complementary, or even preferable, to large models for the purposes of policy analysis and simulations (in addition to Bergstrom's works see, for example, Wymer, 1976, 1979; Reserve Bank of Australia, 1977; Committee on Policy Optimisation, 1978, Deleau et al., 1980; Masson et al., 1980; Richard, 1980; Gandolfo, 1981; Gandolfo and Padoan, 1982; and references therein). It is interesting to note that this idea is not only circulating amongst academics, but has also been put to work by central banks and international organizations. For example, the Reserve Bank of Australia has developed and is using such a model, now in its second edition (Reserve Bank of Australia, 1977; Jonson and Trevor, 1981); the Bank of Canada is currently building another (Masson et al., 1980); and the IMF has built several such models for separate countries (the best being that of Knight and Wymer, 1978).

I also agree with Bergstrom's opinion that such models are better specified as systems of stochastic differential equations and estimated in continuous time. The specification of a macrodynamic model as a differential system is more appealing to the economic theorist for a number of reasons that it would be impossible to go into here (for a treatment see Gandolfo, 1981). From the econometric point of view, recently developed methods (see, for example, Bergstrom, 1976, 1981; Gandolfo, 1981; Wymer, 1976) allow a rigorous estimation of the parameters of a system of stochastic differential equations on the basis of discrete observation such as are available in reality.

After having stated my agreement with Bergstrom's approach, I must now find points of disagreement for, as I understand it, the task of a discussant is also to produce sensible criticism, possibly of the constructive type. In the next sections I will consider the model, both in its theoretical and in its empirical aspects; I will then discuss the policy suggestions that the author draws from his model.

THE THEORETICAL SETTING

We must bear in mind that this is a prototype model—indeed, *the* prototype model—from which all subsequent work on continuous-time models has drawn inspiration. Therefore its pioneering nature has to be kept in mind when discussing it. Nowadays it would be easy to build better models—better in the sense that the financial sector (which is rather rudimentary in this model) and the policy variables (these as well are included in a rudimentary way) are more adequately treated. But these are suggestions of which Bergstrom is certainly aware, as is shown by the fact that he cites the Knight and Wymer (1978) model (which is an extended version of the Bergstrom and Wymer model) where all these problems are dealt with; another model with fully developed financial and policy sectors is the Australian one cited above. Therefore, rather than spending time on minute points, I will comment on the 'vision' (in the Schumpeterian sense) embodied in the model. This model is completely neo-classical (as its original 1976 title suggests), which in my opinion greatly limits its usefulness in institutional contexts that do not conform to the neo-classical paradigm. For example, in Italy (and I suspect also in France and in other countries, though to a lesser extent) the change in the wage rate is practically unrelated to the excess demand for labour (even if the demand for labour is defined as the partial equilibrium level of employment). Similarly, no relation seems to exist (at least in the Italian context) between the partial equilibrium rate of capital formation and the excess of the marginal product of capital over the real interest rate.

Therefore I would say that this model cannot be applied *sic et simpliciter* to other economies and/or periods without radical transformations.

THE ESTIMATES

A general observation is that the model was estimated from UK quarterly data for the period 1955–66. This period would seem to be rather too remote to lead us to believe that all the parameters would remain the same, or not significantly different, were the model estimated from more recent data. In general, a model which may have been accurate 16 years ago is not necessarily accurate today, especially after institutional changes such as the transition from fixed exchange rates to the managed float. It follows that the policy prescriptions that Bergstrom draws from this model (see below) are to be considered with the utmost caution.

A worrying feature deriving from the estimates is the presence of a pair of complex characteristic roots with statistically significant positive real part (table 8.1). This means that the model does not possess an asymptotically stable steady state, for it generates an explosive 21-year cycle. The explanation given on pp. 192–3 is not convincing. In particular, I am not happy with calling the Hicksian limits to help in the way that Bergstrom does. In fact, either the whole model is specified in Hicksian terms since the very beginning, or—if not—the introduction *ex post* of the Hicksian limits is a mere '*ad hockery*' whose consequence is that one should never worry about stability! In fact, if one's model is intrinsically stable (all characteristic roots are of stable type) then all is well; if one's model is intrinsically unstable (at least one characteristic root is of unstable type) then all is equally well, for the Hicksian limits will take care of the instability. I would not agree with this view and, on the contrary, in the presence of an unstable model I would look for a misspecification, for example of the capital or financial sectors of the economy, and in any case I would not use it lightly for policy simulations.

POLICY ANALYSIS

Bergstrom examines the stability of the model under various policy alternatives by giving alternative values to the relevant parameters and recomputing the characteristic roots each time. Perhaps a more fruitful (and in any case complementary) approach would be the use of *sensitivity analysis*. By sensitivity analysis I here mean the analysis of the effects of changes in the parameters on the characteristic roots of the model. This can be performed in a general way by computing the partial derivatives of such roots with respect to the relevant parameters (see, for example, Gandolfo, 1981: 29ff).

As regards the policy results, the conclusion on the comparison between fixed exchange rate and variable rate of growth of the money supply on the one hand, and fixed rate of growth of the money supply and variable exchange rate on the other, which is in favour of the former alternative (see p. 203) is not convincing, for both statistical and economic reasons. When the exchange rate is variable, it is presumable that the parameters of the model—which have been estimated over a period of fixed exchange rates—would be different. Therefore I would re-estimate the model to include the period of managed float before carrying out this simulation. But there is a deeper reason—and indeed the main one—for dissatisfaction: when the exchange rate is variable, the theoretical specification of the model has to be changed accordingly. In fact, a variable exchange rate has diffuse effects on the whole model, which are not considered in the simulations. In any case, even if one were to accept the procedure followed in the paper, the implicit assumption that the price elasticity of the demand for imports (in volume terms) is equal to one would remain highly objectionable.

Finally, the reason given for neglecting optimal control methods is not convincing. There is no need to consider all the variables in the objective function, for one could as a start consider a limited subset of them. Furthermore, I would like to point out that continuous-time models are particularly well suited for optimal control analysis. Consider for example the general problem of control (note that for simplicity's sake I remain in the deterministic field), which can be formulated as follows:

$$\max_{\{z(t)\}} J = \int_{t_0}^{t_1} I(x, z, t)\,\mathrm{d}t + F(x_1, t_1)$$

subject to

$$\dot{x} = f(x, z, t),\ t_0 \text{ and } x(t_0) \text{ given;} \qquad t_1 \text{ given}$$
$$(\text{or } T(x, t) = 0 \text{ for } t = t_1),\ \{z(t)\} \in Z$$

where J is the objective functional, $\mathbf{x}$ a vector of state variables, $\mathbf{z}$ a vector of control variables (belonging to a given control set Z), and the state trajectory is determined by the equations of motion $\dot{\mathbf{x}} = \mathbf{f}(\ \ )$, with the given boundary conditions. For our purposes, the objective functional is supplied by the policy maker or assumed by the model builder, the control variables are the policy instruments, the equations of motion represent the structure of the economy as determined by means of an econometric model. Now, *econometric modelling in continuous time gives the equations of motions immediately, for the model has been built and estimated in such a form:* $\mathbf{x}$ is the vector of endogenous variables, $\mathbf{z}$ the vector of policy variables (instruments), t represents the set of exogenous non-policy variables (by assumption, known functions of time).

CONCLUSION

Bergstrom is to be congratulated for producing a fine paper. However, there are perplexities both on the theoretical side and on the empirical one which, in my opinion, cast some doubts on the policy results that he derives from the model. Therefore it would seem fair to conclude my discussion by saying that I would consider this to be a very important and highly sophisticated exercise (which all those interested in the continuous-time modelling approach should study carefully), rather than a work from which actual policy prescriptions can be drawn.

REFERENCES

Bergstrom, A. R. (ed.) (1976) *Statistical Inference in Continuous Time Economic Models*, North-Holland, Amsterdam.

Bergstrom, A. R. (1981) 'Continuous Time Stochastic Models and Issues of Aggregation over Time', forthcoming in Z. Griliches and M. D. Intriligator (eds), *Handbook of Econometrics*, North-Holland, Amsterdam.

Committee on Policy Optimisation (1978) *Report*, HMSO, London.

Deleau, M., Laffargue, J.-P., Malgrange, P., de Menil, G. and Muet, P.-A. (1980) *Recherches sur les Fondements de la Modélisation Macroéconomique Quantitative*, mimeographed, CEPREMAP.

Gandolfo, G. (1981) *Qualitative Analysis and Econometric Estimation of Continuous Time Dynamic Models*, North-Holland, Amsterdam.

Gandolfo, G. and Padoan, P. C. (1982) 'Policy Simulations with a Continuous Time Macrodynamic Model of the Italian Economy: A Preliminary Analysis', *Journal of Economic Dynamics and Control*, **4**, 205–24.

Jonson, P. D. and Trevor, R. G. (1981) 'Monetary Rules: A Preliminary Analysis', *Economic Record*, **57**, 150–67.

Knight, M. D. and Wymer, C. R. (1978) 'A Macrodynamic Model of the United Kingdom', *IMF Staff Papers*, **25**, 742–78.

Masson, P. R., Rose, D. R. and Selody, J. G. (1980) *Building a Small Macro-Model for Simulation: Some Issues*, Technical Report 22, Bank of Canada.

Reserve Bank of Australia (1977) *Conference in Applied Economic Research*, RBA, Sydney.

Richard, D. (1980) 'International Adjustment, Exchange Rates and Growth', paper presented at the *World Congress of the Econometric Society*, Aix-en-Provence, 28 August–2 September 1980.

Wymer, C. R. (1976) 'Continuous Time Models in Macro-economics: Specification and Estimation', paper presented at the SSRC-Ford Foundation Conference on *Macroeconomic Policy and Adjustment in Open Economies*, Ware, England, 28 April–1 May 1976.

Wymer, C. R. (1979) 'The Use of Continuous Time Models in Economics', unpublished manuscript.

9

A Study of Short-run and Long-run Properties of Macroeconometric Dynamic Models by Means of an Aggregative Core Model

MICHEL DELEAU, PIERRE MALGRANGE
and PIERRE-ALAIN MUET

INTRODUCTION

The construction of 'reduced versions' of large macroeconometric models is now current practice. The objective is generally to produce an instrument easier to handle and able to give a clear and reasonably accurate qualitative and quantitative understanding of the original model.

The study presented below, which also deals with an aggregative macro-model, differs from the previous approach in that it starts not from a given macroeconometric model but from macroeconomic theory; it aims at producing, so to speak, a 'model of models'. It is thus hoped to establish a more continuous and firm link between an essentially qualitative theory, and macroeconometric modelling which is concerned with the quantitative reproduction of economic phenomena.[1] In this respect, such an instrument can help in setting up comparisons between models on a structural basis, beyond a mere external confrontation of multipliers. This approach appears feasible: the common features of macroeconometric models outweigh, in our view, the apparent differences in the details of their specification (see for instance Muet, 1979).

The structure of the paper is as follows: the first section presents the specification of our 'core model'; the second, its long-run properties; the third part deals with the dynamic properties of the model and comparison with some macroeconometric models.

SPECIFICATION OF THE CORE MODEL

General structure

Our core model uses a short-term Keynesian structure as with most macroeconometric models. Production is determined by effective demand. This assumption supposes that demand Q is inferior to full-employment production $\bar{Q}_n$ (excess supply on the labour market) and to production capacity, i.e. the production $\tilde{Q}_c$ which is optimal for a given capital (excess supply on the goods market). The investment demand I, employment demand N and consumption demand C are consistent with these assumptions in the sense that they take into account, as in any Keynesian type model, the anticipated constraints on these two markets.

Given the other specifications, our core model can be viewed as a dynamic IS-LM with standard price and wage relations, i.e. the theoretical paradigm inspiring the bulk of macroeconometric modelling.

The equations of the model are given in table 9.1. It can be seen that they have been specified so as to admit a 'long-run solution', characterized by constant growth rate trajectories with equality between anticipated, optimal and actual values.

TABLE 9.1 The equations

Factor demand

Cost of capital

$$q = r - \tau^a + \delta \qquad (1)$$

Expected production

$$Q^* = [Q^*_{-1}(1 + g)]^{\lambda_2} Q^{1-\lambda_2} \qquad (2)$$

Expected relative capital–labour cost

$$\left(\frac{q}{\omega}\right)^* = \left[\left(\frac{q}{\omega}\right)^*_{-1} \frac{1+n}{1+g}\right]^{\lambda_1} \left(\frac{q}{\omega}\right)^{1-\lambda_1} \qquad (3)$$

Optimal labour

$$N^* = \frac{Q^*}{A} \left(\frac{\beta}{\alpha}\right)^{\alpha} \left(\frac{q}{\omega}\right)^{*\alpha} (1 + \gamma)^{-t} \qquad (4)$$

Actual labour

$$N = [N_{-1}(1 + n)]^{\lambda_4} N^{*1-\lambda_4} \qquad (5)$$

TABLE 9.1 (*cont.*)

Optimal capital

$$K^* = \frac{1}{A}\,[Q^*(1+g)]\left[\left(\frac{\beta}{\alpha}\right)\right]^{-\beta}\left[\left(\frac{q}{\omega}\right)^*\frac{1+n}{1+g}\right]^{-\beta}(1+\gamma)^{-(t+1)} \qquad (6)$$

Actual capital

$$K = K^{*1-\lambda_3}[K_{-1}(1+g)]^{\lambda_3} \qquad (7)$$

Investment

$$I = K - (1-\delta)K_{-1} \qquad (8)$$

Domestic demand and foreign trade

Consumption

$$C = \lambda_5 C_{-1}(1+g) + (1-\lambda_5)\frac{c}{1-\alpha\theta}(Q-\theta\pi) \qquad (9)$$

Imports

$$Im = Q^{e_1}p^{e_2}U_c^{e_3}[(1+g)^{1-e_1}(1+\rho)^{-e_2}]^t\tilde{I}m_0 \qquad (10)$$

Exports

$$Ex = p^{e_4}[(1+g)(1+\rho)^{-e_4}]^t\tilde{E}x_0 \qquad (11)$$

Public expenditures

$$\bar{G} = G_0(1+g)^t \qquad (12)$$

Supply

Work force

$$\bar{N} = \bar{N}_0(1+n)^t \qquad (13)$$

Unemployment rate

$$U_n = \left(1 - \frac{N}{\bar{N}}\right) \qquad (14)$$

Expected real wage rate

$$\omega^{**} = \left(\frac{1+g}{1+n}\,\omega^{**}_{-1}\right)^{\lambda_8}\omega^{1-\lambda_8} \qquad (15)$$

Optimal production capacity

$$\tilde{Q}_c = K(1+m)\left[A\left(\frac{\omega^{**}}{\beta}\right)^{-\beta}(1+\gamma)^t\right]^{1/\alpha} \qquad (16)$$

Capacity utilization rate

$$U_c = Q/\tilde{Q}_c \qquad (17)$$

Continued

TABLE 9.1 (*cont.*)

Wage, price, profits

Nominal wage rate

$$\frac{w}{w_{-1}} = g_1 + g_2 \frac{p}{p_{-1}} + g_3 U_n \qquad (18)$$

Price level

$$p = [p_{-1}(1 + \tau^a)]^{\lambda_7}(U_c/U_{C_c})^{f(1-\lambda_7)}\left(\frac{wN}{\beta Q}\right)^{1-\lambda_7} \qquad (19)$$

Expected inflation rate

$$\tau^a = \lambda_6 \tau^a_{-1} + (1 - \lambda_6)\frac{p - p_{-1}}{p_{-1}} \qquad (20)$$

Real wage rate

$$\omega = w/p \qquad (21)$$

Real profits

$$\pi = Q - \omega N \qquad (22)$$

Money supply and demand

Money supply

$$r = \bar{r} \qquad (23)$$

$$M^+ = r^{\mu_1}[(1 + g)(1 + \rho)]^t \tilde{M}_0^+ \qquad (23')$$

Money demand

$$M^- = [\tilde{M}_0^- pQr^{\mu_2}]^{1-\lambda_9}[(1 + g)(1 + \tau^a)M_{-1}]^{\lambda_9} \qquad (24)$$

Market equilibrium

Goods

$$Q = C + I + \bar{G} + Ex - Im \qquad (25)$$

Money

$$M^+ = M^- \qquad (26)$$

This long-run solution is, in a way, a generalization of the neo-classical growth model, which usually appears, but less explicitly, in macro-econometric models. This explicit introduction has implications at the specification level. This point is discussed in the section on the long-run solution below. We now give some details on the various equations.

Factor demand

Optimal employment and capital are derived through minimization of production cost for anticipated output Q^* and relative cost $(q/\omega)^*$ (equations (4) and (6)). The underlying production technology is assumed to be of the Cobb–Douglas type with constant returns to scale and exogenous technical progress:

$$Q = AK^{\alpha}N^{\beta}e^{\gamma t} \qquad \text{with } \alpha + \beta = 1.$$

Both actual employment and capital have a double lag structure:

(a) anticipated demand and relative cost (equations (2) and (3));
(b) labour and capital adjustment lags (equations (5) and (7)).

Domestic demand and foreign trade

The consumption function is the usual Keynesian function with geometric adjustment lags (equation (9)). Imports and exports depend on three types of factors:

(a) domestic demand (assimilated to production Q) and foreign demand Q_e;
(b) price competitiveness (ratio of domestic to foreign prices in domestic currency); and
(c) capacity utilization rate.

Foreign prices and demand are exogenous. A constant exchange rate assumption is also made. Given these hypotheses, the import and export functions are defined by equations (10) and (11).

Supply and tensions on the goods and labour markets

The notion of capacity used here is a notion of profitable capacity Q_c (optimal production for a given capital) (equation (16)), which consequently depends on the anticipated real wage rate (equation (15)). The labour force is exogenous (equation (13)) and the disequilibrium on the goods and labour markets is defined by the following two variables: capacity utilization (17) and unemployment rates (14).

Prices and wages

As in most models, the general price level is fixed in two steps. The supply, or 'optimal', price (p) is fixed by application of a mark-up upon some unit cost (here marginal cost). This relation can be justified by a short-term profit maximization behaviour of the firm facing a demand curve with a finite elasticity on the goods market. The actual price adjusts then, with a lag, to the optimal price, given the disequilibrium between supply and demand represented by the capacity utilization rate (19). From an economic point of view, it can be noticed that this behaviour is not consistent with the 'quantitative' behaviour of the firms. However, the search for a greater economic consistency would have taken us too far astray from usual macroeconomic specifications.

Lastly, the wage rate is given by a standard Phillips curve which links the nominal wage growth rate to the price growth rate and to the unemployment rate (18). The choice of a specification with growth rates plays an important role in the long-run nominal properties of macroeconometric models, as will be seen later.

Money supply and demand

Two financial assets are considered: money and bonds. The core model offers a standard LM structure with a typical money demand equation.

As for supply, since monetary and financial integration is not the main object of this paper, two alternative simple versions are considered. In the first one, the interest rate is exogenous, which may be interpreted as an infinitely elastic capital inflow, in an open economy with fixed exchange rate. This basic version is the one focused on below. The second version supposes an explicit money supply (23′) independent of the balance of payments. This specification, which corresponds to the traditional hypothesis in a closed economy, will be used only on pp. 236–9 (a more complete study of monetary integration in a closed economy, on the basis of a similar core model can be found in Laffargue (1980)).

List of equations and parameters

The 26 equations are listed in table 9.1 and the parameters in table 9.2. These parameters are of different types:

(a) long-run growth rates (4);
(b) distributed lag coefficients (9); and
(c) structural parameters (20).

As for the distributed lag parameters, λ_i (i = 1–9), we notice that $\lambda_i = 1$ corresponds to an infinitely long adjustment, $\lambda_i = 0$ to an infinitely fast adjustment. The mean lag associated with λ_i is equal to $\tau_i = \lambda_i/(1 - \lambda_i)$.

TABLE 9.2 The parameters

Long-term growth rates
n = Labour force
g = Goods
ρ = Price level
γ = Technical progress

Distributed lag parameters (geometric distribution)
λ_1 = Expected relative capital–labour cost
λ_2 = Expected output
λ_3 = Capital adjustment
λ_4 = Labour adjustment
λ_5 = Consumption adjustment
λ_6 = Expected inflation rate
λ_7 = Price adjustment
λ_8 = Expected real wage rate
λ_9 = Money demand

Structural parameters
α, β = Elasticities of the Cobb–Douglas production function ($\beta = 1 - \alpha$)
c = Long-run propensity to consume
θ = Share of retained profits
m = Average excess capacity
e_1 = Income elasticity of total imports
e_2 = Price elasticity of total imports
e_3 = Elasticity of imports with respect to capacity utilization rate
e_4 = Price elasticity of total exports
g_1 = Constant term of the Phillips relation
g_2 = Price coefficient of the Phillips relation
g_3 = Unemployment coefficient of the Phillips relation
f = Elasticity of price with respect to capacity utilization rate
μ_1 = Elasticity of money supply with respect to interest rate
μ_2 = Elasticity of money demand with respect to interest rate
δ = Rate of fixed capital depreciation

THE LONG RUN: EXISTENCE AND PROPERTIES OF STEADY GROWTH SOLUTIONS

Introduction

One prominent feature of the core model, as compared to the usual macro-econometric models, is the explicit introduction of *long-run constraints.* It should be recalled that, in the present context, a long-run solution is characterized by constant growth rates (not necessarily identical for all the variables of the system) and an identity between expected, or optimal, values and actual values. This requirement of compatibility with a long-run solution has some implications for the specification of the model. As a matter of fact, some homogeneity properties in the relations must hold in order to allow for the existence of such a solution. Furthermore, the way the dynamic adjustments take place should guarantee perfect expectations along these steady growth paths. As will be seen below, it follows that long-run rates of growth have to be incorporated into the dynamic relations.

It is therefore clear that the study of the long-run properties of our core model is a necessary first step.

We give briefly the methodology, before deriving and studying the long run system.

Methodology

Let us call $x^1(t), \ldots, x^n(t)$ the n variables of the dymanic system. A long-run solution will take the following form:

$$x^i(t) = x^i_0(1 + a_i)^t \qquad i = 1, \ldots, n \tag{27}$$

where $((x^i_0), (a_i))$, respectively initial levels and long-run rates of growth, are the $2 \times n$ values to be determined.

It is obvious that the existence of such a solution implies specification constraints on the equations. For example, in a linear relation, all variables must grow at the same rate. If the relation is log-linear, it can readily be seen that the rates of growth may be different, but the multiplicative constant must have a specific trend depending on the parameters of the equation and on the growth rates—see especially the import (10), export (11) and money supply (23) equations.

Beyond these technical constraints, any long-run solution is an equilibrium path along which all expected and optimal values have to be equal to actual values.

This economic requirement implies restrictions on the specification of the dynamic adjustment equations. As it can be seen for example in equations (2), (3), (4) and (5), multiplicative constants depending on the relevant long-run growth rates have to be incorporated.

These methodological remarks explain the 'normalized' aspect of the equations of the core model. For interpreting the long-run system, the dynamic adjustments will generally be supposed to be effective, that is:

$$0 \leq \lambda_i < 1 \qquad i = 1, \ldots, 9.$$

However, in order to disconnect quantities and prices within the same general framework, the special case of $\lambda_1 = 1$ shall be considered (Hyp. $\bar{H}_1$ against $H_1: \lambda_1 < 1$).

A further distinction has to be made according to whether the economy is open (Hyp. H_2: $e_2 \neq 0$ or $e_4 \neq 0$) or closed (Hyp. $\bar{H}_2$: $e_2 = e_4 = 0$) to international competition.

Derivation of the long-run system

The long-run system is the set of equations giving the constant growth rates and the initial levels associated with the long-run solution (27).

The long-run growth rates all derive from the four following basic rates of growth: g = rate of growth of quantities, ρ = rate of growth of prices, n = rate of growth of population, and γ = rate of technical progress. Obviously g, n and γ are not independent. Indeed, the Cobb–Douglas production function implies:

$$1 + g = (1 + n)(1 + \gamma)^{1/\beta}. \tag{28}$$

If we assume n and γ to be exogenous, then g is given by this relation—supply condition—and the growth of demand, especially that of government expenditures, is not freely determined.

The rate of growth of prices ρ results in general from the exogenously given growth of foreign prices. The 'compatible' growth of money supply is at the rate of $(1 + g)(1 + \rho) - 1$.

However, if the conomy is 'closed' w.r.t. foreign prices (Hyp. $\bar{H}_2$), then fixing the growth of money supply at the rate m implies a growth of prices at rate $\rho = (1 + m)/(1 + g) - 1$ (see equation (23′)).

As for long-run initial levels, they are readily determined by writing conditions (27) for time $t = 0$, which yields the equations of table 9.3. No distinction is made between expected/optimal values and realized ones, except for (q/ω).

Several equations require some comments:

(i) The Phillips curve yields a long-run relation between the rate of growth of prices ρ_0 and the unemployment rate U_{n0} (equation (42)).

In other words, this equation determines long-run employment independently of the rest of the system when ρ_0 is exogenously given (equation (47)).

(ii) A progressive adjustment of the price level to marginal cost implies that in the long-run solution the share of real wages is given by neoclassical conditions (equation (44)). The general price level does not appear in this determination.

(iii) As a consequence of (i) and (ii) the determination of the price level p_0 and nominal wages w_0 is implicit.

Properties of the long-run system

In the general case where relative costs are endogenous (case H_1), one can readily compact the long-run system so as to keep only three variables Q_0,

TABLE 9.3 Long-run system

$$q_0 = r_0 - \rho_0 + \delta \tag{29}$$

$$(q/\omega)_0^* = q_0/\omega_0 \text{ if } H_1 \quad \text{or } (q/\omega)_0^* \text{ exogenous if } \bar{H}_1 \tag{30}$$

$$N_0 = \frac{1}{A}\left(\frac{\beta}{\alpha}\right)^{\alpha}\left(\frac{q}{\omega}\right)_0^{*\alpha} Q_0 \tag{31}$$

$$\pi_0 = Q_0 - \omega_0 N_0 \tag{32}$$

$$C_0 = \frac{c}{1 - \alpha\theta}(Q_0 - \theta\pi_0) \tag{33}$$

$$Ex_0 = p_0^{e_4}\tilde{E}x_0 \tag{34}$$

$$\tilde{Q}_{c0} = K_0(1 + m)[A(\beta/\omega)^{+\beta}]^{1/\alpha} \tag{35}$$

$$K_0 = \frac{1}{A}\left(\frac{\beta}{\alpha}\right)^{-\beta}\left(\frac{q}{\omega}\right)_0^{*-\beta} Q_0 \tag{36}$$

$$U_{c0} = Q_0/Qc_0 \tag{37}$$

$$Im_0 = Q_0^{e_1} p_0^{e_2} Uc_0^{e_3} \tilde{I}m_0 \tag{38}$$

$$I_0 = (g + \delta)K_0 \tag{39}$$

$$Q_0 = C_0 + I_0 + \bar{G}_0 + Ex_0 - Im_0 \tag{40}$$

$$U_{n0} = 1 - \frac{N_0}{\bar{N}_0} \tag{41}$$

$$(1 + g)^{1/\beta}(1 + \rho_0) = g_1 + g_2(1 + \rho_0) + g_3 U_{n0} \tag{42}$$

$$\omega_0 = \omega_0 p_0 \tag{43}$$

$$\omega_0 = \beta Q_0/N_0 \tag{44}$$

$$M_0 = r_0^{\mu_1}\tilde{M}_0^{+} \quad \text{or} \quad r_0 = \bar{r} \tag{45}$$

$$M_0 = p_0 Q_0 r_0^{\mu_2}\tilde{M}_0^{-} \tag{46}$$

$$\rho_0 = \rho \quad \text{except for } \{e_2 = e_4 = 0 \quad \text{and} \quad r_0 = \bar{r}\} \tag{47}$$

p_0, r_0, with the following equations:

equilibrium on the goods market

$$sQ_0 - \frac{\alpha Q_0(g + \delta)}{r_0 - \rho + \delta} - G_0 - p_0^{e_4}E\tilde{x}_0 + p_0^{e_2}Q_0^{e_1}I\tilde{m}_0 = 0 \tag{48}$$

equilibrium on the money market

$$r_0 = \bar{r} \qquad \text{or} \qquad p_0 Q_0 - \frac{\tilde{M}_0^{+}}{\tilde{M}_0^{-}} r_0^{\mu} = 0 \tag{49}$$

equilibrium on the labour market

$$Q_0 - \xi \bar{N}_0(r_0 - \rho + \delta)^{-\alpha/\beta} = 0 \tag{50}$$

with

$$s = 1 - c, \qquad \mu = \mu_1 - \mu_2,$$

$$\xi = \frac{[g_1 + g_1(1 + \rho) + g_3 - (1 + g)^{1/\beta}(1 + \rho)]A^{\beta}\alpha^{\alpha/\beta}}{g_3}.$$

Equations (48) and (49) may be interpreted respectively as long-run IS and LM curves. Actually, they do not basically differ from the usual specification of short run IS-LM curves in the context of a small open economy with fixed exchange rate (see e.g. Branson, 1979: chap. 15; Turnovsky, 1977: chap. 9). On the other hand, equation (50) deduced from equations (31), (42) and (44) departs in an essential way from the usual textbook short-term 'supply curve', which gives output as an increasing function of the price level. Here 'labour supply' is rigidly fixed by the long-run Phillips curve (42), and the cost of capital is the crucial price variable to equilibrate this inelastic labour supply with the labour demand as given by equations (31) and (44).

(i) In the case of foreign trade responding to prices (case H_2), and with a monetary policy fixing the interest rate, the LM curve disappears, and the supply curve (50) determines Q_0. p_0 is set in order to reach equilibrium in the goods market (equation (48)). In this case, the long-run model is a pure supply model in which government expenditures have no effect on output.

(ii) If we now suppose a 'closed' economy (Hyp. $\bar{H}_2$) with a fixed money supply, the IS curve, no longer a function of p_0, and the supply curve, together determine Q_0 and r_0 and the LM curve fixes p_0.

In this case, by eliminating r_0 between (48) and (50), we get a single equation in Q_0. It is easy to see that if autonomous expenditures are not too high, this equation may have two solutions, one with high Q_0 and a negative government expenditures multiplier and the other with low Q_0 and a positive multiplier, as has been already pointed out by Laffargue (1980) in a slightly different context.

(iii) Finally, if the two hypotheses $\bar{H}_2$ and $r_0 = \bar{r}$ are jointly made, the rate of inflation must be considered as endogenous; otherwise, there would be two equations (48) and (50) for only one variable Q_0. Here ρ_0, which must replace ρ in equations (48) and (50), plays about the same role as $(-r_0)$ in the previous case. In particular, there may be two symmetrical solutions in (Q_0, ρ_0).

It should be noted that the price level is in this case undetermined.

SHORT-RUN AND MEDIUM-RUN DYNAMICS: A COMPARISON WITH MACROECONOMETRIC MODELS

Introduction

As previously stated, one objective of our core model is to allow a comparative explanatory analysis of the dynamic properties of existing macroeconometric models. In comparing such properties, the need to go beyond a mere impressionistic record of results has long been recognized. A first step consisted of defining homogeneous evaluation procedures (see, for instance, the results of the NBER/NSF comparison seminar—Fromm and Klein, 1976). There were, then, further refinements connected with a 'structural' perspective. For instance, the methodology defined in De Bever et al. (1979) for comparing various Canadian macroeconomic models concentrated on a decomposition of aggregate multipliers into sectoral contributions, so as to attribute the difference in the multipliers to the different sectoral properties.

Our research attempts to go a step further along this line. Our core model is thus intended to offer *a common structural reference* for the previous type of comparisons. If we assume indeed that its structure definitely embodies the main features of macroeconometric models, it should be possible to explain the common characteristics, if any, of these dynamics properties as the reflection of a structurally stable property of the core model relatively unaffected by changes in the values of the parameter, at least over a 'realistic' range. On the contrary, contrasted dynamic evolutions could be traced back to differences in the values of some particular parameters, either characteristic of 'long-term' properties or of adjustment mechanisms.

This section deals with such a study. Our approach is, in a way, very global: we do not try, at this stage, to pinpoint very precise correlations between some particular existing macromodel and a specific numerical 'estimation' of our core model. We rather look for a general explanatory overview of the main dynamic properties of macroeconometric models, with stress put on some salient general conclusions.

Our analysis proceeds as follows and can be paralleled with an approach by 'block simulation'. The next subsection is devoted to *real dynamics*, i.e. the dynamics of real variables when there is no feedback of wage, price and money equations. This can be done, in our core model, by setting some adjustment parameters equal to one (namely λ_1, equation (3): λ_8, equation (15): λ_6, equation (20)) and assuming all profits distributed ($\theta = 0$). Under these same assumptions of no nominal or financial feedback, *wage–price dynamics* are then considered, both from an internal point of view and with respect to the impact of the real block. The last subsection deals with the *integration of real, and wage–price and financial, dynamics.*

The quantitative results for the core model used in these three subsections correspond to three alternative sets of parameters registered in table 9.4, and denoted C_1, C_2 and C_3. They all generate the same long-run solution, and variations are registered with respect to this solution. Numerical data correspond to a yearly basis and are derived from observed data for the French economy in 1970 (initial levels) and common macroeconometric estimates (parameters). Of course, our core model could also be used for a different temporal basis.

TABLE 9.4 Reference values of the parameters

(*a*) *Long-run solution*

Growth rates	Initial levels	
$\gamma = 0.035$	$Q_0 = 1700$	
$n = 0$	$Ex_0 = 320$	$N_0 = 20.0$
$\rho = 0.05$	$Im_0 = 340$	$\hat{N}_0 = 20.5$
	$\bar{G}_0 = 310$	$M_0 = 1000$
	$p_0 = 1.0$	

(*b*) *Parameters constant in all simulations*

$\delta = 0.5$	$\alpha = 0.2$	$c = 0.68$	$m = 0.2$

(*c*) *Other parameters*

	Elasticities, propensities				Lags		
	C_1	C_2	C_3 (full model)		C_1	C_2	C_3 (full model)
θ	0	0	0.6	λ_1	1.0	1.0	0.9
e_1	1.0	1.0	1.0	λ_2	0.5	0.3	0.3
e_2	0	0	0.3	λ_3	0.7	0.75	0.75
e_3	0	1.2	1.2	λ_4	0.5	0.2	0.2
e_4	0	0	−1.0	λ_5	0.5	0.5	0.5
g_1	0.5	0.5	0.5	λ_6	1.0	1.0	0.4/0.8
g_2	1.0	1.0	0.7/1.0	λ_7	0.5	0.3	0.3
g_3	−0.1	−0.1	−0.1	λ_8	1.0	1.0	0.4/1.0
f	0.4	0.4	0.4	λ_9	0	0	0
μ_1	0	0	0				
μ_8	−1.0	−1.0	−1.0				

Real dynamics

It is well known that real dynamics constitute a fundamental component of macroeconometric models. Indeed, in the short run and often over several periods, these dynamics 'dominate' other mechanisms and, as far as real variables are concerned, of course, the dynamic multipliers with, or without, nominal/financial feedbacks are not very different over this range. Real dynamics are, therefore, a very important element accounting for observed differences, or similarities, in the quantitative behaviour of models. In this respect, our analysis focuses, in particular, on a very common feature of macroeconometric models, namely their *general inability to produce any significant deterministic endogenous cycle.*

(a) We first use our macromodel to compare instantaneous multipliers (public expenditures) of various models. The short-run GNP multiplier of the real part of the core model (when all profits are distributed) is given by the following formula:

$$m = \frac{1}{1 + (e_1 + e_3)i_m - \bar{\lambda}_2 \bar{\lambda}_3 k - c\bar{\lambda}_5} \quad \text{with}$$

$$i_m = \frac{Im_0}{Q_0},\ k = \frac{K_0}{Q_0},\ \bar{\lambda}_i = 1 - \lambda_i \tag{51}$$

It can be readily observed that this short-run multiplier (in the range of non-negativity) increases when:

(a) the long-run marginal propensity to consume (c) and capital/output ratio (k) increases,
(b) the long-run average propensity to import (i_m) and short-run elasticities (e_1, e_3) decrease, and
(c) the speed of adjustments of anticipated production (λ_2), desired capital (λ_3) and consumption (λ_5) increases.

Table 9.5 gives the variation and decomposition of this multiplier for changes in those last parameters. It can be observed that, to keep the short-run multiplier in a standard 'realistic' range (not higher than 2.5), *it is necessary to impose rather strict lower bounds on associated delays* (especially on investment; cumulative effect of λ_2 and λ_3). This constraint put on real dynamic adjustments by short-run stability has, of course, important consequences on the medium-run dynamics of macroeconometric models, as is seen below.

In this respect, table 9.6 gives the 'interpretation' of the short-run multipliers of various macroeconometric models in terms of our macromodel. It can be observed, of course, that one main factor of dispersion consists of the foreign trade equations.

(b) The study of the real dynamics of the core model can start from a qualitative basis, given by a formal linearization of the corresponding equa-

TABLE 9.5 Short-run public expenditure multipliers for varying adjustment speeds

λ_i	0	0.1	0.3	0.5	0.7	0.9	1.0
Anticipated demand (λ_2)							
$\Delta Q/\Delta G$	2.78	2.44	1.96	1.64	1.41	1.23	1.16
$\Delta C/\Delta G$	0.95	0.83	0.67	0.56	0.48	0.42	0.39
$\Delta I/\Delta G$	1.39	1.10	0.69	0.41	0.21	0.06	0
$\frac{\Delta Ex}{\Delta G} - \frac{\Delta Im}{\Delta G}$	−0.56	−0.49	−0.40	−0.33	−0.28	−0.25	−0.23
Consumption (λ_5)							
$\Delta Q/\Delta G$	3.70	2.94	2.13	1.64	1.33	1.14	1.05
$\Delta C/\Delta G$	2.51	1.79	1.02	0.56	0.27	0.08	0
$\Delta I/\Delta G$	0.93	0.74	0.54	0.41	0.33	0.29	0.26
$\frac{\Delta Ex}{\Delta G} - \frac{\Delta Im}{\Delta G}$	−0.74	−0.59	−0.43	−0.33	−0.27	−0.23	−0.21
Capital (λ_3)							
$\Delta Q/\Delta G$	50.0	9.10	3.57	2.27	1.64	1.28	1.16
$\Delta C/\Delta G$	17.0	3.09	1.21	0.77	0.56	0.44	0.39
$\Delta I/\Delta G$	42.0	6.83	2.07	0.95	0.41	0.10	0
$\frac{\Delta Ex}{\Delta G} - \frac{\Delta Im}{\Delta G}$	−10.0	−1.82	−0.71	−0.45	−0.33	−0.26	−0.23

tions along the long-run solution. This yields a dynamic system of order 3, with state variables Q^*, C, K; which is in fact a particular form of the 'accelerator–multiplier' scheme:

$$\frac{dQ^*}{1+g} = \lambda_2[1 + mk\bar{\lambda}_2\bar{\lambda}_3]\, dQ^*_{-1} + m\bar{\lambda}_2\lambda_5\, dC_{-1} + m\bar{\lambda}_2 \times \left(e_3\frac{i_m}{k} + \lambda_3 - (1-\delta')\right) dK_{-1}$$

$$\frac{dC}{1+g} = mkc\lambda_2\bar{\lambda}_3\bar{\lambda}_5\, dQ^*_{-1} + \lambda_5[1 + mc\bar{\lambda}_5]\, dC_{-1} + mc\bar{\lambda}_5 \times \left(e_3\frac{i_m}{k} + \lambda_3 - (1-\delta')\right) dK_{-1} \tag{52}$$

$$\frac{dK}{1+g} = \lambda_2[1 + m\bar{\lambda}_2\bar{\lambda}_3]\lambda_3 k\, dQ^*_{-1} + m\bar{\lambda}_2\bar{\lambda}_3\lambda_5 k\, dC_{-1} + \left[\lambda_3 + mk\bar{\lambda}_2\bar{\lambda}_3 k\left(e_3\frac{i_m}{k} + \lambda_3 - (1-\delta')\right)\right] dK_{-1}$$

TABLE 9.6 Decomposition of the short-run public expenditure multiplier for various macroeconometric models

	Core model C_1	French models				US models		Canadian models			
		DMS	METRIC	PITI	DECA	BROO-KINGS	HC	CANDIDE	QFM	RDX 2	TRACE
$\Delta Q/\Delta G$	1.64	1.10	1.38	1.54	1.26	2.79	1.74	1.67	1.37	0.90	1.87
$\Delta C/\Delta G$	0.56	0.31	0.31	0.22	0.37	1.11	0.31	0.93	0.45	0.18	0.74
$\Delta I/\Delta G$	0.41	0.35	0.66	0.82	0.58	0.82	0.53	0.60	0.20	0	0.67
$-\frac{\Delta Im}{\Delta G}+\frac{\Delta Ex}{\Delta G}$	−0.33	−0.55	−0.60	−0.48	−0.69	−p.14	−0.10	−0.86	−0.28	−0.28	−0.54
$1+(\underline{e_1}+\overline{e_3})im$	1.20	1.50	1.43	1.31	1.55	1.05	1.06	1.51	1.20	1.31	1.29
$-k\underline{\lambda_3}\ \overline{\lambda_3}$	−0.25	−0.32	−0.48	−0.53	−0.46	−0.29	−0.31	−0.36	−0.15	0	−0.36
$-c\lambda_5$	−0.34	−0.28	−0.22	−0.14	−0.29	−0.40	−0.17	−0.56	−0.33	−0.20	−0.40
$\frac{\Delta G}{\Delta Q}$	0.61	0.90	0.73	0.64	0.80	0.36	0.58	0.59	0.72	1.11	0.53

Source: The comparative set of multipliers is taken from Artus and Muet (1980) and de Bever et al. (1979).

The consideration of limit cases (putting the λ_i's equal to zero or one) shows that, to get cycles, it is necessary to have 'fast enough' adjustments on consumption and, mainly, on investment.

This statement can be made quantitatively precise by computing the eigenvalues of the system for varying λ_i's. This is done in table 9.7. *It can be noticed that it is not possible to obtain significant 'interesting' cycles* (by this, we mean cycles over the 4–10 year range not quickly dampened) *unless delays on consumption* (λ_5), *and mainly investment* (λ_2, λ_3), *are very short, in any case much shorter than those usually encountered in macroeconometric models* (see tables 9.5 and 9.6).

This rather robust conclusion gives a general explanation of the absence of significant endogenous deterministic cycles in macroeconometric models and of the sluggish increasing evolution of their GNP multiplier (for sustained constant increase in public expenditures and during the first periods, when price effects are not determinant), which has come to be considered as the earmark of a 'well behaved' model.

Wage–price dynamics

The study of wage–price dynamics by themselves is justified on double grounds. First, the 'near-decomposability' of many macroeconometric models, previously mentioned, implies that this study is useful in understanding their actual wage–price dynamics over the first periods of simulation. Secondly, it will be seen in the next subsection that these dynamics are crucial for the medium-run/long-run behaviour of the whole model. It is therefore necessary to have a clear understanding of them.

(a) In the following, we will restrict ourselves to the case of an exogenous long-run anticipated rate of inflation. In this case, the wage and price equations can be written:

$$\frac{w}{w_{-1}} = g_1 + g_2 \frac{p}{p_{-1}} + g_3 U_n \tag{53}$$

$$p = [p_{-1}(1 + \rho)]^{\lambda_7} w^{1-\lambda_7} \left[\frac{N}{\beta Q}\left(\frac{U_c}{U_{eo}}\right)^f\right]^{1-\lambda_7}. \tag{54}$$

This system is linear–homogeneous in w and p. This suggests that the real wage rate be considered, $\omega = w/p$. It can be observed, moreover, that it is the rate of price *growth* $\psi = p/p_{-1}$ which is relevant for the determination of the block.

Using the following notation:

variable exogenous w.r.t. the wage equation

$$u = g_1 + g_3 U_n$$

TABLE 9.7 Eigenvalues of the real block for varying speeds of adjustment

λ_i	0.1	0.3	0.5	0.7	0.9
Anticipated demand (λ_2)					
EV 1	0.35	0.39	0.52	0.57	0.63
Modulus	0.35	0.39	0.52	0.57	0.63
Period	∞	∞	∞	∞	∞
EV 2	0.64 + i0.29	0.75 + i0.25	0.83 + i0.23	0.84 + i0.17	0.89
Modulus	0.70	0.79	0.86	0.85	0.89
Period	15	19	23	32	∞
EV 3	0.64 − i0.29	0.75 − i0.25	0.83 − i0.23	0.84 − i0.17	0.84
Modulus	0.70	0.79	0.86	0.85	0.84
Period	15	19	23	32	∞
Consumption (λ_5)					
EV 1	0.18	0.37	0.52	0.70	0.96
Modulus	0.18	0.37	0.52	0.70	0.96
Period	∞	∞	∞	∞	∞
EV 2	0.76 + i0.35	0.79 + i0.29	0.83 + i0.23		0.65 + i0.17
Modulus	0.83	0.84	0.86		0.67
Period	15	18	23		24
EV 3	0.76 − i0.35	0.79 − i0.29	0.83 − i0.23		0.65 − i0.17
Modulus	0.83	0.84	0.86		0.67
Period	15	18	23		24
Capital (λ_3)					
EV 1	0.52	0.52	0.52	0.52	0.52
Modulus	0.52	0.52	0.52	0.52	0.52
Period	∞	∞	∞	∞	∞
EV 2	0.03 + i0.73	0.59 + i0.54	0.73 + i0.37	0.83 + i0.23	0.78
Modulus	0.73	0.80	0.82	0.86	0.78
Period	4	8.4	13	23	∞
EV 3	0.03 − i0.73	0.59 − i0.54	0.73 − i0.37	0.83 − i0.23	0.89
Modulus	0.73	0.80	0.82	0.86	0.89
Period	4	8.4	13	23	∞

variable exogenous w.r.t. the price equation

$$v = \frac{N}{\beta Q}\left(\frac{U_c}{U_{co}}\right)^f \tag{55}$$

mean price adjustment lag

$$\tau = \frac{\lambda_7}{1 - \lambda_7}$$

one gets the following non-linear system in ω and ψ:

$$\begin{aligned} \omega &= \omega_{-1}[g_2 + u/\psi] \\ \psi &= (1 + \rho)v^{1/\tau}\omega^{1/\tau}. \end{aligned} \tag{56}$$

To study the corresponding dynamics, we first divide each variable by its long-run value (which makes the long-run solution appear as a stationary solution), then linearize the transformed system around its long-run (stationary) equilibrium (see Malgrange, 1981). Noting by ˆ the transformed variables, this yields

$$\begin{aligned} d\hat{\omega} &= d\hat{\omega}_{-1} + \left(1 - g_2\frac{1+n}{1+g}\right)(d\hat{u} - d\hat{\psi}) \\ d\hat{\psi} &= \frac{1}{\tau}(d\hat{\omega} + d\hat{v}). \end{aligned} \tag{57}$$

Noting

$$\gamma = 1 - g_2\left(\frac{1+n}{1+g}\right)$$

which characterizes the rate of 'money illusion', it comes out the following (decomposable) system:

$$\begin{aligned} d\hat{\omega} &= \frac{1}{1+\gamma/\tau}\, d\hat{\omega}_{-1} + \frac{1}{1+\gamma/\tau}\left(\gamma d\hat{u} - \frac{1}{\tau}\, d\hat{v}\right) \\ \widehat{d\psi} &= \frac{1}{\tau}(d\hat{\omega} + d\hat{v}). \end{aligned} \tag{58}$$

The eigenvalue of this system is thus

$$r = 1/(1 + \gamma/\tau) \tag{59}$$

which synthesizes the two fundamental factors for wage–price dynamics:

(a) speed of price adjustment $(1/\tau)$,
(b) indexation of wage growth on price growth (γ).

The more stable the associated dynamics (*'relative' stability* (*Malgrange, 1981*) *in terms of real wage rate and of price inflation*), the weaker these two parameters will be. For usual macroeconometric estimations, this condition of relative stability appears to be fulfilled, γ being positive.

It is straightforward to derive the evolutions of $d\hat{\omega}$ and $d\hat{\psi}$ for initial 'shocks' $d\hat{u}_0$ and $d\hat{v}_0$. If stability is ensured, $d\hat{\omega}$ and $d\hat{\psi}$ will tend to zero for a shock $d\hat{v}_0$, to a finite value for a shock $d\hat{u}_0$ (difference between a shock on a level and on a growth rate).

(b) A quantitative picture of the variations of the autonomous wage–price dynamics of the core model w.r.t. g_2 and λ_7 (i.e. γ and τ) is given in columns 2 to 4 of table 9.8. To simplify comparisons with common practice, these columns register the percentage change in the price level generated by a sustained increase of public expenditures equal to 1 per cent of their long-run value, column 1 giving the results corresponding to various macroeconometric models. *The determinant influence of wage–price indexation appears very clearly.* Indeed, to keep the simulation results of the core model within observed values, it is necessary to assume a *moderate indexation of wage growth on price growth* ($g_2 = 0.7$), which reflects standard estimation results and gives a first reason for the usually moderately inflationist behaviour, in the short–medium run, of macroeconometric models.

In fact, some of these models are not only weakly inflationist, but even *deflationist in the short run.* Results of the core model given in columns 5 to 8 of table 9.8 clearly point out the role of *employment cycles* in this respect. When adjustment of employed labour is slow enough (λ_4), then short-term productivity rises and this yields the observed result. Such slowness in employment adjustment can actually be observed in several macroeconometric models giving short-run deflationist results. It can be noted, moreover, that, in conformity with our previous analytical study, the impact of employment cycles on prices is rather transitory (whereas altering g_3 has a long-run effect).

To sum up this discussion of wage–price dynamics, the results of our core model and their comparison with macroeconometric evolutions yield the following two main conclusions:

(a) The determining factors for wage–price dynamics, *particularly in the medium/long run*, consist of wage–price indexation and speed of price adjustment. The rather gradual evolutions generated by some macroeconometric models can be linked to moderate values of the corresponding parameters,
(b) The short-run deflationist behaviour sometimes observed in macroeconometric models is to be connected with the presence of strong 'employment cycles'. Their influence is, however, stronger in the short run than in the medium/long run.

TABLE 9.8 Wage–Price dynamics for varying parameters (per cent change in the price level for a 1 per cent sustained increase in public expenditures)

Year	Macro-econometric models	Full indexation C_2 $g_2 = 1$ $\lambda_7 = 0.3$	Incomplete indexation C'_2 $g_2 = 0.7$ $\lambda_7 = 0.3$	Incomplete indexation and slow prices $g_2 = 0.7$ $\lambda_7 = 0.5$	Varying parameters w.r.t. C_2			
					$\lambda_4 = 0$	$\lambda_4 = 0.5$	$g_3 = 0$	$f = 0$
1	−0.5 to 0.2	ε	ε	ε	0.4	−0.5	−0.1	−1.0
2	−0.2 to 0.5	0.7	0.5	0.3	1.4	−0.5	0.0	−1.3
3	−0.1 to 0.5	1.9	1.0	0.6	2.7	−0.5	0.9	−0.9
4	0.2 to 1.0	3.3	1.6	1.0	4.2	0.9	1.4	−0.2
5	0.6 to 3.0	5.0	2.1	1.4	5.8	2.1	1.0	1.0
7	1 to 7	8.7	2.9	2.2	9.8	5.5	2.4	4.0
10	3 to 20	15.4	4.2	3.5	16.4	19.2	2.5	10.5

Medium- and long-run dynamics: the interaction of real and nominal-financial dynamics

The two previous subsections dealt with two different types of dynamics, of contrasting characteristics:

(a) real dynamics, which give stable increasing responses of the GNP, without any significant cycle, to sustained increases in public expenditures,
(b) nominal dynamics, which, in the same conditions, produce monotonic divergent evolutions of the price and wage level (but usually with relative stability of the real wage and inflation rate).

It has been mentioned that these dynamics appear in a somehow 'pure' manner in most models, given their 'near-decomposability', during the first periods of simulation.

The present paragraph focuses on the interaction of both dynamics and is, therefore, particularly relevant for the medium- and long-run dynamics of macroeconometric models. It is well known that, in this range, models of similar structure can give contradictory answers, even from a very crude qualitative point of view (downwards, or upwards, divergence of the multiplier, or stabilization, . . .). It follows that, whereas, for the short-run/medium-run pattern of dynamic multipliers there is somehow an agreement among model builders about a standard 'well behaved' shape, no such consensus exists for the medium-run/long-run and comparisons of models are rather mute on this point.

The flexible character of our core model allows a systematic study of this question by successively concentrating on the main factors of nominal/real integration. In this respect, the multiplicity of possible long-run behaviours of models appears very clearly.

(a) The *first source* of integration to be studied consists of *the influence of wages, prices and the rate of interest on production.* For the core model, two mechanisms can operate in this field:

(i) the influence of real wage on production capacity (equations (15) and (16)),
(ii) the influence of relative factor prices on the choice of techniques (equations (1), (3), (4) and (5)).

The first case is illustrative of models with vintage capital and an endogenous extensive margin. Table 9.9 gives the multipliers for a sustained increase of public expenditures equal to 1 per cent of their reference level without (column 1 to 4—$\lambda_8 = 1$) and with (column 5 to 8—$\lambda_8 = 0.4$) an effect of real wage rate on capacity. It can be observed that, in the short

TABLE 9.9 Real wage rate and production capacity

	$g_2 = 1$							
	No feedback, $\lambda_8 = 1.0$				Integration, $\lambda_8 = 0.4$			
	GNP, $\frac{\Delta Q}{\Delta G}$	Capacity, $\frac{\Delta Qc}{\Delta G}$	Price, $\frac{p - pr}{pr}$ (%)	Real wage rate, $\frac{\omega - \omega r}{\omega r}$ (%)	GNP, $\frac{\Delta Q}{\Delta G}$	Capacity, $\frac{\Delta Qc}{\Delta G}$	Prices, $\frac{p - pr}{pr}$ (%)	Real wage rate, $\frac{\omega - \omega r}{\omega r}$ (%)
1	1.2	0	0	0	1.2	−0.1	0.1	0
2	1.6	0.1	0.7	0.1	1.5	−0.1	1.1	0.1
3	1.9	0.6	1.9	0.2	1.7	−0.1	2.6	0.2
4	2.2	1.0	3.3	0.3	1.8	0	4.4	0.2
5	2.4	1.5	5.0	0.4	2.0	0	6.5	0.2
6	2.5	1.9	6.8	0.5	1.9	0	8.8	0.3
7	2.6	2.2	8.7	0.6	1.8	−0.1	11.2	0.3
8	2.7	2.6	10.8	0.7	1.7	−0.2	13.7	0.3
9	2.8	2.8	13.0	0.7	1.7	−0.3	16.2	0.3
10	2.8	3.1	15.4	0.8	1.6	−0.4	18.8	0.4
15	2.9	3.9	29.5	1.1	1.3	−0.8	31.0	0.3
20	3.0	4.2	46.8	1.1	1.2	−1.0	41.7	0.2
40	3.0	4.4	127.8	0.7	1.3	−0.9	69.5	0.1

run, the induced changes are not very important except on prices. In the medium run/long run the depressing effects on the GNP multiplier become noticeable (1.6 after 10 years instead of 2.8).

As for the choice of techniques, the relevant variable is the relative capital labour cost:

$$q/\omega = \frac{r + \delta - \tau_a}{\omega}.$$

Figures 9.1 and 9.2 give five simulations, respectively with full wage–price indexation (figure 9.1—$g_2 = 1$) and incomplete indexation (figure 9.2—$g_2 = 0.7$), for a sustained increase of public expenditures (1 per cent reference level), and with the following assumptions:

simulation 1: no feedback ($\lambda_1 = 1$);
simulation 2: influence of the real wage rate only ($\lambda_1 = 0.9$);
simulation 3: influence of the real wage rate ($\lambda_1 = 0.9$) and of the anticipated inflation rate ($\lambda_6 = 0.6$);

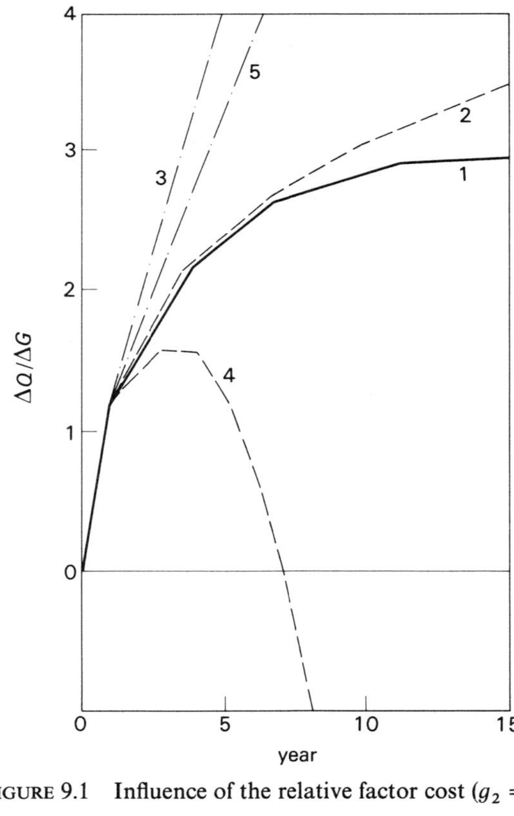

FIGURE 9.1 Influence of the relative factor cost ($g_2 = 1$)

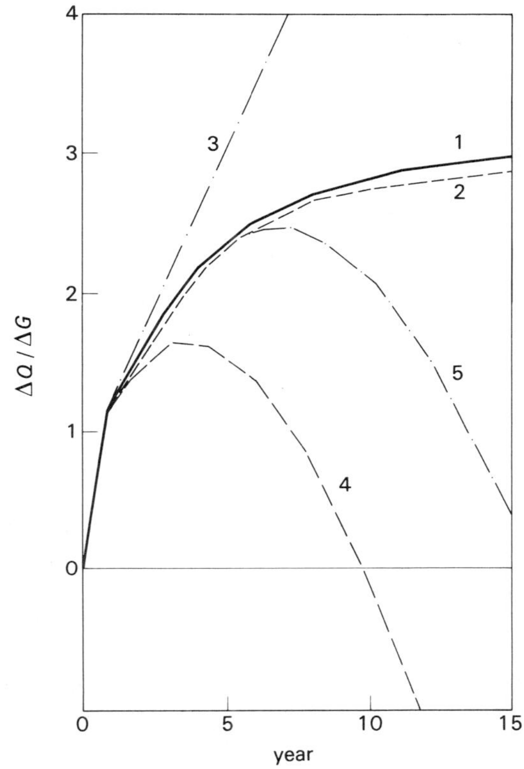

FIGURE 9.2 Influence of the relative factor cost ($g_2 = 0.7$)

simulation 4: influence of the real wage rate ($\lambda_1 = 0.9$) and of the interest rate ($\mu_2 = -1$);

simulation 5: influence of the real wage rate ($\lambda_1 = 0.9$), of the anticipated inflation rate ($\lambda_6 = 0.6$) and of the interest rate ($\mu_2 = -1$).

Two main conclusions can be drawn from these simulations, to be paralleled with the results given by macroeconometric models:

(1) The feedback influence of the real wage rate on the real sector is of secondary importance compared to that of capital cost.

(2) Long-run properties are very sensitive to the numerical estimation of wage–price indexation (which is recalled to be determinative for wage–price dynamics). According to the magnitude of this indexation, the cost of capital will be more ($g_2 = 1$) or less ($g_2 = 0.7$) alleviated by anticipated inflation than increased by interest rates, with a consequent upward or downward divergence of the GNP multiplier.

TABLE 9.10 Income distribution and consumption

Year	$\frac{\Delta Q}{\Delta G}$ $\theta = 0$	$\theta = 0.6$ Exogenous price–wage	$g_2 = 1$	$g_2 = 0.7$
1	1.23	1.18	1.13	1.23
2	1.63	1.46	1.50	1.47
3	1.94	1.75	1.83	1.75
4	2.18	2.00	2.12	1.97
5	2.36	2.19	2.40	2.15
10	2.82	2.86	3.62	2.78
15	2.93	2.94	4.91	3.44
20	2.96	3.04	10.50	3.74
40	2.97	3.06	16.28	3.88

(b) The *second source* of nominal feedback to be considered consists of *the influence of income distribution upon consumption and investment.*

Table 9.10 gives the GNP multiplier for all profits distributed ($\theta = 0$) (column 1) and for some retained profits ($\theta = 0.6$), in this last case with exogenous prices and wages (column 2), full indexation ($g_2 = 1$—column 3), incomplete indexation ($g_2 = 0.7$—column 4). It can be seen that the changes induced through the consumption function are not very important in the short run/medium run (except for some effects of the employment cycle). In the long run, the behaviour of the real wage rate is determining and induces an increase of the GNP multiplier, which is stronger the higher the real wage rate (higher g_2).

As for the influence of income distribution on investment, it is necessary, to test it, to adopt a modified form of the investment function, namely:

$$K^a = (K^*)^{1-\lambda_3}[K_{-1}(1+g)]^{\lambda_3} \tag{60}$$

$$\pi^* = \lambda_{10}(1+g)\pi^*_{-1} + (1-\lambda_{10})\pi \tag{61}$$

$$I = v[K^a - (1-\delta)K_{-1}] + (1-v)a\pi^* \tag{62}$$

$$K = I + (1-\delta)K_{-1}. \tag{63}$$

For $v = 1$, one gets the previous specification, for $v = 0$ a pure profit model.

Figure 9.3 gives the simulations corresponding to:

$$v = 0.5 \qquad \lambda_{10} = 0.6$$

with wages and prices exogenous (simulation 1), full indexation ($g_2 =$ 1—simulation 2), incomplete indexation ($g_2 = 0.7$—simulation 3). The

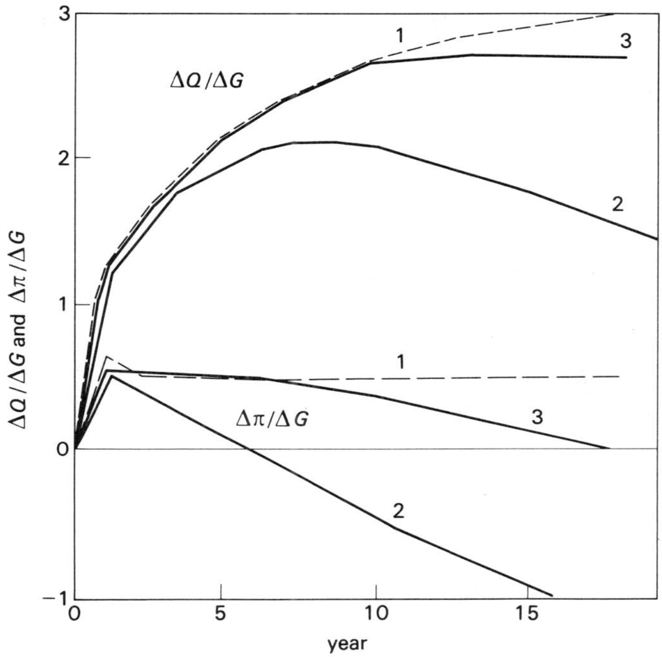

FIGURE 9.3 Profits and investment (see text)

results are qualitatively and quantitatively similar to those obtained for the influence of income distribution upon consumption: moderate effects in the short-run/medium-run, medium-run/long-run behaviour determined by the evolution of real wages.

Figure 9.4 shows how these changes are reinforced when the influence of profits upon investment is increased (simulation for $v = 1$, $v = 0.5$, $v = 0$; $\lambda_{10} = 0.6$, $g_2 = 1$).

(c) The *third and last source* of influence of prices on the real block of our core model is *their effect on demand through imports and exports.*

Figures 9.5 and 9.6 give the simulations obtained with $e_2 = 0.3$ and $e_4 = 1.0$ and, respectively, $g_2 = 1$ (simulation 1), $g_2 = 1$ and $\lambda_7 = 0.5$ (simulation 2), $g_2 = 0.7$ (simulation 3), $g_2 = 0.7$ and $\lambda_7 = 0.5$ (simulation 4). As for prices, simulations 1′ to 4′ correspond to these same values of g_2 and λ_7 with $e_3 = e_4 = 0$ (no integration). *These simulations demonstrate the sensitivity of medium-run/long-run dynamics to the characteristics of wage–price dynamics when the influence of prices upon imports and exports is effective.* When inflationary dynamics are not 'too strong' (3 and 4), integrating price effects upon foreign trade gives a short/medium-run dampening of the multiplier followed by a downward long-run divergence. *This type of evolution is indeed characteristic of many macroeconometric models.* For highly

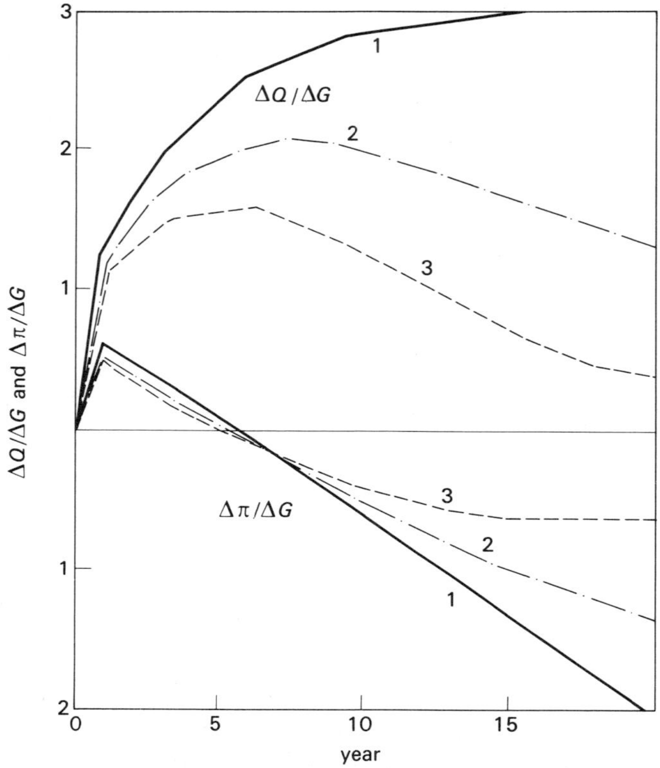

FIGURE 9.4 Profits and investment (see text)

inflationary mechanisms (2 and mainly 1), the depressing effect of prices operates more quickly. Long-run behaviour appears structurally unstable. For full indexation the core model can exhibit strong cycles (more production → increased prices → reduced exports, increased imports → less production. . .), or explosive downward evolution, according to the speed of price adjustment.

(d) Let us sum up the main conclusions of our study of the interaction of real and nominal dynamics and of their impact on the medium/long-run behaviour of macroeconometric models:

(1) The interaction of real dynamics, and of nominal dynamics, of contrasting characteristics, allows a variety of medium/long-run global dynamics. The characteristics of wage–price dynamics are of determining importance, through the speed of price adjustment and, mainly, the wage–price indexation.

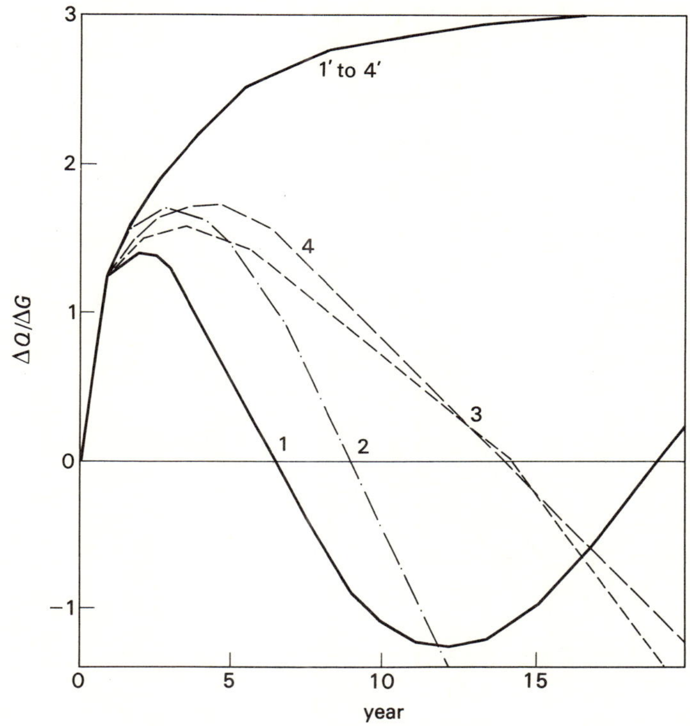

FIGURE 9.5 Prices and foreign trade (see text)

(2) For moderate wage–price dynamics, which is the case in many macro-econometric models, this interaction, except for a very strong effect of income distribution upon consumption, depresses the GNP multiplier in the short/medium run and induces a long-run monotonic decline of this multiplier, through various channels (cost of capital, profits/investment, foreign trade). This appears to be a case frequently encountered in practice.

(3) For strong wage–price dynamics different types of long-run behaviour may occur: upward explosion (for instance, through the decrease of capital cost induced by inflation) or even cycles (foreign trade). The two main channels for contrasted long-run behaviours appear to be first the cost of capital, and second the foreign trade equations.

This long-run structural instability of models suggests that greater caution be used in long-run simulation and that greater attention be paid to long-run structural properties (as already shown).

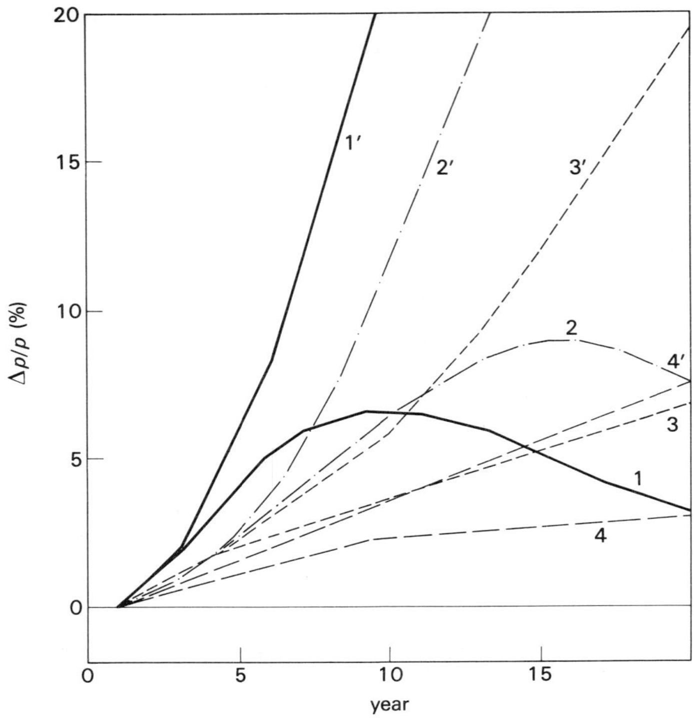

FIGURE 9.6 Prices and foreign trade (see text)

CONCLUSION

Rather than repeat the results given in the previous sections, we would like, in this general conclusion, to broaden the scope of the potential uses of 'core models', of the kind presented here.

First of all, it is our strong conviction that resorting to such instruments is very beneficial for, let us say, 'applied macroeconomic theory'. On the theory side, it is clear that pure qualitative analysis cannot go beyond rather simple schemes. As soon as the theoretical system becomes somewhat complex, because of the number of variables and relations and/or of its mathematical structure itself, it is necessary, in order to obtain any precise conclusion (other than existence results), to practise some kind of quantitative approach. This is obvious, for instance, in the case of fixed price macroeconomic theoretical models, in which analytical results can easily be obtained only for the three goods atemporal paradigm: the study of less elementary structures makes numerical estimation and simulation necessary (see, for instance, Blanchard and Sachs, 1982; Bureau et al., 1981).

Another field in which a careful quantitative approach is needed is clearly the long-run properties of macromodels. On the applied side, namely the construction of macroeconometric models, the reference to core models should help for a more controlled and transparent practice.

It seems thus, to us, that this approach by core models can be of wide use, and concerns both macroeconomic teaching and research as well as macroeconometric modelling. Of course, for this to be possible, advances have to be made. There is first a need for studying macroeconomic mechanisms which have not been systematically taken into account either in this study or in others. In this respect two important areas are the monetary and financial sector and the anticipations phenomena.[2] Another very important, and somehow neglected, aspect is the accessibility of such core models. If one seeks effectively to reach the public of potential users concerned by such instruments, it is necessary to have no technical 'barrier to entry'. In this respect, the development of *flexible interactive computer programs*[3] allowing for easy variations of parameters, exogenous data and equations, giving instantaneous visual and graphic representations, without any preliminary learning cost, is a necessary condition for expanding the use of core models.

NOTES

This paper draws heavily on the following two presentations (in French): Deleau et al. (1981a, b) which are part of a research contract supported by the Commissariat Général du Plan (CORDES no. 41–79) (see Deleau et al., 1980).

1 Several research works using similar methodology and with similar objectives have recently been developed (Bergstrom and Wymer, 1976; Gandolfo, 1981).
2 An extended version of the present core model, encompassing modifications in the underlying production function and the introduction of a detailed monetary/financial sector, is to be found in Jullien and Magnac (1982).
3 Such a program, developed within a cooperative CEPREMAP–ENPC research contract financed by the Commissariat General de Plan, is presently being tested.

REFERENCES

Artus, P. and Muet, P. A. (1980) 'Une Étude Comparative des Propriétés Dynamiques de Dix Modèles Américains et de Cinq Modèles Français', *Revue Economique*, **31**, no. 1.

Bergstrom, A. R. and Wymer, C. R. (1976) 'A Model of Disequilibrium Neoclassical Growth and its Application to the United Kingdom', in Bergstrom (ed.), *Statistical Inference in Continuous Time Economic Models*, North-Holland, Amsterdam.

de Bever, L., Foot, D. K., Helliwell, J. F., Jump, G. V., Maxwell, T., Sawyer, J. A. and Waslander, H. E. L. (1979) 'Dynamic Properties of Four Canadian Macroeconomic Models: A Collaborative Research Project', *The Canadian Journal of Economics*, **12**, no. 2.

Blanchard, O. J. and Sachs, J. (1982) *Anticipations, Recessions and Policy: An Intertemporal Disequilibrium Model*, Working Paper, Harvard.

Branson, W. H. (1979) *Macroeconomic Theory and Policy*, Harper and Row, New York.

Bureau, D., Miqueu, D. and Norotte, M. (1981) *Dynamique des Modèles de Déséquilibre: Une Maquette*, Working Paper no. 223/C31, Direction de la Prévision.

Deleau, M., Laffargue, J. P., Malgrange, P., de Menil, G. and Muet, P. A. (1980) *Recherches sur les Fondements de la Modélisation Macroéconomique Quantitative*, mimeographed, CEPREMAP.

Deleau, M., Malgrange, P. and Muet, P. A. (1981a) *Une Étude de la Dynamique des Modèles Macroéconomiques*, mimeographed, CEPREMAP, no. 8107.

Deleau, M., Malgrange, P. and Muet, P. A. (1981b) 'Une Maquette Représentative des Modèles Macroéconomiques', *Annales de l'INSEE*, no. 42.

Fromm, G. and Klein, L. R. (1976) 'The NBER/NSF Model Comparison Seminar: An Analysis of Results', *Annals of Economics and Social Measurement*, **5**, no. 2.

Gandolfo, G. (1981) *Qualitative Analysis and Econometric Estimation of Continuous Time Dynamic Models*, North-Holland, Amsterdam.

Jullien, B. and Magnac, T. (1982) *Proposition et Étude de Variantes Structurelles d'une Maquette Macroéconomique*, Working Paper, CERAS-ENPC.

Laffargue, J. P. (1980) 'Les Modèles Macrodynamiques de Politique Économique: Dialogue Entre le Théoricien et l'Économètre', *Annales de l'INSEE*, no. 40.

Malgrange, P. (1981) 'Note sur le Calcul des Valeurs Propres d'un Modèle Macroéconométrique', *Annales de l'INSEE*, no. 41.

Muet, P. A. (1979) 'La Modélisation Macroéconomique: Étude de la Structure des Modèles Macroéconométriques', *Statistiques et Études Financières*, série orange, no. hors série.

Turnovsky, S. J. (1977) *Macroeconomic Analysis and Stabilization Policy*, Cambridge University Press.

Comment

G. d'ALCANTARA

In our view the aggregative core model or backbone (BB) model is most suited for educational purposes. We appreciate the fact that the authors have no claim that their instrument is suited for descriptive analysis or alternative simulations oriented towards policy. Maybe their qualification to build a 'model of models' or a 'common structural reference' to all macroeconomic models is somewhat abusive even if their BB model is a relevant introduction to a broad class of Keynesian macromodels. It appears that the Deleau–Malgrange–Muet approach leads to two conclusions.

The first conclusion, which they state themselves, is that economic theory cannot go beyond rather simple schemes, usually irrelevant with respect to the economic issues to be studied. As soon as the theoretical system becomes a little complex, because of the number of variables or the mathematical structure, in order to get any precise conclusion other than existence results, it is necessary to use computerized numerical approaches. This is an important step towards a better interaction between theorists and applied model builders.

The second conclusion, which I would like to develop, is the corrolary of the first. The results of a large econometric model are useless if they cannot be understood and controlled totally through a number of simple instruments. These instruments are those proposed in the paper. They consist of a blockwise analysis of the underlying theory, the dynamics and interpretable parameters of the larger model, starting from a condensed representation of that large model.

These two conclusions lead us to the necessity of a syntax for the construction of macroeconomic models. This syntax would contain a set of rules allowing a common representation of a macroeconomic model by the theoretician and by the applied econometrician. This syntax should represent a model in a nutshell, concisely but exhaustively. It can be checked that, up to a few details, the Deleau–Malgrange–Muet model is equivalent to the following representation which is closer to the usual representation of large macromodels. It is obtained by taking the first difference of the model, by substituting the expected values of the variables and by using a number of operators.

The operators are, for any variable denoted by X,

$$\mathring{X} = \Delta X_t / X_{t-1} \quad \text{or} \quad \Delta \ln X_t \tag{1}$$

$$L_n(X) = (1 - \lambda_n) \sum_{i=0}^{\infty} \lambda^i X_{t-i}. \tag{2}$$

Using the same symbols as in the paper discussed, the complete model comprises eight identities:

$$q_t = r_t - L_7(\mathring{p}_t) + \delta \tag{3}$$

$$I_t = I_t - (1 - \delta)K_{t-1} \tag{4}$$

$$U_{Nt} = N_t / \bar{N}_t \tag{5}$$

$$U_{Qt} = Q_t / \bar{Q}_t \tag{6}$$

$$w_t = W_t / P_t \tag{7}$$

$$\pi_t = Q_t - w_t N_t \tag{8}$$

$$Q_t = C_t + I_t + G_t + E_{xt} - I_{mt} \tag{9}$$

$$M_{St} = M_{Dt} \tag{10}$$

four endogenous long-term equilibria:

$$\mathring{N}_t = L_4\left[L_2(\mathring{Q}_t) + \alpha L_1\left(\frac{\mathring{q}_t}{w_t}\right) - \gamma\right] \tag{11}$$

$$\mathring{K}_t = L_3\left[L_2(\mathring{Q}) - \beta L_1\left(\frac{\mathring{q}}{w}\right) - \gamma\right] \tag{12}$$

$$\mathring{\bar{Q}}_t = \mathring{K}_t - \frac{\beta}{\alpha} L_1\left(\frac{\mathring{q}_t}{w_t}\right) + \frac{\gamma}{\alpha} \tag{13}$$

$$C_t = L_5\left(\frac{c}{1 - \alpha\theta}(Q_t - \theta\pi_t)\right) \tag{14}$$

three endogenous long-term equilibria with temporary discrepancies:

$$\mathring{P}_t = L_7(\mathring{W}_t + \mathring{N}_t - \mathring{Q}_t + f\mathring{U}_{Qt}) + \lambda_7 L_6 \mathring{p}_t \tag{15}$$

$$\mathring{M}_{Dt} = L_9(\mathring{p}_t + \mathring{Q}_t + \mu_2 \mathring{r}_t) + \lambda_9 L_6 \mathring{p}_t \tag{16}$$

$$\mathring{w}_t = g_1 + g_2(\mathring{p}_t - \mathring{p}_{-1}) + g_3(1 - U_{Nt}) \tag{17}$$

three exogenous long-term equilibria with temporary discrepancies:

$$\mathring{I}_{mt} = g + l_1(\mathring{Q}_t - g) + l_2(\mathring{p}_t - \rho) + l_3 \mathring{U}_{Qt} \tag{18}$$

$$\mathring{E}_{xt} = g + l_n(\mathring{p}_t - \rho) \tag{19}$$

$$\mathring{M}_{St} = g + \rho + \mu_i \mathring{r}_t \tag{20}$$

and two exogenous long-term equilibria:

$$\mathring{G} = g \tag{21}$$

$$\mathring{\bar{N}} = n. \tag{22}$$

Since the model is used as an educational tool, this simpler representation is attractive. It makes the model totally transparent and also shows that the simplicity of this model compared to usual 'large' models lies in

(a) the simplified economic theory;
(b) the uniform shape of expectations as well as adjustment lags ($L_n(x)$ represents homogeneous geometrically declining weights over the past);
(c) the high degree of exogeneity of the model: actually after substitution of the identities the model has only seven endogenous variables;
(d) the simple form of the temporary discrepancies which may in usual 'large' models take more sophisticated non-linear forms.

A large number of numerical experiments are presented by the authors, using the various blocks of the model. They provide a number of conclusions concerning the generation of output cycles, the importance of the wage–price dynamics and concerning the reduction of the expenditure multiplier when wage–price or foreign trade feedbacks are introduced which correspond well to the experience of large model builders and users. There may be an exception with an unexpected cyclical behaviour of the foreign trade feedbacks as reported after question (63). The authors also have problems with some explosive responses of the model which illustrate how important this type of exercise can be even when the model is very simple.

Another remark: it may be useful to ask the authors why they have chosen among the infinity of small models to be experimented, an adjustment with respect to anticipations which is not symmetric for all variables.

Except for prices the adjustment processes of the actual values Y_t towards the equilibrium values Y_t^* of the variables are all obtained from

$$\ln Y_t = \lambda \ln Y_{t-1} (1 + u) + (1 - \lambda) \ln Y_t^* \tag{23}$$

where u is the fixed *ex ante* long-term equilibrium rate of change of Y_t. For prices, on the contrary, it is assumed that the rate of change u is not fixed *ex ante* but determined by the model as a function of current and lagged price changes $L_6(\mathring{p})$. This results in a price equation shown in (15) which is homogeneous of degree $(1 + \lambda_7)$ in terms of the equilibrium prices, unlike all other variables which are homogeneous of degree 1 in their equilibrium values.

In the long run this features does not matter since expectations are equal to the equilibrium. In the simulations it does modify the dynamic patterns of response. One would have preferred to use either (23) or

$$\ln Y_t = \lambda \ln Y_t (1 + L_n(Y)) + (1 - \lambda) \ln Y_t^* \tag{24}$$

everywhere in the model.

As a conclusion we would like to make a list of the lines along which BB models can be developed, in order to focus on the analysis of the contribution of each single element of model construction:

(1) for the description or representation of economic reality: relative prices, disaggregate production branches and commodities, institutional representation of financial sector, attitude and tension measures, . . .
(2) for policy simulations: introduction of a large variety of fiscal, parafiscal, budgetry, monetary and financial policy instruments, . . .
(3) for forecasting: large number of predetermined lags, ways to introduce partial information at disaggregated level, controlled econometric estimates of structural coefficients and dynamics, . . .
(4) for the embodiment of theory: introduction of strong non-linearities, temporary equilibrium, disequilibrium, endogenous equilibrium rates of change, endogenous international trade, . . .
(5) for the knowledge of economic facts: large databanks allowing to test or to compare the performances of alternative theories.

Comment

PIERRE-YVES HÉNIN

Large macroeconomic models have been facing a rising stream of criticism, coming partly from the adepts of rational expectations, partly from the advocates of time-series representations or from a too severe appreciation of their predictive failures during an unquiet period of supply or policy shocks. Then, there is a growing interest in small models, which may offer an appropriate answer to several problems, like the question of robustness with respect to policy changes (the so-called Lucas' criticism), of a proper specification of expectation process, of the possibility of using more appropriate estimation techniques. These small models are often seen as substitutes for the large models in the Keynesian tradition.

The approach of the authors, building a core model, is very different, as it aims at a better understanding and a better specification of large models rather than to be the prototype of econometric models of small size to be estimated and used as substitutes for the traditional macromodels.

Large aggregative models can no longer be defended as black boxes: small black boxes offer generally better cost-effectiveness performance than large black boxes. They have to be defended as structural forms, allowing us to identify the proper propagation mechanisms of economic shocks. Thus, their theoretical legitimacy has to be non-disputable, which is not the case for most existing models which do not exhibit consistent long-run properties. The 'core model' methodology can then be interpreted as a convenient way of testing for the theoretical consistency of a typical aggregative Keynesian model, and the expression of 'model of models' used by the authors may be misleading on that point.

Do the authors succeed in providing a model performing with perfect theoretical consistency in the long run? Our comments will indicate that there are some difficulties in the paper as far as the achievement of theoretical consistency is concerned.

It is well known that consistent solution in the long run generally pertains to some kind of growth equilibrium path. But there are strong features to be incorporated in the specification to satisfy the conditions for an equilibrium growth to exist.

A first type of requirement is relative to micro-foundations: they are lacking in the paper and the authors are therefore deprived of a natural way to ensure the consistency of behavioural relationships.

A second type of requirement is connected with the exigency of mathematical homogeneity. The model has to admit a steady state of homothetic growth of a set of correctly defined variables, with relative stability required to justify comparative dynamics exercises according to the correspondence principle argument. These requirements are not difficult to fulfil in a theoretical model, but the authors do not want to get away from the empirical models, and therefore run into difficulties.

Typically, the authors hold a specification in level variables, introducing growth factors of the form $(1 + g)$ so as to accommodate trends. But if the choice of n and γ, the rate of growth in labour force and labour efficiency, is usual in scale factors, it is much more questionable to use for the same purpose the expected rate of growth of demand g or the long-term rate of increase in price level δ, which all have to be taken as exogenous, constant and mutually consistent. Thus, the 'good' long-term properties result from a very peculiar, uncommon, definition of variables.

A standard equation specification in the model is to apply a geometric lag distribution, in a multiplicative form, to variables defined as ratios to their trend values. For instance, equation (2) is equivalent to

$$\frac{Q^*}{Q_0(1 + g)^t} = \left(\frac{Q^*_{-1}}{Q_0(1 + g)^{t+1}}\right)^{\lambda_2} \left(\frac{Q}{Q_0(1 + g)^t}\right)^{1 - \lambda_2}.$$

When applied in a consumption function, this specification implies an adaptative expectation process on the level of income as the ratio to its trend, while for other variables, like prices, a usual adaptive process is applied to the rate of growth.

According to the paper, the authors seem to hold a symmetric view of investment and employment decision, but looking at the equations, it appears that investment results from an adjustment to a K_{t+1} target, while the target employment is relative to date t. There is no explanation given for this asymmetry.

It is very difficult to understand how the import elasticity e_1 may be different from unity, as the only apparent foundation for equation (10) is a specification in terms of partial adjustment of variables in the ratio to their trend value. Similarly the export equation makes sense only if world demand is increasing at the same rate g as domestic public expenditure. These points are examples of the overspecification resulting from the assumption of four different growth rates exogenously given.

We think that it would have been better to adopt a more traditional specification using for instance variables per capita (allowing for labour efficiency) and strictly limiting the number of exogenous trends. A log-linear specification may appear particularly convenient for this kind of model.

The third part of the paper copes with the dynamics of the core models, to be compared with the properties of econometric models. There is a series of interesting numerical exercises, but again we shall comment on some problems.

Concerning the dynamics of real blocks, what is the meaning of multipliers in level in a model with a trend? What is the meaning given to the absence of an eigenvalue with a modulus greater than one? It confirms our interpretation of the specification as essentially a study of variables as ratios over their trend values: we would have appreciated the authors to have been clearer on that point.

Concerning wage price dynamics, it seems useful to refer the results of numerical simulation to two main theoretical debates: Does the model satisfy the natural rate hypothesis? Does it exhibit neutrality or superneutrality? Unfortunately, these qustions are not clearly apparent in the paper because the authors are concerned mainly with the channels of influence of money and prices.

After equation (57) is defined a coefficient γ of money illusion which is null in general for g_r, the coefficient of wage indexation, different from one. It seems a very unnatural condition. The strong effect of inflation on real user cost of capital suggests a non-superneutrality property, which has to be distinguished from the neutrality issue.

So far, we have emphasized specification problems and the theoretical background of the model. Beyond these criticisms it is fair to insist upon the great qualities of the paper, particularly upon the technical cleverness of the authors who provide a fine batch of analytical results. They do succeed in convincing us of the interest in the core model methodology if not in agreeing with their particular model.

10

Planning the Consumption Goods Market: Preliminary Disequilibrium Estimates for Poland, 1955–80

RICHARD PORTES, RICHARD QUANDT, DAVID WINTER and STEPHEN YEO

INTRODUCTION

This paper specifies and estimates a four-equation disequilibrium model of the consumption goods market in a centrally planned economy (CPE). The data are from Poland for the period 1955–80, but the analysis is more general and will be applied to other CPEs as soon as the appropriate data sets are complete.

The work reported here is based on the previous papers of Portes and Winter (1980) and Charemza and Quandt (1982), referred to below as PW and CQ. The former applied to each of four CPEs a discrete-switching disequilibrium model with a household demand equation for consumption goods, a planners' supply equation, and a 'min' condition stating that the observed quantity transacted is the lesser of the quantities demanded and supplied. CQ considered how an equation for the adjustment of planned quantities could be integrated into a CPE model with fixed prices and without the usual price adjustment equation. They made plan formation endogenous and permitted the resulting plan variables to enter the equations determining demand and supply. Depending on the precise specification of the equation determining the plan, the model could adjust towards market clearing in a manner similar to that of disequilibrium models with price adjustment equations.

This paper implements the CQ proposal in the PW context. It differs from PW in several respects: (i) the data are extended beyond 1975, up to 1980; (ii) the main series have been more or less substantially revised, using new information; (iii) a plan-adjustment equation determines the *published plan* for aggregate consumption by households; (iv) this plan enters the equation for the *supply* of consumption goods; (v) the variables constructed by PW to measure deviations from plans for exogenous variables (output, investment, defence expenditure), which proxied the plan series by second-order quadratic trends, now use published plan data. The model here differs from CQ in having a more general form of plan-adjustment equation than they propose.

The work reported here was possible only because we were able to assemble reliable time series for plans for the major macroeconomic variables in Poland and other CPEs. Using this new and unique data set, our empirical work can now go beyond the question posed by PW, which concerned the existence of excess demand in the aggregate consumption goods markets of CPEs, to a range of important questions concerning the planning process and macroeconomic disequilibrium: Are the plans in a CPE properly represented as endogenous, determined by stable economic relationships rather than political caprice? How do plans so determined then influence the planners and the economy? Do the planners plan for macroeconomic equilibrium (i.e. does the plan refer to their planned *supply* or to their intention for the *quantity transacted*)? Is the disequilibrium macro-framework appropriate and useful for the analysis of CPEs (see Portes, 1981a)? There are also interesting theoretical and econometric questions which arise, some of which will provide material for future work. The overall framework is applicable to any large organization which plans economic variables.

THE MODEL

Our general model for Poland is taken from PW with the modifications indicated above. Thus the consumption demand equation is identical to that in PW, derived directly from the Houthakker–Taylor savings function:

$$CD = \alpha_1 DNFA1 + \alpha_2 DYD + \alpha_3 YD1 + u_1 \tag{1}$$

where

CD = household desired expenditure on consumption goods and services in the current period;

$DNFA$ = household saving, measured as the change in net financial assets of households, NFA, during the period (NFA is the end-of-period net stock of financial assets); $DNFA1$ was called $S1$ in PW;

DYD = change in disposable income from the previous to the current period;

YD = disposable income;

1 suffix denotes a one-period lag operator;

$u_1 \sim N(0, \sigma_1^2)$.

The work of Houthakker and Taylor suggests the following *a priori* hypotheses:

$$-1 < \alpha_1 < -1/3, \qquad 0 < \alpha_2 < 1, \qquad \alpha_3 = 1.$$

The modified supply equation is

$$CS = \beta_1 C^* + \beta_2 C^*Z + \beta_4 RNFA1 + \beta_5 CZXD$$
$$+ \beta_6 CZXI + \beta_7 DUM + u_2 \qquad (2)$$

where

CS = supply of consumption goods and services in current period;
C^* = announced plan for consumption (* denotes a plan throughout: the value of a plan variable in period t is the plan for period t, as formulated in period $t-1$);
NMP = net material product;
D = defence expenditure;
I = investment expenditure;
C^*Z = $(C^*/NMP^*) \cdot (NMP - NMP^*)$;
$CZXD$ = $[(D/NMP) - (D^*/NMP^*)] \cdot NMP$;
$CZXI$ = $[(I/NMP) - (I^*/NMP^*)] \cdot NMP$;
$RNFA$ = deviation of current NFA from second-order exponential time trend fitted to observed values of NFA;
DUM = one for the period 1978–80, zero otherwise;
$u_2 \sim N(0, \sigma_2^2)$.

A planned supply function of this form is explained, justified and estimated in Portes and Winter (1977, 1980). The hypothesis is that consumption goods supply will be determined by the announced consumption plan and by *deviations* from plans of output, defence, investment and consumption, as well as deviations from trend of household financial assets. A coefficient β_3 for the lagged values of C^*Z was considered in the general model of PW but the corresponding term dropped out of their estimates for Poland and therefore has been excluded here, while their original numbering of coefficients has been retained to facilitate comparisons. On the other hand, in PW defence and investment expenditure were aggregated, with a single coefficient β_5. *A priori* arguments here suggest $\beta_1 \simeq 1$; $\beta_2, \beta_4 > 0$; $\beta_5, \beta_6 < 0$. The dummy variable was introduced because it was believed that 1978 marked the beginning of an extraordinary sequence of events, including changes in the planners' behaviour, which led to the crisis of 1980 (Portes, 1981b).

In both the demand and supply equations, we expect *a priori* that no constant terms should appear. They were tried in initial estimates, however, and we could not reject the hypothesis that they were zero.

The simple disequilibrium model is completed by

$$C = \min(CD, CS) \tag{3}$$

where C is the quantity observed.

Now we add the plan-adjustment equation

$$C^* = \delta_1 C1^* + \delta_2 C1 + \delta_3 C2 + \delta_4 RNFA2 + \gamma(CD - CS) + u_4 \tag{4}$$

where the suffix 2 denotes a two-period lag and $u_4 \sim N(0, \sigma_4^2)$.

The plan for the current period is normally determined towards the end of the previous period, and we suppose it is a function of the plan for that period and realized quantities for that and the preceding period, as well as the most recent known value of $RNFA$.[1] A final influence on the plan might be excess demand, or $CD - CS$.

Single-equation models of plan formation involving only previous plans and realizations are discussed by Yeo (1982). Planners' behaviour of this kind is discussed by Gacs and Lacko (1973) and by Kornai (1971). Different schemes yield similar relationships of the form of equation (4) with different interpretations of $(\delta_1, \delta_2, \delta_3)$. We discuss below some of the properties of these coefficients.

Our plan-adjustment equation also supposes that the planners will respond to observed 'excess' household liquidity by raising the plan ($\delta_4 > 0$). We use $RNFA1$ in the supply function and $RNFA2$ here because the former is meant to capture behaviour *during* the current period, when $RNFA1$ is known, whereas when the plan for period t is determined in period $(t - 1)$ only NFA at the end of period $(t - 2)$ is known. A similar argument might suggest that $C1$ does not belong in equation (4), but we suppose the planners have better information on a flow variable towards the end of the period during which it is realized than on a stock to be measured at the end of that period. We did try $RNFA1$ instead of $RNFA2$ in equation (4) for some estimates; but although its coefficient was significant and of the correct sign it resulted in considerably poorer estimates of $(\delta_1, \delta_2, \delta_3)$.

A more serious objection to the dating of variables in equation (4) is the use of *contemporaneous* excess demand, which is clearly unknown when the plan is fixed. This might be justified on a 'planners' rational expectations' argument; on the other hand, it might be thought preferable to use lagged excess demand, which would correspond to excess demand in the period during which the plan is formulated. Unfortunately, the model's likelihood function then becomes intractable, unless we suppose that u_4 is identically zero (this is clear by analogy with the analysis in Laffont and Monfort (1979) and Quandt (1981)). We did try estimating such a model, but it gave some silly results, for reasons which we do not yet understand.

One variant which was simple enough to implement was to suppose that *CD* and *CS* enter separately in equation (4) with coefficients γ_1 and γ_2, respectively. When we tried this formulation, we did find $\gamma_1 > 0$, $\gamma_2 < 0$, as expected, and of the same order of magnitude (though surprisingly large); and we often could not reject $\gamma_1 = -\gamma_2$. We therefore report only results for the model as shown above, expecting $\gamma > 0$ *a priori*. We also tried an asymmetrical formulation where only *positive* excess demand influences the planners, so the term in equation (4) is $\gamma \max(D - S, 0)$. This did not work well, and the estimates are not reported.

All estimates use annual data for 1955–80 for Poland, although the two-period lag in equation (4) means that we can report estimates of excess demand only for the 24 observations 1957–80. All variables are in constant prices, with the *CPI* used as deflator. Further information on the data is given in appendix A.

RESULTS

The likelihood function for the model of equations (1)–(4) is derived in appendix B. It is clear that the model is coherent, because the matrix of coefficients of the endogenous variables is the same whether there is excess demand or excess supply. We used the Davidon–Fletcher–Powell algorithm to obtain maximum-likelihood estimates, with numerical first derivatives. The procedure invariably iterated long enough so that the **H** matrix provided good convergence to the inverse of the Hessian and therefore good estimates of standard errors.

We report the results of estimation in tables 10.1 and 10.2. The first column of table 10.1 gives the original PW estimates, the second column estimates for the PW model on the new data (using plans). The third and fourth columns show estimates for two different versions of the model of equations (1)–(4), first with and then without the excess demand term in the plan-adjustment equation. As discussed below, we find the estimates with $\gamma = 0$ to be superior, so table 10.2 gives output only from this run. The first column shows for each observation the probability π that demand exceeds supply, as estimated by PW, and the second gives our estimates of π.

As a first step in the estimation it was decided to estimate the original PW model with data for plans instead of time trend proxies. Estimation of this model for the new data set using a sample from 1957–80 did not yield acceptable results; however convergence was obtained when the observations for 1980 were omitted. The results are given in the second column of table 10.1. The estimates of the demand equation are quite reasonable, the supply equation less so. In particular the estimates of β_5 and β_6 do not have the expected signs.

TABLE 10.1

	PW (1980)	PW model re-estimated	Model of eqns (1)–(4)	Model of eqns (1)–(4), $\gamma \equiv 0$
a_1	−0.965	−0.630	−0.414	−0.494
	(0.085)	(0.236)	(0.213)	(0.222)
a_2	0.970	0.810	0.729	0.747
	(0.055)	(0.136)	(0.107)	(0.126)
a_3	1.001	0.998	0.996	1.000
	(0.004)	(0.007)	(0.006)	(0.008)
s_1^2	3.721	32.30	29.34	55.030
	(1.298)	(11.15)	(11.61)	(6.11)
b_1	1.055	1.028	1.020	1.003
	(0.025)	(0.003)	(0.008)	(0.003)
b_2	0.143	1.179	−0.066	0.499
	(0.562)	(0.085)	(0.237)	(0.106)
b_4	2.572	0.824	−0.424	−0.269
	(1.212)	(0.099)	(0.189)	(0.077)
b_5	−1.718	0.721	−3.332	−5.445
	(0.644)	(0.044)	(2.351)	(1.136)
b_6	—	2.514	0.252	0.527
		(0.723)	(0.175)	(0.086)
b_7	—	—	−33.141	17.42
			(11.118)	(3.55)
s_2^2	15.293	1.247	70.19	2.467
	(11.327)	(0.763)	(3.30)	(1.34)
d_1	—	—	−1.962	−0.751
			(0.645)	(0.184)
d_2	—	—	2.851	2.035
			(0.430)	(0.112)
d_3	—	—	0.223	−0.225
			(0.467)	(0.171)
d_4	—	—	2.820	1.214
			(0.895)	(0.220)
c	—	—	1.526	—
			(0.624)	
s_4^2	—	—	46.36	92.67
			(1.85)	(38.80)
Log L	−48.56	−65.15	−149.89	−154.85
$\bar{C}$	302.7	421.94	448.88	448.88

a_i are estimates of α_i, b_i of β_i, d_i of δ_i, c of γ, s_i^2 of σ_i^2.

Asymptotic standard errors in parentheses.

$\bar{C}$ is the sample mean value of consumption.

b_5 in the estimates for PW (1980) is the estimated coefficient on a term aggregating investment and defence expenditure, but of the same form as *CZXD* and *CZXI*.

The estimation in PW (1980) was carried out over a sample including 1954–75.

Re-estimation of the PW model in column 2 included 1956–79. In this re-estimation the defence and investment deviations were entered as separate variables, and not combined as in PW (1980).

The estimates in columns 3 and 4 were carried out over the sample 1957–80.

TABLE 10.2

	π_t PW (1980)	π_t Model of eqns (1)–(4), $\gamma \equiv 0$
1957	0.00	0.00
1958	0.04	0.00
1959	0.53	0.93
1960	0.03	0.00
1961	0.00	0.81
1962	0.00	0.52
1963	0.00	0.01
1964	0.00	0.00
1965	0.00	0.84
1966	0.00	0.00
1967	0.00	0.00
1968	0.00	0.45
1969	0.00	0.75
1970	0.00	0.00
1971	0.99	0.00
1972	1.00	0.97
1973	0.92	0.00
1974	0.00	0.00
1975	0.00	0.88
1976	—	0.00
1977	—	0.74
1978	—	0.00
1979	—	0.92
1980	—	0.88

The values of π_t taken from PW (1980) are the estimated *marginal* probabilities that the observation was generated by an excess demand regime, i.e. that $CD_t > CS_t$. The probabilities reported in column 2 of table 10.2 (which correspond to the estimates in the last column of table 10.1) are the estimated *conditional* probabilities that the observation was generated by an excess demand regime, i.e. that $CD_t > CS_t$, conditional on the observed C_t. The two estimated π's can nevertheless be compared, since Burkett (1981: 161) reports that there is little or no difference between the marginal and conditional probabilities for Poland in the original PW (1980) model.

Estimation of the new model including the excess demand term in the plan-adjustment equation does produce an estimate of γ which is significant and of reasonable size, and a likelihood ratio test suggests (though not very strongly) that we should reject the restriction $\gamma = 0$. On the other hand, the inclusion of this term affects the estimates of several other coefficients unfavourably (b_2, d_1, d_2, d_3) and gives a less plausible sample separation. Since the rationale for using contemporaneous excess demand in equation (4) is somewhat tenuous (and experiments with separate γ_1 and γ_2 gave no better results and used up yet another degree of freedom), we concluded this informal specification search by choosing the estimates with $\gamma = 0$. Note that the dummy variable for 1978–80 is strongly significant in these estimates, and a run without it was rejected by a likelihood ratio test.

Considering the estimates in the last column of table 10.1, we find that all the estimates for equation (1) satisfy the *a priori* conditions, as do the estimates for β_1, β_2, β_5 and δ_4. The other coefficients in equation (4) look reasonable enough, and we shall discuss them and the anomalous estimates for β_4 and β_6 below.

The estimated probabilities of excess demand regimes look much more acceptable here than they did in PW. PW were themselves sceptical about their π's for Poland (Portes and Winter, 1980: 153, 155). Here, almost half the observations are classified as excess demand, and the pattern is reasonably consistent with a qualitative assessment of events in the Polish economy since the mid-1950s. In particular, the estimates pick up the effects of the investment boom of 1959, the sudden growth of wages in 1971–72, and the strain on the economy from 1975 onwards, which further foreign borrowing could not relieve.

Turning in more detail to the estimates from individual equations and coefficients, there is little further to say about the demand function. The standard errors are somewhat larger than in the original PW estimates, and the estimate of α_1 is significantly different, but the overall picture is quite satisfactory. The coefficients imply a long-run average savings ratio of 2.3 per cent in an economy growing at 5 per cent per annum.

The plan-adjustment equation is much more interesting. First, the coefficients are on the whole quite well determined. Secondly, it seems clear that the plan is adjusted upwards when the planners observe that households are holding 'excess' liquid assets; indeed, they appear to increase the plan more than commensurately (but see the discussion of b_4 below). Thirdly, the long-run properties of the estimated equation (4) are remarkable.

Recall that *RNFA* is a series of deviations from trend. Although this is not a linear but rather an exponential trend, so that the mean of *RNFA* is not zero by construction, it is nevertheless very close to zero (0.7) compared with C. If we therefore disregard *RNFA* and take the estimates with $\gamma = 0$, we have the simplified equation

$$C_t^* = d_1 C_{t-1}^* + d_2 C_{t-1} + d_3 C_{t-2}. \tag{5}$$

What are the implications of a stationary state in which $C_t = \tilde{C}$ for all t? We would have the first-order difference equation

$$C_t^* = d_1 C_{t-1}^* + (d_2 + d_3)\tilde{C}. \tag{6}$$

Provided $|d_1| < 1$, which does hold for the estimates with $\gamma = 0$, this converges to

$$C^* = (d_2 + d_3)\tilde{C}/(1 - d_1) = 1.034\ \tilde{C}. \tag{7}$$

Given the degree of precision of the estimates, this is tolerably close to permitting a stationary state in which the plan is always realized.

Of course, the Polish economy (and aggregate consumption) were in fact growing steadily until the very end of our period. We might then ask what constant growth rate is consistent with exact realization of plans in the estimated version of equation (5)? Taking $C_t = (1 + g)C_{t-1}$ and $C_t^* = C_t$ for all t in equation (5) gives us

$$(1 + g)^2 C_{t-2} = (d_1 + d_2)(1 + g)C_{t-2} + d_3 C_{t-2}. \tag{8}$$

The positive root of this quadratic is $g = 0.075$, which is close to the observed average growth rate of consumption over the period 1957–80 of 6.3 per cent! That is, the observed planners' behaviour does not suggest unrealistic planning. Alternatively, we might say that the consumption planning mechanism was on the whole consistent with the economy's possibilities, and the role of *RNFA* suggests that when exogenous shocks pushed plans and actual consumption off course, the planners sought to return to this path.

Finally, suppose we did introduce an excess demand term equal to a constant proportion e of consumption into the constant growth economy with exact plan realization of equation (8), but with $\gamma = 1$. In other words, for the moment we visualize a centrally planned economy in which there is excess demand for consumption goods in every period, but in which the planners make planned consumption a positive function of excess demand. This would give us

$$(1 + g)^2 C = (d_1 + d_2)(1 + g)C + d_3 C + eC. \tag{9}$$

It is straightforward to establish how the solution to the quadratic in g will vary with e:

$$\frac{\partial g}{\partial e} = +[(d_1 + d_2)^2 + 4(d_3 + e)]^{-1/2} > 0 \tag{10}$$

(for the root with $g > 0$). As excess demand increases so does the consumption plan and so also does actual consumption. Thus the higher excess demand, the higher would be the growth rate of actual consumption required to be consistent with continuous realization of plans (note that this conclusion is not independent of the estimated parameter values, since they determine which root will give $g > 0$, and indeed whether there exists a positive real root).

The estimates of the supply function suggest that consumption is not used as a 'buffer' to absorb unanticipated shocks to NMP ($b_2 < 1$—see PW for this interpretation). Further, they suggest that consumption goods supply would equal the plan ($b_1 \simeq 1$) were it not for the effects of the 'deviation' or shock variables, all of which have means approximately equal to zero.

In this equation, b_4 and b_6 take signs opposite to those expected on *a priori* grounds. For each, we can provide fairly plausible *ex post* rationalizations, but more study will be required.

For b_6, we conjecture that there was a structural change around 1972, when the foreign borrowing constraint was relaxed, so that investment no longer crowded out consumption. Indeed, β_6 might well have become positive, if the planners took account of the multiplier effects of shocks to investment and were willing to accommodate them with additional imports of consumption goods. To test this, we tried an additive dummy on the coefficient β_6 itself for the period 1972–80. The coefficient on the dummy was not significant but at least was positive, as expected, and b_6 also became insignificant, but did not switch sign. This gave partial support to our hypothesis.

The surprising but fairly small negative coefficient on $RNFA1$ in the supply equation must be viewed in the light of the rather large positive coefficient on $RNFA2$ in the plan-adjustment equation. It may be that the end-year measurement of NFA does not correspond to the data to which the planners actually respond when they plan *during* $(t - 1)$, in equation (4), and when they adjust supply *during* t, in equation (2). Thus we also find that $RNFA1$ performs similarly well in equation (4), which is not surprising both because the planners know some of the information going into $RNFA1$ by the time they set C^*, and because the observed positive serial correlation between $RNFA1$ and $RNFA2$ is 0.84.

Moreover it should be noted that the stock of financial assets affects supply in two ways—directly, through the $RNFA1$ term in equation (2) and indirectly through the presence of C^* in equation (2) and the presence of $RNFA2$ in the equation determining C^*. Thus the C^* entering equation (2) already has in it information on $RNFA2$, to which the planners may have overreacted in period $t - 1$ in setting the consumption plan. They may then seek to compensate for this overreaction in period t by adjusting actual supply in the opposite direction, based on $RNFA1$. The total direct and indirect effect of net financial assets on supply can be obtained by substituting the C^* from equation (4) into the supply equation, equation (2). The total effect of $RNFA$ upon CS is then given by

$$\frac{\beta_4 RNFA1 + (\beta_1 + \beta_2 \theta)\delta_4 RNFA2}{1 + \gamma}$$

where θ is $(NMP - NMP^*)/NMP^*$. Now consider a constant unit positive *RNFA*, i.e. a sustained departure of net financial assets from trend. The supply response will be

$$\frac{\beta_4 + (\beta_1 + \beta_2 \theta)\delta_4}{1 + \gamma}.$$

The size of this response of course depends upon θ, which over the sample period ranged in magnitude between -0.05 and $+0.05$. The total effect of *RNFA* upon supply, based on the two versions of the model estimated (with and without the term involving γ), can be summarized as follows:

	$\theta = -0.05$	$\theta = 0.05$
Equations (1)–(4) with γ estimated	0.975	0.967
Equations (1)–(4) with $\gamma \equiv 0$	0.918	0.979

This suggests that the planners, in response to a sustained increase in household financial assets, would adjust the supply of consumption goods by an equal amount. The evidence from the performance of *RNFA* that the planners do seek market clearing thus seems quite strong.

CONCLUSION

We believe we have taken substantial steps towards answering the questions posed in the first section and demonstrating the applicability of the CQ model. Estimation has shown that it is both feasible and informative to use plan data, and to model the regularities in the process of plan construction. The plan for year t, formulated and announced in year $t - 1$, is dependent upon planned and actual consumption and household financial asset behaviour, as known to the planners in year $t - 1$. These announced plans are then embodied in a supply function which reflects, in addition, unforeseen developments in the economy in year t. The role of the financial assets variable suggests that the planners do appear to try to adjust announced plans and actual supply in order to reduce excess demand. The disequilibrium macroeconomic framework, with fixed prices and planned quantities, can be estimated for centrally planned economies and seems to provide insight into their behaviour. The plan-adjustment equation helps in disequilibrium estimation, which was possible even with a relatively small sample.

There are various extensions of the analysis which we shall explore in future work. We should soon have data sets permitting application of the model to three other countries. We shall try further experiments with the model with lagged excess demand in the plan-adjustment equation. We intend also to try a model allowing different coefficients on positive and negative excess demand in equation (4). It may be interesting to run a current-price demand equation with an inflation term, based on a restricted intertemporal linear expenditure system. Finally, the same structure could be applied to other macrovariables and markets, e.g. investment or *NMP* itself.

APPENDIX A

Data

The data used in this study have been drawn from a variety of Polish and other sources, all publicly available (see table 10.3). The earlier study by Portes and Winter (1980) was based on the data described in Rudcenko (1979). There are some important conceptual differences between the variables used here and those constructed by Rudcenko. In addition some of the series reported by Rudcenko and used in PW have been subject to revision by the Polish central statistical agency (GUS).

Realized variables

The series describing actual or realized variables are mainly drawn from the annual statistical yearbook, *Rocznik Statystyczny* (*RS*), the concise annual statistical yearbook, *Maly Rocznik Statystyczny* (*MRS*), or other publications of the GUS (see references).

(i) Real income (*YD*): This is the real disposable income of households, after the deduction of taxes and other obligatory payments. It includes not only income flows from the state or socialized sector to households, but income flows within the private sector. In particular it includes an estimate of the net income of private enterprises and an estimate of the income in kind of private agriculture. In this respect it differs fundamentally from the income series reported in Rudcenko (1979: 447), which included only gross income flows from the socialized sector to households. The income series used in the present study was thought to be the more appropriate for a study of consumer behaviour.

This series has been reported regularly in the *RS* for the years since 1970. A comparable series can be found for the years from 1961 to 1970 and for 1975 in the yearbook of national income, *Rocznik Dochodu Narodowego* (*RDN*), for 1960–65, 1971 and 1976. These issues of the *RDN* contain relatively detailed balance sheets of aggregate nominal household income and expenditure. The income figures, after some adjustment because of definitional changes, appear to be comparable to the figures reported in the *RS* for the years after 1970. We have not yet been able to obtain comparable published income figures for the 1950s. Instead we have applied the percentage changes in the index of 'nominal money income of the population' given in Hodoly (1966: 149) in order to create an income series from 1950 to 1960. The percentage changes in income given by Hodoly have been compared to similar series given in a variety of other publications and monographs. In general all these sources agree closely on the movement in income in the 1950s. This nominal income series for the years 1950–80 is then deflated by the published consumer price index to give the series *YD*.

(ii) Real net financial assets (*NFA*): This variable is equal to the sum of savings deposits and cash held by households, minus the total amount of outstanding loans from the state to households. It is thus financial assets net of the sum owed by

TABLE 10.3 The data

	C	*C**	*NMP*	*NMP**	*I*	*I**	*D*
1950	NA	NA	211.581	NA	42.9248	NA	NA
1951	NA	NA	227.450	NA	48.1616	NA	NA
1952	NA	NA	241.626	NA	57.1758	NA	13.1454
1953	116.034	NA	266.804	NA	65.8466	NA	17.6335
1954	132.633	128.236	294.944	NA	69.7098	67.1635	19.1633
1955	149.609	151.501	319.699	NA	72.5000	68.5248	22.6345
1956	171.323	164.717	342.127	342.078	75.9339	79.6049	17.4762
1957	203.576	207.272	378.942	369.839	81.8576	80.2622	12.6802
1958	220.882	222.657	399.889	401.300	90.3137	88.7336	13.9606
1959	240.681	238.736	420.624	424.282	105.252	101.061	16.7529
1960	243.876	251.165	439.031	444.599	111.433	111.988	16.6505
1961	264.935	261.045	474.788	460.983	119.546	121.685	17.8582
1962	273.665	276.921	484.733	508.024	131.135	131.022	19.4044
1963	285.716	284.067	518.374	509.939	134.612	142.019	21.9837
1964	299.638	299.776	553.285	537.036	140.965	136.901	23.1223
1965	319.077	311.137	592.004	582.056	154.358	153.088	24.5000
1966	337.055	332.587	634.109	613.909	167.278	163.310	26.5967
1967	353.550	355.343	670.290	655.669	186.208	180.827	27.9526
1968	376.077	371.197	730.590	702.463	202.519	197.008	32.1867
1969	392.337	398.892	751.748	767.120	219.045	220.341	35.3429
1970	410.339	415.020	790.891	795.350	227.931	224.521	37.5135
1971	441.644	436.180	855.000	833.599	244.800	244.342	36.7540
1972	487.337	447.533	945.345	907.155	301.117	268.301	36.7534
1973	534.829	533.920	1047.54	1020.03	377.438	339.961	40.2510
1974	579.106	583.522	1156.93	1147.06	461.780	424.240	43.3686
1975	637.987	636.550	1260.81	1270.31	511.191	489.487	44.9683
1976	709.760	742.172	1346.50	1365.46	516.304	511.191	43.1006
1977	766.729	787.825	1413.79	1423.25	532.310	522.499	46.7710
1978	781.604	845.187	1456.10	1490.13	543.488	504.098	48.0826
1979	794.816	803.869	1422.67	1496.87	500.550	494.574	50.0382
1980	817.967	840.438	1337.41	1445.44	438.983	460.506	48.2505

TABLE 10.3 (*contd.*)

	*D**	*YD*	*NFA*	*CPI*	*INVDEFL*	*RNFA*
1950	NA	NA	NA	0.614110	NA	NA
1951	NA	NA	NA	0.673650	NA	NA
1952	13.4233	109.378	6.01553	0.770670	0.464042	−0.0816900
1953	19.2438	115.975	5.93440	1.09261	0.516063	−1.35848
1954	19.5717	134.985	7.75880	1.02426	0.516613	−0.941850
1955	21.9226	151.866	9.70200	1.00000	0.516911	−0.651590
1956	17.0378	178.321	15.6311	0.990080	0.663761	3.34213
1957	12.7324	208.047	18.2042	1.04300	0.764975	3.65546
1958	15.1473	224.929	20.0697	1.07166	0.773603	2.88972
1959	16.3049	244.932	21.0411	1.08269	0.805831	0.806010
1960	17.8090	250.038	24.0691	1.10254	0.852829	0.296640
1961	17.7628	270.914	28.1440	1.11025	0.901548	0.287470
1962	20.6208	280.009	32.7979	1.13782	0.901856	0.239180
1963	23.2949	293.662	37.9076	1.14774	0.900669	−0.0495500
1964	23.7904	308.548	42.7469	1.16207	0.899564	−1.39027
1965	24.9977	328.519	47.1350	1.17310	0.902042	−4.05695
1966	27.0597	350.704	55.6487	1.18743	0.898607	−3.57356
1967	28.3969	366.518	64.9239	1.20507	0.897949	−3.41277
1968	30.8313	388.348	74.2483	1.22492	0.897886	−4.40357
1969	35.1080	404.764	82.4685	1.24146	0.902586	−7.82354
1970	37.1723	418.363	86.1308	1.25579	0.908579	−17.2587
1971	36.6140	463.212	104.102	1.25469	1.00000	−13.9816
1972	37.6451	520.719	128.900	1.25469	1.00592	−5.61996
1973	39.0338	575.597	164.880	1.28986	1.00472	12.0277
1974	42.2350	613.882	200.159	1.38137	1.00833	26.9220
1975	44.6537	677.105	237.270	1.42282	1.05857	41.4322
1976	42.0052	731.565	257.953	1.48545	1.19954	37.1337
1977	43.8104	784.873	267.936	1.55821	1.23320	19.5856
1978	47.2855	791.948	274.193	1.68445	1.24330	−4.40511
1979	47.7857	813.121	290.447	1.80232	1.28438	−21.2824
1980	47.3854	832.127	309.215	1.97133	1.38015	−38.6910

NA means data not available.
INVDEFL is the implicit deflator for gross investment, *I*.
Other variable names are as given in the text.

households to the state. It is measured as an end-of-year stock. This nominal stock figure is then deflated by the published consumer price index.

This variable is constructed from the series reported in Rudcenko (1979: 446–450) and has been updated to 1980 from the data published in the *RS* and the *MRS*. We were not able to obtain a consistent series for credits advanced to and repaid by households. Instead we used the series from Rudcenko, which measures credits advanced to the population, which includes credits to individual farmers and non-agricultural private enterprise.

(iii) Real household consumption of goods and services (C): This series is obtained as the difference between real income (YD) and the annual change in real financial assets, $DNFA$. Note that the net financial assets variable is deflated before being differenced to obtain $DNFA$.

(iv) Net material product (NMP): This is net material product, in constant prices. The series is taken from the *RS*, but rescaled to give an implicit deflator equal to 1 in 1971, in conformity with the practice in PW.

(v) Investment (I): This is total investment in both the socialized and private sectors, in constant prices. The series is taken from the *RS*, but rescaled in the same way as net material product.

(vi) Defence (D): This is current defence expenditure, as given in the *RS*. The figure in the *RS* is in current prices, and is deflated using the implicit deflator for investment, I. This implicit deflator is calculated as the ratio of current to constant price total investment figures as published in the *RS*.

(vii) Consumer price index (CPI): This is the price index for goods and services purchased by the population, as published in the *RS*. The published series has been linked and rescaled so that 1955 = 1.0, in accordance with PW.

Plan variables

The annual economic plan for Poland is announced during November or December of the preceding year in the official gazette of the Polish government, *Monitor Polski* (*MP*). The plan figure for year t is usually given only as a percentage increase over the (unspecified) actual or realized figure for year $t - 1$. In some cases the *level* of the planned series for year t is also given, but this is not always the case. The figures in *MP* have been supplemented and confirmed from the figures given in the planning journal *Gospodarka Planowa* (*GP*) and in the United Nations *Economic Survey of Europe*. In some instances in the 1950s and 1960s additional information was obtained from the Polish monthly statistical bulletin, the *Biuletyn Statystyczny* (*BS*), and the United Nations *Economic Bulletin for Europe*.

(i) Planned net material product (NMP^*): This series is available in *MP*, *GP* and the UN sources, given as a percentage increase over the preceding year's actual figure. It has been converted to a planned level by applying this percentage increase to the latest available published figure for the previous year, which is just the series NMP.

(ii) Planned investment (I^*): This series is available on the same basis as the NMP figures, although planned levels are given for some years. The series I^* is generated in the same manner as the series NMP^*.

(iii) Planned defence expenditure (D^*): This series corresponds to budget appropriations for current defence expenditure announced by the government. The series is taken from Alton et al. (1980: 32–33).

(iv) Planned supply of consumption goods and services: There is no published plan series available which corresponds exactly to our notion of consumption, although a variety of retail sales plan figures are available. We have used here a series for the planned 'volume of retail sales' or 'retail sales turnover', taken from the United Nations *Economic Bulletin for Europe* and the *Economic Survey of Europe*. This corresponds to a fairly complete coverage of retail sales of goods, but not of services. There are some plan figures available for services for the 1970s, but not earlier. We generated planned consumption levels in the following manner: We applied the published planned percentage increases in the 'volume of retail trade turnover' to the published series on actual retail sales of goods, *RSG*. This generated a series of planned *levels* for retail sales, *RSG**. We then regressed our real consumption series, *C*, on the published actual retail sales of goods *RSG*. Because our consumption data are somewhat different in origin for the 1950s, 1960s and 1970s, we allowed slope and intercept dummies for each of these periods in the regression relating *C* and *RSG*. We then generated *C** by substituting *RSG** for *RSG* in this estimated relationship. The alternative and more direct way of generating *C** would be to apply the planned percentage increases in *RSG* directly to the actual level of *C* in $t-1$, as if they were the planned percentage increases in *C* itself. This yielded a very similar series.

APPENDIX B

The likelihood function

The equations of the model are

$$D_t = z_{1t} + u_{1t} \tag{A.1}$$

$$S_t = \beta_1 Q_t^* + \beta_2 z_{4t} Q_t^* + z_{2t} + u_{2t} \tag{A.2}$$

$$Q_t = \min(D_t, S_t) \tag{A.3}$$

$$Q_t^* = z_{3t} + \gamma_1 D_t + \gamma_2 S_t + u_{3t} \tag{A.4}$$

where Q_t^* represents plans, z_{1t}, z_{2t}, z_{3t} and z_{4t} contain only parameters and predetermined variables, and u_{1t}, u_{2t}, u_{3t} are distributed as $N(0, \Sigma)$ with scalar covariance matrix. The p.d.f. of D_t, S_t, Q_t^* is immediate from (A.1) to (A.4):

$$f(D_t, S_t, Q_t^*) = \frac{|1 - \gamma_2(\beta_1 + \beta_2 z_{4t})|}{(2\pi)^{3/2}\sigma_1\sigma_2\sigma_3} \exp\left[-\frac{1}{2}\left(\frac{(D_t - z_{1t})^2}{\sigma_1^2} + \frac{[S_t - (\beta_1 + \beta_2 z_{4t})Q_t^* - z_{2t}]^2}{\sigma_2^2} + \frac{(-\gamma_1 D_t - \gamma_2 S_t + Q_t^* - z_{3t})^2}{\sigma_3^2}\right)\right]. \tag{A.5}$$

The p.d.f. of the observable random variables Q_t, Q_t^* is

$$h(Q_t, Q_t^*) = \int_{Q_t}^{\infty} f(Q_t, S_t, Q_t^*)\, dS_t + \int_{Q_t}^{\infty} f(D_t, Q_t, Q_t^*)\, dD_t. \tag{A.6}$$

It is easy to show by completing the square that the integrals in (A.6) can be obtained as

$$\int_{Q_t}^{\infty} f(Q_t, S_t, Q_t^*)\, dS_t = \frac{|1 - \gamma_2(\beta_1 + \beta_2 z_{4t})|}{2\pi\sigma_1(\sigma_3^2 + \gamma_2^2\sigma_2^2)^{1/2}} \exp\left[-\frac{1}{2}\left(\frac{(Q_t - z_{1t})^2}{\sigma_1^2} + \frac{B_t - A_t^2}{\omega_1^2}\right)\right] \times \left[1 - \Phi\left(\frac{Q_t - A_t}{\omega_1}\right)\right]$$

$$\int_{Q_t}^{\infty} f(D_t, Q_t, Q_t^*)\,\mathrm{d}D_t = \frac{|1-\gamma_2(\beta_1+\beta_2 z_{4t})|}{2\pi\sigma_2(\sigma_3^2+\gamma_1^2\sigma_1^2)^{1/2}}$$

$$\times \exp\left[-\frac{1}{2}\left(\frac{(Q_t-(\beta_1+\beta_2 z_{4t})Q_t^*-z_{2t})^2}{\sigma_2^2}+\frac{E_t-C_t^2}{\omega_2^2}\right)\right]$$

$$\times\left[1-\Phi\left(\frac{Q_t-C_t}{\omega_2}\right)\right]$$

where

$$A_t = \frac{\sigma_3^2(\beta_1 Q_t^* + z_{2t}) - \sigma_2^2\gamma_2(\gamma_1 Q_t - Q_t^* + z_{3t})}{\sigma_3^2+\gamma_2^2\sigma_2^2}$$

$$B_t = \frac{\sigma_3^2(\beta_1 Q_t^* + z_{2t})^2 + \sigma_2^2(\gamma_1 Q_t - Q_t^* + z_{3t})^2}{\sigma_3^2+\gamma_2^2\sigma_2^2}$$

$$C_t = \frac{\sigma_3^2 z_{1t} - \sigma_1^2\gamma_1(\gamma_2 Q_t - Q_t^* + z_{3t})}{\sigma_3^2+\gamma_1^2\sigma_1^2}$$

$$E_t = \frac{\sigma_3^2 z_{1t}^2 + \sigma_1^2(\gamma_2 Q_t - Q_t^* + z_{3t})^2}{\sigma_3^2+\gamma_1^2\sigma_1^2}$$

$$\omega_1^2 = \frac{\sigma_2^2\sigma_3^2}{\sigma_3^2+\gamma_2^2\sigma_2^2}$$

$$\omega_2^2 = \frac{\sigma_1^2\sigma_3^2}{\sigma_3^2+\gamma_1^2\sigma_1^2}$$

and where $\Phi(\ )$ is the standard normal distribution function. The likelihood is

$$L = \prod_t h(Q_t, Q_t^*).$$

NOTES

Quandt gratefully acknowledges support from the National Science Foundation under grant SES-8012592. Portes, Winter and Yeo thank the Social Science Research Council (UK) for support under its Programme for Quantitative and Comparative Macroeconomics at Birkbeck (Grant HR6235). Portes has also benefited from the assistance of the Maison des Sciences de l'Homme. We are especially indebted to T. Bauer, W. Charemza and M. Gronicki for assistance with time series for plan variables, and to I. Grosfeld for help with Polish data. I. Brunskill and A. Milne provided research assistance.

1 The plan for year t is formulated in the last quarter of year $t-1$. At that time the planners know $NFA2$ exactly, since it refers to financial assets at the end of year $t-2$. They also know part of $NFA1$, the first 6 or 8 months, since it refers to financial assets at the end of year $t-1$.

REFERENCES

Alton, T. P., Bass, E. M., Lazarik, G. and Znayenko, W. (1980) *Military Expenditures in Eastern Europe, Post World War II to 1979*, New York, Research Project on National Income in Eastern Europe, Occasional Paper no. 63.

Burkett, J. (1981) 'Marginal and Conditional Probabilities of Excess Demand', *Economics Letters*, **8**, 159–162.

Charemza, W. and Quandt, R. (1982) 'Models and Estimation of Disequilibrium for Centrally Planned Economies', *Review of Economic Studies*, **49**, 109–116.

Gacs, L. and Lacko, M. (1973) 'A Study of Planning Behaviour on the National-Economic Level', *Economics of Planning*, **13**, 91–119.

Hodoly, A. (1966) *Problemy Spozycia w Polsce*, Warsaw, PWE.

Kornai, J. (1971) *Anti-equilibrium*, Amsterdam, North-Holland.

Laffont, J. J. and Monfort, A. (1979) 'Disequilibrium Econometrics in Dynamic Models', *Journal of Econometrics*, **11**, 353–361.

Portes, R. (1981a) 'Macroeconomic Equilibrium and Disequilibrium in Centrally Planned Economies', *Economic Inquiry*, **19**, 559–578.

Portes, R. (1981b) *The Polish Crisis*, London, RIIA.

Portes, R. and Winter, D. (1977) 'The Supply of Consumption Goods in Centrally Planned Economies', *Journal of Comparative Economics*, **1**, 351–365.

Portes, R. and Winter, D. (1980) 'Disequilibrium Estimates for Consumption Goods Markets in Centrally Planned Economies', *Review of Economic Studies*, **47**, 137–159.

Quandt, R. (1981) 'Autocorrelated Errors in Simple Disequilibrium Models', *Economics Letters*, **7**, 55–61.

Rudcenko, S. (1979) 'Household Money Income, Expenditure and Monetary Assets in Czechoslovakia, GDR, Hungary and Poland, 1956–1975', *Jahrbuch der Wirtschaft Osteuropas*, **8**, 431–450.

Yeo, S. (1984) *Some Simple Models of Plan Adjustment*, Birkbeck Discussion Paper in Economics (forthcoming).

Official Polish Publications

Biuletyn Statystyczny (monthly statistical bulletin)

Gospodarka Planowa (monthly planning journal)

Maly Rocznik Statystyczny (concise statistical yearbook)

Monitor Polski (government gazette)

Rocznik Dochodu Narodowego (yearbook of national income) 1960–65, 1971 and 1976

Comment

JEAN-PASCAL BÉNASSY

The first estimated disequilibrium models of the consumption goods market in centrally planned economies consisted of a demand equation, a supply equation and the 'minimum condition'. This paper estimates a new system with an additional equation describing the formation of planned consumption (i.e. expected consumption as it appears in the published central plan). This addition is an extremely welcome one, both because it brings us closer to the institutional reality in CPEs and because it gives us a starting point for the construction of models of dynamic adjustment, since the planned consumption in one period depends upon some past quantities. I shall make a few remarks here aimed towards clarification and further development of the model.

A first suggestion which comes naturally to mind would be to relate both planned consumption and the supply of consumption goods to the productive capacities of the economy. These productive capacities themselves could be related to investments and work force, as in standard production functions analysis. This would allow one to give a better endogenous explanation for the feasible growth rate of consumption, which should then be related to the investment effort (and of course work force growth). The inclusion of investment on the supply side would also allow one to differentiate better its role from that of defence expenditures, while they currently appear very symmetrically in the model as two alternative ways of crowding out consumption.

Another question pertains to the theoretical status of the supply equation (equation (2)). Indeed if we were in a closed economy, with no imports or exports, and neglecting inventory variations, we would have the following definitional identity:

$$CS = NMP - I - D$$

which simply tells that what is supplied for consumption purposes is what is left from national product once investment and defence expenditures have taken their share. Now another identity is the following:

$$C^* = NMP^* - I^* - D^*.$$

Indeed, if the planner is rational, planned consumption, investment and defence expenditures must sum to planned national product.

Using the two above identities and the definitions of C^*Z, $CZXI$ and $CZXD$ we obtain a new identity:

$$CS = C^* + C^*Z - CZXD - CZXI$$

which is equation (2), where $\beta_1 = \beta_2 = 1$, $\beta_5 = \beta_6 = -1$ and the other coefficients are equal to zero. Inasmuch as external trade and inventory variations are present, equation (2) will differ from the above identity. But it could be useful to specify the supply block in a little more detail, giving the relevant accounting identities, and indicating more explicitly what the underlying assumptions are in terms of external trade and inventories.

Comment

JACQUES MAIRESSE

Being chosen as a discussant of this paper has provided me with an excellent learning opportunity, because I was led not only to read the article itself, but also to consult the authors' past articles and the literature on disequilibrium in which I was not extremely well versed. This was necessary since this study by Portes and his co-authors cannot be fully appreciated unless it is viewed as the continuation of their earlier work on centrally planned economies (CPE), and more generally, unless it is seen in the context of overall research in the field of the theory and the econometrics of disequilibrium.

No-one can any longer be unaware of the fact that the theory and the econometrics of disequilibrium have become, in recent years, an extremely fertile area of research, both in terms of the results obtained, and the sheer quantity of studies to which it has given rise. Here are several figures gleaned from a bibliography of Quandt (which is, I think, relatively complete): over the past eight years, from 1975 to mid-1983, there are some 200 references, 85 of them classified as theoretical, 115 as econometric. Overall, 60 per cent of the entries date back less than four years. The econometric articles are not only somewhat more recent but also tending to be more plentiful than the theoretical ones. The record year seems to have been 1980, which alone accounts for 46 of the publications. Thus, the extent of the research is impressive. It is only right that such research should be represented in a symposium devoted to recent developments in macroeconomic modelling, and also fortunate that this representation should include the present authors. Quandt, for one, has focused highly successfully from the outset upon methods of estimation and tests that are properly adapted to disequilibrium models; Portes on his part—most often in collaboration with Winter—has undertaken in the preceding years to apply models of this type empirically.

The research programme of Portes and Winter is particularly exemplary. Their basic aim has been to apply macroeconomic modelling to the countries of Eastern Europe, or centrally planned economies, and to conceive this modelling in terms of disequilibrium models. In pursuit of this goal, they have gathered, assessed and processed the necessary economic data and have implemented the appropriate econometric methods. It is impressive that they undertook such an ambitious project at least eight years ago, and have since then continuously kept in step with the progress in analysis, methods and data in the field.

The present contribution is, in fact, a direct outgrowth of three of their earlier articles. The first is their 1977 article of the *Journal of Comparative Economics*, in which Portes and Winter introduced and estimated for Poland, as well as for Czechoslovakia, Hungary and East Germany, a consumption goods supply function analogous to the one considered in this paper. The estimation, however, remained traditional. Next, came the 1978 article in the *Review of Economics and Statistics*, in which Portes and Winter justified and estimated—though again in a traditional manner—a consumption goods demand function for these same countries. The particular function in this case was also similar to the one found in the present paper. Lastly, there was the 1980 article in the *Review of Economic Studies*, involving a joint study of supply and demand functions in the framework of a disequilibrium model. There Portes and Winter assumed the 'minimum condition' that the observed quantity transacted is the lesser of the quantities supplied and demanded. They also estimated the full model by computing and maximizing its likelihood function.

As compared with these three articles, the present study constitutes new progress in three areas. (i) It incorporates new data—the goals, forecasts, or expectations of the planners (that is, insofar as they are known). Thus, the consumption plan enters the consumption goods supply equation, as do the deviations from plans of total output, investment and defence expenditures. (ii) The article enlarges the model by attempting to describe the plan formation for consumption. It summarizes the behaviour of the planners in this area by means of an additional equation. (iii) In the framework of the overall estimation of the model, this last additional equation plays a role analogous to the price adjustment equation in a disequilibrium model for a market economy. The purpose is especially to improve the estimates of the probabilities of periods of excess demand (or regime of repressed inflation) and excess supply (or Keynesian regime).

To these general remarks on the background, I would like to add several criticisms or questions about content. Since the quality of a disequilibrium model, like that of any model, is closely linked to the quality of the equations of which it is composed, I will do this simply by reviewing these equations rapidly.

(i) The consumption goods demand equation (1) is of the Houthakker–Taylor type and appears to be clearly justified and interpretable. It has been estimated with success, revealing that households in Eastern Europe tend to consume the entirety of their disposable income and not to accumulate financial assets.

(ii) Unlike the demand function, the supply function (2) seems to be rather open to criticism as it is not the outcome of a clear formalization but basically *ad hoc*. It is a kind of reduced-form equation of the effort of the central authorities to achieve the planned total output and its distribution between planned consumption, investment and defence expenditures. If we suppose that, in the economy under consideration, there is no possibility for inventory building nor variations in imports and exports, we can easily perceive that the supply equation proposed must amount to the equality of sources and uses: $NMP = C + I + D$. This equality must be verified *ex post*, as well as *ex ante* within a coherent plan, and would imply $\beta_1 = \beta_2 = 1$, $\beta_5 = \beta_6 = -1$, and $\beta_4 = 0$. Thus the departures from these values in the estimates of the supply equation probably only reflect the omission of imports and exports and changes in inventory.

(iii) The disequilibrium condition of the minimum of supply and demand has the advantage of being both simple and practicable. Nevertheless, it should be remembered that this condition need not hold at the macroeconomic level, that is, when equilibrium or disequilibrium is the result of an aggregation of numerous microeconomic equilibria or disequilibria.

(iv) The plan-formation equation (4) is relatively straightforward. The plan for consumption C^* in year t is the outcome of the revision or adjustment of plan C_1^* for the year $(t-1)$ and the plan realizations C_1 and C_2 for the years $(t-1)$ and $(t-2)$. The revision in household net financial assets $RNFA$ for the year $(t-2)$ and possibly the contemporaneous excess demand $(CD - CS)$ also enter the equation. Given the multicollinearity between C^*, C_1^*, C_1 and C_2, it is not surprising that the fit is good and that the long-term implications are reasonable (with parameter estimates $d_1 + d_2 + d_3 \sim 1$). On the other hand, the adjustment profile is odd (with $d_1 < 0$ and $d_2 \sim 2$). Thus, I have far more reservations than the authors do about their plan-formation equation. I agree with them, both for theoretical reasons and in view of the results, that the variable $(CD - CS)$ ought best not be included (or $c = 0$). On the other hand I feel that they do not sufficiently emphasize the interesting fact that the variable of revision in net financial assets $RNFA$ comes into play significantly ($d_4 = 2.8$ and $c = 1.5$, or $d_4 = 1.2$ and $c = 0$). Rough calculations of the total effect of $RNFA$ on consumption supply, moreover, would seem to show that it would be preferable to eliminate this variable in the supply function and to suppose that it enters only in the plan-formation equation. The estimated coefficient of $RNFA$ in the supply function has the 'wrong sign' and is not statistically very significant. If it were eliminated there, it is likely that its estimated coefficient in the plan-formation equation would be more stable and show

$d_4/(1 + c)$ of about 1. Thus, it could be more clearly established—as is most interesting—that Polish planners are sensitive to 'excess' household liquidity and try to absorb such 'forced' savings by raising the plan for consumption.

I would like to close my comments with a general remark on the results. On the one hand, it can be observed in table 10.2 that the separation between excess supply and excess demand regimes is relatively clearcut. A Keynesian situation seems to have prevailed for 13 years and a situation of repressed inflation for nine years, with the situation ambiguous or in-between for only two years. In examining table 10.1, on the other hand, one cannot help but be struck by the differences in the estimates of supply for the different specifications (coefficients *b*), and also by the difference in the quality of the demand and supply fits (s_1^2 and s_2^2). The instability of the supply function estimates and the predominance of Keynesian situations in an economy such as that of Poland are perhaps not so surprising if, as we suggested before, the supply function specification is not entirely adequate. The likelihood of the model as a whole appears, indeed, as a sort of average of the supply and demand likelihoods, weighted by the probabilities of one regime or the other. If we suppose that the supply function, unlike the demand function, is affected by large specification errors, then we can expect an overestimation of the probability of excess demand regimes. Such a conjecture may have rather general application, but to my knowledge has not been analysed in the econometrics of disequilibrium. Perhaps it bears consideration by the authors in their future research along with problems of better specification of supply and extension of the model.

11

The Evaluation and Comparison of Large Macroeconomic Models

R. P. SMITH

INTRODUCTION

Disputes about the relative merits of individual macromodels generate great heat without any clear resolution despite the existence of a substantial though heterogeneous literature on methods of model assessment.[1] The apparent confusion in criteria results from the fact that the large models reside in an uncomfortable intersection between the spheres of influence of econometricians, economic theorists and practical people of commerce and policy. This results in an ambiguity about what is assessed, why it is being assessed and which measures of success or failure are appropriate. For instance with respect to what is being assessed, sometimes model means a specified set of equations, more often it means the operation of a team, as in 'The ABC model forecast a fall in output in 1983'. Econometricians and economic theorists have devoted considerable effort to clarifying the ambiguities about what, why and which, and proposing if not agreeing criteria. Practical people, being far too busy, have not. Yet these models are largely designed for practical purposes, so assessment should be in terms of how useful they are for such purposes. Kmenta and Ramsey (1981: 10), after making a very similar distinction between business and scientific models, and saying that they should be evaluated according to different criteria, merely suggest judging business models 'mainly on whether they provide the desired product to clients at a competitive price' before restricting the remainder of the chapter to evaluation of scientific models. This seems inadequate. First it begs the interesting questions. What is the desired product? How do you judge whether it is well provided? What is the total cost? Secondly, it is not clear that scientific criteria are directly relevant, in that the existing large models are not designed, and would not be built, for purely scientific purposes. The intention of this paper is to try to systematize assessment from the point of view of practical people, within a loose framework of decision theory. The looseness arises largely from the recognition of practical problems. Any assessment of macromodels raises major problems of computational load and definitional detail which preclude formal implementation of statistical decision theory.

The first stage in this process is to clarify what is being assessed. Macromodels are not small linear simultaneous equations models nor theoretically coherent general equilibrium systems despite the tendency of econometricians and economic theorists respectively to discuss them as if they were. Their large size, non-linearity, instrumental role, judgemental input, eclectic evaluation procedures and heterogeneity are inherent characteristics produced by their functions. The significance of each of these aspects is discussed in the second section. Assessment must be relative to some purpose, and the third section discusses the purposes for which macromodels are used. The fourth section discusses two examples of user-oriented assessment procedures and the following section attempts to put them within a more general framework. The final section contains conclusions.

The models with which the paper will be concerned are the large client-oriented macromodels like Wharton or DRI in the US, or LBS or NIESR in the UK. Such models have been widely criticized for being fundamentally misdirected, and in particular as subject to the Lucas critique.[2] Although these issues are important they will not be dealt with here. Instead the models will be assessed on their stated purposes. Just as the criticisms of theorists will be ignored, so will those of econometricians and questions related to appropriate estimation procedures will not be discussed.[3] This is not to deny that such 'scientific' criteria have an important role, merely to suggest that their role is as an indirect contribution to usefulness. In general the term 'evaluation' will be confined to within-model assessment procedures based on general performance criteria and 'comparison' to between-model assessments based on relative performance criteria.

CHARACTERISTICS OF MACROMODELS

Size

Although macromodels are typically large in the sense of having hundreds of equations, there is no single measure of size which is appropriate for all purposes. The problem of size has two dimensions—inadequate sample information and interpretive complexity. The sample information is inadequate in two respects. First, the number of stochastic equations is greater than the number of observations, so maximum-likelihood estimation of the system is precluded without severe implausible and untestable restrictions on the covariance matrix. Estimates and tests cannot therefore be justified on likelihood grounds, and estimates of the structural parameters obtained will not be consistent. The second problem is that the number of predetermined variables is greater than the number of observations, so that even were the model linear we could not estimate the unrestricted reduced form. For most policy and forecasting purposes it is the multipliers that are the parameters of interest and these are calculated as the restricted reduced-form coefficients obtained from estimates of the structural parameters, which will rarely even be consistent. Inadequate samples mean that we cannot test the implicit restrictions required to determine the multipliers, or obtain unbiased estimates of the multipliers. The multipliers are also likely to be very sensitive to variations in the individual structural parameters, the inverses of which play a large part in their calculations. As a result a system in which each equation seems *a priori* acceptable can generate unacceptable multipliers. System properties cannot therefore be evaluated on an equation-by-equation basis, but only by reference to the multipliers. However the large number of multipliers produced by these models makes it difficult to check them all systematically to determine whether they accord with prior expectations.

With regard to interpretive complexity, models can be large as measured by the number of equations, but be simple and comprehensible because the structure of each equation is the same. This is the case for models like Input–Output, Johansen General Equilibrium, complete systems of demand and production equations, etc. This is not the case for most policy models, which tend to have very complex systems properties because they are composed of hand-crafted and heterogeneous individual equations. This complexity of structure precludes clear analytical examination of system characteristics and makes it difficult to explain why the model gives the results it does. To users and even sometimes operators it acquires the status of a big black box.

Non-linearity

Although it is usual to have each equation linear in transformed variables, to ease estimation of equation parameters, the system as a whole is highly non-linear. The use of different transformations in different equations and the combination of additive identities linking expenditure categories with multiplicative ones linking prices and quantities make the non-linearities inherent. As a result it is not possible in general to write down an explicit reduced form for the model. However, the derivatives can usually be evaluated numerically at a specific point. Unlike the linear case these multipliers, the theoretical derivatives, are not parameters, but random variables, functions of the predetermined variables and disturbances. It is often not clear how sensitive they are to the choice of the point of evaluation, and since the estimates are unlikely to have first or second moments, being obtained as ratios of random variables, interpretation of their expected values and standard errors presents difficulties. Although it is convenient to call these derivatives multipliers, they are quite different from the reduced-form coefficients in a linear model or the analytical multipliers derived from comparative statics exercises.

Policy models also tend to have quite complex dynamic structures, but given size and non-linearities there is no analytical way to examine the global stability of the models. Numerical simulation with specified values can be used to check for local stability, but the prevalence of imposed ceilings and floors on variables in models designed for simulation by outsiders suggests that proprietors are uncertain about even local stability.

Instrumental nature

Models may be constructed and used for a variety of purposes: methodological illustration; teaching; testing economic theories; simulation of historical counterfactuals; forecasting; policy evaluation; or policy formulation. Models that are designed for one purpose may not be so useful for another purpose, and if one is used for multiple purposes there will be trade-offs involved. Macromodels are largely designed for policy and forecasting purposes. Because of their size, complexity and analytical and statistical structures they are not well suited for theoretical and methodological investigations. Correspondingly they should not be evaluated as displaced academic models. The output of the model is sets of conditional solutions. Depending on how they are conditioned (i.e. initialization and the choice of values for exogenous and policy variables not determined by the model), these solutions might be called historical simulations, forecasts, or exploration of policy alternatives. These outputs are used by decision-makers as the basis for action. The value of the output then depends on the consequences of the actions taken as a result of it, while the output itself, i.e. the conditional solution, is a product of both model structure and choice of conditioning.

In this context it is impossible to assess the model in isolation, and it is the usefulness of its output that is of concern. The usefulness of a model can only be specified relative to a particular purpose and particular conditioning. This raises problems for model comparison because purpose and conditioning vary. Macromodels are used for both forecasting and policy analysis and these purposes may conflict. A pure forecasting model, e.g. Box–Jenkins, which provides unconditional predictions, might provide more accurate forecasts than an econometric model. But since it cannot answer questions of the form 'What would be the effect of changing Z?' its use in policy formation is less. If a model which combines the advantages of both is not available, the choice between them must rest on the weights given to the two purposes.

With respect to conditioning, pure forecasting models are also a polar case in that predictions are not conditional on any future variable. But econometric models also differ in the degree of conditioning. The more variables a model treats as exogenous the better it should fit in *ex post* simulations since it uses more information. However, the more variables treated as exogenous the less use it is for analysing linkages and feedbacks and the more variables that have to be forecast off model. How these aspects should be traded off is an open question.

Judgement

Practical discussion of policy modelling emphasizes the role of judgement. Whether it is described as tender loving care, use of extraneous information, fine tuning or a feel for the system, judgement plays a major role in the production of the outputs. Macromodelling for policy and forecasting purposes is not an objective, replicable procedure, it is a machine-intensive art. The model provides a consistent framework within which identities can be imposed, information stored, judgement and experience applied, and questions formulated. The success of a system may be related more to its ability to elicit extraneous information, impose consistency and provoke alternatives than to its economic or statistical character. Judgement enters at three stages—specification, estimation and solution. At the specification stage it influences choice of theoretical paradigm, coverage (which variables are to be explained), causal structure (what they are to be explained by) and parameter restrictions. The bulk of potential system parameters (on lags and excluded endogenous and exogenous variables) will be set to zero *a priori.* No allowance will be made for the uncertainty about these priors. At the estimation stage many parameters may be set at values different from their data-based estimates. This may be done because the estimated parameter value conflicts with theoretical preconceptions (e.g. homogeneity in prices), does not agree with strong extraneous evidence, produces unacceptable systems behaviour, or does not reflect likely changes in economic behaviour known to the modeller. Modellers behave as informal Bayesians and emphasize that their information set is much wider than the data used for estimation.[4] At the solution stage judgement is used to choose values for exogenous variables, policy and residuals. The widespread practice of constant adjustment can be thought of as choosing equation residuals.

Separating the modeller from the machine is made more difficult because teams differ in whether the judgement is entered primarily through parameters, exogenous variables or residuals. One may put all extraneous information into setting the parameters and then use the model mechanically. Another keeps the model data determined and uses its extraneous information to set future residuals.[5] There is some evidence that this use of judgement improves *ex ante* forecast performance. On occasions models are used backwards—the endogenous and exogenous variables are forecast judgementally and the model used to check identities and solve for implicit residuals. The role of judgement is also well illustrated in the UK by the half-a-dozen groups who use the Treasury Model. Despite using a common system, their forecasts and policy analysis diverge substantially.

Model outputs are parameters of posterior distributions which reflect both data and the priors of proprietors. Given the complexity of the process by which these are combined there is no unique way to separate the two. Although we shall distinguish between the system of equations and its operation, it is important to remember how much judgement is embodied in the system itself.

Evaluation

Although there is no way to assess the system itself directly, practical modellers have developed a whole variety of more or less *ad hoc* procedures for checking the inputs to the system (the individual equations) and the outputs (the conditional solutions). The procedures vary between teams, but might involve the following elements with substantial feedback between the stages.[6]

(1) Inspection and testing of individual equations for theoretical plausibility, fit, serial correlation, etc.
(2) Solution and numerical checks.
(3) Inspection of multipliers.
(4) Backward simulations over historical data to check system fit, replication of cyclical properties of the economy, turning points, etc. The simulations involved may be static or dynamic, deterministic or stochastic.
(5) Forward simulations to check stability, long-run solutions, response to large perturbations, sensitivity to parameter variation, etc.
(6) Derivation of optimal control solutions for policy instruments to check plausibility of implied policies and trade-offs.
(7) Analysis of previous *ex ante* forecasting performance to identify source of errors.

Evaluation involves judging whether model outputs conform either with data, in which case there are a variety of statistical techniques that can be employed, or more often with some subjective prior expectations based on theoretical, institutional or historical considerations. With regard to the latter judgement, the more the model conforms with expectations the greater the degree of belief in it. The more extensive the testing of its properties the more confidence the proprietor has about its performance in different circumstances. If it does not pass these tests it is respecified until it does. Multicollinearity and inadequate samples put a premium on the use of prior information to reduce parameter uncertainty. Priors on structural coefficients tend to be used extensively in traditional specification searches. Most simulation checks are ways of using priors about reduced- or final-form coefficients in the estimation of equation parameters—Rasche in Kmenta and Ramsey (1981) discusses this.

Comparison

Comparison raises difficulties because models differ with respect to data frequency, variables forecast, variables treated as exogenous, degree of disaggregation, theoretical orientation, statistical methodology, purpose for which they were constructed, etc. Comparable summary statistics can be constructed only with the use of auxiliary hypotheses introduced to convert the models to a comparable base. In addition models change because they are regularly re-estimated and updated. Thus comparisons only refer to previous versions of the model which proprietors can claim have been superseded.

All *ex post* comparisons of models are plagued by the difficulty that different models use different information sets. This can be avoided by the comparison of *ex ante* forecast errors. Predictions of the future made at a given date should share the same potential information set. Nonetheless, many economists have been sceptical of the informativeness of the *ex ante* forecast performance, for four main reasons. It is argued that a combination of model and modeller performance is being measured and that it is difficult to draw lessons from the judgemental input. Secondly, the forecasts are conditional on a specified policy vector being realized, yet they are assessed as being unconditional. This problem can be mitigated by decomposing the forecast error into that due to wrong exogenous variable assumptions, data revisions, system error, judgemental adjustment, etc.,[7] but this requires repeated resimulation of the model. Thirdly, forecast performance in the past may not be a good guide to future performance, if the model or circumstances change. Finally, forecasts may affect outcomes and so be self-defeating or self-fulfilling.

Although the problems of comparison are severe, they are not unique to assessing macromodels and they are not a reason to abandon comparison. One can make an analogy between a model and a race horse. On considering the horse on its own there are a number of criteria upon which it can be evaluated—breeding, conformation, condition, etc. Each observer can assess these and combine them with some subjective weighting to make an overall judgement. This can be compared to an economist reading the technical manual of a large model (not least in terms of the similar degrees of scepticism required). But the observer would be foolish to put money on the horse without knowing what sort of race was involved (distance, obstacles, the going, etc.) and how it was to be ridden (jockey, handicap, etc.). Likewise the economist would want to know for what purpose the model was to be used and with what judgement it would be operated.

The betting public relies on 'form', detailed records of performance and conditions in past races. They are well aware that past performance is no guarantee for the next race, but it is the most reliable information they have. Since there are no races for models, evaluation and comparison exercises involve reconstructing them, under well specified conditions. Nor can there be races merely between models, they must be between teams comprising both the model and the proprietor who provides the essential conditioning. Comparison exercises thus should involve the reconstruction of well specified competitions which relate directly to the intended use of the model. This requires discussing use in more detail.

THE USE OF MODELS

Models are used for a wide variety of purposes, and evaluation and comparison can only be conducted relative to a specific purpose. Most practical uses of these models are designed to inform decision-makers and provide the basis for improved policy actions. The effectiveness of the model should thus be judged in terms of the consequences of the actions taken on the basis of it. One could identify a range of possible decision-makers: business firms making investment and employment decisions, governments deciding economic policy, or academics seeking to improve their understanding of the structure of the economy. The most interesting case for our purposes is that of the use of models by government to set macroeconomic policy. Below, the process by which the model is used for this purpose is examined in a schematic way. The approach could be applied to business use in the same way. The objective function would be profitability; the instruments, investment, employment, price, etc.; and the framework below adapted accordingly.

The policy model will be characterized by

$$G(y_t, z_t, x_t, e_t) = 0 \tag{1}$$

where y_t is a vector of endogenous variables, z_t of policy instruments, x_t of predetermined variables (current exogenous and lagged variables), e_t of residuals. $G(\ )$ is taken to include the parameters estimated or imposed. In this form the model always fits the data in that there are values of e_t for which (1) is satisfied. Forecasting and policy analysis involve solving the model for some hypothetical y_r^f for period r conditional on some z_r^f, x_r^f, e_r^f specified by the modeller. In this notation we treat residuals as a special sort of exogenous variable on which there are observations from the past generated by solution of the model and which are forecast for the future. Let us assume that the model is being used to advise on policy formation (the choice of z) and that the government has a loss function $L(y)$. Although specifying the loss function is difficult and controversial, doing so is an essential part of clarifying the use of the model. For computational purposes it is convenient to regard the loss function appropriate to macro-policy as being a quadratic in present and future deviations of a small set of variables like growth, inflation and unemployment from their target values. In these circumstances we wish to ask how much the model contributes to reducing this loss function. The objective endogenous variables will be a small subset of the endogenous variables actually generated by the model, but the endogenous variables not in the objective function can be solved out. Although models will differ in the number of variables, it is likely that they will all contain the target subset and the relevant instruments. If it does not do so there is a *prima facie* case for regarding the model as unsuitable for the purpose at hand. Even if it is not useful for the purpose at hand, the model may of course be useful for other purposes, and it is likely that the decision-maker will have available a 'portfolio' of models each used for different things. Disaggregation has advantages since in general the more disaggregated the model and the greater the number of instruments specified, the more precise the potential control and hence the lower the loss function could be made, in principle.

Before we can assess how the information in model and forecasts contributes to reducing the loss function it is necessary to specify how it influences action, i.e. the setting of the instruments. Policy formation involves three stages: the prediction of the predetermined variables and the residuals to obtain x_r^f, e_r^f; the investigation of the effects of various possible policies z_r, conditional on the predictions; and finally the choice of a desired policy. Efficient ways to implement this process are of considerable practical importance but we shall assume that there is a known loss function and that the government uses optimal control methods to minimize this subject to predictions and model. This provides us with a decision rule determining actions which maps the information set (model and predictions) into settings of the instruments. Some form of decision rule is necessary to allow us to assess the value of the information, and optimal control provides a convenient, model-consistent, form. Estimated government reaction functions or rules specified *ex ante* by model proprietors could be used instead, but in general these are not available. It is common practice to use a model of the economy to assess policy makers' performance. What is suggested here is that a model of policy making should be used to assess economists' performance. We wish to ask what the value of the information provided by forecasts and model would be if the policy makers acted optimally upon that information.

Initially the process will be split into two parts. First, what is the information in the unconditional forecasts x_r^f and e_r^f for a given model? Secondly, what is the value of the information in the different models? The section on decision-oriented assessment then brings the two together. Throughout, the emphasis is on evaluation and comparison procedures which set up well defined competitions with a specified purpose (assumed to be embodied in the loss function) and specified decision rules (assumed to be optimal control).

TWO EXAMPLES

Forecast evaluation

For macro-policy formation it is the unconditional forecasts of the exogenous variables and residuals that are of interest. In policy models the predictions of the instruments are primarily illustrative, obtained by assuming current policy continues for instance. In a model used by business, however, forecasts of government policy instruments would be important. The predictions of the endogenous variables follow automatically given the unconditional forecasts, assumed policy and model. Although presenting models in the form of solutions for endogenous variables is an economic way of summarizing the results, it contains no extra information.

We shall therefore be concerned with forecasts of exogenous variables and residuals made for period r at time t ($t < r$), i.e. the vector (x_r^f e_r^f) which will be called w_r^f. Once the realizations w_r are observed (e_r being the *ex post* system residuals corresponding to historical (y_r, x_r, z_r)) it is necessary to summarize the performance. Some constructed measure is necessary to draw inferences about whether performance is improving or deteriorating, how serious the errors are, etc. The summary statistic is often a weighted average of the form

$$Cr = \sum b_i(w_{ir} - w_{ir}^f) \qquad i = 1 \ldots n$$

where there are n variables forecast. A common choice for the weights is

$$b_i = 100(w_{ir} - w_{ir}^f)/w_{ir}^2 n$$

and then Cr is the percentage mean square error. Alternatively, the weights may be related to the variance of w_i as a reflection of its difficulty to forecast as in the Theil statistics. Weights are necessary to average over variables. Variance–covariance matrices alone are inadequate for comparison between forecasters, because the usual result is that one forecasts better on one variable, another on a different one. The usual processes for forming weights are *ad hoc* in the sense that they do not relate directly to the cost of forecast error. The weights should reflect the relative loss resulting from the incorrect decisions made as a result of the forecast error. What we wish to do is to compare the outcome that would result from adopting the incorrect forecasts with the outcome that would result from adopting correct forecasts. For a given model, loss function and decision rule this can be calculated. The procedure will first be illustrated with a simple linear model and then applied to realistic models.

Suppose we have a linear reduced form and the same number of instruments as objectives:

$$Y = AZ + BX + U \tag{2}$$

where Y is a k vector of objective variables, Z a k vector of instruments, X a g vector of exogenous variables, and U a k vector of residuals. The loss function is

$$(Y - Y^*)'H(Y - Y^*)$$

where Y^* are the target levels for the objective variables. Given forecasts of X and U, X^f and U^f, optimal *ex ante* deterministic policy is

$$Z^f = A^{-1}(Y^* - BX^f - U^f) \tag{3}$$

optimal perfect foresight policy is

$$Z^* = A^{-1}(Y^* - BX - U). \tag{4}$$

If Z^* is adopted

$$Y = Y^*$$

and

$$L = 0.$$

If Z^f is adopted,

$$Y = AZ^f + BX + U$$

$$Y = Y^* + B(Ex) + Eu$$

where $Ex = X - X^f$ and $Eu = U - U^f$ and the loss is

$$\begin{aligned} L^f &= (BEx + Eu)'H(BEx + Eu) \\ &= Ex'B'HBEx + Eu'HEu + 2Ex'B'HEu. \end{aligned} \tag{5}$$

Since the loss with Z^* is zero, the extra loss that results from the forecast errors is essentially the covariance matrix of the forecast errors weighted by the priorities H and the parameters B. The derivatives of L^f w.r.t. the elements of *Ex* and *Eu* provide information on which variables it is most important to forecast well and thus suggest where the returns to forecast accuracy are greatest and effort should be directed. Linearity, adequate instruments and the assumption of static deterministic control make this example very simple. In more general cases the weights would be the products of the derivatives of the instruments w.r.t. the forecast variable, the targets w.r.t. the instruments and the loss function w.r.t. the targets. To implement the procedure requires calculating the optimal policy settings of the instruments corresponding both to the forecast and to the actual values of the predicted variables. The model is then simulated with both settings of the instruments, using historical values for exogenous variables and residuals and calculating the loss for each case. The difference is the increase in loss as a result of forecast error. In calculating this measure it is important to recognize that forecast errors have effects into the future and these must be allowed for directly. This can be done using the procedure suggested by Fair (1978) for policy. Essentially this measures the loss in this period from this period's forecast errors, plus the loss in future periods from this period's error given that no further errors are made. The effect of the error in the future is then only that caused by being in the wrong initial position at the beginning of the next period. Using this procedure a cost of forecast error for each period can be calculated. This can then be used by model proprietors to assess whether track record has improved or deteriorated.

An example of the cost of forecast errors can be found in the Craine et al. (1978) examination of the performance of US monetary policy. The loss function was

$$L = \sum_{t=1}^{n} 2(u_t > 4.8)^2 + (p_t > 2.5)^2$$

$$+ 5\,(\Delta TBR_t| > 1.5)^2 + 0.0001(M_t - M_t^{\alpha})^2$$

where u is the unemployment rate, p the inflation rate, TBR the Treasury Bill rate, M demand deposits, and M^{α} target value of M corresponding to 5.1 per cent annual growth. The policies were evaluated over 1973 III to 1975 II. Optimal policies were derived using historical values of the exogenous variables and error realizations. Simulated on the model these produced a value of L of 600.8. This is perfect foresight policy. Optimal policies were then derived by open loop with feedback conditional on the forecasts, the optimal policy being updated each quarter as new forecasts become available. Simulating this open loop with feedback policy produced a value of L of 677.8. The difference, 77, measures the increase in L caused by the forecast errors. The paper discusses the sensitivity of this estimate to model and loss function, and compares other policies.

Comparison

If one accepts the instrumental function of models, the obvious way to compare them is in terms of the quality of the policy performance they generate. Chow (1981: 166) discusses how this might be done. The argument is that we should choose the model which produces the best policy. However, we cannot be certain which is the best policy since that depends on the unknown state of the world—the true nature of the economy. To get around this problem we also use the models to represent the possible states of the world. Choice of policy, and by implication choice of model on which to base policy, then becomes a problem of decision under uncertainty.

Suppose there are two competing models, *M* and *W*, and for each the optimal policy is derived for a common loss function. The two policies are then run through the two models to represent possible states of the world and the loss function values for the four policy–model combinations evaluated. The pay-off matrix for Chow's illustrative calculations with policy as the decision variable are:

		Model	
		M	*W*
Policy	*M*	731	27739
	W	1257	1624

On these numbers, *M* policies could give either the best outcome, or the worst outcome. Risk aversion or a minimax strategy would therefore suggest that *W* is a better model on which to base policy, for this loss function. On an expected utility criterion *M* would only be chosen at odds of worse than 4 to 1 against *W*. The same sort of procedure could be used to investigate the sensitivity of outcomes to choice of loss function.

The models are used for two purposes above: as the basis for policy, the decision variable; and to represent the unknown state of the world. It will be noticed that one does not necessarily choose the model in which one has a higher degree of belief, i.e. the one more likely to represent the state of the world. The choice also depends on relative consequences. In practice choice of model will also depend on the relative accuracy of the forecasts associated with the two models. A model which has a low prior probability of being true may have a proprietor with flair and judgement which is only obtainable in conjunction with the model. The model may provide a more stimulating framework for eliciting extraneous information about future developments. Policy under the more likely model may be very sensitive to exogenous variables which are difficult to predict.[8] Thus our payoffs must reflect both policy effectiveness and forecast effectiveness.

DECISION-ORIENTED ASSESSMENT

The forecast evaluation and model comparison procedures discussed in the previous section can both be put in a decision framework by reconstructing *ex post* the *ex ante* choices available to policy makers. Suppose the government has a choice between two models:

$$g_i(y, z, w) \qquad i = 1, 2$$

where w includes both the usual predetermined variables and the system residuals. Having chosen a model it gets one of a set of potential forecasts corresponding to that model. *Ex ante* the forecasts are random variables with some joint distribution. In the decision tree (figure 11.1) two possible realizations, which can be observed *ex post*, are shown: the values actually observed *ex post* w_i^{a}, corresponding to perfect foresight forecasts, and those historically forecast by the model team, w_i^{f}.

Assuming it has a known loss function $L(y)$, conditional on model $g_i(\ )$ and forecasts w_i^j, the government adopts an optimal policy $z(i, j)$, $i = 1, 2$, $j = \mathrm{a, f}$, to minimize $L(\ )$. The state of the world realized may then be represented by either $g_1(\ )$ or $g_2(\ )$. Thus there are eight possible outcomes denoted by $y(i, j/s)$, $i = 1, 2$, $j = \mathrm{a, f}$, $s = 1, 2$, with corresponding losses $L(i, j/s)$. These are the losses associated with the outcomes resulting from optimal policy given by model i, with forecasts j, when model s is the state of the world. The state of the world being s corresponds to simulating the hypothetical policies on model s with the historical values of the exogenous variables and the systems residuals generated by observed data. This involves assuming that the residuals are independent of policy. Actual observations will not of course tell us *ex post* which model did actually represent the state of the world.

Each of the losses $L(i, j/s)$ in figure 11.1 can be calculated *ex post*. Thus the decision tree essentially defines a competition reconstructed from historical data. It could be elaborated by deriving the w_i by stochastic simulation using observed distributions for forecast errors, and the state of the world by stochastic simulations of g_1 and g_2 using calculated distributions for parameter estimates. However, the tree given combines the exercises given in the two examples discussed. In the notation of the decision tree, the cost of forecast error discussed in the first example are:

for model 1

$$L(1, \mathrm{f}/1) - L(1, \mathrm{a}/1)$$

and for model 2

$$L(2, \mathrm{f}/2) - L(2, \mathrm{a}/2).$$

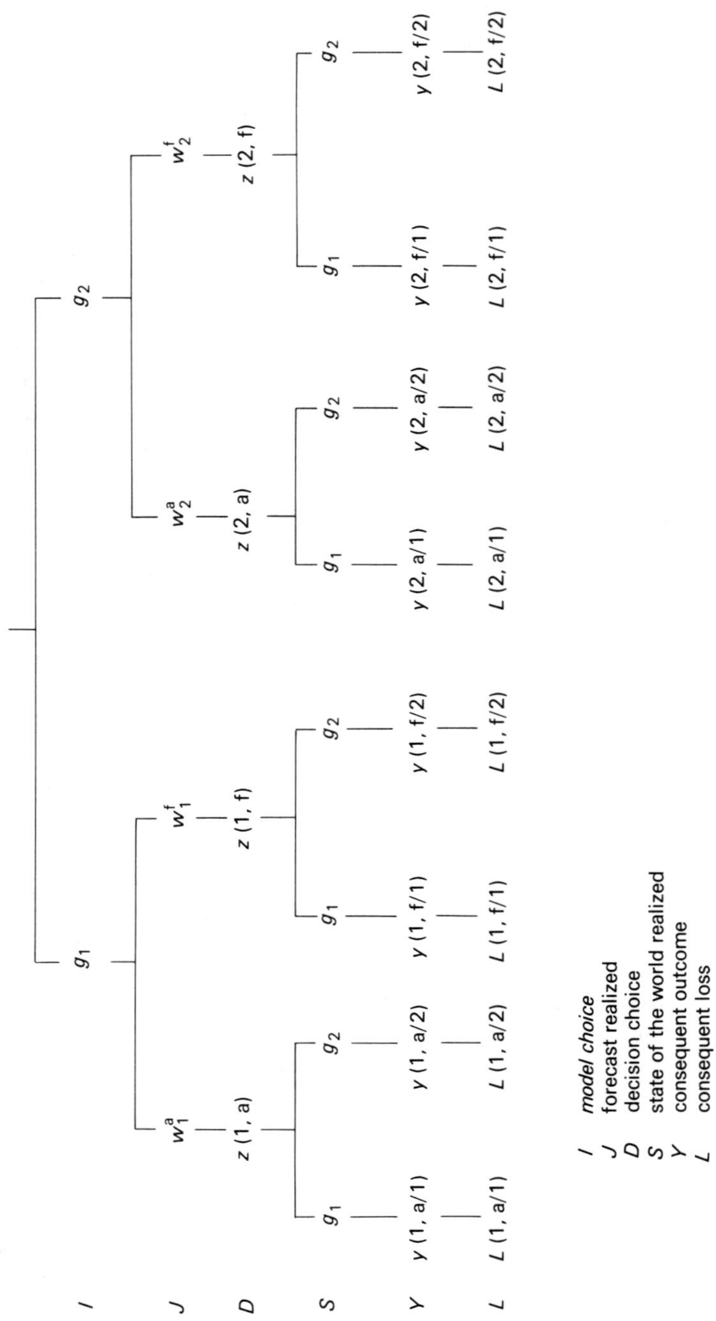

FIGURE 11.1 Decision tree

The perfect foresight payoff matrix in the second example is:

		Model	
		1	2
Policy	1	L(1, a/1)	L(1, a/2)
	2	L(2, a/1)	L(2, a/2)

The historical forecast payoff matrix would be:

		Model	
		1	2
Policy	1	L(1, f/1)	L(1, f/2)
	2	L(2, f/1)	L(2, f/2)

Notice that although L(1, a/1) must be no greater than L(2, a/1), because optimal policies are by definition a minimum for that model, L(1, f/1) may be greater than L(2, f/1), because of the contribution of forecasting accuracy. Thus it is possible for one team to dominate unambiguously whatever the state of the world.

If this is not the case, and we wish to choose between models on the basis of an expected utility criterion, then in order to make decisions we need to assign probabilities. Because we have assumed model parameters as given, and forecast and actual exogenous variables and residuals are fixed at historical values, in the *ex post* decision problem above we only need to assign probabilities to whether g_1 or g_2 represents the state of the world. If we call π the probability that model 1 is the state of the world, we would be indifferent between the two models if

$$\pi = \frac{L(2, f/2) - L(1, f/2)}{L(1, f/1) + L(2, f/2) - L(2, f/1) - L(1, f/2)}$$

but choose model 1 if π is higher, and 2 otherwise.

Clearly π measures only our degree of belief in model 1 relative to competing models used in the exercise, not our belief that model 1 was the true state of the world. π is a conditional probability, in the sense that it measures the belief we attach to the model conditional on the realized numerical values of the parameters, etc., associated with that model. Inherently it is a subjective probability combining together a personal weighted view of the theoretical plausibility of the model, its statistical performance, accord with extraneous evidence, etc. For *ex ante* comparison between models we require another two sets of conditional probabilities: the sampling distributions of the forecasts, and the sampling distribution of the parameter estimates. These are both calculated conditional on the model being true. Unlike the probability distributions over models, the probability distributions over parameter estimates and forecast errors can be given a frequentist interpretation and calculated 'objectively'. Approximate procedures for calculating and combining these are available, e.g. Fair (1980).[9]

Given information on the relevant probabilities the problem becomes a standard statistical decision theory problem, with choice of model corresponding to the choice of experiment in Raiffa and Schlaifer (1961). In principle, models could be chosen and parameters estimated to minimize expected loss. In practice, the characteristics of the models, analytical intractability and computational burden preclude this. Rather than being a formal rule for choosing optimal models and estimators the decision framework provides a systematic structure, a grammar, within which the comparison-relevant information can be organized. Simulation exercises like that set out in figure 11.1 are computationally feasible and set up policy-relevant competitions. This procedure does not remove the subjective element from comparison, since judgements about theoretical plausibility, accord with extraneous information, etc., must play as large a role in assessing a model as in constructing it. What the framework does is to separate these from the other issues and put bounds on the range over which they are influential. In the second example, only estimates of π above 0.8 would make any difference to the ranking.

CONCLUSION

Size, non-linearity and complexity make analytical interpretation and evaluation of macromodels in terms of economic theory very difficult. Inadequate sample size and differences in conditioning preclude likelihood-based statistical evaluation. The central role that judgement and subjective prior information play in model construction and operation preclude the replication, transferability of information, and integration of results into general theoretical structures, on which scientific assessment and development rests. For academic purposes these characteristics constitute serious objections to their use and small models which do not suffer from these difficulties have a major role.

These are not reasons to disparage the characteristics of large models, since for practical purposes they are functional adaptations to the environment in which they are used. The point is that the models should be assessed on the basis of criteria relevant to that environment. The loss function approach summarized in the last section was an attempt to systematize such procedures. What is required is (1) a clear statement of the object of the model, i.e. what it is going to be used for, embodied in loss function and decision rule; (2) information on the sampling distributions of the parameter estimates and forecast errors conditional on the model; and (3) quantified subjective judgements on confidence or degree of belief in the model reflecting theoretical and institutional criteria. A decision framework provides a structure within which this information can be combined.

NOTES

1 An excellent survey of the issues is provided in Kmenta and Ramsey (1981), which emphasizes US models; UK models are discussed in Ormerod (1979).

2 Lucas (1976), Sims (1980), Malinvaud (1981) and Bank of England (1981) also consider the usefulness of macromodels.

3 Maddala surveys the estimation issues in Kmenta and Ramsey (1981). Deaton also discusses them in Bank of England (1981) as does Sargen (1975).

4 Leamer (1978) provides some interpretations of such informal Bayesian procedures. Ando in Kmenta and Ramsey (1981: 363, note 19) summarizes the sort of 'extraneous' information used to confirm an equation.

5 Artis (in Bank of England, 1982) gives examples of such differences in approach. McNees discusses the impact of judgement on forecast performance in Kmenta and Ramsey (1981).

6 Howrey et al. in Kmenta and Ramsey (1981) and Bray in Ormerod (1979) report on development and evaluation procedures for a number of teams.

7 The *National Institute Economic Review*, February 1981, p. 26, provides an example of such forecast decomposition.

8 Kelejian and Vavrickek in Kmenta and Ramsey (1981) discuss other circumstances in which the wrong model may forecast better.

9 Although Fair (1979) uses these measures to compare models, his procedure does not deal with the problem of trade-offs between variables.

REFERENCES

Bank of England (1981) 'The Usefulness of Macroeconomic Models', *Papers Presented to the Panel of Academic Consultants*, No. 14.

Bank of England (1982) 'Why Forecasts Differ', *Papers Presented to the Panel of Academic Consultants*, No. 17.

Chow, G. C. (1981) *Econometric Analysis by Control Methods*, Wiley.

Craine, R., Havenner, A. and Berry, J. (1978) 'Fixed Rules vs. Activism in the Conduct of Monetary Policy', *American Economic Review*, **68**, no. 5, December, 769–783.

Fair, R. C. (1978) 'The Use of Optimal Control Techniques to Measure Economic Performance', *International Economic Review*, **19**, no. 2, June, 289–309.

Fair, R. C. (1979) 'An Analysis of the Accuracy of Four Macroeconometric Models', *Journal of Political Economy*, **87**, August, 701–718.

Fair, R. C. (1980) 'Estimating the Expected Predictive Accuracy of Econometric Models', *International Economic Review*, June, 355–378.

Kmenta, J. and Ramsey, J. B. (eds) (1981) *Large-Scale Macro-Econometric Models*, North-Holland.

Leamer, E. E. (1978) *Specification Searches: Ad Hoc Inference with Non-Experimental Data*, Wiley.

Lucas, R. E. (1976) 'Econometric Policy Evaluation: A Critique', in K. Brunner and A. H. Meltzer (eds), *The Phillips Curve and Labour Markets*, North-Holland.

Malinvaud, E. (1981) 'Econometrics Faced with the Needs of Macroeconomic Policy', *Econometrica*, **49**, no. 5, November, 1363–1376.

Ormerod, P. (ed.) (1979) *Economic Modelling*, Heinemann.

Raiffa, H. and Schlaifer, R. (1961) *Applied Statistical Decision Theory*, MIT Press.

Sargen, J. D. (1975) 'Asymptotic Theory and Large Models', *International Economic Review*, **16**, 75–91.

Sims, C. A. (1980) 'Macroeconomics and Reality', *Econometrica*, **48**, January, 1–48.

Comment

PASCAL MAZODIER

Exactly ten years ago, one could read in one of the first issues of the late *Annals of Economic and Social Measurement* an important article whose title 'Criteria for Evaluation of Econometric Models', stated purpose 'to develop a framework for systematically evaluating large scale econometric models' and even conclusion 'Models will be used for decision making, and their evaluation, therefore, ought to be tied to optimization of these decisions' were surprisingly close to those of Smith's present communication.

The main apparent difference between then and now is that the 4 : 1 proportion—pessimists would no doubt say 'odds ratio'—between theoretical and practical considerations has been inverted. The feeling of this discussant is that such a switch should not be taken to mean that most of the theoretical difficulties have been overcome, but rather that the increased use of large-scale macroeconometric models has led to realize the extent of their deficiencies when they are used as all-weather navigational devices.

In the first part of this text, Smith reviews these main practical shortcomings. Everyone familiar with these models will not dispute his insistence on the following three points: the point of view of model users should not be forgotten (i.e. remember Edsel); the model itself should not hide the model makers (i.e. the speaker usually is at least as important as the loudspeaker, McLuhan notwithstanding); a large model is inevitably a 'big black box' (of which everybody pretends not to be afraid).

These general reminders should not come as any surprise for experienced model makers, who might, however, wonder whether they can amount to more than mere lip service. For instance, can this 'practical model user' be identified precisely enough to be of any true operational utility to model builders? Of course, they already take him into account when they decide to introduce or not to introduce government reaction functions in their models, or to insist on unconditional rather than conditional forecasts, depending on whether their customer is a private firm or the government itself.

The problem is: can they go far beyond such an obvious step? Frankly, has the main Leviathan decision-maker suggested by Smith—the government, or even a given governmental agency—ever assigned a clearcut purpose to any macroeconometric model? And even so, would the publicly avowed purpose be the real one? One suspects that more than a bit of administrative sociology would be welcome here. It may be flattering for the ego of model-builders to think that their customer is no less than 'the government', but they would be myopic indeed if they believed that they play a decisive part in the governmental decision process.

More generally, even if it is certainly sound for applied econometricians to have in mind their clients' purposes when elaborating and evaluating macroeconometric models, they should also be aware of a second-type error: by sticking too closely to their customers' preferences, they run the risk of losing at least some of the academic standards of excellence and independence—some might think here of Laffer's curve's fate.

The second part of Smith's communication is devoted to presenting practical tools for evaluating and comparing macroeconometric models which take into account the points made in the first part. To this purpose, Smith elaborates an approach based upon statistical decision theory and optimal control theory. Provided they are somewhat aware of the developments in these fields, most model builders would probably react in the same way: the tools proposed by Smith do have some internal coherence and look attractive from a logical point of view; for the time being, however—and possibly for an indefinite future as well—they are useless for 'practical people' who work on large models, not only because of the sheer complexity and costs of such exercises when they are implemented life-size (as Smith himself recognizes), but also—and possibly even more—because of the conceptual difficulties which have been mentioned previously: eliciting a realistic government loss function is no trivial job indeed, and regarding it as a 'quadratic one in present and future deviations of a small set of variables like growth, inflation and unemployment from their target values'—as Smith does 'for practical purposes'—is but an oversimplifying pedagogical device which dates back at least to Theil's work on economic forecasts and public policy in the late 1950s. It is very dubious whether such back-of-an-envelope computations can tell much about the relevance of small models, and even less be extended to large ones.

In short, about half of Smith's paper is realistic enough, but mostly critical; the other half purports to be constructive, but is largely idealistic. To this discussant, at least, the message is clear: the importance of macroeconometric models is still mainly an educational one, so that it is dubious whether the point of view of practical model users should be given more weight than the point of view of economic theorists, who use these models mainly to test their hypotheses and to help improve their understanding of the underlying economic mechanisms. In that respect, the recent work done by various econometricians on dynamic models and specification tests seems at least as promising for the evaluation of models as Smith's concern about 'practical purposes'.

As for the elaboration of economic policy, perhaps macroeconometric models can be viewed as the counterpart of confidents in classical tragedies: although characters of minor importance, they often turn out to give briefly the essential clues to catch the significance of a plot in which they play no decisive part otherwise, so that the question of their lifelikeness is, at best, a secondary one.

Comment

CLIFFORD R. WYMER

Smith's paper provides a summary of some of the major characteristics of large macroeconomic models, particularly those models directed towards macroeconomic policy making, such as size, complexity, use and properties, and then discusses how these models should be evaluated. Specifically, he suggests that it is the forecasting ability of the model which is important for macro-policy and that models should be compared on the basis of their forecasts. I should like to discuss this aspect of his paper first and then to look at other criteria which I consider as important in assessing models for their usefulness in policy making.

Smith argues that a model's forecasting performance should be evaluated by the use of a loss function and he provides a decision framework for making this assessment. From the point of view of macro-policy, the difficulties of specifying a satisfactory loss function reduce the usefulness of this approach. Although broad targets of economic policy could be specified fairly readily, the weights which should be placed on deviations from these targets are likely to be poorly defined. The problem here is the same as that which arises in the use of optimal control for macro-policy; that question was considered, for example, by Ball (1980). Moreover, as the parameters of the model have been estimated, and the exogenous variables are not known with certainty, it is an expected loss function which should be used, but the size of the models being considered are almost certain to preclude getting a reasonable estimate of the expected loss. For example, in the models considered in this paper, estimates will be available for the covariances of the parameters within a given equation but not the covariances between parameters of different equations. Comparison of the reliability of models for forecasting is then reduced to a comparison of indicators such as the root-mean-square error of forecasts of a small set of variables (for example, see Christ, 1975).

The costs of specifying, testing and using large models are high so they are preferable to smaller models only if they produce more useful information or significantly better results. Even if a model is to be used primarily for forecasting it need not be large. At the macroeconomic level, and especially at the international level, policy makers are interested in relatively few variables. For these purposes, a high degree of disaggregation is required only if it is necessary in order to obtain a satisfactory representation of the economy. An aggregate model will contain the major feedbacks in the economy, so the need for disaggregation depends on whether the additional distribution effects are significant in determining the variables of interest. If such a core model of the economy is satisfactory, more detailed results can be produced when required by the use of satellite models which, in effect, disaggregate the macro-variables but do not feed back into the core model. An advantage of this structure is that it is highly flexible, and new satellite models can be included for specific purposes without respecifying the core system.

I agree with Smith that the purpose of the model helps determine its nature, but in evaluating such models I should wish to place much greater emphasis on the theoretical basis and properties of the model and its validation during estimation. The main functions of a model for macro-policy purposes are often not forecasting but rather to provide a framework for policy analysis and research. A model is used to complement more theoretical work, allowing the policy implications of theory to be developed more fully. Policy makers, or their advisors, may wish to investigate changes in the structure of the system, such as the movement from fixed to floating exchange rates, or the increase in energy prices in the 1970s. Changes of this magnitude require the structure of the models or the values of the parameters to be modified, but as data would not be available to re-estimate the complete new model the new parameters must be inferred indirectly using whatever information is available, perhaps from other countries or other periods. For this purpose a much smaller, more rigorously specified, model could be more useful than the large models being considered by Smith. It is much easier to understand and explain the overall properties of such a model, an important feature if the model is to be used to support policy recommendations.

Economic theory provides information on the long-run equilibrium relationships in macroeconomics, information which is fairly well accepted by the profession, but it provides much less information on the dynamic behaviour of the economy when the system is out of full long-run equilibrium. If a macromodel is to be plausible, therefore, its long-run equilibrium properties should be consistent with theory, whether or not this equilibrium is ever reached. Secondly, there is the question of stability of the model. Since most economies seem to be relatively stable over quite long periods this should be reflected in the dynamic properties of the model. Although a model need not necessarily be stable, a highly unstable model raises a question of whether some feedbacks have been omitted from the system. More generally, the properties and behaviour of the model must be credible. It is not uncommon for models to exhibit medium- to long-run behaviour which is at variance with theory and which cannot be easily explained. It is this lack of credibility which has led policy makers to be sceptical of the usefulness of macromodels.

Finally, there is the question of estimation. For eight to ten major industrial economies 20–30 years of quarterly data are available on the main macroeconomic variables, but for the remaining countries only annual series, or much shorter quarterly series, are available. As Smith indicates, the estimates of the models he is considering, which may have several hundred endogenous variables and well over a thousand predetermined variables, cannot be justified on likelihood grounds, the properties of the estimators are poorly defined or unknown, and many tests are inappropriate. Under these circumstances it is difficult or impossible to test the validity of the models and, if their theoretical and statistical properties are unsatisfactory, it is questionable whether it is worth while comparing their forecasting abilities.

REFERENCES

Ball (1980) *Report of the Committee on Policy Optimization*, Cmnd. 7148, HMSO, London.

Christ, C. F. (1975) 'Judging the Performance of Econometric Models of the US Economy', *International Economic Review*, **16**.

12

Conclusion

EDWIN KUH

My assigned task—to offer some concluding remarks on these papers—is easy from one perspective but hard from another. It has been made easy since, beginning with the lucid overview of Malinvaud, the papers were admirably presented and discussed, thus avoiding the need for a detailed summary. My job has been made harder because so much of substantive merit was presented, thus making it difficult to contribute new ideas that are germane to the purposes of the conference. I therefore have chosen a different tack, which is to offer an individual perspective on how the main themes developed here can deepen our understanding of some current controversies about macroeconomics and models. These remarks will be made on four related aspects:

(1) growth in model complexity and size;
(2) how modelling relates to macroeconomic controversy;
(3) contributions of this volume towards resolving some controversies; and
(4) a summary conclusion.

GROWTH IN MODEL SIZE AND COMPLEXITY

In a general discussion about the state of econometric models more than a decade ago, Jan Tinbergen aptly asserted:[1]

> In several parts of our science, and I presume other sciences as well, we must beware of following *vogues* too easily. Model building has become a vogue. . . Sometimes indeed some of our followers *overdo* model building.

Since then there has been still further acceleration in size (several thousand endogenous variables) and complexity, the latter principally arising from lengthy equations with numerous non-linear elements.[2] Macromodels typically contain both ingredients. There are well understood reasons to explain what happened. First and foremost, there was the correct perception that in reality there are many different modes of behaviour; this commonsense observation, coupled with an awareness of aggregation biases, led to substantial disaggregation. Secondly, model clients have an insatiable and understandable desire for detailed information about endogenous variables (e.g. automobile sales by size, domestically produced or imported, and sales areas such as a region or a city). Furthermore, policy actions often cannot be understood unless there are numerous policy instruments represented. Thirdly, costs of computation have been falling dramatically both for statistical estimation and simulation or even more computer-intensive applications including Monte Carlo simulations and optimal control. It is possible, for instance, to have eight or ten simulation runs in a day that will cost \$10–\$20 for a 500-equation model. The urge to try out numerous scenarios at these bargin prices is hard to resist, a temptation that is only equalled by the inclination to estimate 20 or 30 variants of an individual equation at half a dollar or less per trial.

To compound our difficulties, economic theory is often regrettably vague about critical aspects of behaviour—institutions, dynamics and expectations. Thus modellers usually build their enlarged model with minimal theoretical guidance and with data whose properties (seldom more than 100 observations for highly autocorrelated time series) are unfavourable for sharp tests of hypotheses; many alternatives fit the data about equally well. Since model building is dominated by forecasters and their pragmatic response to client needs, the prevailing situation is one in which large models that have slight theoretical justification and much empiricism are the rule. Aspects of these models are often superficial because of pressures to respond quickly to urgent questions of the day.

Thus, while adding to knowledge in some circumstances and perhaps improving forecasts (a seriously debated issue, however), growth in size and complexity has been accompanied by a substantial dilution in disciplinary content and intuitive understanding. To mix a couple of metaphors, many macromodels are black boxes with shaky foundations. This raises serious questions about how much macromodels have contributed to advancing the academic discipline[3] of macroeconomics.

HOW MODELLING IS RELATED TO MACROECONOMIC CONTROVERSY

The point I wish to elaborate further is that (to reiterate Tinbergen) there has been an 'overdoing' and a consequent dilution, so that the scope for controversy has been enlarged.

Current disputes in macromodelling and macro-theory bear a resemblance to those of the 1930s and 1940s in two respects. One respect is that exchanges are often ferocious, not to say rancourous. Intensity of feeling often overflows the boundaries normally observed in a naturally contentious area. The second resemblance is that there are overtones of religious fundamentalism ('born again' rational expectation proponents at times, their harder-to-classify adversaries at other times).

It is only sensible to restate the widely recognized proposition that economics is inherently controversial, especially but not exclusively where policy matters are at issue. Beliefs and feelings about ideology, distributional matters and ethics are bound to differ among professional economists even though we sometimes pride ourselves, not always with justification, that we are adept at separating these from the more objective aspects of economics. Models are supposed to be devices that aid clear thinking on such separation but these alone cannot overcome the controversial nature of the social sciences.

Confronted by large, complex models and without widely accepted, reasonably objective rules of evidence, the possibilities of avoidable or unnecessary controversy are increased. While controversy will always remain part and parcel of social science including economics, advances in the more objective elements of economics is a matter of major importance to which this volume has made a valuable contribution, which is the main topic of my remarks.

CONTRIBUTIONS OF THIS VOLUME TOWARDS ALLEVIATING SOME CONTROVERSIES

While proclamations of dramatic advances that are revealed here would surely be exaggerated, some propositions emerged that should advance the disciplinary content of macromodelling in ways that strengthen rules of evidence and thus are closely related to the ideas discussed above. Since many of the papers are at the forefront of knowledge, this welcome further cause of debate was also present.

Much attention has been given to subjective aspects of modelling. Beyond cursory mention of Bayesian methods (there was insufficient time to include detailed discussion on estimation), questions about subjective elements in modelling arose at several points. All I wish to point out here is that their involvement in the modelling process is very different in model formulation or estimation than in the use of models either for policy or forecasting. The principal subjective element in model-structure/model-theory is widespread concern with expectations. For policy, however, welfare criteria matter most, sometimes in the context of optimal control.

Add factors, other parameter adjustments and scenarios based on different subjective assumptions about policy or future exogenous variable paths are the main subjective aspects faced by forecasters.

From the perspective I have chosen for these summary remarks, the papers can most conveniently be separated into two groups:

(1) back to the drawing boards to reintroduce greater theory content;
(2) expectations.

Several contributions in the first category warrant further comment. Deleau, Malgrange and Muet have assembled a 26-equation, theory-based core macromodel that puts heavy emphasis on factor supply and demand (half the equations). It is a dynamic IS-LM model with standard price–wage relations which possesses a long-run solution that 'is, in a way, a generalization of the neo-classical growth model, which usually appears, but less explicitly, in macroeconometric models'. Dynamic behavioural equations have first-order lags (nine altogether). The model is used to study what effects on model structure are implied by parameter constraints from steady-state growth requirements, and which dynamic coefficients are most critical for short- and medium-term dynamics. They contrast the behaviour of several versions of their core model (with several assumed sets of parameters) with results from larger empirical econometric models, such as multipliers. This is a convincing demonstration that small models with many strategic attributes of large models can be constructed that provide insight into the qualitative implications of quantitative models. This is an extremely interesting starting point for what we trust will be many subsequent studies. It avoids the pitfalls of larger models lacking sufficient theoretical content.

Bergstrom's model is a methodological demonstration of how a continuous-time econometric model of the UK can be an effective vehicle to study monetary, fiscal and exchange rate policy. Earlier work with Wymer, and that of Gandolfo in the same vein, uses much theory leading to cross-equation constraints and full information maximum-likelihood methods to estimate first-order approximations of small linear continuous-time (first-order differential equation) models. The implications of these models are studied through simulation and linear systems analysis (e.g. characteristic roots). While potentially a significant contribution to the solution of a crucial aggregation problem—aggregation over time—the systems studied to date have been highly aggregated over behavioural variables, for analytical convenience and computational tractability.

Wymer, in discussing Bergstrom's paper from the floor, suggested that an aggregate macromodel that acts as a driver for more detailed subsectors should be considered as one approach to gaining the benefits of simplicity and continuous time at the macro-level. The benefits of such a hierarchical approach depend of course on the actual recursive structure of economies. Continuous-time procedures pioneered by Bergstrom are relatively new. In contrast to Deleau, Malgrange and Muet, whose model has numerous non-linearities, they have obtained FIML consistency theorems for the estimation of linear differential equations. These approaches are complementary, although each has different dynamic implications, and both approaches to core models are from different perspectives.

There are two small-scale, theory-based macroeconomic disequilibrium models of estimation methods pioneered by Quandt. Along with co-authors Portes, Winter and Yeo, Quandt has participated in constructing a disequilibrium planning model for Poland. The level of behavioural aggregation is even greater for these switching regression regimes than for the earlier-mentioned core models because the computational burden becomes excessive as the number of equations and possible combinations of regimes grows so rapidly. While estimation methods and the general model structure are similar, a paper by Patrick Artus, Guy Laroque and Gilles Michel, which was presented at the conference but is not included in this volume, is about capitalist macroeconomic model structure, not planning models. Their estimates of an eight-equation disequilibrium macromodel (five behavioural, three disequilibrium rationing equations) enable them to distinguish four types of macroeconomic behaviour—Keynesian unemployment, classical unemployment, repressed inflation, and underconsumption (excess demand for labour, excess supply of goods). These results are among early experimental efforts to model explicitly excess supply or demand. Since it is hard to estimate disequilibrium models, their range of applicability so far has been restricted, but together with their recent precursors (cited in the two papers) this new way of modelling macroeconomies is potentially a major addition to realistic representations of economic behaviour.

Turning now to assessment, the paper by Smith on large-model evaluation makes the valid point that the purposes and clients served by large forecasting models should provide the criteria for judgment. Smith offers some suggestions on how this might be done. The large vs. small model issues raised at the outset of this talk, in terms of the contribution such models make to the disciplinary parts of economics, is not addressed by Smith. He is interested in using large models and understanding them better. This conference has helped to sort out some issues involved in the small vs. large debate so that Smith's paper is helpful in marshalling arguments for his point of view.

Expectations are fundamental to much of economic theory. Operational versions of economic theory in the context of quantitative and estimable (i.e. econometric) form often have only fragile theoretical support because of the inherent complexity of expectation formation. Stock adjustment models seem relevant in some contexts but involve intermediate assumptions (e.g. expected = current actual output) that are reasonable enough sometimes, but not always. Rational expectations, a fad of the sort that preoccupies economists from time to time, have rekindled interest in the general topic of expectations. In the long run, I expect this renewed attention will be their major contribution, which ought not be discounted. Three papers are about expectations. These have been written from disparate perspectives, a reflection of the innate problems alluded to earlier. Two of the three papers test various hypotheses about some version of rational expectations and all the tests find rational expectations deficient.

The broadest expectational framework is that presented by Pesaran, who distinguishes between behavioural uncertainty (e.g. uncertainty about competitive responses in an imperfectly competitive market) and exogenous uncertainty (e.g. the effect of weather on crop output). Constant returns to scale, perfect competition is amenable to uncertainty of the latter type and lends itself most readily to rational expectations hypotheses. Since the author believes behavioural uncertainty dominates many economic sectors, he proposes interesting ways to convert direct information on expectations from survey data about expected direction of changes (in prices or quantities) to quantitative per cent changes, by regressing observed series of the latter on transformations of the qualitative data (such as per cent of respondents who expect price increases and per cent of respondents who expect price decreases). This is an impressive paper.

Shiller sets himself the task of understanding a century of annual stock market price indices using several models of rational behaviour. He looks hard at graphs of the market stock price index and its presumed rationally based determinants, such as the present discounted value of future year dividends, based on the efficient market hypothesis. The time plots of price and its determinants behave differently. Prices have more variability and different cyclical turning points. This suggests a wide open area of research. The random walk hypothesis for changes in stock prices is partially rejected. Stock price levels contain systematic elements that have not yet been explained. Since equity prices are important in rational models of investment behaviour, these negative results cannot be ignored. Shiller uses graphical exploration and more formal hypothesis testing: both lead to the same negative conclusions.

The last test of rational expectations is by Henry and Wren-Lewis in the context of labour demand functions. They test two models, one based on rational expectations. A valuable aspect of their paper is that the performance of the two models initially fitted to 1965–79 data is used to predict post-sample data on the succeeding eight quarters. Output and employment dropped much further and more rapidly in 1980–81 than during the period of fit. This is noteworthy because (a) post-sample or out-of-sample data are ordinarily the most effective way to test econometric relations and (b) the unusually large post-sample variability substantially increases the power of the test. On both of these counts and the care with which they have analysed this problem, their paper is highly commendable.

Branson incorporates a version of rational expectations into a model of floating exchange rate determination in the presence of central bank policy intervention. From the viewpoint of exchange rate determination, he uses residuals or innovations from vector autoregressions for the United States, Germany, United Kingdom and Japan as indicators of new information. The sign patterns of these innovations when correlated with policy variables are used to infer dominant central bank modes of behaviour. I am unsure of how secure these inferences are (vector autoregression residuals can lack adequate robustness), but Branson's paper squarely confronts expectational aspects together with institutional behaviour in a novel way.[4]

CONCLUSION

The dominant conclusion is that macroeconomics–macromodelling is alive and well, once we sweep aside accumulated intellectual debris. Solid ground for the future possibilities of quantitative macroeconomics have been demonstrated at this conference.

The 'small can be beautiful' theme dwelt on in this summary is predicated on the view that solid advances on the objective side of this discipline need a highly consolidated base from which to start. This is now being achieved. Another step in this process is needed. We must test the theoretical restrictions imposed (e.g. constant returns in the Deleau et al. maquette, many cross-equation constraints in the continuous-time models) from the basis now established. Yes, we must also see where aggregation is unduly restrictive, but we are now happily in a strong position to do so systematically and thus avoid the more helter-skelter accretions that have typified previous model expansions.

We should, also, resist the temptation to assert that our models are revealed truth. The basic complexity of most economic behaviour, relatively short time series, imperfect correspondence between theory and data and our inability to experiment and obtain sharp or powerful tests of alternative structures set limits to what we can seriously expect to attain. Realism in our aspirations for the objective disciplinary content of models and less hard selling of forecasting models would increase the credibility of macromodelling. Such credibility is presently at low ebb.

We should also consider models as vehicles for testing competing theories. In that process we can sometimes extract orders of magnitude for critical parameters. This in turn will open up opportunities to understand some major attributes of model dynamics, e.g. which aspects of model structure are responsible for short-, intermediate- and long-term dynamics. This 'order-of-magnitude' viewpoint contrasts with the calculation or comparison of multipliers with four or five 'significant' digits. The latter may be part of a forecast but presupposes much more precision than actually exists or which can be solidly based on the objective discipline of applied economics.

The need for sound quantitative macroeconomics has never been greater. It is essential for the discipline of economics, for whatever economics can contribute to sensible economic policy, and even to improve forecasts.

By way of a final comment, I want to thank profusely Monsieur Fourgeaud, who is Director at CEPREMAP, and Pierre Malgrange and Pierre-Alain Muet, also at CEPREMAP, who organized this conference that has had such interesting and substantial results.

NOTES

1 Nobel Lecture in Stockholm, 1969—reprinted in the *American Economic Review*, December 1981.

2 Large models can be simple (e.g. input–output with many sectors) and small models can be complex (highly non-linear, discontinuities, etc.).

3 I have deliberately abstained from using the term 'science', which is irrelevant for many purposes and misleading as well, especially since economics more closely resembles engineering than scientific disciplines.

4 Aglietta and Oudiz are concerned with real exchange rates as opposed to nominal rates. Their interesting paper is about how to model real exchange rates, a central problem for both policy and theory. Turnovsky has a purely theoretical model that describes for 'an expository model' the effects of optimal policy intervention in an open economy. Since these papers are adjacent to the principal two topics I have used to focus my discussion, readers are referred to the well discussed and presented papers by these authors.

Contributors

M. AGLIETTA Professor of Economics at the University of Paris X-Nanterre. Research in international economics: macroeconomic modelling of the world economy, prospectives and scenarios for the world economy.

G. D'ALCANTARA Research Associate at CES (Katholieke Universiteit Leuven) and at CORE (Université Catholique de Louvain). Works on various projects of macroeconomic and international modelling.

JEAN-PASCAL BENASSY Maître de Recherche at CNRS and CEPREMAP works on the microeconomic foundations of macroeconomics and non-Walrasian macroeconomic theory.

A. R. BERGSTROM Professor of Economics at the University of Essex. Research on economic dynamics and continuous-time disequilibrium models.

WILLIAM H. BRANSON Professor of Economics and International Affairs, Princeton University. Research on international trade and finance.

JEAN-MICHEL CHARPIN Head of Division at INSEE (medium term studies and forecasts). Research on macroeconomic planning and policy models.

R. COURBIS Professor of Economics at the University of Paris X-Nanterre and Director of GAMA (Group for Applied Macroeconomic Analysis). Research on macroeconomic theory, national and regional modelling, forecasting and economic policy.

MICHEL DELEAU Vice Chairman at Direction de la Prévision, Paris and Maître de Conférences in Economics at Ecole Polytechnique. Published contributions on decisions under uncertainty, and on the study of the structural properties and theoretical foundations of dynamic macro models.

GIANCARLO GANDOLFO Professor of International Economics and Director of the Instituto di Economia Politica, Facoltà di Economia e Commercio, University of Rome. Author of several books and articles on mathematical methods and models in economic dynamics and econometric estimation of continuous-time dynamic models.

C. GOURIEROUX Professor at the University of Paris IX-Dauphine. Published articles on econometrics, time series, rational expectations.

PAUL DE GRAUWE Professor at the University of Louvain. Research on monetary and fiscal theory and institutions, international economics.

PIERRE-YVES HENIN Professor at the University of Paris I. Fields of research: macroeconomic theory, disequilibrium economics, applied macroeconomics, open economy macroeconomics.

S. G. B. HENRY Senior Research Fellow at NIESR, London. Published articles on macroeconomic policy, employment and inflation.

EDWIN KUH Professor of Economics and Finance at MIT and Director of the Center for Computational Research in Economics and Management Science. Research on investment, aggregation, macroeconomics and model diagnostics.

JEAN-PIERRE LAFFARGUE Professor of Economics at the University of Paris-Panthéon Sorbonne, and Research Associate at CEPREMAP. Author of numerous publications dealing mainly with aspects of macroeconomic modelling applied to international finance.

VIVIEN LEVY-GARBOUA Currently Directeur Adjoint at the BNP (Banque Nationale de Paris) and Maître de Conférences in Economics at Ecole Polytechnique. Fields of interest: macroeconomic policy, balance of payment analysis and banking theory.

JACQUES MAIRESSE Director of ENSAE and Directeur d'Etudes at Ecole des Hautes Etudes en Sciences Sociales. Main topics of interest: the study of productivity and technical change and the econometrics of panel data.

PIERRE MALGRANGE Maître de Recherche at CNRS and CEPREMAP. Published contributions on decision under uncertainty and on the study of the structural properties and theoretical foundations of dynamic macro models.

EDMOND MALINVAUD Directeur Général of INSEE. Devotes his current research to both theoretical and applied macroeconomics.

PASCAL MAZODIER Head of the short-term forecasting service at INSEE. Has taught econometrics at ENSAE and at the University of PARIS-I, and done some research in econometric theory (mainly econometrics of panel data and simultaneous equations methods).

JACQUES MELITZ Member of the Research Unit at INSEE and Professor of Economics at the Institut des Etudes Politiques in Paris. Research mainly in the area of money and international macroeconomics.

ALAIN MONFORT Member of the Research Unit at INSEE and Professor of Statistics at ENSAE. Publications concerned with the application of statistical methods to the econometric models.

PIERRE-ALAIN MUET Director of the Econometric Department at Observatoire Français des Conjonctures Economiques and Maître de Conférences in Economics at Ecole Polytechnique. Research on investment and macroeconometric modelling.

G. OUDIZ Administrateur at INSEE. At present a visiting scholar at MIT and NBER. His research interests include macroeconomic policy evaluation, exchange rate policy and economic policy coordination among western countries.

M. H. PESARAN Fellow of Trinity College and University Lecturer in the University of Cambridge.

RICHARD PORTES Director of the Centre for Economic Policy Research, London, Professor of Economics at Birkbeck College, University of London, and Directeur d'Etudes Associé at Ecole des Hautes Etudes en Sciences Sociales, Paris. Works on disequilibrium macroeconometrics, open economy, macro, centrally planned economies and East–West economic relations.

RICHARD QUANDT Professor of Economics at Princeton University. Published extensively in econometrics, microtheory, financial economics and transportation.

ROBERT J. SHILLER Professor of Economics at Yale University and Research Associate, NBER. Research on macroeconomic fluctuations and financial markets.

R. P. SMITH Reader in Applied Economics at Birkbeck College, University of London.

JEAN TIROLE Research Associate at CERAS, Ecole des Ponts et Chaussées, Paris. Main research interests: microfoundations of macroeconomics, industrial organization and planning.

STEPHEN J. TURNOVSKY Professor of Economics at the University of Illinois at Urbana-Champaign and Research Associate, NBER. Research on macroeconomic theory in international and domestic context and stabilization policy.

JEAN WAELBROECK Professor at the Free University of Brussels.

UWE WESTPHAL Professor of Economics at the University of Hamburg. Research on quarterly econometric models of the German economy.

DAVID WINTER Lecturer in Econometrics at the University of Bristol, and currently a Visiting Professor at the University of California, Santa Barbara. Main research interests: the macroeconomics of centrally planned economics and the methodology of applied macroeconometrics.

S. WREN-LEWIS Research Officer at NIESR. His research has concentrated on earnings behaviour, macroeconomic policy, and models of asset accumulation.

CLIFFORD R. WYMER Senior Economist with the Research Department of the IMF. Has written on the use of continuous disequilibrium models, particularly for macroeconomic policy, and on econometric studies of financial and commodity markets.

STEPHEN YEO Research Officer in the Department of Economics, Birkbeck College, University of London.

Index